Basic Accounting
Concepts, Principles, and Procedures

Volume 1

Building the
Conceptual Foundation

Basic Accounting
Concepts, Principles, and Procedures

Volume 1

Building the
Conceptual Foundation

Gregory R. Mostyn, CPA, MBA
Mission College

Worthy & James Publishing

About the Author

Greg Mostyn is an accounting instructor at Mission Community College and is a practicing certified public accountant. He is a member of the American Institute of Certified Public Accountants and the California CPA Society. He is a past accounting department chairman and has extensive experience in accounting curriculum design and course development, and has written two previous books.

Before you buy or use this book, you should understand . . .

© 2007 Worthy & James Publishing

Cataloging-in-Publication Data
Mostyn, Gregory R.
    Basic accounting. Volume 1, Building the conceptual
foundation / Gregory Mostyn.
    p. cm.
    Includes index.
    "Concepts, principles, and procedures."
    LCCN 2006939188
    ISBN-13: 978-0-9791494-8-1
    ISBN-10: 0-9791494-8-7

    1. Accounting.   I. Title.

HF5636.M67 2007   657'.042
                         QBI07-600006

For more information about our products, contact us at:

Worthy & James Publishing
P.O. Box 360215
Milpitas, CA 95036
www.worthyjames.com

Suggestions, comments, criticism? E-mail us: mail@worthyjames.com

Printed in Canada

*To my parents, Bob and Melita, who by word and deed
have taught me the value of lifelong learning*

And

*Daisy, who has always been exactly right about
the importance of long walks in the park*

BRIEF Contents

Contents

SECTION V   USING A BASIC ACCOUNTING SYSTEM

Learning Goal 19:   Explain the Five Kinds of Information   385

Learning Goal 20:   Explain the Use of Accounts   394

Learning Goal 21:   Use the Owner's Capital Accounts   411

Learning Goal 22:   "Debits on the left, credits on the right"   427

Learning Goal 23:   Use a Ledger   442

Learning Goal 24:   Use a Journal   449

Learning Goal 25:   Use a Basic Accounting System   479

Computer Disk (Back of Book)
Solutions to All Problems by Learning Goal
Essential Math for Accounting
Accounting Paper Templates for Volume 1

Preface

Basic Accounting Concepts, Principles, and Procedures provides a new pedagogical approach for introductory accounting. The content does not begin with a focus on the accounting profession and introductory accounting procedures. Instead, the text first explains the basic concepts and structure of a business to create a meaningful context for the accounting concepts that follow. The conversational, relaxed approach is built on a research-based instructional design that improves comprehension and retention, and minimizes stress. The system's special design becomes immediately apparent by viewing the appearance of the material.

As any experienced accounting instructor can relate, accounting knowledge is very much a building-block architecture. Accounting skills rest on the foundation of critical basic concepts. Instructors know that introductory accounting students who miss the early concepts seldom successfully complete a course. *Basic Accounting Concepts, Principles, and Procedures*, particularly Volume 1, is specifically designed to address this weakness in traditional texts, in which *early foundation concepts receive no greater emphasis than later content*. These two volumes provide the reader with guidance that strongly reinforces key foundation concepts, particularly those that beginning students often find most difficult. Volume 1, for example, places great emphasis on building a clear understanding of transaction analysis. In Volume 2, each type of adjusting entry is treated as a separate learning goal before all adjusting types are combined in a single learning goal. This approach provides special emphasis for key concepts as well as for difficult concepts and is applied to all topics. In our experience, this builds the confidence that assures future progress and creates curiosity about the value (and shortcomings) of accounting. At the same time, the flexibility of the design allows readers to move quickly through the parts of the material with which they are comfortable.

Particularly in Volume 2, Applying Principles and Procedures, the reader will also benefit from real-world practical help. Some examples are: what to do if a bank reconciliation will not balance, how to handle partial payments, a checklist for an accounting software purchase, and how to identify the hidden costs of accounting software.

Basic Accounting Concepts, Principles, and Procedures is a complete self-study package. The two volumes contain full coverage of the traditional first accounting principles course plus a complete first-course coverage of corporate accounting and financial statements analysis. The importance of ethics in business and accounting is reinforced by exposition as well as by articles and questions, including Internet exercises. Volume 2 contains two complete merchandising practice sets with solutions. The disk included with each volume contains detailed solutions to all learning goal questions and problems, a complete basic math review with problems and solutions, and templates that provide an unlimited supply of various types of accounting paper, worksheets, journals, and ledgers.

Acknowledgments No book can ever be written alone. I wish to especially acknowledge the following practitioners and educators for their excellent suggestions, useful criticism, and creative ideas. They have fixed mistakes and generously shared their wisdom in more ways than I can describe.

William Bernacchi, CPA, MBA
William E. Bjork, JD, CPA, MBA
Randy Castello, CPA, MBA
Jennifer Chadwick, CPA, EA, MBA
George Dorrance, CPA, MBA
Richard Hobbs, MA
John Hui, CPA, MPA

Christopher Kwok, CPA, MBA
Shellie Mueller, MBA
Ernestine Porter, CPA, MBA
Diana Smith, CPA, MBA
James Van Tassel, PhD, MBA
Guoli Zhang, MA

And a Special Thanks to

Mary Douglas, Rogue Valley Publications, for the excellent project management and editing services that materially improved the quality of this book.

Cover Design: David Ruppe, Impact Publications
Interior Design: Mark Ong
Typesetting: ICC Macmillan Inc.

Cover Images

Skyline: Stockbyte/Getty Images
Basketball Players: Jim Cummins/Taxi/Getty Images
Office: Stockbyte/Getty Images
Golden Gate Bridge: Andrew Gunners/Digital Vision/Getty Images
Market: David Buffington/Photodisc/Getty Images

How to Use This Book

MANY RESOURCES FOR YOU

Overview

This book is designed in a way that will maximize your ability to learn and remember information. The design is an application of researched-based methods that will make your learning experience more interesting and enjoyable and will build your confidence as you use the book.

To achieve the greatest benefits from the book, be especially sure that you use the features described below.

"Overviews" and "quick reviews"

- Each *section* has an overview to direct you to the parts of the book that are most important for you. Be sure to read each section "overview" when you come to it.
- Each *learning goal* has a short overview of the content of the goal. Read this overview before you begin. Then, after you study a learning goal, read the "quick review" and "vocabulary."

Answers to questions and problems

All the learning goal questions and problems in this book (except for Internet exercises and some special instructor-assigned problems) have detailed solutions. These solutions are in the computer disk that is located on the inside back cover of this book. For Internet exercises, be sure to create a folder to keep all the useful financial links that you are going to accumulate.

Cumulative tests

This book includes cumulative tests with answers after each test. Each test also has a **Help Table**. After you check the answers, use the **Help Table** to specifically identify your strong and weak knowledge areas. Use this for review.

Accounting paper

The disk at the back of the book contains a complete selection of all types of accounting paper that you can use for the solution of any problem type in the book. You can print out an unlimited supply of accounting paper by using the disk.

Complete math review

The disk at the back of the book also contains a comprehensive, step-by-step math review beginning at the most basic level. The review contains many types of problems, all with solutions. The review continues on the disk for Volume 2 with fractions, ratios, and basic algebra.

How to Study Accounting

Overview

Acquire a Balanced Understanding

Accounting is a system of activities that analyzes, processes, and communicates and interprets financial information about a business or other entity. If you wish to acquire a clear understanding of this system, you will need to spend some time studying three important areas of accounting knowledge:

- how a business operates
- analyzing and processing business data
- communicating and interpreting financial reports

Each of these areas is very important in its own right and should not be underestimated. For example, an understanding of:

- "how a business operates" is needed by accountants, business owners, managers, management consultants, operations specialists, investors, and lenders.
- "analyzing and processing business data" is needed in bookkeeping, auditing, and information system use (or design), especially in new "intranet" systems that integrate all kinds of accounting and other information.
- "communicating and interpreting financial reports" is important for accountants and managers. Interpreting financial reports is also very important for business owners, investors, bankers, voters, union members, and everyone and anyone with a financial or social interest in business and the economy.

At some point in your future career, you might become a specialist or be involved in work that is related to any of the three areas just mentioned. However, because all of these areas interact with and affect each other and because you cannot be entirely sure where your career will take you, it is wise to be sure that you acquire some working knowledge in each area. This book and other good introductory accounting textbooks introduce you to each of these areas in a balanced and careful way.

Study Techniques for Students

Overview

The following suggestions are study tips that really work. Each additional one that you are able to consistently use is "money in the bank" toward success in your accounting study.

What Is a Business?

OVERVIEW

What this section does	This section introduces you to the fundamental features of a business:

- purpose
- how a business operates
- basic financial structure
- economic entities
- ownership types

Use this section if . . .	. . . you are unfamiliar with *any* of the features above. Learning Goal 3, Learning Goal 4, and Learning Goal 5 are especially important.
Do not use this section if . . .	. . . you already understand all the elements listed above. You can begin with Section II starting on page 76, analyzing the transactions that change a business.

LEARNING GOALS

"Welcome to the territory of business!"

LEARNING GOAL 1

Explain What a Business Is and What It Does

Welcome

Speak the Language of Business . . .

Welcome! Thank you for selecting me as your guide in this part of your journey through the territory of business and commerce. To prosper in this territory and to enjoy your journey, you will need to learn the languages of the region. The most important language to learn is called "accounting."

When educated people in this region want to describe a business or explain what has happened to it, they often use the language of accounting. When you use this book, you will be carefully and thoroughly trained in the fundamentals of this language.

. . . But First Learn What a Business Is

A common dilemma for beginning accounting students is the double burden of struggling to learn accounting while at the same time being expected to understand what a "business" is—the thing that the accounting is trying to describe. The student is expected to learn what a business is by having to learn the language that describes it. This would be like me telling you, in a new language, all the details about some beautiful tree even though you are not exactly sure what a tree is.

I suggest that we try something more interesting and fun. Instead of beginning right away with the details of accounting, let's first take a little time to understand what a business is and how it operates. After that, accounting discussions will make more sense to you.

If you decide to extend your study of accounting, you will later learn that, with small modifications, accounting can also be used to describe non-business activities, such as governments and charities. However, business is where accounting is used the most.

In Learning Goal 1, you will find:

Identify a Business

Business Operations

Identify a Business

Business Characteristics

Definition: A Business

A "business" is an organization with the primary goal of accumulating wealth by creating valuable new resources and selling them to customers.

Note: Valuable resources have a dollar value, so they are also called **economic resources.**

Examples of businesses . . .	Desired resource created . . .
An automobile manufacturer	Automobiles
An automobile dealer	A selection of automobiles to buy
A veterinarian	Medical services for animals
An accounting firm	Accounting and tax services
A movie theater	Entertainment
A bakery	Delicious bread and desserts

Business Characteristics, *continued*

Not a Business	■ A public university (primary purpose is not accumulating wealth) ■ A charitable organization (primary purpose is not accumulating wealth) ■ A city government (primary goal is public service, not accumulating wealth)
Important Difference	Government or nonprofit organizations (such as charities) do carry on business-like activities such as detailed record-keeping, paying bills, incurring expenses, commercial transactions, and so on. However, because the primary goal of these organizations is not the accumulation of wealth, none of them is called a "business."

The Two Kinds of Resources

Overview	Only two kinds of resources can be created: property and services.
Property and Services	A business creates and sells valuable resources that people want. Only two possible kinds of resources can be created and sold:

[handwritten: AKA: Goods & Services.]

■ ***Property:*** Any resource that can be *owned*. Property generally (but not always) has a dollar value. Examples are a computer, a book, or a car.
■ ***Services:*** The *use of* labor or the *use of* someone else's property. Services generally (but not always) have a dollar value. Examples are repairing a truck, delivering a pizza, giving financial advice, teaching a class, renting out a copy machine, or renting out an apartment.

Synonym	Property and services are often referred to as "goods and services."

Classifying a Business

Classify by Type of Resource Created	■ A *service business* creates services. Examples of services are repairs, communication, legal advice, entertainment, and health care. ■ A *merchandising business* offers a convenient selection of merchandise to customers. Merchandising businesses do not make products. Examples of merchandising businesses are a grocery store, a bookstore, a clothing store, and an automobile dealer. ■ A *manufacturing business* creates new property. Examples are an automobile manufacturer, a food manufacturer, and a computer manufacturer.
Combined Types	It is not unusual for one business to combine activities. Examples are an automobile dealer (a merchandiser) that may also do repairs (services), or a bakery (a manufacturer) that may also sell to the public (a merchandiser).

Business Operations

What Is Wealth?

Overview

Because the primary goal of a business is to accumulate wealth, it is important to understand exactly what "wealth" means in business language.

Wealth Defined

Wealth is property that has a dollar value.

The Idea of Wealth

"Wealth" refers to the *dollar value* characteristic of property. If the property is in the form of money, its value is easy to know, and it can be used to buy things and pay debts. Other property that has value, but that is not money, can be sold or exchanged for money (example: selling equipment).

Although most property is also physically useful (like equipment), the concept of wealth ignores this utility and focuses only on the dollar value.

Wealth is important because its value can be used to acquire any other resource.

"I'm bored. Let's go into business!"

What Is Wealth, *continued*

Wealth Examples

- Money
- Equipment that you could sell for $500
- *Account receivable* (the *legal right* to collect money from a customer)
- Shares of stock that you could sell
- Clothing for sale in a store
- Land that is worth $100,000
- A car that you can sell for $5,000
- A calculator that you can sell for $5
- Office supplies worth $900

Note: All of these examples have dollar value *and* can be owned.

Not Wealth

This item . . .	is not wealth because . . .
Old broken equipment that no one wants	it has no value.
Shares of stock in a bankrupt business	it has no value.
Food that is spoiled and dangerous	it has no value.
The services of an employee	a service cannot be owned (because it is immediately consumed).
The telephone service you receive	a service cannot be owned (because it is immediately consumed).
The financial advice that you receive from an accountant	a service cannot be owned (because it is immediately consumed).
The rental of a computer	a service cannot be owned (because it is immediately consumed).

Property and Services Compared

The table below helps you compare property and services, and indicates whether or not they can be called wealth.

Resource	Useful?	Can it have dollar value?	Can it be wealth?
Services	Yes	Yes	No, because it cannot be owned.
Property	Yes	Yes	Yes, because it can be owned.

Coming Up Next . . .

Exactly *how* does a business operate so that it can accumulate wealth?

Check Your Understanding

Write the completed sentences on a separate piece of paper. The answers are below.

A business is an organization that creates and sells new resources and that has the primary goal of accumulating ·········. This is property that has a dollar ·········.

Only two kinds of resources can be created and sold. They are ········ and ·········. Only ········ can be wealth because it can be owned.

Answers

A business is an organization that creates and sells new resources and that has the primary goal of accumulating wealth. This is property that has a dollar value.

Only two kinds of resources can be created and sold. They are property and services. Only property can be wealth because it can be owned.

How a Business Accumulates Wealth

Overview

A business accumulates wealth by creating and selling goods or services (resources) that people (customers) need. Because these resources have value, the business is paid other valuable property by the customers. A business creates value!

Examples

The table below shows you some examples of how a business creates resources and accumulates wealth.

A business does this:	so it created the valuable resource of . . .	and the business accumulates wealth because . . .
performs computer repairs for $300	computer repairs (service)	the customer pays $300 cash for the value of the repairs received
shows a movie	entertainment (service)	the customers pay for the value of the tickets and to be entertained
makes and sells 1,000 loaves of fresh bread	loaves of bread (property)	it receives money for the value of the bread
makes and sells 100 new computers for $200,000	computers (property)	the customers pay $200,000 cash for the value of the computers
operates a grocery store that sells 1,000 loaves of bread and other foods	providing a selection of bread and other foods (service)	the customers pay the store for the value of the food and the service provided

How a Business Creates a New Resource

Overview

Now you know that a business creates and sells new resources, but that does not explain *how* a business creates the new resources. The discussion coming up tells you how that is done.

Resources Are Used Up

A business creates valuable new resources by using up other valuable resources. In other words, a business creates new property and services by using up other property and services.

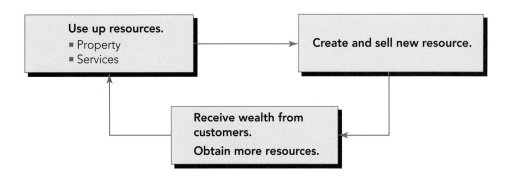

In the table below, notice that the only two kinds of resources used up are property and services, in order to create new and different property or services.

Business action:	The resource created is . . .	and examples of resources used up by the business are . . .
Richland Bakery makes and sells 1,000 loaves of fresh bread.	1,000 loaves of bread, a resource, which did not exist until it was produced,	the flour, water, and other ingredients of the bread dough; employee and manager labor; the equipment wear and tear.
Brookhaven grocery store sells the bread to shoppers.	the service of providing access to a selection of different breads,	employee and manager labor; electricity for light, heat, and power; the bread that the store had to purchase in order to sell.
El Paso Company manufactures 100 new computers.	a computer, which did not exist until it was manufactured,	employee and manager labor; metal and plastic components in the computer; the air and water of the city where the business is located.
Your local theater group presents Shakespeare's "Hamlet."	the service of entertainment,	the rental of the theater; the use of actors' labor; the wear and tear on the costumes.

continued ▶

How a Business Creates a New Resource, *continued*

Business Term: Expenses

People in business have a name for the dollar amount of a resource consumed in the operations that create a new resource. The *dollar cost* of any resource used up in the process of creating a new resource is called an *expense.*

> *Note:* "Used up" or "consumed" means not replaced by any other resource.

It does not make any difference what kind of resource is consumed. Services, supplies, equipment, merchandise, or any other kind of resource can be used up to create a new resource. Whatever the cost of the resource consumed, that is the amount of the expense.

Examples of Expenses

- $100 of office supplies used up is called "Office Supplies Expense."
- $2,000 value of employees' services is called "Wages Expense."
- A grocery store buys bread for a cost of $500. When the bread is sold to the store's customers, the store has $500 "Cost of Sales Expense."
- A furniture maker uses wood, nails, and fabric to make chairs. When the chairs are sold, the cost of these materials are "Cost of Sales Expense."
- The value of advertising services is called "Advertising Expense."

Not Expenses

- A business uses up $10,000 to pay off a bank loan. This is not an expense because paying a debt is not part of the process of creating a new resource for customers.
- A business gives up $100 cash to buy $100 of supplies. This is not an expense because one resource is simply replacing another (supplies for cash). Total value of resources remains the same.

How Much Value Is Created?

Overview

The entire purpose of using up resources is to create a new resource *that is valuable.* A business does not want to create something that has little or no value because no one will buy it. A business tries hard to create as much value as it can for every dollar of resources used up.

How Much Value Is Created? *continued*

Added Value

The total dollar value of a new resource that a business creates is called the *added value*. The process of incurring expenses to create a new valuable resource is sometimes called *adding value*.

The table below shows you some examples of added value and the expenses that create it.

The resource created:	so the added value is . . .	and value was added by incurring expenses such as . . .
Blinn Bakery makes *muffins* that can be sold for $1 each,	$1 each,	Wages Expense, Supplies Expense, and Cost of Sales Expense.
Blinn Bakery makes *walnut muffins* that can be sold for $1.25 each,	$1.25 each,	walnuts, which increased expense, but also increased the added value by $.25 per muffin.
Laredo Plumbing Service does *plumbing repairs* and charges the customer $375 for the job,	$375 for the job,	Labor Expense and Parts Expense.
Computers are manufactured by San Antonio Company. A computer can be sold for $1,000,	$1,000 each,	Labor Expense, Utility Expense, Rent Expense, Supplies Expense, and Cost of Sales Expense.
Kilgore Nursery offers *a selection* of young pine trees for $20 each,	$20 each,	Utilities Expense, Fertilizer Expense, and Labor Expense.

Warning to Businesses!

Expenses Do Not Always Add Value

As you have seen in the examples, a business consumes resources because it is trying to create added value. Unfortunately, while producing a new resource, businesses often consume resources that actually create very little or even no value. These expenses are wasted because little or no value is added. The customer will not pay for the amount of these expenses as part of the price of the resource created. A successful business eliminates as much of this nonvalue-added resource consumption as possible.

continued ▶

How Much Value Is Created? *continued*

Examples of NO Value Added

The resource created:	The business has this expense:	and the expense does not add value because . . .
Jones Company manufactures and sells a computer.	$10,000 for *storing the computers* before they are sold,	customers do not want to pay more just because the company made too many computers and had to pay for storage.
Jones Company manufactures and sells a computer.	the company president *uses the company airplane* to fly his dog back and forth between New York and Los Angeles,	the cost of these flights, and wear and tear on the airplane, do not make the computers more useful or valuable to customers. Using the company airplane in this way will not add value, even though it makes the dog happy.
Jones Company manufactures and sells a computer.	$25,000 *labor time* required to repair manufacturing mistakes,	customers do not want to pay for the cost of fixing new merchandise. Customers want a product that works properly the first time.

*"Really? And just how much value do
you add with that stupid flag?"*

How Much Value Is Created? *continued*

Added Value Is Difficult to Predict

In reality, the amount of added value that a business creates is only an educated guess until the resource is actually sold. A business can never be completely sure of the total added value until it sells what it has created. It is the customer who finally determines the actual added value by purchasing the resource and paying for it.

 Regardless of how carefully a business designs or sells the resource it creates, "value" is still just a feeling in the mind of the customer—a feeling that can change at any time. Moreover, customers are different, and some customers perceive value differently than others.

Here are some interesting examples of how added value can be unpredictable:

If a company . . .	then we would guess that the added value will be . . .	because . . .
uses higher quality parts in the toasters it makes,	probably greater than before	many people want improved reliability and quality and will pay more for it.
offers Christmas tree ornaments for sale on December 1 for $25 each,	$25 each	customers are willing to pay this amount because they are excited about Christmas and want new ornaments.
offers the same Christmas ornaments on February 1 for $25 each,	probably a lot less than $25 each	people are not so excited about Christmas anymore. Changing the time of the year reduced the total amount of added value.
angers potential customers because it damages the environment,	anywhere from a little less to a lot less than before	people become so angry that they refuse to purchase the company products. (This actually happens. For example, customers boycotted tuna products until tuna sellers agreed to stop killing dolphins in tuna nets.)
pays for a big advertising promotion for a product, although not changing the product in any way,	probably greater	even though the product itself has not changed, it may have improved in the *minds* of the customers! Resources used for repeated advertising can add significant value, even if a product is actually unchanged.

continued ▶

How Much Value Is Created? *continued*

The Value Chain	Every business has a value chain. The **value chain** is the sequence of all the activities that consume resources for the purpose of adding value. Together, all the expenses in the value chain result in the total cost of all resources consumed. *Note:* The term "value chain" may be a little misleading because, as we know now, all resources consumed do not always add value.
Example of Value Chain	Bad Apple Cider Company has to pay for fertilizer, water, and labor to maintain the apple trees. Then it pays for processing the apples into cider. After that, it pays for the cost of distributing and selling the cider. During all of these operations, the business also pays for the cost of management. *Question for the owner:* Do all parts of this value chain add significant value?

Check Your Understanding

Write the completed sentences on a separate piece of paper. The answers are below.

A business accumulates wealth by creating and selling new resources. New resources can only be created when a business uses up other · · · · · · · ·. The business term for the dollar cost of resources used up for this purpose is · · · · · · · ·.

The dollar value of the new resources that a business creates is called · · · · · · · ·   · · · · · · · ·. This is usually (easy/difficult) · · · · · · · · to precisely predict. As a general rule, (all/not all) · · · · · · · · expenses will add significant value.

Answers

A business accumulates wealth by creating and selling new resources. New resources can only be created when a business uses up other resources. The business term for the dollar cost of resources used up for this purpose is expense.

The dollar value of the new resources that a business creates is called added value. This is usually difficult to precisely predict. As a general rule, not all expenses will add significant value.

Confirming the Value Created

Overview	You know that added value is difficult to predict. The point at which a business finally knows exactly how much total value has been created is when a sale is made to a customer.

Confirming the Value Created, *continued*

Business Term: Revenue	When a business actually makes a sale to a customer, the true total of added value is confirmed. Businesspeople have a special name for the "confirmed" added value: revenue. ***Revenue* is the dollar value of a sale.** It is the amount the customer pays for the resource created.

Example #1 of Revenue

Blinn Bakery incurs expenses and makes 100 muffins that can be sold for $1 each. So far, the company has sold 70 muffins for a total of $70.

- The total amount of added value that the company believes has been created is $100 because 100 muffins normally sell for that amount.
- The total revenue is $70 because this is the actual dollar value of sales up to now. The company has received $70 from customers. This means that $70 of added value has been confirmed so far.

Example #2 of Revenue

Vancouver Company makes glazed clay pots for gardens. The company incurs expenses to make 20 blue pots and offers the pots for sale at $10 each, based on past experience. So the added value of the 20 pots *appears to be* $200.

- The company sells 10 of the clay pots, so it has $100 of revenue. This confirms the added value of 10 clay pots as $100.
- However, the company is unable to sell the remaining 10 blue pots and must reduce the price to $8 per pot. At this price, all the remaining pots are sold. The company has $80 of revenue for the remaining 10 pots, thus confirming their added value.

The total revenue of $180 for all 20 pots confirms that their real added value is actually $180. (The company has received $180 in wealth from customers.)

Example #3 of Revenue

Artie, the golf pro, owns the golf shop next to the municipal golf course. Artie offers golf lessons for $100 per hour. Artie sold 20 hours of golf instruction this month. Artie says, "The business earned $2,000 of instruction revenue." This means that the business wealth increased by $2,000 because the business created and sold $2,000 of added value in the form of golf instruction.

Not Revenue

- Burnaby Company collected $10,000 from a bank loan. This money is not revenue because it does not come from making a sale. It must be repaid.
- The owner of Surrey Company invests $10,000 in his business. This money is not revenue because it does not come from making a sale.

continued ▶

Confirming the Value Created, *continued*

Do Not Confuse Revenue with Wealth	"Revenue" refers to the dollar amount of a sale. Making a sale is one particular source of wealth.
	"Wealth" is the dollar value of the *property* that is received from a sale. This property could be anything—cash, accounts receivable, gold, supplies, land—although, in reality, wealth is almost always cash or accounts receivable.

Success or Failure?

Two Requirements for Success	To be successful, a business must do two things:

- It must create value.
- It must be sure that the cost of the resources consumed are less than the value created.

The owners and managers of businesses must determine which combination of resources adds the most value. This is not easy to do because, as we have seen, the amount of value added is only an estimate until whatever is created is actually sold. Then, the managers must also be sure that resources consumed do not exceed the total value added.

Example of Combining Resources	Bad Apple Cider Company makes and sells apple cider. The company makes 200 gallons of apple cider that the managers estimate can be sold for $10 per gallon, an added value of $2,000. When the cider is actually sold, the company has $2,000 of revenue, confirming the amount of value created.

The owners of Bad Apple Cider Company say, "We have earned $2,000 of cider revenue." The owners must also figure out precisely what combination of resources can create the most added value at the lowest cost. Is it some combination of the types of apples used to make the cider? How about the method of processing? The quality of the apples? The convenience of the store? The selection of ciders in the store? The time of year? . . . Business is tricky.

Success: Net Income	If a business creates and sells more value than the cost of the resources consumed, it will be successful. This means that revenues are greater than expenses. When *revenues are greater than expenses,* the business has a *profit.* People in business call this **net income.** Net income makes the wealth of a business increase and the business grows.

Success or Failure, *continued*

Failure: ***Net Loss***	If *revenues are less than expenses,* the business has a loss. This is called a ***net loss.*** Net loss is bad because the business is using up a greater value of resources than it is receiving from customers. Wealth is decreasing. There are two possible reasons for this: ■ The expenses (resources used up) cannot add enough total value. ■ The business is not charging enough for the actual value that it is creating. These are reasons why businesses lose money and go out of business.

Example #1:
Net Income

Swell Computer Manufacturing Company charges $2,500 per computer, and the company makes and sells 100 computers. The cost of the resources consumed (expenses) is $1,500 per computer. So, the business has total revenue of $250,000 and total expenses of $150,000. This is a net income of $100,000. Even though some of the $150,000 expenses might not add value, other expenses created enough value to result in a net income.

Example #2:
Net Loss

At the end of the year, Jiffy Tax Services has $300,000 of revenue for all the tax returns that it prepared. Expenses were $400,000. Jiffy has a net loss of $100,000. There are two possible reasons:

■ The expenses do not add enough total value. The business must change the way it uses resources or go out of business. This means:

   • Use the resources more efficiently so total expenses are less.
   • Use the resources in a different way so greater value is created.

■ The business is not charging enough for the actual value that it is creating. In this case, the business should increase what it charges customers.

TIP

Sometimes the word "revenue" is confused with "net income" (profit). Revenue is the total amount of the sales price. Net income is what is left over after subtracting expenses from the revenue.

QUICK REVIEW

- A business is an organization that has the primary goal of accumulating wealth by creating and selling new and valuable (economic) resources.

- There are only two economic resources: property and services.

- "Wealth" is property that has value.

- A business creates a valuable new resource by consuming other resources. The total value of the new resource is called the "added value." The cost of a resource consumed to add value is called an "expense."

- Unfortunately, not all expenses add value, and final added value is difficult to predict.

- "Revenue" is what the new resource actually sells for. Revenue confirms the actual added value.

- In a successful business, revenues exceed expenses. In an unsuccessful business, revenues are less than expenses.

VOCABULARY

Account receivable: the legal right to collect an amount owed by a customer (page 7)

Added value: the value created when a new resource is created (page 11)

Economic resource: a resource that can be valued or measured in dollars (page 4)

Expense: the cost of a resource used up in the process of creating a new resource (page 10)

Net income: when revenues are greater than expenses (page 16)

Net loss: when expenses are greater than revenues (page 17)

Property: any resource that can be owned (page 5)

Revenue: the dollar value of a sale—what a customer pays (page 15)

Services: the use of labor or the use of someone's property (page 5)

Value chain: the sequence of activities that consumes resources for the purpose of adding value (page 14)

PRACTICE   Learning Goal 1

Solutions are in the disk at the back of the book and at: www.worthyjames.com

Learning Goal 1 is about defining and identifying a business. Use these questions and problems to practice what you have learned about a business.

Multiple Choice
Select the best answer.

1. A business is
   a. an easy way to get rich.
   b. an organization that has the purpose of accumulating wealth.
   c. an organization that always adds value.
   d. an activity that provides little or no benefit to society.
2. The way a business operates is by
   a. borrowing and obtaining investments.
   b. using up resources.
   c. avoiding all risk.
   d. using up resources to create and sell new resources.
3. When a business creates a new resource that customers will want, the business is said to be
   a. adding value.
   b. making sales.
   c. doing market research.
   d. advertising.
4. "Bad Apple Cider Company had $200 of revenue." This statement refers to
   a. cash, in the amount of $200.
   b. an increase in business wealth in the amount of $200, caused by making a sale.
   c. a profit of $200.
   d. all of the above.
5. To add value, a business always has to
   a. make a profit.
   b. consume resources.
   c. make a sale.
   d. both (b) and (c).
6. Expenses
   a. will always add significant value.
   b. may add little or no value.
   c. require a nonvalue-added activity.
   d. none of the above.
7. Added value results from any expense that
   a. is not excessive.
   b. is cost effective.
   c. makes the final product more valuable or useful to customers.
   d. uses up resources.
8. The actual amount of revenue (total added value) is always determined
   a. by business management.
   b. by the productivity of the employees.
   c. by how much the customers decide to pay for the resource created.
   d. by a predetermined mathematical calculation for each product.
9. A business knows that it has net income when
   a. revenues are greater than expenses.
   b. expenses are greater than revenues.
   c. it is still able to repay its loans.
   d. it is certain that it is adding value.

Solutions are in the disk at the back of the book and at: www.worthyjames.com

PRACTICE   Learning Goal 1, continued

10. Which of the following expenses probably do not add any value?
    a. The $500 cost of the utilities to air-condition an accounting office.
    b. The $15,000 cost of the employee wages in the computer assembly operation.
    c. The $2,000 cost of the cookie dough that was spoiled in the bakery refrigerator.
    d. The $750 cost of the janitorial service.

Reinforcement Problems

LG 1-1. How is value being added? For each of the following situations, write a short and clear explanation of how the business is adding value.

a. A restaurant prepares a meal.

b. A bank advertises its new services and low loan rates.

c. An automobile manufacturer crash-tests the new models.

d. A doctor studies new surgical techniques.

LG 1-2. Determine the amount of added value. In each situation below, give your advice about what you think the final value will be.

a. Thinking that they have created the greatest new product since sliced bread, executives at Great Products Company produce liver-flavored toothpaste. Each tube costs $1.50 to produce, and this cannot be changed. The management wants to sell the product for $2 per tube. The managers have heard about added value, and they want you—a consultant—to tell them if their proposed selling price is a good estimate of the added value of their product.

b. Management at Green Bay Company is thinking about spending $100,000 to install on-site exercise and child-care facilities for its employees. However, to pay for this, the company will have to cancel the purchase of four new delivery trucks. Management wants to maximize added value and is not sure how their decision will affect the added value of the products. Write a brief response to the managers.

LG 1-3. Learning Goal 1 Cumulative Review. Jerry Berg recently graduated from veterinary school and received his license to practice veterinary medicine. A few months ago, he opened a veterinary clinic. The clinic provides medical care for animals and also sells pet-care merchandise that customers frequently need. Last month, the clinic billed customers a total of $38,500 for medical care services. At the beginning of the month, the merchandise was marked up to a total selling price of $2,500. However, for various reasons, the merchandise sold for only $2,200. $10,000 of the cash received from customers was used to purchase new equipment.

To operate the clinic, Dr. Berg employs a medical staff of five people. Employee wages last month totaled $21,200. The clinic also pays $2,000 per month for rent and $450 for utilities. The cost of the merchandise was $2,000. Repair services for equipment that was damaged by a poorly trained employee cost $1,100. Supplies were an additional $800. The clinic advertises its services in local magazines and papers at a cost of $400 per month. Finally, accounting and management services are $750 per month.

LG 1-3, *continued*

Answer the following questions about the clinic.

a. Would you classify this business as service, merchandising, or manufacturing?

b. How does this business add value? What kind of new resource is being created?

c. What was the actual added value as determined by the revenue? Was this different in any way from what was expected?

d. What kinds of resources does this clinic use up in order to add value?

e. Describe the value chain for this business. What was the total expense in the value chain?

f. Did all expenses in the value chain add significant value?

g. As a business, was the clinic successful or unsuccessful for the month? How much did the wealth of the business change?

LG 1-4. Challenging questions

a. **Accounts receivable as property.** In this learning goal, we said that wealth is property; that is, something that the business owns that has money value. How does an account receivable qualify as property? Or should we just say that it is the same as cash?

b. **Exchanges.** In this learning goal, we said that a business accumulates wealth by creating and selling things that people need, and then the business in turn receives other valuable property from its customers. Suppose that two companies exchange services with each other. Although services are valuable resources, we know that services cannot be owned. Can an exchange of services qualify as part of the process of accumulating wealth?

Your Questions?

It is *very* important to be aware of what you need to understand better. What do you need to understand better about this learning goal? On a separate piece of paper, write the questions that you want to discuss with your classmates, instructor, or supervisor. Try to be very specific about what is bothering you, such as explanations that you do not fully understand.

Do You Like a Good Story?

It Might Help You to Remember Better

Sometimes people remember information better when the information is part of an interesting story. The story that begins on the next page tells about how humanity first discovered what a business really is. The story has adventure, mystery, and romance—all for your enjoyment! So, if you think a story might help you remember better, or if you just want to have some fun, go ahead . . . the adventures of Darius await you.

Technical Content

This part of the story contains the following technical content:

■ The basic financial structure of any business
■ The definition of "asset"
■ Asset valuation basics
■ Claims on assets
■ Using the accounting equation

You Can Skip the Story

If you prefer to study the technical content listed above more quickly, you can skip the story and go directly to page 33, where the standard presentation and practice continue.

The Wealth of Darius
Part I

How Darius Came to Be a Merchant

Long, long ago, when civilization was just beginning, when the world was fresh, and when the Greek people believed that gods lived far above the clouds on the heights of great Mount Olympus, there lived a youth named Darius. What happened to Darius changed the world forever.

Darius was the child of a poor family, with many brothers and sisters, but he was lucky. The gods had given Darius the gifts of the artist. Everyone in the village admired the child for his fine drawing and painting. His skill surprised everyone, for none of his brothers or sisters nor his mother or father had ever shown the slightest of such talents.

Darius grew into a dark-haired and athletic young man, and he became an apprentice to a painter who painted wall designs and frescoes, and sometimes pottery for wealthy collectors. Darius had such exceptional talent that it was not long until he became more skilled than his master, a friendly man named Ammon.

One day Ammon came to Darius and said, "Young man, it is time for you to be on your own. There is nothing more that I can teach you now. Your beautiful designs, bright colors, and expert painting show the world that you are already better than the master. I am getting old, and it is time for me to enjoy the rest of my life without the worries of business."

Ammon continued. "You have such great talents, Darius. I would be honored if you would buy my shop from me and carry on the name of this honorable business. I will sell it to you for 7,000 gold coins, even though I might be able to get more."

When he heard Ammon say these things, Darius' heart rose and then fell. Darius had very little money. He had no chance to buy the business.

But Ammon continued. "I know that you are still a poor apprentice. I will wait seven years, and then you can pay me for the business. By that time, I think you will be a rich and famous painter. In the meantime, I only ask that you allow me to work for you as your employee for two gold coins per week so that I may have some income. I also ask two additional gold coins per week for allowing you to have the seven years to pay me."

Darius' eyes filled with tears of gratitude. He and Ammon signed an agreement according to Ammon's terms. Poor but talented young Darius was now the owner of his own business. He soon earned the admiration of all who saw and purchased his beautiful and original paintings and designs.

Darius' Troubles

Darius worked very, very hard to prove to Ammon that he could succeed. However, Darius was worried, and every day he prayed to the gods on Mount Olympus to help him.

Darius had the talents of an artist, not a businessperson. So, when Darius began to be responsible for the business, he soon felt confused and frightened. He did not dare ask Ammon for too much advice because he did not want to worry and trouble the old man. Besides, Darius was sure that neither Ammon nor any other merchant would have the answer to his most frightening worry of all.

What worried Darius most of all was that he did not know a way to determine what kind of condition the business was in. How does one know if a business is successful or unsuccessful? Even if there were many customers, would there be enough money to pay back the debt to Ammon? A few times, Darius asked other merchants how they would know if a business was successful, but he always received different answers from different people.

One merchant answered, "Well, that is easy! The more gold you have, the more successful you are." Another merchant said, "Success is when the business does not have debts." Still another said, "Many customers means success." Darius just became more confused than before.

At first, Darius sometimes wondered whether he was more prosperous because he owned a business. But after a while, he stopped thinking about his own prosperity because all he thought about was paying Ammon. Even worse, Darius then remembered the other people to whom the business owed money: Aulis, the merchant who sold paint and glaze; and Hela, the merchant who supplied the paper, ink, and drawing tools Darius used for designs.

Darius tried to think: "Let me see . . . the business has some gold now. The business owes money to Aulis and Hela and will have to pay Ammon four gold coins per week. But there is still some paint that I bought last month, and the prince Cronos has not yet paid for the large wall painting that was finished last week, and there are brushes and drawing tools, and . . . aaahh! How does all that tell me if the business is any better or worse than when I bought it? How do I know if I will ever be able to pay Ammon? I will be shamed in front of the world. I am sorry Ammon, sorry, *sorry*!"

When Darius returned to his house that evening and lay down to sleep, the worry demons whispered and giggled in his ears the entire night, and he never closed his eyes.

The Gods Intervene

The mysterious and immortal gods, who can observe all that mortal humans do, had been watching Darius. The gods reposed in the garden of eternity on Mount Olympus and debated what they should do with Darius. The god Hermes (pronounced *HER-meez*) was especially interested. Hermes wore winged sandals and was the god of commerce and the marketplace. Of all the gods, Hermes was the cleverest and most cunning, and he was forever causing discord and arguments among the other gods.

"I think it is time for humans to learn a secret of commerce from us," Hermes said. "These foolish mortals pretend to do business, they buy and they sell, they count their worthless little coins, and still they have almost no idea of what a business is or what they are doing. Let us give them new knowledge."

"Yes," said Apollo, the god of music, truth, and light. "It is time to give humanity a secret. After all, we already make the dull little beasts suffer enough with our games."

"What! Give them a secret of the gods? Never!" said Artemis, the goddess of hunting and of all wild things. "What a waste it would be. They would never know what to do with a secret of ours, and this fool Darius only knows how to paint pictures."

"Well," rumbled Hades (pronounced *HAY-deez*), the god of the dead and the world below, who had heard the discussion and appeared from his lands under the earth, "it will do them no good when they come to spend their time with me," at which Hades and Artemis laughed heartily, while Apollo frowned.

Hermes had started another argument and felt pleased with himself. Now he was ready for his next trick. "So," he said, "if none of the gods themselves can decide, let us wager that Darius can decide for us! I will test this mortal, and if he passes my test, I will reward him with a secret of the gods that will end his worries. If he fails my test, then Artemis may turn him into a wild pig to be hunted anytime she wishes."

"Yes, excellent!" they roared, Artemis shouting the loudest.

Hermes was happy with himself again. He had tricked the gods into gambling one of their secrets on the test of a human which, as we all know, no one can ever be sure about.

A Strange Event

Darius felt exhausted, confused, and full of worry when he left his house the next morning. He walked down the road to a small favorite lake, where he planned to bathe and regain his energy after a night with no sleep. He had been walking for perhaps ten minutes when he observed a dark form next to the road. As he approached the object, Darius began to notice a foul odor coming from the shape. To his surprise, the form was a filthy old beggar woman, disgustingly soiled and infested with lice.

The woman screeched, "I am hungry! I have no place to stay. Give me food and a place to stay! I am too tired to walk. Carry me to a place to rest!" Darius was already burdened with his own worries and concerns. He did not want another problem, so he walked away from the repellent woman. After a few steps, however, he thought, "Her problems are just as important to her as mine are to me. Who knows? If I fail in my business, as seems likely now, someday I may be nearly the outcast she is today."

With that thought he turned, picked up the disgusting woman, and carried her back to his house. He gave her bread, what meat he had left, heated some water for her bath, and told her to rest as long as she wished. As Darius prepared to leave his house the second time, a brilliant light filled the room, momentarily blinding him. As he regained his vision, he saw the old woman disappear. A large, powerful-looking man wearing winged sandals replaced her at the center of the light.

"You have passed," proclaimed the figure. Darius also heard the sounds of laughter and angry voices, but he could not see anyone else in the room. In that moment, he knew that he was in the presence of a god. Darius threw himself to the floor, trembling.

"Yes," said Hermes, who had disguised himself as the foul old woman, "you may be full of your own concerns, but you did not abandon someone even more hopeless than yourself, poor mortal." With that, the imposing god threw back his head, his thundering laughter filling the room, and pronounced, "You have defeated the gods!"

The huge, brilliant figure spoke again. "And now, Darius, as the god of commerce, I reward you with a secret of the gods that will end your present confusion. I thereby bring you peace of mind, for now. Rise up and listen, so that I may give you the secret of knowing the condition of your business at any time you wish."

As Darius slowly rose, the god continued. "Listen carefully to what I tell you now, mortal. The true picture of a business is simply this: wealth and claims on the wealth. That is all.

"At any time you choose, you may determine the condition of your business. First, determine the wealth of the business. Business wealth means any valuable things that belong only to the business. These things are called 'assets.' Assets are the business wealth. They are also used by the business to operate.

"Next, determine the claims on the assets. There are no more than two kinds of claims. The owner, of course, has a claim on the assets. But if there are business debts, which are the claims of creditors, then the creditors have first claim. Whatever value of all assets exceeds the claims of the creditors, then this excess may be claimed by you, the owner."

Finishing, the god said, "Here is how to remember what I have told you today: First, determine the value of all the assets. Next, determine the claims on the assets—the creditors and the owner. The total claims always equal the total assets . . . but the creditors have first claim.

"Remember this well, mortal, for it is the essence of every business. I expect you to understand this. I will visit you again in one year, when I will decide if you have learned to properly use the gift of knowledge that I have given to you."

With that, the god and the bright light disappeared in a shower of arching golden sparkles, leaving Darius dazzled and speechless. There was a roll of parchment paper on the wooden table in the center of the room. Written on the paper in gold print were the words:

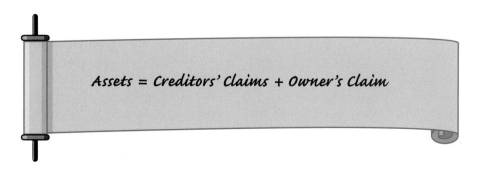

Assets = Creditors' Claims + Owner's Claim

Darius Tries Out the Secret

When he recovered his senses, Darius looked at the words on the paper and felt happier than he had felt since he had bought the business. He thought, "No longer will I operate my business in darkness! I will learn to use this at once!" Excitedly, Darius grabbed the paper and raced toward town, passing the place where he had met the old woman, and ran the entire distance to his shop.

Ignoring everyone else in the shop, Darius flew straight to his table in the back, where he did his planning and drawing. Slowly he took a deep breath, found a piece of paper to write on, and began to think.

"Let me see," he thought, "first I determine the wealth of the business. The name for this is assets. Hermes himself told me that an asset is anything with value that belongs to the business. So, what assets does my business have?"

Slowly and carefully, Darius began to list the assets belonging to the business, along with their values:

Gold *$2,500*
Receivable from Prince Cronos *500*
Painting equipment . . . .

As he was about to write down a number for the painting equipment, Darius began to hesitate. "What is the value of this equipment? I think I could sell it for $3,000 because Thrice, that bandit, offered me only $1,500 for it last week. Everyone knows that he never offers more than half." Still hesitating, Darius thought, "Yet, I cannot be certain until I actually sell it."

Then Darius had an excellent idea. "I know! I will use the cost that I paid for the equipment when I bought it. At least this is a number of which I can be completely certain. Only when I actually sell the equipment will I find out if it has some other value. This is acceptable."

And so, using this rule, he continued writing:

Painting equipment . . . . *2,700* (*my cost*)
Painting supplies . . . . *1,900* (*my cost*)
Other supplies . . . . *300* (*my cost*)
Other assets . . . . *800* (*my cost*)

These were all the assets that he could see. He tried to think if there were any other assets that might belong to the business. "The building!" he thought. But then he remembered that the building was actually owned by Amar, the landlord, and Darius paid Amar $25 in gold each month to use the building. So, the building really belonged to Amar.

Then Darius thought about Ammon. "Is Ammon an asset?" he wondered. Ammon was still a very valuable employee, but did he actually belong to the business like the equipment and supplies?

What Do You Think?

If you could help Darius answer this question before he decides what to do, how would you advise him? Should Ammon be considered a business asset? Write your answer on a separate piece of paper.

After giving the problem much thought, Darius remembered that Hermes said that an asset must not only have value, but that it must also belong to the business. So Darius decided that he could not include Ammon, because Ammon did not belong to the business like a table or a chair.

Darius then added up the assets and wrote the total on a piece of paper:

Total assets: $8,700

This was beginning to make sense! Under his breath, he thanked the gods one more time. Anxiously, Darius now began to write down the total business debts:

Owing to Ammon....................*$7,000*
Owing to Aulis 400
Owing to Hela........................ 600

He could not think of any more debts, except he wondered if Ammon's future wages were a business debt. Also, Darius owed his neighbor one gold coin for some meat he bought when he prepared dinner for his family last week. He stopped writing and thought hard about these two items.

If you could help Darius answer this question before he decides what to do, how would you advise him? Are Ammon's future wages a business debt right now? How about the money that Darius owes to his neighbor? Write your answer on a separate piece of paper.

Darius thought for a long time. He slowly began to realize that Ammon's wages could not be a debt if Ammon had not yet done the work. The business did not owe money for things that it had not yet received, and so it did not owe Ammon for work that was not yet done.

As to the one gold coin owing for the meat—well, that was a debt, all right, but it was not a business' but a personal debt because he was the one who had received the meat. Again, the business itself had not received anything, and so it did not owe anything.

Darius then added up the total business debts: $8,000.

Darius looked again at the words on the paper Hermes had left for him. He remembered that Hermes said that the owner's claim on the business wealth was whatever value of assets exceeded what was owed to the creditors.

The Owner's Claim

Darius realized that now all he needed to do was simply make the totals on each side be equal. To do this, he needed to determine if the assets' value exceeded the creditors' claims. This excess would be the amount of owner's claim, if there was any. Darius started writing down the total assets and total creditors' claims. He already knew the total assets and creditors' claims, so he only had to fill in . . .

Assets	=	Creditors' Claims	+	Owner's Claim
$8,700		$8,000		_____

Before Darius could write more, he realized what was happening and his heart leaped into his throat. He held his breath. Electricity flashed down his spine. He stood up and sat down. He stood up and sat down again. And again. Then he jumped into the air and shouted out, "Oh yes, by the gods, I am worthy!" People in the shop stopped and looked at him.

What made Darius so deliriously happy was what the calculation showed: The condition of his business was such that the business had enough wealth ($8,700) to pay *all* the $8,000 of debts (including Ammon!) and still have $700 which Darius could claim for himself as owner. He had not failed as a business owner!

Finally, when his heart was beating more slowly, Darius sat down again and finished writing the calculation:

Assets	=	*Creditors' Claims*	+	*Owner's Claim*
$8,700		*$8,000*		*$700*

Darius was an artist, so he drew a picture of the condition of his business, because he knew this would help him to remember it better. His picture looked like this:

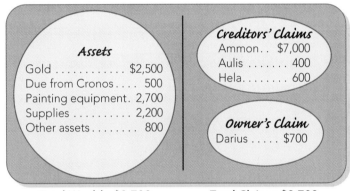

Total Wealth: $8,700	Total Claims: $8,700

It was all as clear as day to him. Darius realized that now he had the power at any time to clearly see the picture of his business. This made him remember what Hermes had said: "The picture of a business is simply wealth and claims on that wealth."

How Darius Used His Knowledge

At first, Darius was so excited about his newfound power that he wanted to calculate the condition of his business almost every day. However, because the condition changed so little from one day to the next, he began the habit of calculating the condition at the end of each month. When he did this, Darius could clearly see the change in the condition of the business every month.

He discovered that the total wealth—that is, the total of the assets—often changed. Sometimes the total of the assets increased a little and sometimes a lot, and sometimes it even decreased. Not only did the total amount of the assets change, but Darius discovered that the individual assets also changed. For example, sometimes the business had more gold or less gold than before, or more supplies or less supplies than before, and so on.

Also, the total amount owing to the creditors sometimes changed. Sometimes the business owed more to creditors than before and sometimes less. Darius watched the debts carefully.

Darius felt so good that he found a piece of paper and made a list of all the wonderful things that the calculation had made possible:

What I can see now but I could not see before:

- *I now see that the condition of my business is made up of assets and an equal amount of claims on those assets:*
  - *Assets are wealth (and are also used by the business).*
  - *The two types of claims on the assets are the creditors' and the owner's.*
- *I can know the condition of my business any time I want to by calculating these values.*
- *I can observe how the condition of my business is changing by doing the calculation every month.*
- *By watching the changes, I can make better decisions.*

Because of the success of the business, Darius was able to withdraw a little more money from the business for himself. His greatest enjoyment was to share his money and have dinners and parties for his mother and father and brothers and sisters, who had always been poor.

As the seasons passed, Darius continued on in this way. He worked hard, calculated the condition of his business, and was good to his family and friends.

But Darius had forgotten something important: Hermes' promise. It was now exactly a year since Hermes had promised to return.

To be continued . . .

LEARNING GOAL 2	# Define and Identify Assets

Overview

Introduction

In business, the word for property is "assets." Assets (especially the right kind) make a business wealthy, successful, and powerful.

However, before we begin discussing business assets, we will do a quick review of all resources—property and services—just to make sure that these basic ideas are clear.

In Learning Goal 2, you will find:

A Review of Resources

Resources in a Business

Resources Consumed to Add Value

A business consumes resources for the purpose of creating and selling more valuable resources. This is often called "adding value."

Only Two Kinds of Resources

On the planet Earth, only two kinds of resources can be bought and sold: property and services. These resources are also called "goods and services."

- **Property** is any resource that can be owned.
- **Services** are the use of labor or the use of someone else's property.

  Note: Because they can be bought and sold at some money amount, goods and services are sometimes called "economic" resources.

A Business Creates Both Kinds

A business can add value by producing either property or services, or both.

Example

Your business makes and sells fresh bread. The business has created bread, a valuable resource that can be owned. Your business also delivers the bread to restaurants and charges for this service. The delivery service is another valuable resource that customers want. However, the delivery service—although valuable—is not something that can be owned (because services are immediately used up).

Which Resource Is Most Important?

Both property and services are essential to any business, because both are needed to make a business operate. For example, a bread company needs ovens (property) and oven repairs (services) to operate.

However, in addition to being a useful resource, another feature of property makes it more important than services: property is also wealth.

The Dual Nature of Property

Property as Resource and Wealth

**Property Provides
Two Benefits**

Most property has a dual nature that allows it to be used in two ways. First, property can be consumed as a *useful resource* in the adding-value process. Secondly, property is also *wealth*.

**Property as a
Useful Resource**

A business obtains benefits by *consuming* property. In the examples below, each property item provides benefits as the item is used up or worn out in the adding-value process of operations.

Property	Benefits
Computer equipment	Calculations, projections, document preparation
Book	Knowledge
Insurance policy	Protection from losses
Truck	Delivery and transportation
Coffee supplies	Nourishment

Property as Wealth

Wealth is property that has a dollar value. Because wealth is property, wealth can be owned and kept for future use. This makes it extremely useful for obtaining other resources.

Wealth (property)	which has value because . . .
Computer equipment	it could be sold for cash (used to obtain other resources).
Book	it could be sold for cash (used to obtain another resource).
. . . and so on, for all the other property listed above.	

Exceptions

Some property has only monetary value. This kind of property is not a resource that is physically consumed in the adding-value process. Money is the best example of this kind of property. Another example is accounts receivable. These items are strictly wealth.

The Two Essential Characteristics of Assets

Overview

Introduction

People spend a lot of time thinking about assets. It probably has been that way from the time that two cavemen argued about who was entitled to sleep on the bearskin. Assets seem to appease deep psychological needs for security, power, and pleasure.

Human beings are amazing in how many ways they can think of for creating different assets and exchanging them back and forth. Common examples of business assets can be simple things like cash, office supplies, automobiles, or land. Sometimes assets can be strange and unusual things, like a "capitalized lease" or a "financial market derivative." (Whoever thought up those things?) You will learn more about assets as you progress in your study of accounting and business.

Assets: The Everyday Meaning and the Business Meaning

Everyday Assets

It is important to distinguish the everyday meaning of the word "asset" from the business meaning. In everyday language, we usually use the word "asset" to mean anything useful or beneficial, such as:

- Cash (because you can buy things with it)
- A car (because it provides transportation)
- A computer (because you can use it to do calculations)
- An education (because it will help you get a good job)
- Beauty (because it helps you meet people and get invited to parties)
- A sense of humor (because it helps you make friends)

Assets: The Everyday Meaning and the Business Meaning, *continued*

"Assets, sir. Everywhere you look!"

Business Assets

In business, the general idea of **asset** is similar to the everyday meaning—something useful or beneficial. However, for business purposes, *general beneficial qualities are not enough*. An asset must be property, and the property must have the following two specific qualities to qualify as an asset:

 The property must provide future economic benefits to a business.
 The property must be owned by a business as a result of a past event.

continued ▶

Assets: The Everyday Meaning and the Business Meaning, *continued*

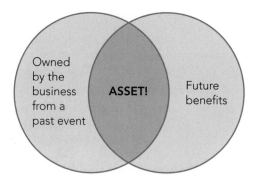

You can visualize the necessary qualities of an asset as two circles. An asset is described only in the space where the circles intersect.

The "Future Benefit" Characteristic

Future Benefit
(Property Is Useful)

A future benefit of an asset is whatever benefit or advantage an asset will bring to a business at any time in the future. The benefit can be either physical use of the asset or its cash value.

The asset must benefit the business in some way in the future, whether the benefit is five minutes in the future, five years in the future, or any other future time. Past benefits are gone. Only future benefits can help a business.

Note: Sometimes these future benefits are called **service potential**.

Examples of Future Benefits (Service Potential)

	For a business to . . .	Using the asset releases benefits
Cash	. . . get a different asset, it might exchange its cash for a computer. . . . operate and grow, it might exchange its cash for employee services. . . . pay a debt, it might use its cash to pay a bank loan.	By exchanging its cash for assets or services or by using its cash to pay debts, a business can . . . 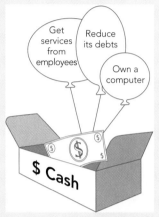
Noncash: Computer	. . . operate and grow, it might consume its computer by using it to: ■ record revenues and expenses ■ create marketing documents ■ e-mail bills to customers *Analogy:* driving a car wears it out and therefore uses it up. Similarly, using office equipment wears it out.	As it uses up or wears out its computer, a business can . . . 
Noncash: Supplies	. . . operate and grow, it might use up or consume its office supplies to: ■ write letters to customers and vendors ■ make copies of documents ■ prepare bills for customers	By using up or consuming its supplies, a business can . . . 

The "Owned by the Business as a Result of a Past Event" Characteristic

Ownership from a Past Event	■ ***Ownership:*** As a characteristic of an asset, "ownership" means complete control over all uses of property, provided that the uses are legal. Having this control means that a business has the legal right to receive any and all benefits from the property, including use in operations, selling, exchanging, and disposing in any manner.
	■ ***Past event:*** This means a completed transaction; in other words, the event has already taken place at some time in the past.
Examples of Ownership	■ A business buys a computer to use in its operations.
	■ A business creates an account receivable by a sale to a customer.
Not Ownership	■ A business rents a computer from another company. (Renting is not ownership. *Note:* Renting is also called **leasing**.)
	■ A business pays employees who work for the business. (People are not property.)
Examples of a Past Event	■ Last month a business bought a computer.
	■ Yesterday a business made a sale to a customer.
Not a Past Event	■ A business creates a budget that includes buying a new computer. (A budget is a plan, but the new computer has not yet been purchased.)
	■ A very good customer tells us that he will make a purchase tomorrow. (This is only an intention; the sale has not actually happened yet.)
More Benefits of "Past Event"	By requiring "past event" to be a characteristic of an asset, two important benefits happen. First, the past event provides *objective evidence*. Second, *historical cost* is identified.
	Objective evidence refers to documents that prove the amount of cost as well as when and where the asset was acquired. Examples of objective evidence are documents such as invoices, receipts, and canceled checks.
	Historical cost refers to the asset value used in the past event. This provides a reliable method of determining the dollar-value amount of the asset. Even though an item qualifies as an asset, a dollar value is still necessary to record it.

More Examples of Assets and Their Characteristics

Cash

Cash is the most useful of all assets. Its dollar value is clear, and it provides the most kinds of possible future benefits. This is because cash can easily be used to obtain any other kind of resource—whether property or services—or to pay debts.

"Cash is the most useful of all assets."

Non-Cash Assets

Non-cash assets are any assets other than cash. Non-cash assets have a money value and also are frequently used physically or consumed as part of the business operations.

Non-Cash Examples

- Office supplies: small items that are quickly used up in the office such as pens, pencils, paper, computer disks, and coffee for employees
- Office equipment: long-lasting equipment that is used in the office such as desks, file cabinets, computers, and copy machines
- Accounts receivable: the legal right to collect money from customers
- Automobiles
- Land
- Prepaid services: advance payments such as prepaid insurance and prepaid rent

Monetary Assets

Some assets have only money value. These assets are not physically used or consumed as part of the value-adding operations of a business. Common examples of monetary assets are cash and accounts receivable. Notes receivable, a more formal right to collect money, is also a monetary asset.

continued ▶

More Examples of Assets and Their Characteristics, *continued*

Not Assets

- *Employees:* Although employees are a valuable resource, people are not property, and *they do not belong to the business.*
- *Rented truck:* Although the truck is useful to the business that uses it, the truck *does not belong to that business.* It is an asset of the business that actually owns it and rents it to other businesses. (Renting is a service.)
- *Broken calculator:* If the calculator is broken and cannot be repaired, it will never function and will not provide future benefits (no service potential). It will not work and cannot be sold, so it will give *no future benefits.*
- *Repair service: Services cannot be owned* because they are immediately consumed. Services are never assets.
- *Good credit:* The good credit does belong to the business, is very important, and surely will provide future benefits. However, *it was not acquired from an identifiable past event,* and no dollar value can be identified.

QUICK REVIEW

- Only two kinds of economic resources are available to a business:

  - services, which are useful in the operations, and
  - property, which is both useful *and* is wealth.

- A business property is called an "asset."

- To qualify as an asset, the property resource must meet two requirements:

  - It must provide future benefits.
  - It must belong to the business as the result of a past event.

- A business has both cash and non-cash assets.

VOCABULARY

Asset: business property (page 37)

Historical cost principle: the requirement that transactions be recorded at actual cost (page 40)

Leasing: renting property (page 40)

Objective evidence: proof provided by a past transaction (page 40)

Service potential: the future benefits that any asset provides (page 38)

PRACTICE   Learning Goal 2

Solutions are in the disk at the back of the book and at: www.worthyjames.com

Learning Goal 2 is about defining and identifying assets in a business. Use these questions and problems to practice what you have learned about assets.

Reinforcement Problems

LG 2-1. **Characteristics of an asset.** This exercise will help you remember and understand the correct definition of the word "asset." Write the completed sentences on a separate piece of paper.

An asset is · *property* that is *owned.* · · · by a business. Every asset must be able to provide a future *benefit* · · to the business to which it belongs. The asset must be *owned* · by the business as a result of a *past* · · · event.

On a separate page, write a short, clear answer to each of the following questions:

LG 2-2. What is the everyday, nontechnical meaning of the word "asset"?

Something useful & beneficial

LG 2-3. Name the two essential qualities of an asset for business purposes.

Provide future benefits & must belong to business as result of past event.

LG 2-4. **Make up an example of an asset.** Using a bicycle as your subject, create your own example that compares the bicycle used as an everyday asset (meaning a non-business asset) to the bicycle used as a business asset. (*Tip:* when writing the example, think of the essential qualities of a business asset. An everyday asset will be missing some or all of those essential qualities. A business asset will have all of them.)

LG 2-5. **Identify assets and non-assets.** Use a blank sheet of paper to complete the table. Identify what items are assets and what items are not. If an item is *not* an asset, identify the *missing* quality. Use the first two items as examples.

Business item	It is . . .		Missing quality	
	an asset	not an asset	Future benefits	Owned as a result of a past event
a. The supervisors of a business		✓		✓
b. Office supplies	✓			

PRACTICE   Learning Goal 2, continued

Solutions are in the disk at the back of the book and at: www.worthyjames.com

LG 2-5, *continued*

Business item	It is . . .		Missing quality	
	an asset	not an asset	Future benefits	Owned as a result of a past event
c. Cash in the checking account	X	(Reminder: Use a separate sheet of paper to complete the table.) X		
d. The legal right to collect $500 that customers owe the business	X			
e. The new airport to be built next year, five miles from your business		X		X
f. A 12-year-old computer that is no longer functional		X	X	X
g. An expensive French impressionist painting purchased to hang in the lobby of your office	X			
h. A building that your company rents from Multnomah Company		X		X
i. A prepaid $700 fire insurance policy	X			
j. The business owner's master's degree	X			
k. The computer that your business <u>rents</u> and uses to produce marketing brochures		X		X
l. A promise by a good customer to buy $10,000 of merchandise from your business				
m. The $5,000 increase in value of the French painting your business bought six years ago.	X		X	
n. A mission statement explaining company goals that managers prepared	/			
o. The employees of a business	X		X	
p. A budgeted amount to buy office equipment				
q. Money that your business owes to vendors				

PRACTICE   **Learning Goal 2, continued**   *Solutions are in the disk at the back of the book and at: www.worthyjames.com*

LG 2-6. Identify the type of resource. On a separate piece of paper, identify each resource item in the table below as property or service by placing a mark in the correct box. The first item has been done for you as an example.

Item	Property	Service
a. The aircraft of a commercial airline company	✓	
b. A medical examination by your doctor	(Reminder: Use a separate sheet of paper to complete the table.)	
c. The medical equipment in the doctor's office	✓	
d. The gasoline in your car	✓	
e. The cash in a savings account	✓	
f. The classroom lecture from your accounting instructor		✓
g. The rental of a computer to a business that does not own one		✓
h. A six-month fire insurance policy paid in advance	✓	

LG 2-7. Challenging questions

a. Suppose that your business owns an old machine. The machine is no longer functional and cannot be repaired. However, the machine can still be sold for salvage value of $250. Would you still call the machine an asset for accounting purposes?

b. Suppose that the machine is still functional and useful in the business operations and helps create cash flow into the business. However, it has no market value and cannot be sold for any amount. Would you still call the machine an asset for accounting purposes?

c. Suppose that the machine cannot be sold at any price and is also no longer useful to the business. However, the machine is still functional. Is it still an asset to the business?

d. Could an item be acquired at a zero dollar value and still be an asset?

Instructor-Assigned Problems

If you are using this book in a class, these review problems may be assigned by your instructor for homework, group assignments, class work, or other activities. Only your instructor has the solutions.

IA-1. Identify assets and non-assets. On a piece of paper, draw a table like the one below. Identify which items are assets and which items are not by entering a checkmark. If an item is not an asset, identify the missing quality.

Business Item	Asset	Not an Asset	Future Benefits	Owned as a Result of a Past Event
a. A computer that was purchased last year				
b. A computer that is being leased from another company				
c. A computer that was purchased last year but is no longer functional and cannot be repaired				
d. The legal right to collect money from customers				
e. A promise by a good customer to purchase merchandise tomorrow				

PRACTICE   Learning Goal 2, continued

IA-1, *continued*

Business Item	Asset	Not an Asset	Future Benefits	Owned as a Result of a Past Event
f. Office supplies				
g. Airline tickets that our company paid for in advance, but that have not been used yet				
h. Cash in the company savings account				
i. Employees of our business				
j. An amount in the company budget to purchase office supplies				
k. A bill from the telephone company for telephone service				
l. An appraisal report that indicates an increase in the value of land owned by the company				
m. A major improvement in the road in front of our store				
n. Computer repair and maintenance services we paid for				
o. Merchandise inventory that your company will sell to customers				
p. Office furniture that our company owns that we are renting to another company				
q. A new roof for a building				

INTERNET EXERCISES

Develop a business startup checklist. Do an Internet search for "small business startup" and "small business."

a. Use the links you locate to develop a **checklist** for a person who wants to begin a new business. Look for a link to the Small Business Administration (*www.sba.gov*). Many states have general checklists and state-specific checklists for new businesses. So check state government home pages. For example, the state of Idaho Department of Commerce provides a checklist called "Starting a Business in Idaho" at *www.idoc.state.id.us*. An interesting general-purpose link is *www.ideacafe.com*. (Use bookmark/favorites to save the locations in an "Accounting References" folder.)

b. What important training and/or resources does the checklist indicate that you had not anticipated? Explain why you feel they are important.

c. What do you think are the most important items in your checklist? Why?

d. Did you have search results that were primarily advertising that you excluded from your checklist? Give three examples.

Your Questions?

It is *very* important to be aware of what you need to understand better. What do you need to understand better about this learning goal? On a separate piece of paper, write the questions that you want to discuss with your classmates, instructor, or supervisor. Try to be very specific about what is bothering you, such as explanations that you do not fully understand.

| LEARNING GOAL 3 | # Define and Identify the Two Claims on Assets |

Overview

Introduction

In the previous learning goal, you learned how to identify business assets. In this learning goal, you will learn who gets to claim these assets and why . . . and it is not always just the owner!

Rules for Claims on Assets

- There is always at *least* one kind of claim on business assets—the owner's.
- There are never more than two possible claims—the owner's and the creditors'.

"Equity" Means a Claim

Equity, as used in business, means the legal right to claim the value of assets. Another way of expressing the same idea is to say that equity means a legal claim on the business wealth.

In Learning Goal 3, you will find:

The Owner's Claim and the Creditors' Claims

The Owner's Claim and the Creditors' Claims

Owner's Equity and Creditors' Equity Defined

Two Possible Kinds of Equity

There are two kinds of legal claims on assets:

- The owner's equity
- The creditors' equity

Definition of Owner's Equity

Owner's equity is the owner's legal claim on the value of business assets. This is the most basic claim on the assets. There is always an owner's equity for every business.

Other terms used for owner's equity are **net worth** and **net assets**.

Example of Owner's Equity

Ramos Enterprises has a $10,000 value of various kinds of assets, consisting of cash, accounts receivable, supplies, equipment, and so on. Andy Ramos (the owner) has the legal right to claim the entire $10,000 value of the business assets for himself if there are no business debts to pay.

Definition of Creditors' Equity (Liability)

Creditors' equity is a legal claim on the value of business assets by a creditor. This kind of claim is usually called a *liability*. Liability simply means a debt of the business.

Examples of Liabilities

- An unpaid bank loan (the bank is the creditor)
- Amounts owing to suppliers (for items purchased on credit)
- Wages owing to employees (who are creditors until they are paid)
- An unpaid telephone bill (the telephone company is the creditor)

What Is the Amount of a Liability?

The amount of a liability is the unpaid value of the resources provided. When a business fully pays a creditor, the liability disappears.

Owner's Equity and Creditors' Equity Defined, *continued*

Examples:
Not Liabilities

- A company purchases various items of office supplies and pays cash. The seller is fully paid, so no liability exists.
- A contract is signed for $5,000 of accounting services to be received next month. No resources (services) have yet been provided, so no liability exists.
- Totally defective supplies are received from a seller. No acceptable resources (supplies) have yet been provided, so there is no liability to the seller.

Check Your Understanding

Write the completed sentences on a separate piece of paper.

· · · · · · · · · · · · · · · · is the owner's claim on the value of the business assets. Other terms that mean the same are · · · · · · · · · · · · · and · · · · · · · · · · · · · · . The word · · · · · · · · is used to describe the total creditors' equity claim on assets. If a business purchased $900 of supplies and paid $500 to the seller, a liability of $· · · · · · · · would exist. The creditors' claims have (higher/lower) · · · · · · · priority than the owner's claim.

Answers

Owner's equity is the owner's claim on the value of the business assets. Other terms that mean the same are net worth and net assets. The word liabilities is used to describe the total creditors' equity claim on assets. If a business purchased $900 of supplies and paid $500 to the seller, a liability of $400 would exist. The creditors' claims have higher priority than the owner's claim.

Why the Two Claims Exist

Overview of the
Two Claims

Directly or indirectly, the owner and the creditors provide all the resources to a company, both assets and services.

- *The owner* invests his/her own assets into a business. The owner also invests services—time and energy—and by doing this creates a business operation that adds value and obtains wealth from customers.
- *Creditors* directly supply both assets and services to a business.

Why Owner's
Equity Exists

The owner's equity claim exists because the business belongs to the owner.

continued ▶

Why the Two Claims Exist, *continued*

Why Creditors' ***Equity Exists***	The creditors' equity (liabilities) exists because the creditors provided goods and services resources to the business that the business has not yet paid for.

When . . .	and . . .	then . . .
resources are pro-vided by someone other than the owner	the resources are not immedi-ately paid for,	a liability is cre-ated (creditor's equity).

Claims Are Usually ***on the Total Assets***	The liability claims and owner's equity claim are normally against the entire dollar value of all assets, up to the amount of the claim, and not against the value of any specific asset.

> *Exception:* Sometimes a creditor's claim may be "secured" by a particular asset. This means that a creditor has the right to seize and sell a particular asset to pay a debt, if the debt is not paid on time. The particular asset is said to be **security** for the debt.

TIP

A supplier of goods or services is sometimes called a **vendor**. "Vendor" means the same as "seller."

Compare the Claims

The Most Important ***Difference***	Owner's equity claim and the liability claim are different in several ways, which are listed for you in the comparison table on page 52. However, the *most important difference* is that they do not have the same priority for payment.

Liabilities Have ***First Priority***	Liabilities have first priority over owner's equity. This means that if a business does not have enough assets to pay both the creditors and the owner, then the creditors must be paid first.
	If all liabilities are fully paid, any remaining asset value can be claimed by the owner.

Compare the Claims, *continued*

Examples of
Liability Priority

- Tishomingo Enterprises has a $10,000 bank loan coming due this week. The owner must make sure there is sufficient asset value to pay the loan before considering how much asset value might be available for himself.
- Wilmington Company has $90,000 of assets and $50,000 of liabilities. The company decides to cease operations and go out of business. Therefore, all company debts are now due and payable. The owner must wait and make sure that all the debts are fully paid before he can claim any of the asset value for himself.

Owner's Equity
Is Residual

Whenever there are liabilities, the owner's equity is the amount of asset value that would be left over if all the liabilities were fully paid. Therefore, the owner's equity is always a residual amount. The formula is:

$$\textbf{Assets} - \textbf{Liabilities} = \textbf{Owner's Equity}$$

Example of Owner's
Equity Residual

Georgetown Company has $52,000 of total assets and $35,000 of various liabilities. To calculate the amount of the owner's equity, calculate the value of assets that would be left over if the business were to pay off all its liabilities: $52,000 − $35,000 = $17,000 owner's equity.

continued ▶

"It says: 'There are no more than two kinds of claims on assets.'"

Compare the Claims, *continued*

Liabilities Compared to Owner's Equity

This table compares the three important characteristics of liabilities and owner's equity.

Compare . . .	Liabilities . . .	Owner's Equity . . .
priority of payment	always have first priority	is second priority
when it must be paid	■ the day a debt becomes due, according to its terms, or ■ when the business terminates	has no requirement to be paid at a particular time—it is a residual
intended risk	none, because the creditor expects to be fully paid	resources that are invested can be lost

TIP

Sometimes the word "liability" is confused with the word "expense." We discuss expenses in Learning Goal 6. "Liability" only means a debt.

Check Your Understanding

Write the completed sentences on a separate piece of paper. The answers are below.

There are two kinds of claims on the assets of a business. The owner's claim is called · · · · · · · ·
· · · · · · · · and the creditor claims are called · · · · · · · · ·. Directly or indirectly, the owner and the creditors together provide all the · · · · · · · · to a company, both assets and services.

The (owner's equity/liabilities) · · · · · · · · always has (have) legal priority for payment. Claims are usually against (total assets/a particular asset) · · · · · · · ·.

Answers

The liabilities always have legal priority for payment. Claims are usually against total assets.

There are two kinds of claims on the assets of a business. The owner's claim is called owner's equity and the creditor claims are called liabilities. Directly or indirectly, the owner and the creditors together provide all the resources to a company, both assets and services.

Management of a Business Changes the Owner's Equity

Good Management

Regardless of whether an owner manages a business or employs other people to manage it, management can be good or bad. Good management will cause the business assets to grow because the managers will operate the business so it will create and sell more value than the value of resources it uses up. When assets increase this way, owner's equity also increases.

Bad Management

Bad management will cause the business to use up more resource value than the value that is created and sold. This will cause assets to decrease as more resources flow out than come in. When assets decrease this way, owner's equity decreases.

Example Using Equation

Good: Assets $\uparrow$ = Liabilities + Owner's Equity $\uparrow$

Bad: Assets $\downarrow$ = Liabilities + Owner's Equity $\downarrow$

QUICK REVIEW

- There are only two possible types of claims on business assets:
  - creditors' claims, which are called liabilities.
  - owner's claim, which is called owner's equity.
- The owner's equity exists because the owner owns the business and provided assets and services to the business. The creditors' claim exists because the creditors provided assets and services which have not been paid for.

- The claims do not have equal rights; the creditor always has priority. This means:
  - Debts must be paid when they are due.
  - Debts have first claim if a business is liquidated.
- Liabilities are normally against the entire total dollar value of the assets.
- The most important cause of change in the owner's equity is the manner in which a business is managed.

VOCABULARY

Equity: a claim on asset value (page 47)

Liability: a debt; a creditor's claim on assets (page 48)

Net assets: a synonym for owner's equity (page 48)

Net worth: a synonym for owner's equity (page 48)

Owner's equity: an owner's claim on assets (page 48)

Security: the particular asset or assets a creditor can claim for nonpayment of a debt (page 50)

Vendor: any seller of goods or services (page 50)

PRACTICE   Learning Goal 3

Solutions are in the disk at the back of the book and at: www.worthyjames.com

Learning Goal 3 is about identifying the claims on assets. Use these questions and problems to practice what you have learned about a business.

Reinforcement Problems

LG 3-1. **What creates and changes claims on assets?** Claims on the wealth of a business (the assets) result from only two providers of resources.

   a. Who are these two providers of resources? What do they provide?

   b. Why do they have claims on the wealth of a business?

   c. Why isn't the owner's claim equal to the value of whatever assets the owner invested minus the value of whatever the owner has withdrawn?

   d. Do the owner's services have a fixed dollar value, like wages of an employee?

LG 3-2. **Explain changes in equities.**

   a. A supplier sells merchandise to a business for $800 on credit. Does the supplier have a claim on the assets? How much?

   b. A computer repair service charges a business $500 on credit for repairs made. Does the repair service have a claim on the assets? How much? If the business later pays $100 of the liability, does the claim change?

   c. An owner invests $5,000 in his small video store. Does this affect the owner's claim on the assets? By how much?

   d. The owner of a video store invests 500 hours of his time managing the store. He thinks his time is worth $30 per hour. Does this affect the owner's claim on assets? By how much?

LG 3-3. On a separate piece of paper, write a short, clear definition of "owner's equity."

LG 3-4. On a separate piece of paper, write a short, clear definition of "liabilities" and give three examples.

PRACTICE   **Learning Goal 3, continued**   *Solutions are in the disk at the back of the book and at: www.worthyjames.com*

LG 3-5. YOU be the teacher! While I was writing this book, a student made the following suggestion about how to describe the meaning of equities. He said:

> "Why not just say that equities are a claim against assets because the equities are the source of those assets? So, you could look at equities as *simply direct sources of assets and also as claims on assets.* That's all there is to it!"

I appreciated his good suggestion, but why is he not quite complete in his description of equity claims? How do I answer him? (*Hint:* Is there more than one kind of resource that a business has to pay for?)

LG 3-6. Explain the priority of liabilities. "The creditors' liability claims always have priority over the owner's claim." Does this mean that an owner cannot withdraw money from his business until he pays off all the debts first?

LG 3-7. Identify the kind of claim. For each separate item described, indicate if it is a creditors' equity claim or an owner's equity claim. Use a blank sheet of paper to complete the table.

Description of Equity Characteristic	Creditors' Equity	Owner's Equity
a. It always has the first claim on assets.	(Reminder: Use a separate sheet of paper to complete the table.)	
b. It is increased by the owner's hard work and risk-taking.		
c. It is usually called "liabilities."		
d. It is known as a "residual" claim on assets.		
e. They are the debts of the business.		
f. It is increased when the owner invests in his/her business.		
g. It is created when someone other than the owner provides assets or services to the business that are not immediately paid for.		
h. Together they always add up to the total amount of assets.		

Your Questions?

It is *very* important to be aware of what you need to understand better. What do you need to understand better about this learning goal? On a separate piece of paper, write the questions that you want to discuss with your classmates, instructor, or supervisor. Try to be very specific about what is bothering you, such as explanations that you do not fully understand.

| LEARNING GOAL 4 | **Use the Accounting Equation to Show the Condition** |

Overview

The Most Basic Question

The most fundamental and basic question about any business is: "What is the condition *right now*?" Every business owner and every investor will ask this question hundreds of times during the life of a business.

What "Condition" Means

The "condition" of a business as used in this book means the total value of the assets and the total claims on the assets, at any specified point in time. This simply means the wealth and the claims on the wealth.

Synonym

Another word used to refer to the condition of a business is *position*.

Purpose of This Learning Goal

In this learning goal, we will study how the condition of a business can always be expressed by the accounting equation. Then we will practice using the equation to show condition.

You will also learn a way to visually picture the condition of a business.

In Learning Goal 4, you will find:

The Financial Condition of a Business

The Financial Condition of a Business

The Accounting Equation

The Final Result of Business Activities

The daily operations of a business can be quite complex, involving marketing, finance, production, research and development, and a complex flow of resources into and out of the business. **But the final result of all these activities always shows up like this simple picture:**

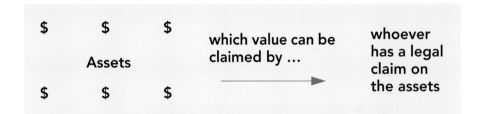

This is the fundamental condition of any business.

Assets and the claims on assets are the essential elements of the condition of any business entity. That is why we have taken such a long time to talk about them. No matter how complex the business operations might be, the result of all the activities can still be expressed like this simple picture.

The Accounting Equation

Instead of drawing a picture, we can use the accounting equation as a clear and powerful way to describe the condition of a business:

$$\text{Assets} = \text{Liabilities} + \text{Owner's Equity}$$

or

$$A = L + OE$$

This means that the total dollar value of the assets is claimed by no more than two providers of resources: the creditors and owner. This is a very powerful idea and it applies to any business. In fact, it even applies to charities, governments, or you and me! We all have assets and claims on the assets.

Rearranging the Equation

The equation can also be rearranged to show:

- Liabilities: $A - OE = L$
- Owner's equity: $A - L = OE$

Last month, your aunt Minnie opened up an appliance repair business. She is thinking about applying for a loan and wants to know how to show the bank the financial condition of her business at the end of the first month. At the end of the month, she provides you with the following information from her business records:

- Cash in the bank: $7,500

- Debts to suppliers: $2,000

- Office supplies on hand: $300

- Car belonging to the business: $10,000

- Tools belonging to the business: $4,000

- Owing to employee: $500

On a separate piece of paper, show the condition of aunt Minnie's business at the end of the month by using the accounting equation. To do this, identify each of the individual asset and equity items and then show their totals.

What do you think about the financial condition of aunt Minnie's business?
Do you think the business looks strong or weak now? Using the accounting equation, what would you say to explain to aunt Minnie what would make her business be stronger or weaker?

Answers

Assets	=	Liabilities	+	Owner's Equity
$21,800		$2,500		$19,300
($7,500 cash + $300 supplies + $10,000 car + $4,000 tools)		($2,000 debts to suppliers + $500 owing to employee)		(assets of $21,800 less the liabilities of $2,500)

The business looks strong now. Creditors have only a $2,500 claim on $21,800 of assets. (This is only 11.5% of assets needed to pay debts.) Stronger or weaker? If the liabilities were lower or the assets were greater, the business would be stronger because more wealth would be available for operations. The reverse situation would make the business weaker. Owners and managers spend a lot of time worrying about this!

Visualizing the Condition

Most People Are Visual Learners

Most people learn a lot by remembering mental pictures. Using a picture in your head is called "visualizing." If I were to say the word "car," the first thing you probably would think of is a picture of some kind of car. This is a very good way to remember and understand.

Visualize the Condition of a Business

For many people, it is helpful to visualize the condition of a business in addition to using the accounting equation of $A = L + OE$.

Suppose for a moment that I give you a "magic" camera. You can point this magic camera at any business and the camera will give you an accurate picture of the condition of the business in its most basic form. The picture would always come out like this:

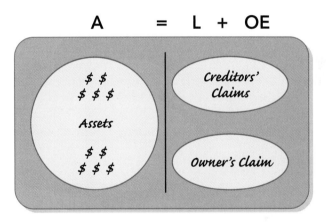

Continue to Visualize . . .

Soon, we will spend a lot of time watching how business events can cause changes in the three parts of the picture, but remember that the financial condition of every business can always be visualized like this picture.

Any change or business event you might encounter in an accounting book (or in "real life") can always be understood by visualizing how it affects the three basic parts of the business condition. Try to keep this picture in mind as you study the rest of the book.

Learning Goal 4 is about using the accounting equation. Use these questions and problems to practice what you have learned.

Reinforcement Problems

LG 4-1. Make the equation balance. In the table below, calculate the missing amounts in the accounting equation.

	Total Assets	= Total Liabilities	+ Owner's Equity
a. Mohawk Company (June 30, 2008)	$251,000	$200,000	?
b. Nez Perce Company (December 31, 2008)	?	$18,500	$22,200
c. Lakota Company (October 31, 2007)	$50,000	?	$35,000
d. Modoc Company (March 31, 2007)	?	$45,000	$180,000
e. Cherokee Company (April 30, 2008)	$200,000	$251,000	?
f. Seminole Company (December 31, 2008)	$815,000	?	$645,000

What is the meaning of situation (e) in the table above? Is situation (e) actually possible?

LG 4-2. Identify specific items in the accounting equation. Use a blank sheet of paper to complete the table. In the space to the right of each item, indicate if the item is an asset (A), a liability (L), owner's equity (OE), or none of the above (none).

Item	A, L, or OE
a. Money owed to a supplier	(Reminder: Use a separate sheet of paper to complete the table.)
b. Cash	
c. Office supplies	
d. Money owed to the bank for a loan	
e. The amount of assets that would go to the owner after the all creditors are paid	
f. A signed contract requiring us to provide services next month	
g. A computer	
h. Computer software	
i. A bill from the telephone company for this month's service	

PRACTICE   Learning Goal 4, continued

LG 4-2, *continued*

Item	A, L, or OE
j. Land	
k. An employee	
l. An office building our company is renting	
m. Money owed to us by our customers	

LG 4-3. **What does the accounting equation explain?** Someone in another business class who has never studied accounting wants to know if it is true that the accounting equation somehow "explains any business." Write a brief, but complete, answer to this person here:

LG 4-4. **A practical application.** The Schuykill River Rowing and Sailing School has a bank loan. The bank requires that total liabilities including the loan (which is $80,000) can never be more than 40% of the company's assets. What is the minimum amount of assets that the company must maintain if there are no other debts? What is the minimum amount of owner's equity?

INTERNET EXERCISES

What is the difference? What are the differences among the following professions?

- Certified public accountant auditor
- Certified fraud examiner
- Forensic accountant

a. Briefly describe the main activities and the type of work described by these titles. To help with your research, you can use the following Internet websites. (Use bookmark/favorites to save the locations of links you use in an "Accounting References" folder.)

  - www.startheregoplaces.com
  - www.aicpa.org (follow the links for: students, landing a job, career path)
  - www.cfenet.com
  - www.forensicaccounting.com

b. If you are interested in protecting the environment, how could being a CPA help you in your goals?

Your Questions?

It is *very* important to be aware of what you need to understand better. What do you need to understand better about this learning goal? On a separate piece of paper, write the questions that you want to discuss with your classmates, instructor, or supervisor. Try to be very specific about what is bothering you, such as explanations that you do not fully understand.

| LEARNING GOAL 5 | # Define "Entity" and Identify Different Types |

Overview

Introduction

In the prior learning goal, you learned how to calculate the basic financial condition of a business. In this learning goal, you will see that to calculate a condition, something else must be done first: an "entity" must be identified. Unless this is done, it is impossible to calculate the condition of a business.

In Learning Goal 5, you will find:

Economic Entities

The Economic Entity Explained

Definition of an Entity

An *economic entity* is any activity for which the financial condition or financial information is to be reported separately. An economic entity is also called an *entity*.

Examples of Economic Entities

- A candy store business is an economic entity. A hardware store business is a different economic entity. Another candy store is a different entity.
- The owner of a business and the business that she owns are two separate economic entities.
- A charity is an economic entity.

The more specific the entity, the more detailed the financial information can be.

- A large company is an economic entity. However, the management of the company wants more detailed information about the operations of the company. The company is therefore divided into different divisions, and financial records of business activity will be kept for each division. Each division is an entity. If each division is divided into departments and financial records are kept for each department, then each department is an entity.
- A government is an economic entity. Each department within the government is also an entity, if the department must report its operations separately.

Not Economic Entities

- Your Wednesday night chess group is not an economic entity because the group is a social entity and not an economic one. There is no intention of preparing financial reports concerning the group.
- You own three businesses and you do not keep separate records for any of the individual business activities. The individual operations are not economic entities because there is no way to identify their separate activities. It is impossible to report their financial information individually. Only the combination of the three activities is an economic entity. This combined information is not very useful.

The Economic Entity Assumption

Assumption	The ***economic entity assumption*** states that it must be possible to correctly identify an economic entity for which accounting is to be done.
A Priority Requirement	The economic entity assumption is the most fundamental requirement in accounting.
Why Is It Important?	If there is no identifiable entity, then accounting will be impossible.
	Before you can calculate financial condition or report financial activities, you must identify the entity for which you are doing the calculating and reporting. If no entity can be identified, no reporting can be done. If the operations of different entities are all mixed up like scrambled eggs, then financial reporting will be all mixed up like scrambled eggs.
Example	You own a video rental store, an ice cream store, and a real estate sales office. You do not identify them as separate entities, and you make no effort to keep separate records of the business activities.
	Result: You will not be able to determine the condition of any of the businesses or analyze the operations of each business.

How to Identify an Economic Entity

Follow these Steps

Step	Action	
1	Identify an activity.	
2	**IF** someone needs to make financial decisions concerning this activity . . .	**THEN** go to Step 3. Otherwise, this is not a economic entity.
3	Maintain separate financial records concerning only this activity.	

How to Identify an Economic Entity, *continued*

Examples of Separate Record-Keeping

When an economic entity is identified, the entity must keep separate records of its financial activities, apart from any other entity. This is the only way to accurately identify the true financial condition of an entity.

- Dave's dry cleaning business has $275,000 in various assets such as cash, supplies, and equipment, as well as business debts. Dave personally owns another $190,000 in various assets that are not part of the business. Dave wants to make financial decisions about the operations of the business and about his own personal affairs, so he must keep completely separate records for the business and for himself. These records will show assets, claims on assets, income, expenses, and so on.
- Eduardo owns a yogurt shop and a motorcycle repair shop. Therefore, he must keep separate records for three entities: the yogurt business, the motorcycle repair business, and himself.
- Diana owns a beauty salon business and uses only one credit card for purchases of beauty supplies and cash advances. She uses some of the purchases and cash in her beauty salon business; the rest of the beauty supplies and cash she uses personally. Without a tremendous amount of reconstruction and analysis, Diana will *not* know:
  - how much credit card debt is personal and how much is business.
  - how much cash and beauty supplies were used in the business and how much were personal. (Where did the cash and supplies go?)

Check Your Understanding

Write the completed sentences on a separate piece of paper. The answers are below.

The · · · · · · · assumption means that each economic · · · · · · · · can be · · · · · · · · · . After this is done, separate · · · · · · · · must be maintained. An airline company (is/is not) · · · · · · · · an economic entity, and each individual ticket agent for the airline (is/is not) · · · · · · · · an economic entity of the airline.

You are tutoring accounting. A student asks you this: "Why keep a separate checking account for my business? If I own the business, then I own the cash in the business. So why not just keep that cash with my personal cash all in one account?"

Answers

The entity assumption means that each economic entity can be identified. After this is done, separate records must be maintained. An airline company is an economic entity, and each individual ticket agent for the airline is not an economic entity of the airline.

The issue is not just that all the cash belongs to her. The issue is knowing how to account for it. Otherwise, she will manage her business poorly.

Can the student identify exactly where all the cash came from—how much from business activities and how much from personal activities? The student probably will not know how much cash is business cash and how much comes from personal activities, such as investments, loans, gifts, or another job. If she says, "I keep a record of all the deposits and checks," then she has the potential to reconstruct separate records for each entity, but it will be a very slow and difficult process.

"Darling, of course I'll learn accounting!"

How Businesses Are Owned

Classification by Ownership

Three Classifications

It is common practice for people to classify a business entity by the way in which the business is owned. The three common forms of business ownership are:

- Proprietorship
- Partnership
- Corporation

Each of these forms of ownership has certain advantages and disadvantages, and there is no one "best" type for everyone.

The Proprietorship

Definition

A **proprietorship** (also called a *sole proprietorship*) is a business that is owned by one person. The business cannot be a corporation.

Attributes of a Proprietorship

The following table describes the important attributes of a proprietorship.

Proprietorship Attribute	Description
Number of owners	One
Who manages it?	The owner
How difficult to start?	A proprietorship is easy to start. Only a limited amount of money is needed, and very little documentation is required for legal approval (business license, resale application, etc.).
How common is it?	It is the most common form of business. There are more proprietorships than any other kind of business.
Type of business	Any kind of business can be a proprietorship, but usually small service businesses and small retail merchant operations are proprietorships.

continued ▶

The Proprietorship, *continued*

"Economic Entity" Compared to "Legal Entity"

As you know, every business must be identified as a separate *economic* entity. "Economic" refers to identifying financial activity for record-keeping purposes. This is done so the operations are correctly identified and the financial condition is properly reported.

However, legal rights and responsibilities are also a part of being in business. These legal rights and responsibilities must always connect to some particular person. A **legal entity** is a person with legal rights and responsibilities.

For a business, a legal entity can be different from an economic entity. A perfect example of how these two entities can be different for a single business is the proprietorship. A proprietorship is a separate *economic* entity from its owner and other businesses. The owner keeps separate records for the business and himself or herself.

But *legally*, there is no distinction between the owner and the business! It is the owner who has the ultimate obligation to pay the business debts and who legally owns the business assets. There is **one** *legal* entity—the person who is the owner. However, for financial record-keeping, there are **two** *economic* entities: the business and the owner.

Example 1

Al owns a flower shop proprietorship that has $75,000 of assets, including a $35,000 delivery van. Even if the van is used only by the business, Al's name is on the state motor vehicle department records that show he owns the van. If Al permanently withdraws the van asset from the business operations and uses the van personally, the van still belongs to the same legal entity—Al.

However, for the purpose of identifying financial assets and claims on assets, the van has moved from one economic entity (the business) to a different economic entity (Al).

Example 2

Al's flower shop has $50,000 of liabilities. Suppose the business cannot sell its assets for enough money to pay these business debts. Al, the owner of the business, is *personally* responsible to pay the business debts with his own personal assets. The personal obligation to pay business debts is called **personal liability**. Even though the business is a separate economic entity for record-keeping purposes, the *legal* entity, Al, has the ultimate obligation to pay the debts.

The Proprietorship, *continued*

Example 3

If Al works in the business and pays himself cash from the business, this is not an expense of the business even though Al calls it a "salary." Like all the other proprietorship assets, the cash is already owned by Al. Even though Al might be taking the money out of the business bank account, he is simply paying himself what he already owns. It is just a withdrawal of an asset by the owner.

The Partnership

Definition

A ***partnership*** is a business that is owned by two or more people acting together as partners.

Attributes of a Partnership

The following table describes the important attributes of a partnership.

Partnership Attribute	Description
Number of owners	Two or more, acting together as partners
Who manages it?	The partners
How difficult to start?	Technically, as easy as a proprietorship. Only a verbal agreement is legally required, but this is very unwise. For practical purposes, partnerships can be extremely tricky to form properly. A written partnership agreement should be used, along with the help of a lawyer and an accountant experienced in partnerships.
How common is it?	Less common than proprietorships and corporations.
Type of business	Any kind of business can be a partnership. Usually partnerships are businesses that require more investment than a proprietorship.

continued ▶

The Partnership, *continued*

General vs. Limited Partnership	The kind of partnership we are discussing is called a ***general partnership***.
	Like a proprietorship, the partners in a general partnership have personal liability for partnership debts.
	A different kind of partnership is a ***limited partnership***. These are special partnerships in which certain partners do not have personal liability; however, these partners cannot manage the business.

TIP

There are also other limited liability entities called "limited liability companies." These can be operated as partnerships or by one person. A lawyer can explain the details.

The Corporation

Definition

A ***corporation*** is a business that is *one* combined legal *and* economic entity given "life" by the laws of the state in which the corporation was formed.

General Features of a Corporation

- The document that creates a corporation is called a ***charter***.
- The charter creates the corporation as a legal "person." The corporation is *both* a combined legal and economic entity, and the owners of a corporation do *not* have personal liability or ownership of the business assets.
- The ownership of a corporation is divided into many small shares, called ***common stock***. Anyone can buy shares of the stock, so it is possible that the stock may be owned by just one or many thousands of people. These people are called ***stockholders*** or ***shareholders***. Large corporations obtain millions of dollars of investment money because there can be many stockholders. Corporations are the largest type of business.
- A corporation has an unlimited life.
- A corporation is the most complex of all businesses to form and operate.

Section VI provides more obtails about corporations and corporate accounting.

The Same Basic Principles for All Business Types

All Entities Use the Same Principles

Regardless of the type of entity, the same principles determine the financial condition of the business. The business classification does not alter these principles.

Example

Bill Smith owns a proprietorship but changes it to a partnership by signing a partnership agreement with Louise and Dave. The basic principles of business condition are exactly the same. The only difference is that the ownership claim is divided among three people, which is more time-consuming to analyze.

Later on, if the partners agree to make the business a corporation, the basic accounting principles will still be exactly the same, even though there might be many stockholders. Now the ownership claim is called "stockholders' equity." Even though there may be certain special stockholder equity transactions, that is only a refinement of the basic principles, which still apply.

Visual Picture of Condition for the Three Types

The pictures below show the condition of the business as a proprietorship, partnership, and corporation. The idea of assets and claims on assets is unchanged. In all cases, the accounting equation is still A = L + OE. The only difference is how the owner's equity is described.

A Proprietorship

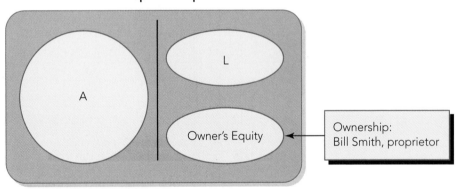

A Partnership

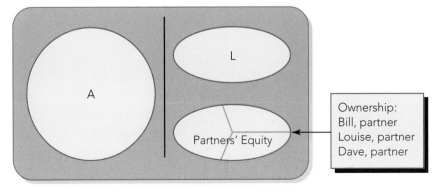

continued ▶ 71

The Same Basic Principles for All Business Types, *continued*

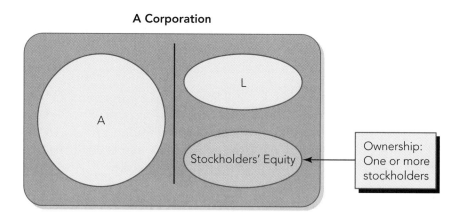

A Corporation

A | L

Stockholders' Equity

Ownership:
One or more
stockholders

Overview of Organization Features

Feature	Proprietorship	Partnership	Corporation
Ownership	1 owner	2 or more partners	1 or more stockholders
Owner personal liability?	Yes	Yes (unless a limited partnership)	No
Life	Limited (to termination or life of owner)	Limited (fixed period or same partner group)	Unlimited
Separate records kept?	Yes	Yes	Yes
Same accounting rules?	Yes	Yes	Yes
Main advantages	■ Easy to start ■ One person controls the business ■ Simple records	■ Greater resources than a proprietorship ■ Greater flexibility in allocating profits and losses to owners than a corporation	■ No personal liability (with limited exceptions) ■ Potentially greater resources ■ Often easier ownership transfer
Main disadvantages	■ Personal liability ■ Limited resources	■ More complex and expensive to start, operate, and manage ■ Personal liability ■ Potential for partner conflict is high	■ Most complex and expensive to start, operate, and manage ■ Corporate income is taxed twice: on the profits and on the dividends (special elections can eliminate double taxation for small corporations)

QUICK REVIEW

- An economic entity is any activity or operation for which financial condition or financial information is to be reported.

- The economic entity assumption means that it must be possible to correctly identify an economic entity for which accounting is to be done.

- Once an entity is identified, separate financial records must be maintained for that entity.

- It is necessary to distinguish between economic entities and legal entities.

- Business entities are commonly classified by the nature of their ownership:
  - proprietorship (one owner)
  - partnership (two or more owners acting as partners)
  - corporation (one or more stockholders)

VOCABULARY

Charter: the legal document that creates a corporation (page 70)

Common stock: ownership shares of a corporation (page 70)

Corporation: a business that is a combined legal and economic entity and is owned by one or more individuals as stockholders (page 70)

Economic entity: any activity or operation for which the financial condition or financial information is to be reported (page 63)

Economic entity assumption: assumption that it is possible to identify an individual economic entity for which financial reporting is to be done (page 64)

Entity: another term for economic entity (page 63)

General partnership: a partnership where all partners have personal liability and full management authority (page 70)

Legal entity: the entity that has legal ownership of assets and legal responsibility for debts (page 68)

Limited partnership: a partnership in which certain partners do not have personal liability (page 70)

Partnership: a business with two or more owners acting as partners (page 69)

Personal liability: being personally responsible to make good all business debts (page 68)

Proprietorship: a noncorporate business that is owned by one person (page 67)

Shareholder: another word for stockholder (page 70)

Stockholder: an owner of stock of a corporation (page 70)

PRACTICE   **Learning Goal 5**

Solutions are in the disk at the back of the book and at: www.worthyjames.com

Learning Goal 5 is about defining the meaning of "entity" and identifying different types of entities. Use these questions and problems to practice what you have learned about entities.

Multiple Choice
Select the best answer.

1. A general partnership
   a. is not an economic entity.
   b. is not a legal entity.
   c. cannot be created by only a verbal agreement.
   d. all of the above.
2. A proprietorship
   a. is not a separate economic entity from the owner.
   b. is difficult and time-consuming to start.
   c. cannot be easily managed by the owner.
   d. is the most common form of business organization in the United States.
3. The economic entity assumption means that
   a. separate recording-keeping is important.
   b. it must be possible to correctly identify a particular financial activity.
   c. if an entity cannot be identified, accounting cannot be done.
   d. all of the above.
4. Which of the following is *not* an economic entity?
   a. a bowling club
   b. a stockholder
   c. the marketing department of a corporation
   d. a group of accountants who meet every Wednesday night just to go bowling
5. Which of the following is a combined economic entity *and* a legal entity?
   a. the De Anza Partnership Company
   b. the West Valley Corporation
   c. the Mission Proprietorship
   d. none of the above.
6. The owners of a corporation are usually called
   a. stockholders.
   b. partners.
   c. proprietors.
   d. investors.
7. For which of the following would "A = L + OE" *not* apply?
   a. Proprietorship
   b. Partnership
   c. Corporation
   d. none of the above
8. You have a business that manufactures gasoline tanks for cars. Which form of entity would you select for your business?
   a. Proprietorship
   b. Partnership
   c. Corporation
   d. none of the above

PRACTICE   **Learning Goal 5, continued**   *Solutions are in the disk at the back of the book and at: www.worthyjames.com*

Reinforcement Problems

LG 5-1. **What are the characteristics of the entity?** Write the correct answer on a separate piece of paper.

a. How many owners form a proprietorship?
b. What document brings a corporation into existence?
c. What is the length of life of a partnership?
d. What entity is most difficult to form?
e. What entity is technically easy to form but for practical purposes has many potential complications?
f. What entity is a legal "person" that incurs liability separate from the owners of the entity?
g. The owners of what business are called "stockholders" or "shareholders"?
h. As an owner, you will have personal liability if you form what type of entity?
i. What is the most common form of business?
j. What form of business is easiest to create?
k. What are the three biggest advantages of a corporation?
l. How many owners form a partnership?
m. How many owners form a corporation?
n. What is the length of life of a corporation?
o. What are the main disadvantages of a proprietorship?
p. The owner of a proprietorship writes herself a check from the business bank account. What is this payment called?
q. What indicates ownership in a corporation?
r. What is the type of entity that potentially can obtain the most money from investors?

Transactions—Analyzing and Visualizing

OVERVIEW

What this section does	This section shows you how to analyze and see the effects of transactions so you can understand how they change the condition of a business.
Use this section if. . .	. . . you do not fully understand how transactions affect a business, or . . . you want more practice analyzing transactions before studying debits and credits.
Do not use this section if. . .	. . . you already know how to analyze the effects of transactions. If you want to learn about debits and credits, go to Section V on page 427. To get an easy introduction to debits and credits, go to Section III on page 235.

LEARNING GOALS

Do You Like a Good Story?

It Might Help You to Remember Better

Sometimes people remember information better when the information is part of an interesting story. The story that continues on the next page is the second part of a three-part adventure, mystery, and romance story. If you have not read the first part of the story, you can return to the beginning on page 23 to find out how it all began—or you can start here. So, if you think a story might help you remember better, or if you just want to have some fun, go ahead! The adventures of Darius continue.

Technical Content

This part of the story contains the following technical content:

- Identifying transactions
- How to analyze the effects of transactions
- Revenues and expenses explained
- Identifying all changes in owner's equity

You Can Skip the Story

If you prefer to study the technical content listed above more quickly, you can skip the story and go directly to page 94, where the standard presentation and practice continue.

The Wealth of Darius
Part II

It happened when Darius least expected it. Early in the morning, just after sunrise, Darius was walking in the marketplace toward the vegetable seller's stall when he felt a hand on his arm.

A cackling voice called to him, "Come here, young man!"

He turned instantly and saw the old woman, dressed in black, grasping his sleeve. It was the same woman he had helped a year ago. She pulled his sleeve and her voice rattled, "You come with me."

Remembering her and what she had become, Darius felt the strength drain from his body. He fought to keep his legs from folding. In a moment, the old woman pulled Darius out of the market and around a corner. Darius was at once blinded by a flash of intense white light. For an instant, he felt himself being lifted off his feet by a strong wind, and then he remembered nothing.

When Darius awoke, he was standing in his shop. The large, dazzling Hermes loomed before him. They were alone. "Well?" Hermes boomed. "I promised you that I would return in exactly one year, and here I am!"

Darius threw himself down and whispered into the floor, "I have used what you have given me, and I have given it much thought. I am grateful beyond words! I thank you daily!"

"Up, mortal!" the god ordered. A force snapped Darius back into a standing position. "Yes, I know," Hermes continued, "and I am pleased that you say you have given this valuable gift much thought. Tell me what you have thought about it."

Darius tried hard to think clearly. Then with relief he remembered that he had made a list of all the things that the formula, which he had received from the god, had made possible. He found the paper and timidly handed it to Hermes. In a shaky voice, Darius said, "I have given much thought to the correct value to use for the assets when I calculated the condition of my business."

"You did well to use the price that you paid for the assets," Hermes responded.

"I gave much thought to what assets and debts to use in the calculation. I have never included assets or debts that did not belong to the business."

"You did well again," the voice rumbled.

"Each time I prepared the calculation, I carefully watched the changes in the total assets and the changes in the total debts. Sometimes this helped me make better decisions about when to buy more assets and how much debt I would allow the business to have."

Hermes looked down at Darius and spoke. "You have done correct things, but I expected no less from you. After all, you have received a great gift, have you not?"

"Yes, a very great gift." Darius bowed his head.

"Very well, then. You spoke of changes in the condition of your business. How do you explain those changes?"

Darius began to tremble because he had nothing else to say. His mind raced. What had he overlooked?

"You have nothing else to tell me or to ask me after an entire year?" The force of Hermes' voice was now vibrating the tools lying on the table. "You have no other questions about the changes in your business?"

As if he were a forest animal caught in a bright light, poor Darius was so paralyzed that he could only stare, transfixed by the sparkling brilliance around Hermes. Darius could no longer think.

Hermes softened his voice. "Darius, you have calculated the condition of your business. You learned to use the special formula $A = L + OE$ to see the wealth and claims on wealth. That is good. But isn't there something else that you need to know each time you use the formula?"

Silence.

"Mortal, you try my patience!" The tools bounced off the table. "Very well, the gods will teach you!"

In a white blaze, Hermes was gone. Darius remained frozen, staring into the space Hermes had just occupied. In the distance, like a faraway echo, Darius heard, ". . . gods will teach you . . . gods will teach you. . . ."

What Darius Forgot

Another perfect day warmed the fields of blooming clover on the distant heights of Mount Olympus. Gentle zephyrs puffed and nudged the sweet blossoms and borrowed their fragrance to bring to the gods, who relaxed among a grove of oak trees in a grand garden.

"So, Hermes," said Artemis, goddess of hunting and all wild things, "tell us about your visit to that mortal Darius."

"He demonstrates that mortals remain flawlessly impaired."

"Yes," replied Artemis, "in their own way, they are as perfect as we are."

Aphrodite (pronounced *afro-DYE-tee*), the goddess of love and beauty, asked, "He is such a handsome young man. What did you find deficient in him, Hermes?" She lifted a silver cup of ambrosia to her lips.

"What I find deficient," replied Hermes, "is that Darius faithfully calculates the condition of his business, yet he does not bother to ask himself *why the condition changes!* He watches the changes but does nothing to discover the reasons. He does not appreciate my gift! After all I did for him!"

"Really. They are such simple beings," said Athena, the goddess of wisdom and courage.

"And worst of all, worst of all," Hermes continued, "is that he has done nothing to explain the reasons why his owner's claim on the wealth has changed. What could be more important to a merchant or a businessperson than explaining why the owner's claim on the business wealth has increased or decreased?"

Apollo, god of truth and music, had been listening the whole time and added, "I would think that explaining all the changes in his claim on the business wealth would be the first thing an owner would always do. It would be the first thing the owner would want to understand. After all, if an owner can explain the reasons why his claim on the wealth has changed, then he can begin to control the causes of the change! He is thereby sure to improve his claim."

"Exactly," replied Hermes. "You describe it perfectly, Apollo."

"Perhaps he has become too satisfied," Apollo said. "After all, his owner's claim has only been increasing. Why should he trouble himself to find out?"

"Yes," Hermes said. "So far, he has not had a good reason to learn what causes the changes in his business—especially the changes in the owner's claim. I believe it is time for me to give him a reason to learn. I will ask Aphrodite to help me."

"What are you going to do?" all the others asked at once, as they turned to look at Aphrodite.

"Oh, nothing really," smiled Hermes. "I will simply give him reasons to want to know."

Hermes' First Trick on Darius

After the second visit from Hermes, Darius tried to go about his business as if nothing had happened, and for a while nothing at all was different.

He watched his business grow. He was grateful and thanked the gods. Darius now prayed to the gods even more frequently, but in his heart he was not sure if he wanted his prayers answered or not.

He worked hard. He carefully observed the calculation each week, and observed the changes in the amounts of assets and claims on assets. What more could the gods want?

One day, Darius had been working in the back of his shop and did not notice the increasing buzz of conversation and gossip in the front. Then Ammon's daughter, Dana, who now sometimes worked in the shop, said, "Darius! Can you believe it? What are you going to do?"

"Do about what?" Darius asked.

Dana smiled gently at him. Darius was always too intent on his work to notice that Ammon's attractive daughter never smiled in the same way for anyone else. "Look across the street, Darius."

As Darius looked out the front of his shop, he saw that the shop directly across from him did not look the same. It had been a sandal maker's shop, but the sandal maker was gone. To Darius' great amazement, paintings of every size were displayed in front of the shop.

Another painter had moved into the shop directly across from Darius' painting business! The new painter's name was Somnus. He had traveled many miles from his old town to settle in Darius' village and open a new shop. Somnus later told people that he moved because of a powerful dream that he had. In that dream, he heard the god Hermes telling him to move. Then, in the dream, he had seen Darius' village.

Darius soon discovered that Somnus was an artist of great experience and talent. He was about the same age as Darius but, unlike Darius, Somnus was a businessman. Somnus always spent extra time with customers or gave them small gifts. He would tell each customer what great artistic understanding the customer had.

Because there was another painter right across the street, Darius noticed that customers did not buy paintings from his shop quite so quickly as before. Even regular customers did not always choose to have Darius design a fresco or wall painting anymore. Now they would always speak to Somnus before deciding.

Darius began to notice something else happening when he did his monthly calculation. The assets of the business no longer seemed to be increasing so quickly, and the owner's claim hardly changed at all.

After two months, something happened that Darius had never seen before: slowly at first, then faster, his owner's claim began to decrease. As the business lost its wealth, the owner's claim began to diminish. Darius did not understand the reasons for this, and so he could only watch helplessly as the business began to dissolve like a small piece of candy.

Unexpected Help from a Friend

Month after month, Darius watched as his owner's claim decreased. Finally, at the end of a year, to Darius' dismay, the calculation showed:

$$\text{Assets} = \text{Creditors' Claims} + \text{Owner's Claim}$$
$$\$14,700 \qquad \$7,700 \qquad \$7,000$$

The creditors' claims were now again greater than the owner's claim—something Darius had promised to never let happen again.

While Somnus continued to create new wall designs and find new customers, Darius watched his own business sink further. At the end of the next month, his calculation showed:

$$\text{Assets} = \text{Creditors' Claims} + \text{Owner's Claim}$$
$$\$10,400 \qquad \$7,700 \qquad \$2,700$$

To Darius, the causes of the changes seemed unknowable and beyond his control. Darius had no idea what to do!

Darius tried to find some comfort with friends. He still gave his dinners for neighbors, especially the poorest ones. On the evening of the same day that he had done his last calculation, Darius prepared a large birthday dinner for Ammon and his family.

Darius was unable to enjoy the party. He smiled and wished Ammon a happy birthday, but each time he spoke with Ammon the old worries returned. At a quiet moment, after the toasts were finished, Ammon's daughter, Dana, approached Darius and looked into his eyes.

"Darius, I know you. I watch you every day in the shop. Something is troubling you. What is wrong?"

Darius began to say that everything was fine and deny that he was worried, but instead he found himself saying, "Dana, you are a clever girl. I have seen how well you bargain with the other merchants. If you can keep a secret, I will show you something tomorrow at the shop. If you have any of your clever ideas, now is the time that I can use them."

The next day, Darius showed Dana the formula he had received from Hermes and how to calculate the condition of a business. At first, Dana was amazed at how this worked, but then she began to frown. "Darius, lately your owner's claim has been decreasing rapidly. It has gone from $7,000 to $2,700 in only one month. Soon you will not be able to claim any of the wealth of the business. It will all go to the creditors!"

"Now you know why I am worried," he said. "I have no idea what is making my owner's claim decrease in such a way."

Dana looked at him for a long time and said, "Darius, you are a wonderful artist. That is what you do best. I will go home tonight and think more about the condition of your business. Together we can think of something." She smiled in the way that she saved just for Darius.

Early the next morning, when Dana entered the shop she went to Darius at his table and said, "I have an idea. We will carefully observe every business event that might affect the condition of your business. Then we will see which ones affect your owner's claim. We can use the good picture that you drew, with the three circles, to visualize the condition."

Darius looked at her with admiration and, for the first time, noticed her beautiful smile.

Transactions: Why the Picture Changes

For the next week, Darius and Dana watched as many business events as they could. To analyze an event, they wrote a description and drew a picture of the change in the condition of the business. Inside the circles, they showed only the particular item that was affected by the change. They analyzed the circles one at a time by asking three specific questions.

The first event they observed was when the business used five gold coins to purchase some paint supplies.

First: Did any *assets* change? Yes (Gold decreased by $5 and paint increased by $5; one asset was given up for another asset.)

Second: Did any *creditors' claims* change? No (Debts were not affected.)

Third: Did the *owner's claim* change? No (The owner's claim was not affected because the total assets are the same and the total debts are the same.)

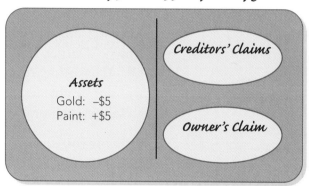

Purchase $5 of paint supplies for $5 of gold

Assets
Gold: –$5
Paint: +$5

Creditors' Claims

Owner's Claim

Total Wealth: $10,400   Total Claims: $10,400

The picture showed them that there were more supplies than before—and less gold—but that was the only change in the condition of the business. None of the claims seemed to be affected at all by this event. Exchanging one asset for another asset only affected the assets.

In the next event that they observed, the business used $20 to pay Hela, a creditor.

Again, Darius and Dana wrote a description of what happened. Then they drew a picture of the business, showing the changes. One at a time, they analyzed each circle:

First: Did any *assets* change? Yes (Gold decreased by $20, and this change reduced total wealth to $10,380.)

Second: Did any *creditors' claims* change? Yes (The creditors' claims also decreased, so the total claims on wealth decreased to $10,380.)

Third: Did the *owner's claim* change? No. Although paying a debt reduced assets, it also reduced a creditor's claim on the assets. Thus, the owner's claim stayed the same. So Darius and Dana saw that paying a debt only had an effect on the creditors' claims but not on the claim of the owner.

Pay $20 debt owing to Hela

Total Wealth: $10,380   Total Claims: $10,380

The next event occurred when Aulis visited the shop to tell Darius that he would be raising the price of many of the paints, beginning next month. When Aulis left, Darius and Dana talked about what happened. They decided that although this was a business event, it did not yet affect the financial condition of the business. The information did not change any part of the picture.

Darius and Dana continued watching the events. They even gave the events a special name. Any event that changed the picture of the condition of the business they called a "transaction."

What Do You Think?

Darius and Dana are developing a procedure to find out how each transaction makes a change in the condition of the business. What are the three questions they ask in the procedure?

1. **Assets:** Did the transaction cause any assets to change?
2. **Creditors' claims:** Did the transaction cause any creditors' claims (liabilities) to change?
3. **Owner's claim:** Did the transaction cause the owner's claim (owner's equity) to change?

In the meantime, Darius watched as Somnus continued to attract even more customers. Two days later, in a moment of desperation, Darius decided to take all of his savings and invest them in the business. The business would then have money to purchase some special and rare paint colors. Darius went home and took $250—his entire savings—from a secret hiding place. He went back to town and placed the $250 in a metal box under the floor in his shop. The money now belonged to the business. With this new money, the business would buy the special paints and, therefore, might take some customers back from Somnus.

Transactions That Affect the Owner's Claim

Fortunately, Darius told Dana what he had done. She said, "Darius, I think that this is a transaction, and an important one." As before, they wrote a description of the transaction, and drew a picture of the change in the condition.

Again, they analyzed the circles one at a time:

First: Did any *assets* change? Yes (The business now has $250 more gold; no other asset is affected.)

Second: Did any *creditors' claims* change? No (The asset did not come from a creditor.)

Third: Did the *owner's claim* change? Yes! (The gold came entirely from the owner. This must be an increase in the owner's claim!)

Darius invests $250 in his business

Assets
Gold: +$250

Creditors' Claims

Owner's Claim
Darius: +$250

Total Wealth: $10,630   Total Claims: $10,630

Sure enough, when they drew the picture of the business, they could see the increase in assets and the increase in the owner's claim. Dana and Darius had discovered the first transaction that affected the owner's claim: the owner's investment in the business.

Then Dana began to think some more. "If an owner's investment increases the owner's claim, then would an owner's withdrawal of assets decrease it?" She asked, "Darius, did you withdraw gold from the business this month to pay any of your own personal debts?"

"Yes," he said. "This month I obtained the money to pay for your father's birthday party by withdrawing $80 from the business."

"Let us draw a picture of an owner's withdrawal of $80," Dana said. Before completing the picture, they analyzed each circle, one at a time, as they did before:

First: Did any *assets* change? Yes (Gold decreased by $80; the wealth is reduced to $10,550.)

Second: Did the *creditors' claims* change? No (No debt was paid or changed.)

Third: Did the *owner's claim* change? Yes! (The owner's claim is only the excess of the assets over the debts. If the total assets decrease and the debts (creditors' claims) do not change, then the owner's claim must decrease.)

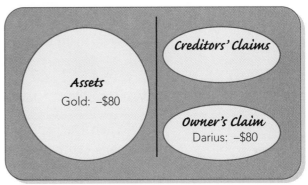

Darius withdraws $80 from his business

Creditors' Claims

Assets
Gold: –$80

Owner's Claim
Darius: –$80

Total Wealth: $10,550   Total Claims: $10,550

Together they made their second discovery: when an owner withdraws assets, the decrease in assets also decreases the owner's claim. Now they had found two causes for changes in the owner's claim: investments and withdrawals. They hoped that these changes would explain the entire change in the owner's claim.

They would be disappointed. They had not yet discovered two more important changes to the owner's claim.

At the End of the Month

When Darius prepared the calculation of the condition at the end of the current month, to his shock he saw the condition was even worse than before:

Assets	=	Creditors' Claims	+	Owner's Claim
$9,300		$7,400		$1,900

This time, Darius drew two pictures: a picture of the condition at the end of the prior month and a picture of the condition at the end of the current month. These pictures showed the total assets and the total claims after all the transactions were completed for each month.

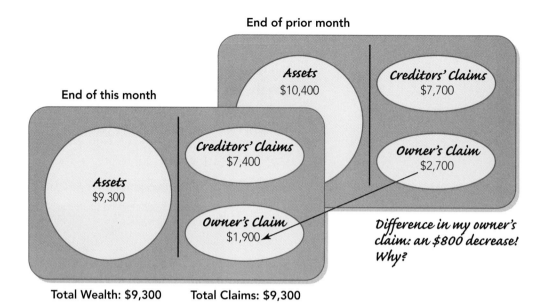

End of prior month

Assets
$10,400

Creditors' Claims
$7,700

Owner's Claim
$2,700

End of this month

Creditors' Claims
$7,400

Assets
$9,300

Owner's Claim
$1,900

Difference in my owner's claim: an $800 decrease! Why?

Total Wealth: $9,300   Total Claims: $9,300

When Darius showed this to Dana, she looked concerned. "Your owner's claim is down another $800, Darius, and we still have not explained all the reasons why."

Then they wrote down how much of the change in the owner's claim they had been able to explain so far:

Owner's investment:	+	$250
Owner's withdrawal:	−	80
Net change identified:	+	170

"Well, we certainly have more work to do," Dana said. "The total change in the owner's claim was a *decrease* of $800. So far, we have only identified the part of the change that is an *increase* of $170. There must be $970 of some other decrease hidden somewhere. We are still far from a complete answer! And at this rate of decrease, Darius, you will only have a few more months to operate your business."

What Do You Think?

What are the two causes of the changes in the owner's claim that Darius and Dana have discovered so far? They have not yet discovered two more causes of change in the owner's claim. Any guesses?

Changes in owner's claim identified so far:
1. An investment by the owner, which increases the owner's claim
2. A withdrawal of assets by the owner, which decreases the owner's claim

The Other Transactions That Affect the Owner's Claim

Darius made a suggestion. "I have an idea. Because I have no more money left to invest, there will be no increases in my owner's claim. Next week, I will not withdraw any gold or other assets from the business, so there will be no changes caused by withdrawals. . . ."

Dana finished his thought. ". . . so any change in your owner's claim will have to be caused by whatever is missing. Correct?"

"Yes, and this time, we will watch every transaction until we find what is missing," Darius answered.

Because they were alert and watching every transaction, it did not take much time to find something interesting. The next afternoon, a customer came into the shop, and Darius painted a small portrait of her. When she left, she paid Darius $25. Both Darius and Dana immediately saw that assets had increased by $25.

As before, they wrote a description of the transaction and drew a picture showing how the condition changed:

First: Did *assets* change? Yes (Gold increased by $25, and this increased total assets to $9,325.)

Second: Did the *creditors' claims* change? No (Creditors were not involved; we did not borrow $25.)

Third: . . .

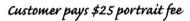

Customer pays $25 portrait fee

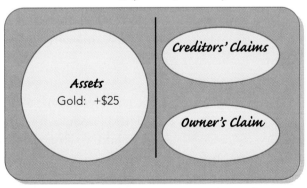

"What do you think, Darius?" Dana asked. "What is the only thing left?"

Darius' eyes opened wide. "I think I understand! The owner operates the business and takes the risks. Therefore, the owner claims any increase in wealth that the business gets from customers. The assets increase because of the efforts of the owner, so the owner's claim also increases."

Dana said, "Yes, I agree. Fees do increase assets. So fees cause an increase in the owner's claim. I think we should give this kind of increase in the owner's claim a special name to show that it comes from making sales to customers."

Dana chose the word "revenue," which is derived from a word meaning "to return, or to come back home after being away." She finished drawing the picture:

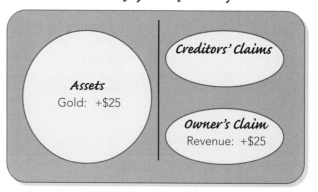

Customer pays $25 portrait fee

Assets
Gold: +$25

Creditors' Claims

Owner's Claim
Revenue: +$25

Total Wealth: $9,325   Total Claims: $9,325

Dana could see that Darius was thinking about something. "What is it?" she asked.

"Well, I think we are correct in what we just did," he said, "but now I am even more confused than I was before."

"Why is that?"

"Because my owner's claim has been decreasing, not increasing! This transaction we just found is an increase! So we still have not yet explained why my owner's claim has been decreasing so quickly."

Dana was quick to respond. "Darius, I thought about this before when I watched you working. I think the answer has to do with what we have just seen. Tell me, do you think that customers give you money just because they want to be generous?"

"Of course not," he said. "I have to provide them with something they want—something valuable."

"Yes," she continued, "and are you able to do that at no cost to yourself? Do the gods just give you your supplies free?"

"No, no. What are you saying? I buy supplies and tools, I pay employees, I use up paints and glazes, I use up candles and incense in the shop, I use up gold, I . . ." He stopped.

"Now do you see what I am saying?" she asked.

"Well . . . ," he said, "I have to use up assets to operate the business. When assets are used up in my operations so I can create something to sell, there are less assets than before. My owner's claim is less!"

He continued, "So the 'operations' is almost like a race. Operations increase the owner's claim when I make a sale but decrease the owner's claim when assets are used up."

Dana said, "I can look at your operations and see two examples of using up assets right now. First, how much paint did you use up for the portrait you just painted?"

"I am not exactly sure. I can guess it would be about $10."

"So, let us draw a diagram of that and see if it changed your owner's claim and the condition of your business."

Use up $10 of paint and glaze to operate

Assets	Creditors' Claims
Paint supplies: −$10	
	Owner's Claim
	Darius: −$10

Total Wealth: $9,315   Total Claims: $9,315

Darius and Dana thought in the same slow, careful way as before:

"I know that $10 of the asset supplies was used up," Darius reasoned. "There was no reduction in creditors' claims. Therefore, using up assets as part of business operations must cause a decrease to my owner's claim."

Dana said, "It is very clear to me now. Because of its operations, the business will receive the value of what it creates. That was $25: the fee you charged the customer. This increases the owner's claim."

She continued, "At the same time, to create something of value, the operations also consume assets: the $10 of paint supplies used up. This decreases the owner's claim."

Dana chose the word "expense" to mean the value of the assets used up that helps to create revenue.

Just to be sure, they looked at another example of an expense. That morning, Darius had paid the rent to Opheron, the landlord. The monthly rent was $250 which Darius always paid on time. In this case, the asset used up was gold:

Use up $250 of gold to pay rent to operate

Assets
Gold: –$250

Creditors' Claims

Owner's Claim
Darius: –$250

Total Wealth: $9,065   Total Claims: $9,065

If the rent was not paid, there would be no shop to work in. The business needed a shop to operate and create value. So, paying rent was another example of using up assets as part of business operations, even though it did not involve a job for some particular customer.

During the remainder of the week, Dana and Darius continued to carefully watch the transactions. They drew pictures of how the transactions changed the condition of the business. Except for operations, they were not able to discover anything else that increased or decreased the owner's claim. At the end of the week, they decided that business operations were the cause for the rest of the change in the owner's claim.

After thinking about the operations for several days, Darius asked, "Dana, do you think the business is using up assets in operations faster than it is receiving them from customers?"

"Yes, I think that is your problem," Dana suggested. "That would cause your owner's claim to decrease."

"But how can I be sure?"

"Darius, I do not know for certain. All I can suggest is that every day you keep a record of all the transactions. Then you can identify which ones are affecting your owner's claim the most. Whatever you find, you need to begin making changes soon."

"By the gods, that would be a great amount of effort! And I have never tried such a thing."

From far above, Hermes smiled as he watched the two mortals and thought to himself, "If Darius—poor mortal—thinks that business is difficult now, he has much to learn! I will soon favor him with a much bigger surprise."

Hermes' second trick would be of surpassing quality.

To be continued . . .

What Do You Think?

Darius and Dana spent much time searching for all the causes of change in the owner's claim (owner's equity). They discovered four kinds of events that affect the owner's claim—two cause increases and two cause decreases. Do you remember what the four kinds of transactions are?

The two increases: Owner's investment and revenue
The two decreases: Owner's withdrawals and expenses
Revenues and expenses are caused by business operations.

| LEARNING GOAL 6 | # Analyze Individual Transactions |

Overview

Introduction

In this learning goal, we will begin the most basic analysis of *changes* in the condition of a business. After some practice looking at changes, you will begin to see something pretty amazing: most of the events that change the condition of a business fall into typical patterns. Learning to analyze these patterns will give you a lot of confidence in your ability to understand the transactions of any business.

Fundamental Principle

Because the condition of any business has only three basic parts, the effect of any change should be analyzed according to how it affects these three basic parts: A = L + OE. This is the essential idea for this learning goal.

"Double-entry" Accounting

Using an equation approach to analyze and record transactions is called **double-entry** accounting. Double-entry accounting has two basic requirements:

- Analyze every change by how it affects the three parts of the equation.
- The equation must always stay in balance.

  Reminder: Because we are forced to keep the equation in balance, every transaction always creates *at least two changes* within the equation. This is the only way to keep the equation in balance. That is why the method is called "double-entry"—at least two changes with every transaction.

What Is "Single-entry"?

Single-entry accounting is a simple, very old-fashioned system in which some items in the accounting equation are recorded, but there is no concept of describing a business by using an equation to describe all the changes.

For example, if you keep a record of the balance of your checking account and all the deposits and checks, but you do not keep a record of how the deposits and checks affected the other items in the accounting equation, you are doing single-entry accounting.

In Learning Goal 6, you will find:

Introduction to Transactions

What Is a Transaction?

Definition

A **transaction** is any event that causes a change in the accounting equation.

"Well, boys, I'd say a 'transaction' is any event that causes a change in the accounting equation."

**Examples of
a Transaction**

- Owner investment
- Paying a debt
- Borrowing money

- Selling to a customer
- Using up supplies
- Buying more supplies

Not a Transaction

- Signing a contract (because the accounting equation is not affected)
- The bank offering to loan money (because nothing has happened yet)
- A proposed law affecting business (because nothing has changed yet)

Note: Some accountants make a technical distinction between the words "transaction" and "event." However, what really matters is knowing if the equation is affected.

Overview of Transactions

Four Ways to Classify

Transactions can be generally classified by the type of event that causes them:

- External
- Internal
- Exchange
- Non-exchange

External and Internal Events

External events are transactions that take place between an entity (for example, a business) and some other entity. Internal events occur only within an entity.

Exchange and Non-exchange Transactions

Exchange transactions are always external. Exchange transactions result from events in which separate entities give or receive something of value between each other. Non-exchange transactions are events in which an entity gives up or receives something with nothing in return.

Examples

The table below shows examples of general classification of transactions.

	Exchange	Non-exchange
External	<ul><li>Buy equipment</li><li>Borrow money</li><li>Pay a bill</li><li>Perform services</li><li>Sell a product</li><li>Use services</li><li>Collect from a customer</li><li>Trade assets</li></ul>	<ul><li>Owner investment</li><li>Owner withdrawal</li><li>Fire or other casualty loss</li><li>Theft of property</li><li>Give or receive a gift</li></ul>
Internal		<ul><li>Consume supplies</li><li>Wear out equipment</li><li>Use materials to put into a product</li></ul>

continued ▶

Overview of Transactions, *continued*

Coming Up . . .

Coming up now are some examples of transactions that always involve assets. These are the most common kinds of transactions. For each example you will see the three steps of analysis. Under the three steps you will see the visualization using the accounting equation *and* the illustration. We will label each illustration as a "snapshot" of the event.

Go slowly and let yourself absorb each example at a comfortable pace, being careful and methodical. You do not have to rush because the analysis will become easier and easier as you practise.

Note: Also watch for events that do not qualify as accounting transactions.

Watch out for the owner's personal transactions. The owner's personal transactions are never part of the business activity and are never recorded by the business. (Example: The owner buys a computer for use at home.)

Check Your Understanding

Write your answers on a blank piece of paper.

1. Briefly and accurately define the word "transaction."

2. Write an overview that explains the main types of transactions.

3. What does "double-entry" mean?

Answers

1. A transaction is any event that causes a change in the accounting equation.

2. Transactions can be generally classified by the events that cause them. In this way, transactions are classified as external, internal, and non-exchange. External transactions occur between two or more entities. Internal transactions occur within a single entity. Exchange transactions are external transactions in which each entity gives and receives something. Non-exchange transactions are external transactions in which an entity gives or receives something with nothing in return.

3. "Double-entry" means keeping the accounting equation in balance. Keeping the accounting equation in balance requires that at least two items within the equation must change with each transaction. This is the only way the accounting equation can remain in balance. For example, if a business borrows $1,000, the assets increase and so do the liabilities. Or, if a business uses $100 of cash to purchase supplies, cash decreases by $100 and supplies increase by $100.

Transactions That Always Involve Assets

Examples of Analysis and Patterns

The Three Analysis Steps

To analyze the effect of any event on a business, always ask these three questions:

Step 1: Are *assets* affected?
Step 2: Are *liabilities* affected?
Step 3: Is *owner's equity* affected?

Visualize: Two Useful Methods

As part of the analysis, it is very helpful to visualize the effects of transactions on a business. Students often find two visualizing methods helpful when they are first learning how to analyze the effects of transactions:

Method 1: Use the accounting equation. The best way to do this is to write the equation and use up or down arrows to help you see the effects on the equation. Example: Suppose the owner invests $100,000 cash in a new business. Using the equation, you can visualize this as:

$$A\uparrow \ = \ L \ + \ OE\uparrow$$
$$100{,}000 \qquad\qquad 100{,}000$$

Method 2: Draw a picture of the business, showing the changes. Using the same example, you would draw:

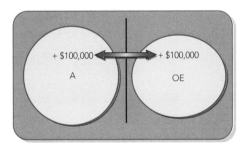

Use Either Method— We Will Show Both

It does not make any difference which method you prefer. Some people prefer to use the equation, and other people prefer the illustration.

To help you decide which method works best for you, we will show both methods in each of the examples that follow.

continued ▶

Examples of Analysis and Patterns, *continued*

Analysis	Effect on Condition
Step 1: Are *assets* affected? Yes (Cash goes up by $100,000.)	↑ A = L + OE
Step 2: Are *liabilities* affected? No (No debt is involved.)	
Step 3: Is *owner's equity* affected? Yes (Owner's equity increases by $100,000.)	↑ A = L + ↑ OE

$$\text{A} \uparrow \quad = \quad \text{L} + \text{OE} \uparrow$$
$$\text{100,000} \qquad\qquad\qquad \text{100,000}$$

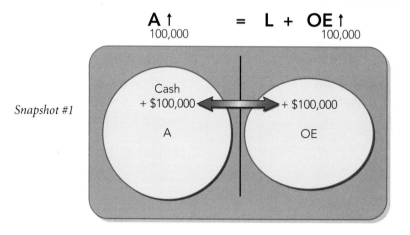

Snapshot #1

Use Cash to Purchase an Asset

The business buys $500 of computer software for cash. One asset is given up (Cash) for another asset (Computer Software), so total assets do not change.

Analysis	Effect on Condition
Step 1: Are *assets* affected? Yes (Cash decreases by $500; software increases $500.)	↓ ↑ A = L + OE
Step 2: Are *liabilities* affected? No	
Step 3: Is *owner's equity* affected? No	

$$\text{A} \uparrow \;\; \downarrow \qquad = \quad \text{L} + \text{OE}$$
$$\;\; \text{500} \;\; \text{500}$$

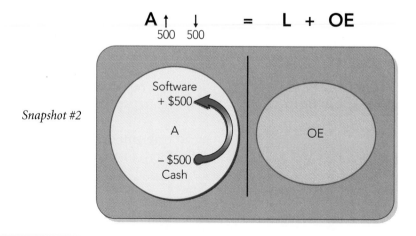

Snapshot #2

Examples of Analysis and Patterns, *continued*

Purchase Asset on Credit

The business buys $50,000 of testing equipment "on account." Total asset value increases, but now there is a creditor's claim because the equipment is not paid for.

Analysis	Effect on Condition
Step 1: Are *assets* affected? Yes (Equipment increases by $50,000.)	↑A = L + OE
Step 2: Are *liabilities* affected? Yes (Accounts Payable increases by $50,000.)	↑A = ↑L + OE
Step 3: Is *owner's equity* affected? No	

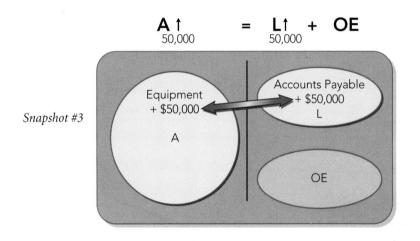

Snapshot #3

Borrow Money

The business borrows $25,000 from a bank. Total assets increase, but so do creditors' claims.

Analysis	Effect on Condition
Step 1: Are *assets* affected? Yes (Cash increases by $25,000.)	↑A = L + OE
Step 2: Are *liabilities* affected? Yes (Loan Payable increases by $25,000.)	↑A = ↑L + OE
Step 3: Is *owner's equity* affected? No	

continued ▶

Examples of Analysis and Patterns, *continued*

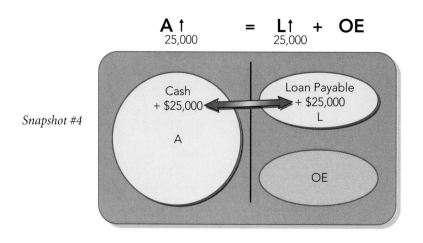

$$A \uparrow \quad = \quad L \uparrow \quad + \quad OE$$
$$25{,}000 \qquad 25{,}000$$

Snapshot #4

Use Up an Asset in the Operations

The business uses up $275 of supplies during operations. This event is completely within the business, so it is an *internal* transaction. This is an expense that decreases owner's equity because resources (in this case, supplies) are consumed in the process of operations to produce revenue.

Analysis	Effect on Condition
Step 1: Are *assets* affected? Yes (Supplies decrease by $275.)	$\downarrow A = L + \quad OE$
Step 2: Are *liabilities* affected? No (Nothing happens with creditors.)	
Step 3: Is *owner's equity* affected? Yes (Owner's equity decreases by $275.)	$\downarrow A = L + \downarrow OE$

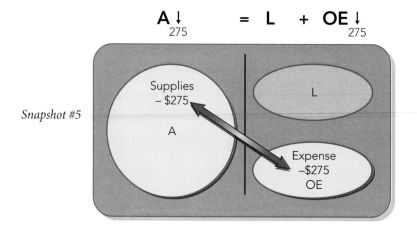

$$A \downarrow \quad = \quad L \quad + \quad OE \downarrow$$
$$275 \qquad\qquad\qquad 275$$

Snapshot #5

Examples of Analysis and Patterns, *continued*

Payment of a Liability

The business uses $500 cash to pay the liability from the software purchase on account. The creditor (the supplier) is the *external* party to the transaction. Assets are used to reduce creditor claims.

Analysis	Effect on Condition
Step 1: Are *assets* affected? Yes (Cash decreases by $500.)	$\downarrow A = \ \ L + OE$
Step 2: Are *liabilities* affected? Yes (Account Payable decreases by $500.)	$\downarrow A = \downarrow L + OE$
Step 3: Is *owner's equity* affected? No	

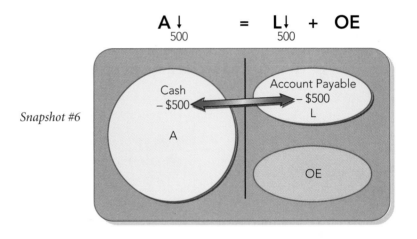

$$A\!\downarrow_{500} \quad = \quad L\!\downarrow_{500} \ + \ OE$$

Snapshot #6

Perform Services for Customers

The business completes a diagnostic job for a customer and receives $2,500 cash. Providing services is revenue. It increases owner's equity because the new asset (Cash) was earned by the business. It did not come from creditors.

Analysis	Effect on Condition
Step 1: Are *assets* affected? Yes (Cash increases by $2,500.)	$\uparrow A = L + \ \ OE$
Step 2: Are *liabilities* affected? No	
Step 3: Is *owner's equity* affected? Yes (Owner's equity increases by $2,500.)	$\uparrow A = L + \uparrow OE$

continued ▶

Examples of Analysis and Patterns, *continued*

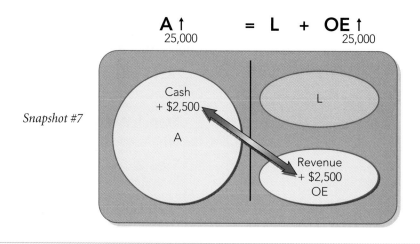

Snapshot #7

Sale on Account

The company performs $1,200 of diagnostic services. The company sends a bill to the customer for the amount of services. Accounts Receivable increases by $1,200 and owner's equity increases by the same amount.

Analysis	Effect on Condition
Step 1: Are *assets* affected? Yes (Accounts Receivable increases by $1,200.)	$\uparrow A = L +\ \ OE$
Step 2: Are *liabilities* affected? No	
Step 3: Is *owner's equity* affected? Yes (Owner's equity increases by $1,200.)	$\uparrow A = L + \uparrow OE$

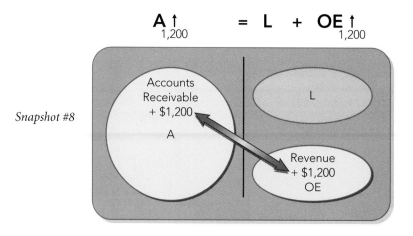

Snapshot #8

Note: It is not necessary to receive cash when the revenue is earned. Any asset can be received (such as accounts receivable).

Examples of Analysis and Patterns, *continued*

Collect an Account Receivable

The company collects $1,500 cash from a customer's account receivable. Cash increases and Accounts Receivable decreases the same amount. Total assets do not change—they simply shift as one asset increases and the other decreases.

Analysis	Effect on Condition
Step 1: Are *assets* affected? Yes (Cash increases by $1,500 and Accounts Receivable decreases by $1,500.)	A ↑↓ = L + OE
Step 2: Are *liabilities* affected? No	
Step 3: Is *owner's equity* affected? No	

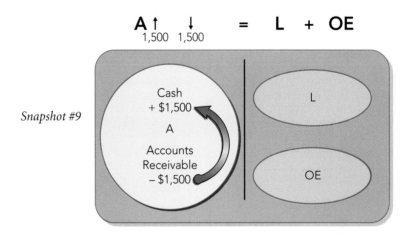

Snapshot #9

Expense: Cash is Used to Pay for Services

The business uses up $150 cash to pay the telephone company for telephone service as soon as the bill is received (so liabilities are not affected). This is an expense that decreases owner's equity. Owner's equity decreases because cash decreases to pay for the resource (telephone service) consumed to help create revenue.

Analysis	Effect on Condition
Step 1: Are *assets* affected? Yes (Cash decreases by $150.)	↓A = L + OE
Step 2: Are *liabilities* affected? No	
Step 3: Is *owner's equity* affected? Yes (Owner's equity decreases by $150.)	↓A = L + ↓OE

continued ▶

Examples of Analysis and Patterns, *continued*

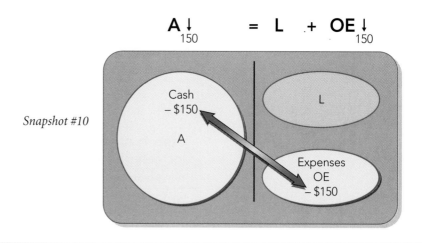

Snapshot #10

Use Cash and a Note Payable to Purchase Equipment

The company buys $9,000 of equipment by paying $2,000 cash and signing a note payable for the balance of the price. (*Result:* Total assets increase by $7,000 and total liabilities increase by $7,000.)

Analysis	Effect on Condition
Step 1: Are *assets* affected? Yes (Equipment increases by $9,000 and Cash decreases by $2,000.)	$A \uparrow \downarrow = L + OE$
Step 2: Are *liabilities* affected? Yes (Liabilities increase by $7,000.)	$A \uparrow \downarrow = \uparrow L + OE$
Step 3: Is *owner's equity* affected? No	

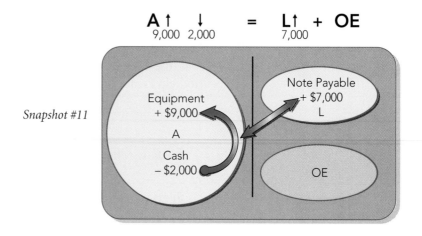

Snapshot #11

Examples of Analysis and Patterns, *continued*

Casualty Loss:
Fire Destroys Assets

A fire destroys $10,000 of uninsured office equipment. The fire is the *external* agent of change in this non-exchange transaction. Owner's equity decreases because the owner of a business always assumes the risk of losses.

Analysis	Effect on Condition
Step 1: Are *assets* affected? Yes (Equipment decreases by $10,000.)	$\downarrow A = L +\ \ OE$
Step 2: Are *liabilities* affected? No	
Step 3: Is *owner's equity* affected? Yes (Owner's equity decreases by $10,000.)	$\downarrow A = L + \downarrow OE$

Snapshot #12

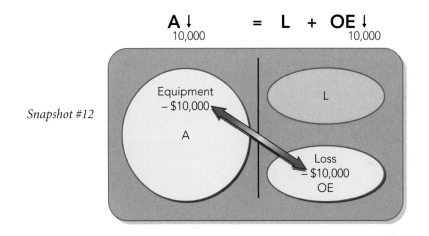

$$A \downarrow \quad = \quad L \ + \ OE \downarrow$$
10,000   10,000

Unrecordable Event

The business signs a new contract with the employee labor union. This is a legal event. No economic event will happen until the employees are actually paid. There is no change to the condition of the business.

Analysis	Effect on Condition
Step 1: Are *assets* affected? No	
Step 2: Are *liabilities* affected? No	
Step 3: Is *owner's equity* affected? No	

continued ▶

Examples of Analysis and Patterns, *continued*

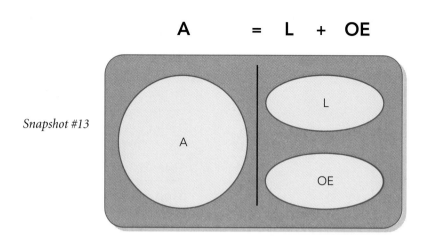

Snapshot #13

Use Cash to Pay Expense and Make Prepayment

The company makes a $4,000 payment to the landlord for office rent. $1,000 of the payment is for the current month's rent. The remaining $3,000 is a prepayment for the next three months' rent. (Three items are affected by this transaction: Cash decreases by $4,000, Prepaid Rent increases by $3,000, and Owner's Equity decreases by $1,000 because of the rent expense.)

Analysis	Effect on Condition
Step 1: Are *assets* affected? Yes (Prepaid Rent increases by $3,000 and Cash decreases by $4,000.)	$A \uparrow \downarrow = L + OE$
Step 2: Are *liabilities* affected? No	
Step 3: Is *owner's equity* affected? Yes (Owner's equity decreases $1,000 because of the expense.)	$A \uparrow \downarrow = L + OE \downarrow$

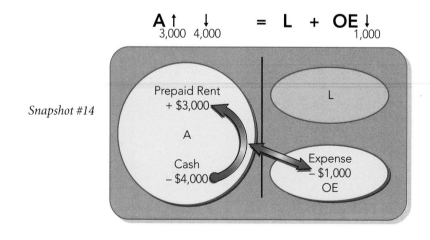

Snapshot #14

Examples of Analysis and Patterns, *continued*

Owner Withdraws Assets from a Business

The owner of the business needs some cash for personal expenses, so she withdraws $2,000 cash from her business. Assets are reduced and not used to pay creditors, so owner's equity is the claim that decreases.

Analysis	Effect on Condition
Step 1: Are *assets* affected? Yes (Cash decreases by $2,000.)	$\downarrow A = L + \quad OE$
Step 2: Are *liabilities* affected? No	
Step 3: Is *owner's equity* affected? Yes (Owner's equity decreases by $2,000.)	$\downarrow A = L + \downarrow OE$

$$A \downarrow_{2,000} \quad = \quad L \quad + \quad OE \downarrow_{2,000}$$

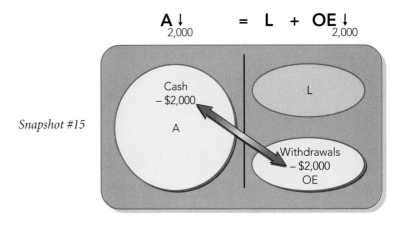

Snapshot #15

Owner's Personal Expenditure

The owner spends the $2,000 she withdrew from the business on the purchase of furniture for her home. This is not a transaction of the business, so the condition of the business is not affected.

Analysis	Effect on Condition
Step 1: Are *assets* affected? No	
Step 2: Are *liabilities* affected? No	
Step 3: Is *owner's equity* affected? No	

$$A \quad = \quad L \quad + \quad OE$$

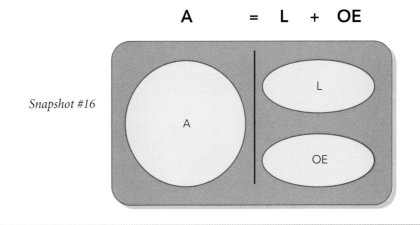

Snapshot #16

continued ▶

Examples of Analysis and Patterns, *continued*

Summary: Three Types of Asset Transactions

If you take a moment to review all the transactions that you have just analyzed, you will notice that every recordable transaction always involved an asset in some way. All of these transactions can be classified into three possible types of asset transactions (or combinations of the three):

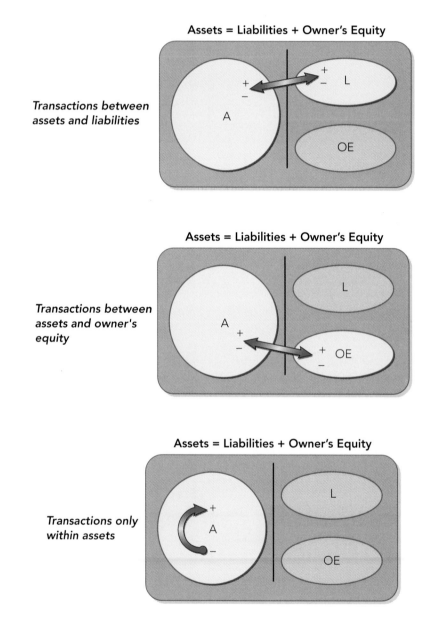

Transactions between assets and liabilities

Transactions between assets and owner's equity

Transactions only within assets

You can see that so far every transaction has involved an asset. Sometimes total assets did not change, sometimes total assets decreased, and sometimes total assets increased.

Check Your Understanding

For each of the transactions given to you, write the change in the accounting equation and draw a diagram that illustrates the change in the condition of the business.

1. A purchase of $800 of supplies for cash

2. A $1,000 loan payment

3. A purchase of $200 of supplies on credit

4. Using up $300 of supplies in operations

5. A $700 sale to a customer on credit

6. Purchase $5,000 of equipment by paying $1,000 cash and signing a $4,000 note payable

Answers

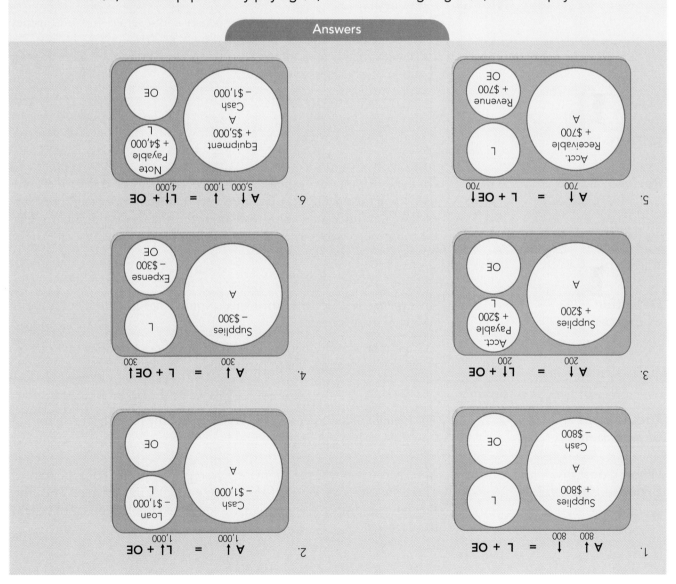

Expenses and Revenues in More Detail

Overview

The Need for Precision

One of the most common errors that students make in basic accounting is the misinterpretation of the words "expense" and "revenue." It is vital that you have a clear understanding of these words for the following reasons:

- Expenses and revenues are the most powerful force of change on any business.
- You will always be dealing with expenses and revenues in your business classes and/or business practice.
- The next major topic shows how expenses and revenues affect the condition of a business in a new way.

Expenses

Review

On page 10, you saw "expense" described as the dollar cost of a resource used up in the operations to create a new resource. This is still true. However, we now understand how to describe the financial condition of a business more precisely, so let us use a definition for expense that is more precise.

Definition of Expense

An *expense* is a decrease in owner's equity that is caused by using up resources in operations.

> *Note:* The word "operations" still means those activities that create a new resource and sell it to customers.

The Amount of an Expense

The *amount* of an expense is the dollar cost of the resources used up.

When Does an Expense Happen?

An expense happens the moment a resource is consumed in operations. There are only two kinds of resources: property and services. Therefore, the moment property or services are consumed in operations, an expense has occurred.

Expenses, *continued*

___

Using up Resources Always Decreases Assets

A business operates by consuming property resources and services resources. Using up these two resources always causes assets to decrease. Assets decrease like this in two possible ways:

- *Noncash asset used up:* Often, an asset itself is the resource (property) that is consumed in the operations. When the noncash asset is used up, total assets decrease. (Examples: Using up supplies or wearing out equipment.)
- *Cash used up:* The asset cash is used to pay for services consumed in the operations. When the services resource is consumed, total assets decrease because cash is used to pay for the services. (Examples: Paying employees for their services or paying the telephone company for telephone service or paying rent.)

___

Examples of Expenses

The table below shows some expenses. In each case, a property or services resource is consumed in operations. This causes total assets to decrease and also decreases the owner's equity.

Description	Amount of expense	What resource used up?	What asset decreased?
Waterville Company used up supplies costing $400. The supplies would have cost $475 to replace.	$400	Supplies (property)	Supplies (The asset is also the resource used up.)
Augusta Company received a telephone bill for $200 and immediately paid it.	$200	Telephone services	Cash (to pay for telephone services)
Bangor Enterprises completely wore out a machine that had cost $5,000.	$5,000	Machine (property)	Machine (The asset is also the resource used up.)
Portland Company paid $7,500 for employee wages in the current month's production.	$7,500	Employee services	Cash (to pay for employee services)

continued ▶

Expenses, *continued*

Not Expenses

All of the following transactions or items do not involve an expense. The missing quality is indicated to the right.

Transaction or Item	Missing Quality
A liability is paid.	Assets decrease, but liabilities decrease the same amount, so owner's equity is not affected.
Cash is used to purchase supplies.	Owner's equity is not affected. There is no decrease in resources—one asset is given up but another is obtained.
An uninsured fire loss destroys equipment.	The resources are not consumed as part of *operations*. (A "loss" is an incidental decrease in owner's equity caused by casualty, theft, or other incidental event.)

Why Does an Expense Make Owner's Equity Decrease?

When assets decrease as a result of the business operations, the owner's equity decreases. The accounting equation clarifies how the owner's claim decreases:

When assets decrease, we know that part of the change in the condition of the business will show up like this: $\downarrow A = L + OE$

To keep the equation in balance, what else must happen? *Owner's equity* also decreases: $\downarrow A = L + \downarrow OE$

(The creditors are not going to let *their* claim be decreased!)

More Examples of Expenses

This expense...	would be called...	This expense...	would be called...
Consuming office supplies	Office Supplies expense	Consuming repair services	Repairs expense
Wearing out equipment	Depreciation expense	Consuming advertising services	Advertising expense
Consuming gasoline	Fuel expense	Using city services	Property Tax expense

Note: Each business decides what name to use for an expense, so there is always some variation in the exact names that are used.

Expenses That Increase Liabilities, *continued*

Analysis	Effect on Condition
Step 1: Are *assets* affected? No (Assets are not used to pay the bill.)	
Step 2: Are *liabilities* affected? Yes (Accounts Payable increase by $120.)	$A = \uparrow L + \quad OE$
Step 3: Is *owner's equity* affected? Yes (Owner's equity decreases by $120.)	$A = \uparrow L + \downarrow OE$

$$A \quad = \quad L\uparrow \quad + \quad OE\downarrow$$
$$\qquad\qquad\quad 120 \qquad\quad 120$$

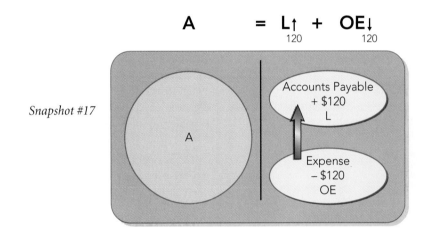

Snapshot #17

Stage 2: The Liability is Paid

The business in the example above pays the $120 telephone bill on August 2. As assets decrease, the creditor's claim also decreases. Owner's equity is unaffected by the payment to creditors.

Analysis	Effect on Condition
Step 1: Are *assets* affected? Yes (Assets decrease by $120.)	$\downarrow A = \quad L + OE$
Step 2: Are *liabilities* affected? Yes (Accounts Payable decrease by $120.)	$\downarrow A = \downarrow L + OE$
Step 3: Is *owner's equity* affected? No	

continued ▶

Expenses That Increase Liabilities, *continued*

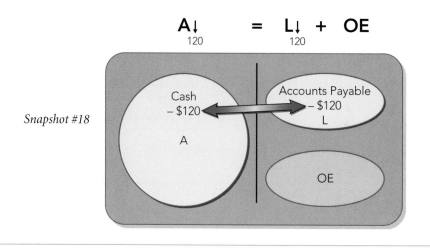

Snapshot #18

Caution!

Remember that not every increase in a liability happens because of an expense. Expenses and liabilities usually occur together when there are unpaid services consumed in operations.

For example, if a company borrows money or buys supplies on credit, no expense is involved. Can you use the equation (or draw the picture) to verify this?

Analysis	Effect on Condition
Step 1: Are *assets* affected? Yes (Cash or Supplies increase.)	$\uparrow A = \quad L + OE$
Step 2: Are *liabilities* affected? Yes (They increase.)	$\uparrow A = \uparrow L + OE$
Step 3: Is *owner's equity* affected? No (no expense)	

Caution! Don't Confuse "Liability" and "Expense"

Beginning students often confuse the word "liability" with the word "expense." I am not exactly sure why this happens; perhaps they both seem like negative or bad kinds of things or because they sometimes occur together.

An expense can happen with or without a liability, and a liability can happen with or without an expense. The fact that they sometimes occur in the same transaction does not mean that they are the same thing.

A liability is not an expense, and an expense is not a liability. (*Suggestion:* Go to the glossary at the back of the book and review the definitions of "expense" and "liability.")

"He thinks a 'liability' is the same thing as an 'expense.'"

Check Your Understanding

Write the completed sentences on a separate piece of paper. The answers are on page 126.

An asset is not always used up at the same time an expense occurs. Sometimes, there is a · · · · · · · · decrease in assets. Instead of decreasing assets, · · · · · · · · are increased. This usually happens when a (property/service) · · · · · · · · resource is consumed and not immediately · · · · · · · ·.

Use up and/or down arrows (↑ ↓) in the accounting equation to show these transactions:

- Beebe Company used $5,000 of accounting services in June, but did not pay for them.

- In July, Beebe Company paid the amount owing for the accounting services.

Revenues That Decrease Liabilities

Assets Increase in Advance

On page 116, you read that a revenue always causes assets to increase. Frequently, assets increase at the same time a revenue is earned. That is what you have studied up to now.

However, sometimes a business receives an advance payment from a customer *before* goods or services are provided to the customer. When this happens, the business has increased its assets *before the revenue is earned.*

Examples

- Louisville Corporation receives a $2,000 advance payment from a customer one month before the merchandise is sold.
- Bowling Green Legal Services requires a $1,000 advance payment from a client before they begin doing the legal work.

The Advance Receipt Creates a Liability

Suppose that Blarney Advertising Company receives an advance payment of $800 from a customer in October. The advertising service will begin in November. Assets increase by $800 when payment is received in October. However, no revenue is recorded. Why? Because no services have been provided yet!

Because Blarney Advertising Company received cash and has not yet performed services, *the company has a liability.* Until the services are provided, the company is obligated to return the money.

At this point, the accounting equation will show this: $\uparrow A = \uparrow L + OE$
$$\$800 \quad \$800$$

Revenues That Decrease Liabilities, *continued*

Earning the Revenue Decreases the Liability

When Blarney Advertising Company provides the advertising service in November, it has earned the revenue. At this point, the liability will disappear because the service has been provided. Now owner's equity increases. The customer's claim on the cash payment has now shifted to the owner because the business provided the service.

The accounting equation will now show this: $A = \downarrow L + \uparrow OE$
$ \$800 \quad \$800$

Name of the Liability

The name of the liability created by receiving an advance payment from a customer is **unearned revenue**. It is also sometimes called **deferred revenue**.

Summary

The following table shows the stages of the condition of a company as these transactions happen:

Stage	Event	Accounting Equation
1	Company receives advance payment.	$\uparrow A = \uparrow L + OE$
2	Company provides service or product and earns the revenue.	$A = \downarrow L + \uparrow OE$

Final Result

The final result for Blarney Advertising Company is that cash increased by $800 and owner's equity increased by $800. The liability is gone.

Note: If the company had not performed the services, it would have to return the money. Both cash and liabilities would decrease by $800.

More Examples

Each of the following examples show how the condition of a business changes for businesses that receive advance payments from customers.

continued ▶

Revenues That Decrease Liabilities, *continued*

Stage 1: Company Receives Advance Payment

White-Knuckle Airlines receives $550 for a standard ticket. The flight will be in two weeks. The customer is a creditor until the flight is provided. Notice that the airline cannot yet record an increase in owner's equity because the service has not been provided.

Analysis	Effect on Condition
Step 1: Are *assets* affected? Yes (Cash increases by $550.)	$\uparrow A = \ L + OE$
Step 2: Are *liabilities* affected? Yes (Liabilities increase by $550.)	$\uparrow A = \uparrow L + OE$
Step 3: Is *owner's equity* affected? No	

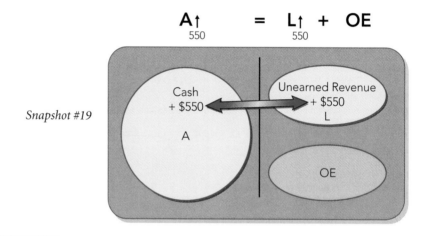

Snapshot #19

Stage 2: Revenue Is Earned

Two weeks later, the customer uses the ticket and takes the flight. The service is provided to the customer, so the liability is gone and revenue is earned.

Analysis	Effect on Condition
Step 1: Are *assets* affected? No	
Step 2: Are *liabilities* affected? Yes (Liabilities decrease by $550.)	$A = \downarrow L + \ OE$
Step 3: Is *owner's equity* affected? Yes (Owner's equity increases by $550.)	$A = \downarrow L + \uparrow OE$

Revenues That Decrease Liabilities, *continued*

$$A \quad = \quad L\downarrow \quad + \quad OE\uparrow$$
$$ _{550} _{550}$$

Snapshot #20

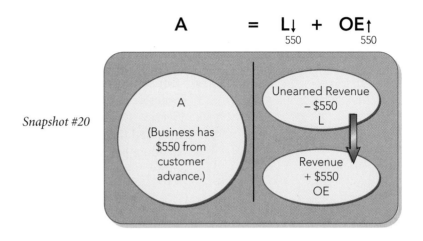

Stage 2: Different Example

Last month, a lawyer received a $2,000 advance (called a "retainer") from a client. The lawyer now performs the services and earns the revenue.

Analysis	Effect on Condition
Step 1: Are *assets* affected? No	
Step 2: Are *liabilities* affected? Yes (Liabilities decrease by $2,000.)	$A = \downarrow L + OE$
Step 3: Is *owner's equity* affected? Yes (Owner's equity increases by $2,000.)	$A = \downarrow L + \uparrow OE$

$$A \quad = \quad L\downarrow \quad + \quad OE\uparrow$$
$$ _{2,000} _{2,000}$$

Snapshot #21

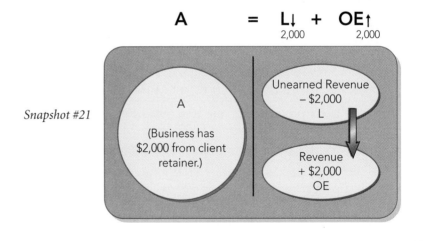

continued ▶

Revenues That Decrease Liabilities, *continued*

Naming Revenues

To give decision makers detailed information, each company identifies a revenue by the type of sale that is made.

Examples:
- "Consulting Fees" means that consulting revenues increased the owner's equity.
- "Service Revenue" means that some kind of service activity revenue increased the owner's equity.
- "Product Sales" means that sales of merchandise increased the owner's equity.

Check Your Understanding

Write the completed sentences on a separate piece of paper. The answers are on page 131.

Sometimes a business receives an advance payment from a customer. This creates (a/an) ·········. When the business later provides the service or product to the customer, revenue is earned and the ········· will (increase/decrease) ·········.

Comparing revenue types. The table below shows various transactions. For each transaction, place a mark in the correct box to show if the transaction is a revenue with an immediate increase in assets, a revenue with a decrease in liabilities, or is not a revenue.

Transaction	A revenue with a:		Not a Revenue
	Immediate Increase in Assets	Decrease in Liabilities	
1. A company receives a $300 cash advance payment from customer for repair services.	(Reminder: Use a separate sheet of paper to complete the table.)		
2. A company provides service to a customer who had previously made a $300 advance payment.			
3. A customer pays a company $300 immediately upon completion of repair services.			
4. A business increases its cash when it borrows $4,000 from a bank.			
5. An accountant prepares a tax return and sends a bill to his client.			

Answers

Sometimes a business receives an advance payment from a customer. This creates a liability. When the business later provides the service or product to the customer, revenue is earned and the liability will decrease.

Transaction	A revenue with a:		
	Immediate Increase in Assets	Decrease in Liabilities	Not a Revenue
1. A company receives a $300 cash advance payment from customer for repair services.			✓
2. A company provides service to a customer who had previously made a $300 advance payment.		✓	
3. A customer pays a company $300 immediately upon completion of repair services.	✓ (Cash)		
4. A business increases its cash when it borrows $4,000 from a bank.			✓
5. An accountant prepares a tax return and sends a bill to his client.	✓ (Accounts Receivable)		

"How could I forget! A revenue can either increase
an asset or decrease a liability."

Nonasset Transactions: Other

Overview

Well Done!

You have already covered the most frequently occurring transactions in a business! Most business transactions you see fall into one or a combination of these basic categories that you have studied.

The Last Two Types

The only basic types of transactions that remain are the following:

- Transactions only within the liabilities
- Transactions only within the owner's equity

These transactions happen much less frequently than the others, so we will not spend much time on them.

Transactions Within Liabilities

Why They Happen

These transactions happen when a company replaces old debts with new debts. For example, if a loan is coming due, a company can go to a new bank and obtain a new loan that pays off and replaces the old loan.

The accounting equation would show: $A = \downarrow \uparrow L + OE$

Picture Example

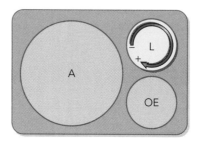

Transactions Within Owner's Equity

Why They Happen

These types of transactions involve reorganizing the owner's equity accounts. The most important kind is called "closing the books," which is discussed in Volume 2 of this series. The other transactions of this type involve certain partnership and corporation transactions. Corporate stockholders' equity transactions are discussed in Learning Goals 28–30.

The accounting equation will show: $A = L + \downarrow \uparrow OE$

Picture Example

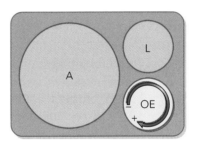

The Six Basic Patterns of Transactions

A Summary of All Transaction Patterns

Now You Have Seen Them All

Congratulations! Now you know all the basic types of transactions that can happen to a business. Although there are thousands of possible different transactions that can occur, they all fall within six patterns as to how they change the condition of a business. You have now seen all six patterns. The last two types you will not see very often, so it is the first four that you need to practice the most. These are:

Type 1:   Transactions between assets and liabilities
Type 2:   Transactions between assets and owner's equity
Type 3:   Transactions within assets
Type 4:   Transactions between liabilities and owner's equity

continued ▶

A Summary of All Transaction Patterns, *continued*

All Six Transaction Patterns

Type 1: **Assets and Liabilities** (see Snapshots #3, #4, #6, #11, #18, and #19)
Type 2: **Assets and Owner's Equity** (see Snapshots #1, #5, #7, #8, #10, #12, #14, and #15)
Type 3: **Within Assets** (see Snapshots #2 and #9)
Type 4: **Liabilities and Owner's Equity** (see Snapshots #17, #20, and #21)
Type 5: **Within Liabilities**
Type 6: **Within Owner's Equity**

Note: Practice the first four types as often as you can until you become comfortable with them.

Type 1: Assets and Liabilities

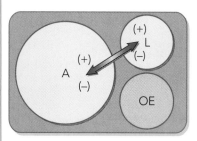

Examples:
- Borrowing money (+)
- Buying on credit (+)
- Paying off debts (–)

Type 2: Assets and Owner's Equity

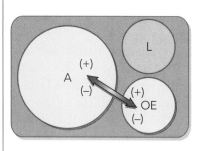

Examples:
- Owner investment (+)
- Revenue: sales of goods and services (+)
- Owner drawing (–)
- Expenses: using up assets in operations (–)

Type 3: Within Assets

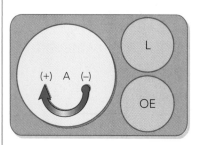

Examples:
- Using cash to purchase another asset
- Collecting an account receivable

Type 4: Liabilities and Owners Equity

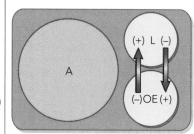

Examples:
- Expenses: debts incurred while consuming services in operations (↑)
- Revenue: reducing debts as a result of selling goods and services (↓)

Type 5: Within Liabilities

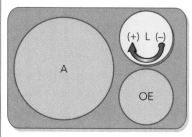

Example:
Incurring new debts to pay off old debts. The old debt decreases, but a new debt takes its place.

Type 6: Within Owner's Equity

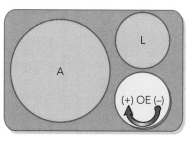

Examples:
- Closing entries (see Volume 2)
- Certain transactions in corporations and partnerships

A Summary of All Transaction Patterns, *continued*

**Combinations
Are Possible**

Sometimes one transaction type can occur in combination with another. An example of this is Snapshot #11 on page 106 and Snapshot #14 on page 108. However, these are not new transactions; they are just combinations of the other transaction types you already know.

VERY IMPORTANT RULE

Don't just memorize—analyze! Do not even think about memorizing all the possible individual transactions. It is totally impossible. Instead, analyze each transaction by doing this:

Step 1: Are *assets* affected?
Step 2: Are *liabilities* affected?
Step 3: Is *owner's equity* affected?

When you are doing the analysis, use the accounting equation or the six basic pictures to visualize the change in the condition. You will be surprised at how easily you can train yourself. You will become confident that you can analyze how any transaction affects a business.

"Not 'sex,' you idiot! I said 'SIX'! There are six basic transaction patterns!"

QUICK REVIEW

- A transaction is any event that changes the financial condition of a business. Transactions can result from:

  - Internal or external events
  - Exchange or non-exchange events

- Using A = L + OE to record the effects of each transaction is called "double-entry."

- *Always analyze* the effects of a transaction by either drawing a picture of the condition of a business or by using the accounting equation. Do this analysis:

  - **Step 1:** Are *assets* affected?
  - **Step 2:** Are *liabilities* affected?
  - **Step 3:** Is *owner's equity* affected?

- When an expense occurs, owner's equity decreases, and either an asset decreases or a liability increases. If a liability increases, eventually it must be paid, and this will cause assets to decrease. Sooner or later, expenses always decrease total assets.

- When a revenue occurs, owner's equity increases, and either an asset increases or a liability decreases. The liability that decreases is called "unearned revenue" and previously caused assets to increase. Sooner or later, revenues always increase total assets.

- Of the six basic types of transactions, only four types happen frequently. Every transaction will be one of the basic types or sometimes a combination of types.

VOCABULARY

Deferred revenue: another name for unearned revenue (page 127)

Double-entry: a system of recording financial changes that requires at least two changes in the accounting equation so it will stay in balance (page 94)

Expense: a decrease in owner's equity caused by using up resources in operations (page 112)

Revenue: an increase in owner's equity caused by making sales to customers (page 116)

Single-entry: an outdated method of recording transactions in which only a part of the change in the accounting equation is recorded (page 94)

Transaction: any event that causes a change in the accounting equation (page 96)

Unearned revenue: a liability created by receiving a payment from a customer before services are performed (page 127)

"Don't just memorize—analyze!"

PRACTICE   Learning Goal 6

Learning Goal 6 is about analyzing individual transactions. Use these questions and problems to practice what you have learned about analyzing individual transactions.

Multiple Choice
Select the best answer.

1. Which of these transactions would increase an asset and increase a liability?
   a. an owner's investment into a business
   b. borrowing money by signing a note payable
   c. purchasing supplies for cash
   d. performing services for a customer on account
2. Which of these transactions would increase an asset and decrease an asset?
   a. collecting an account receivable
   b. purchasing supplies for cash
   c. purchasing supplies on account
   d. both a and b
3. Which of these transactions would decrease an asset and decrease a liability?
   a. an owner's withdrawal of assets
   b. borrowing money by signing a note payable
   c. purchasing supplies on account
   d. paying a debt
4. Earning revenue by performing services on account would
   a. increase total assets and decrease total liabilities.
   b. decrease total assets and decrease total liabilities.
   c. increase total assets and increase owner's equity.
   d. decrease total assets and decrease owner's equity.
5. If San Jose Circuits Company bought $10,000 of equipment by paying $3,000 cash and signing a note payable for the balance, then
   a. total assets decrease and total liabilities increase.
   b. one asset increases and one liability increases.
   c. one asset increases, one asset decreases, and one liability increases.
   d. none of the above.
6. If $500 of supplies were used up in business operations, then
   a. total assets decrease and total liabilities increase.
   b. total assets increase and total liabilities decrease.
   c. total assets decrease and owner's equity decreases.
   d. total assets decrease and owner's equity increases.
7. The payment of an account payable would
   a. decrease total assets and increase total liabilities.
   b. increase total assets and increase total liabilities.
   c. decrease total assets and decrease total liabilities.
   d. not change total assets, total liabilities, or owner's equity.
8. Collection of an account receivable would
   a. increase total assets and increase owner's equity.
   b. increase total assets and increase total liabilities.
   c. decrease total assets and decrease total liabilities.
   d. not affect total assets or owner's equity.

PRACTICE **Learning Goal 6, continued**

Solutions are in the disk at the back of the book and at: www.worthyjames.com

Reinforcement Problems

LG 6-1. Give examples based on the information. Give at least one example of a transaction that would cause the following changes to happen. Also identify any change described that cannot happen.

a. Assets increase and liabilities increase.

b. One asset decreases while another asset increases.

c. Owner's equity decreases and assets decrease.

d. Assets decrease and liabilities increase.

e. Owner's equity decreases and liabilities increase.

f. Assets decrease and liabilities decrease.

g. Liabilities decrease and owner's equity increases.

LG 6-2. Using the three steps to analyze a transaction. Use a blank sheet of paper to complete the table. In the table below, columns 1, 2, and 3 are for the three steps to use in analyzing each transaction. If any step results in a change in the condition of a business, write in the amount of the change with a ↑ to indicate an increase or a ↓ to indicate a decrease. Use the first item as an example.

Transaction	A =	L +	OE
	Step 1: Are assets affected?	Step 2: Are liabilities affected?	Step 3: Is owner's equity affected?
a. The owner of Ellisville Enterprises invests $10,000 in his business.	↑ $10,000	No	↑ $10,000
b. Senatobia Company borrowed $5,000.	(Reminder: Use a separate sheet of paper to complete the table.)		
c. Youngstown Service Company earned $1,000 of revenue that had already been prepaid by a customer last month.			
d. Canton Corporation used $5,000 of cash to purchase supplies.			
e. Brownsville Company provided $2,500 of consulting services to a customer on credit.			
f. Harlingen Partnership received a telephone bill and paid it at once.			
g. Chula Vista Corporation used $2,500 of consulting services and did not pay for them immediately.			
h. Redding Company purchased $10,000 of equipment by paying $2,000 cash and borrowing $8,000.			
i. Shasta Company collects $1,000 owed by a customer on account.			

PRACTICE   Learning Goal 6, continued

Solutions are in the disk at the back of the book and at: www.worthyjames.com

LG 6-3. Explain the changes that are shown. Print out copies of this problem from the disk at the back of the book. Write a brief, accurate explanation next to each of our "business photographs," describing the possible kind of transaction(s) that could have happened to the business in each snapshot.

a.

Business Photograph	Explanation
$A = L + OE$	

b.

Business Photograph	Explanation
$A = L + OE$	

c.

Business Photograph	Explanation
$A = L + OE$	(Assume that this happens as part of business operations.)

PRACTICE   **Learning Goal 6, continued**

LG 6-3, *continued*

d.

Business Photograph	Explanation
A = L + OE	(Assume that this transaction is not part of business operations.)

e.

Business Photograph	Explanation
A = L + OE	

f.

Business Photograph	Explanation
A = L + OE	

Solutions are in the disk at the back of the book and at: www.worthyjames.com

PRACTICE   Learning Goal 6, continued

LG 6-3, *continued*

g.

Business Photograph	Explanation
A = L + OE	(Assume that this happens as part of business operations.)

h.

Business Photograph	Explanation
A = L + OE	(Assume that this transaction is not part of business operations.)

i.

Business Photograph	Explanation
A = L + OE	(Assume that this is not a prepayment by a customer.)

PRACTICE   **Learning Goal 6, continued**

LG 6-3, *continued*

j.

Business Photograph	Explanation
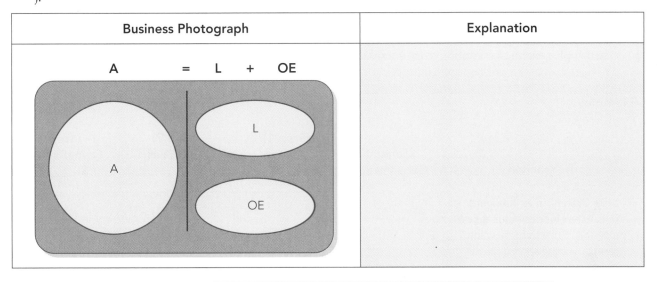	

LG 6-4. What could have made the equation change? Each situation below changes the prior balances and shows new balances in the three elements of the accounting equation. Assuming that just one transaction caused each new balance, on a separate piece of paper, write a brief, accurate explanation of what possible kind of business transaction it could be. There is at least one business transaction for each situation. The solution to the first situation is shown as an example.

	BALANCES			EXPLANATION
	Assets =	Liabilities +	Owner's Equity	
	$5,000		**$5,000**	**Beginning Balances**
a.	$12,000	$7,000	$5,000	a. Business borrowed $7,000 or purchased $7,000 of assets on credit or received an advance of $7,000 from a customer.
b.	$17,000	$7,000	$10,000	**(Reminder: Use a separate sheet of paper to complete the table.)**
c.	$11,000	$1,000	$10,000	
d.	$11,000	–0–	$11,000	
e.	$8,000	–0–	$8,000	
f.	$8,000	–0–	$8,000	
g.	$8,000	$4,000	$4,000	

PRACTICE   Learning Goal 6, continued

Solutions are in the disk at the back of the book and at: www.worthyjames.com

LG 6-5. **A comprehensive review for identifying and analyzing individual transactions.** Print out copies of this problem from the disk at the back of the book (so you can use this problem again). The following problem consists of different transactions. Complete the visualization box by drawing the circles, and indicating plus or minus, as needed, to show what assets or equities are affected by the transaction. Above the box, show the dollar *changes* in the accounting equation. Then apply general classification to each transaction by type of event as internal (Int), external (Ext), exchange (Ex), or non-exchange (N-Ex). Here is an example for the first transaction:

Example:

Transaction	General Classification	(Step 1) Assets $ _____	=	(Step 2) Liabilities $ _____	+	(Step 3) Owner's Equity $ _____
a. Mike Craven, an ex-firefighter but an interior decorator at heart, invests $15,000 in his new interior decorating service called "Hot Spots."	___					

Solution:

General Classification	(Step 1) Assets + $15,000	=	(Step 2) Liabilities $ _____	+	(Step 3) Owner's Equity + $15,000
Ext, <u>N-Ex</u>					

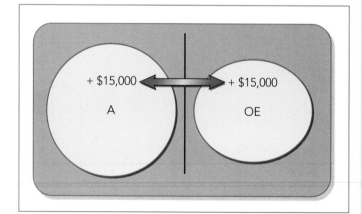

LG 6-5, *continued*

Transaction	General Classification	(Step 1) Assets $ _____	=	(Step 2) Liabilities $ _____	+	(Step 3) Owner's Equity $ _____
b. The company purchases $1,000 of supplies for cash.	—					

Transaction	General Classification	(Step 1) Assets $ _____	=	(Step 2) Liabilities $ _____	+	(Step 3) Owner's Equity $ _____
c. The company purchases another $1,000 of supplies, but this time on credit.	—					

Transaction	General Classification	(Step 1) Assets $ _____	=	(Step 2) Liabilities $ _____	+	(Step 3) Owner's Equity $ _____
d. A large bank pays $5,000 to Hot Spots for decorating consulting services for its new corporate offices.	—					

PRACTICE

Learning Goal 6, continued

Solutions are in the disk at the back of the book and at: www.worthyjames.com

LG 6-5, *continued*

Transaction	General Classification	(Step 1) Assets $ _____	=	(Step 2) Liabilities $ _____	+	(Step 3) Owner's Equity $ _____
e. The company pays the office help $1,200 in wages.	___					

Transaction	General Classification	(Step 1) Assets $ _____	=	(Step 2) Liabilities $ _____	+	(Step 3) Owner's Equity $ _____
f. The business pays $750 of the amount owing for the supplies.	___					

Transaction	General Classification	(Step 1) Assets $ _____	=	(Step 2) Liabilities $ _____	+	(Step 3) Owner's Equity $ _____
g. The company uses up $250 of supplies.	___					

LG 6-5, *continued*

Transaction	General Classification	(Step 1) Assets $ _____	=	(Step 2) Liabilities $ _____	+	(Step 3) Owner's Equity $ _____
h. The company receives a telephone bill showing $150 of telephone services. The bill is not paid immediately.	___					

Transaction	General Classification	(Step 1) Assets $ _____	=	(Step 2) Liabilities $ _____	+	(Step 3) Owner's Equity $ _____
i. The company signs a contract with a new client. The client advances Hot Spots $1,200 before any services are performed.	___					

Transaction	General Classification	(Step 1) Assets $ _____	=	(Step 2) Liabilities $ _____	+	(Step 3) Owner's Equity $ _____
j. Hot Spots fully performs all the work that was required according to the terms of the contract in the previous transaction.	___					

PRACTICE

Learning Goal 6, continued

Solutions are in the disk at the back of the book and at: www.worthyjames.com

LG 6-5, *continued*

Transaction	General Classification	(Step 1) Assets $ _____	=	(Step 2) Liabilities $ _____	+	(Step 3) Owner's Equity $ _____
k. Mike Craven withdraws $1,500 cash for his own personal use.	—					

Transaction	General Classification	(Step 1) Assets $ _____	=	(Step 2) Liabilities $ _____	+	(Step 3) Owner's Equity $ _____
l. Mike Craven uses the $1,500 that he withdrew to make an investment in land.	—					

Transaction	General Classification	(Step 1) Assets $ _____	=	(Step 2) Liabilities $ _____	+	(Step 3) Owner's Equity $ _____
m. Hot Spots purchases $3,500 of equipment by paying $1,000 cash and signing a note payable for $2,500.	—					

Asset Types, *continued*

Kind of Asset	Examples
Notes receivable: A stronger legal right to collect money as the result of a borrower signing a *written promise* to pay, called a "promissory note." It normally involves receiving interest (the opposite of notes payable).	▪ Money is loaned to a borrower. The borrower signs a formal written promise to repay according to specified terms. ▪ A sale is made, and the seller requires the buyer to sign a promissory note.
Comment: Receivables that are created *by sales to customers*—either accounts receivable *or* notes receivable—are said to be "on account" and are called **trade receivables.**	
Interest receivable: The amount of interest that is earned and not yet received on a note receivable. Interest receivable is always recorded separately from the note receivable.	▪ The borrower must make regular payments to pay off the amount of a loan AND pay interest on the loan.
Prepaid expense: An advance payment *paid* to a provider for services *before* the services are received (usually for services to be received in a year or less)	▪ The next 12 months of fire insurance is paid in advance (Prepaid Insurance). ▪ The next three months of rent is paid in advance (Prepaid Rent). ▪ Sometimes supplies are also referred to as a prepaid expense.
Inventory: The goods that a merchant has in stock for the purpose of selling to customers	▪ Golf clubs in a sporting goods store ▪ Meat in a grocery store ▪ Video camera in an electronics store
Furniture, fixtures, and equipment: Long-lived (more than a year) non-real estate assets used in operations	▪ A computer ▪ A truck ▪ A desk
Comment: The key difference between supplies and equipment is that supplies are used up quickly (in a year or less) whereas equipment is used up over a longer period of time. For example, "office supplies" (such as paper, pencils, computer disks, and binders) are used up relatively quickly, whereas "office equipment" (such as furniture, filing cabinets, and computers) provide their benefits over a period of years.	

continued ▶

Asset Types, *continued*

Kind of Asset	Examples
Real estate: Land, buildings, and improvements to land.	■ Land ■ Building ■ Parking lot
Intangible assets: Assets that have no physical substance—you cannot touch them! Intangible assets are usually legal rights.	■ Patent ■ Trademark ■ Franchise right—you can't open a MacDonald's hamburger operation without permission from the company. This permission is called a **franchise,** which gives you the legal right to operate someone else's business (in this case, MacDonald's) in a certain location.

Liability Types

Definitions and Examples

The table below defines common kinds of liabilities and gives examples.

Kind of Liability	Examples
Accounts payable: A legal obligation to pay money, usually as the result of a purchase and usually requiring payment in less than 90 days (the opposite of accounts receivable).	■ $50 of supplies are purchased and not paid for immediately. A bill is received from the vendor. An account payable of $500 is owed to the vendor. ■ A $200 bill is received from the telephone company. $200 is the account payable to the telephone company.
Comment: Accounts payable are promises to pay made using the general credit of a business, are often referred to as made "on open account," and are called **trade payables.**	

Liability Types, *continued*

Kind of Liability	Examples
Notes payable: A stronger obligation to pay money as the result of a borrower signing a *written promise* to pay, called a "promissory note." It normally requires the payment of interest (the opposite of notes receivable).	▪ Money is loaned to a borrower. The borrower signs a formal written promise to repay according to specified terms. ▪ A sale is made and the seller requires the buyer to sign a promissory note.
Interest payable: The amount of interest that is due and unpaid on a note payable. It is always recorded separately from the amount of the note payable.	▪ The borrower must make regular payments to pay off the amount of a loan *and* pay interest on the loan.
Unearned revenue: An advance payment *received* from a customer *before* goods or services are provided to that customer (usually for goods or services to be provided in a year or less).	▪ An insurance company receives an advance payment for 12 months of fire insurance. ▪ A landlord receives an advance payment for the next three months of office rent.
Comment about comparing unearned revenue and prepaid expense: Unearned revenue is a liability that is created because a business *receives cash* before a service or product is provided to the customer. Prepaid expense is an asset that is created because a business *pays cash* before a service or product is received.	

continued ▶

Liability Types, *continued*

TIP

Unearned revenue is *always* a liability. Unearned revenue is *always* a liability; it is *never* a revenue. Remember that any time you see the word "revenue" with the word "unearned" in front of it, it's a liability.

TIP

A creditor does not own the asset. Sometimes people think that a creditor's claim on assets is the same as the creditor actually owning the assets. This is not true. Remember that one part of the definition of an asset requires that it belong to a business. For example, even though your car is security for a bank loan, *you* still own the car—the bank doesn't own it—and you can use the car as you wish without asking the bank for permission. You can also sell the car, as long as you pay off the loan. You are the owner of the car, even though you owe money on it.

"Unearned revenues are . . . L I A B I L I T I E S !"

PRACTICE   **Learning Goal 7**

Learning Goal 7 is about defining and identifying common assets and liabilities. Use these questions and problems to practice what you have learned.

Reinforcement Problems

LG 7-1. **Can you identify the assets and liabilities?** On a separate piece of paper, write the name of the item.

a. A formal written promise by someone else to pay cash to our business
b. Amounts owing suppliers or service providers, usually due in 30–90 days
c. Items needed for the daily operation of a business and consumed in a year or less
d. Money that is collectible in addition to a note receivable
e. Currency on hand, plus amounts in checking and savings accounts
f. A formal written promise by our business to pay someone else
g. Amounts owed to us by our customers, usually due in 30–90 days
h. Money that is owed because of item (f), above, but is not yet paid
i. A payment to a provider of services or goods before they are received
j. The receipt of a prepayment from a customer before providing goods or services to that customer

LG 7-2. **Explain the difference.** Briefly and accurately explain the difference between an account receivable, a note receivable, and interest receivable:

LG 7-3. **Explain the difference.** Briefly and accurately explain the difference between office supplies and office equipment:

Your Questions?

It is *very* important to be aware of what you need to understand better. What do you need to understand better about this learning goal? On a separate piece of paper, write the questions that you want to discuss with your classmates, instructor, or supervisor. Try to be very specific about what is bothering you, such as explanations that you do not fully understand.

Do You Like a Good Story?

It Might Help You to Remember Better

Often people remember information better when the information is part of an interesting story. The story that continues on the next page is the third part of a three-part adventure, mystery, and romance story. If you have not read the first two parts of the story, you will probably want to go back to the beginning on page 23 or the second part which begins on page 78. If you think a story might help you remember better, or if you just want to have some fun, go ahead! The adventures of Darius continue.

Technical Content

This part of the story contains the following technical content:

- Identifying all changes in owner's equity
- Summary statement: statement of owner's equity
- Identifying the operational changes in owner's equity
- Summary statement: income statement
- Business decision making: use the income statement to analyze operations

You Can Skip the Story

If you prefer to study the technical content listed above more quickly, you can skip the story and go directly to page 187, where the standard presentation and practice continue.

The Wealth of Darius
Part III

Hermes' Second Trick

It was morning on the day of rest, and Darius was walking to Dana's house. He carried a basket of white roses and blue wildflowers that he had picked for her. Darius had decided that no matter what happened with his business, it was time to show Dana that he valued her special friendship. He smiled when he thought about seeing her again.

Hermes, however, had a surprise for Darius that day. Hermes had decided that Darius needed to fall in love, but not with Dana. To his regret, the god did not possess the power to make this happen by himself. Instead, Hermes persuaded Aphrodite, the goddess of love and beauty, to help him make things happen in the way he wanted.

Aphrodite had a son named Cupid who could make people fall in love. Cupid was not a small baby with wings as we often see depicted, but rather a beautiful youth, a young man who himself yearned to be loved by a mortal woman. However, Cupid lived with a terrible curse. Cupid could never allow himself to be seen by any mortal. So great was Cupid's beauty that all who gazed upon him would become hypnotized by desire and lose the power to love, or to think, or even to live. Because of his beauty, Cupid forever lived without the love he wanted.

Even so, Cupid had the power to make others fall in love. He had a bow that shot invisible magic arrows. Cupid would wait until someone was looking at another person. At that moment, Cupid would shoot one of his arrows. Whoever was hit by one of Cupid's arrows would fall desperately, madly, hopelessly, and completely in love with the person he or she was gazing upon at that moment.

Cupid waited until he saw Darius walking on the road to the village. Cupid watched as Darius passed by a wealthy local trader walking with his family. As Darius went by, he happened to see the trader's oldest daughter. She was a tall, graceful, black-haired woman named Lamia. In the next second, Darius felt himself overcome by admiration, love, and desire for this woman whom he had never seen before. Darius rushed up to her, introduced himself, and told her that she was the most beautiful woman he had ever seen. Then he anxiously asked her father for permission to visit the next day. Because Lamia was already past the age at which a woman was usually married, her father readily agreed to the visit.

Darius, who normally worked very hard, foolishly forgot his important business problems. He forgot that he was going to see Dana. Instead, Darius withdrew precious money from the business to buy rare eastern perfumes and silks as gifts for Lamia.

The next day Darius, holding the same flowers that he had intended for Dana, knocked on the door of Lamia's house and was shown into the main room to wait for her. As Darius walked into the room, he stopped in amazement. There, standing in the room and coldly staring back at him, was Somnus, who was also holding gifts and flowers.

The Test Is Revealed

Perhaps you have decided by now that it is best to never try to guess what the gods will do. That would be a wise decision, particularly with Hermes. The trickster Hermes had persuaded Aphrodite to ask her son Cupid to make Somnus fall in love with the same woman as Darius. Somnus, while he was in the market, also received one of Cupid's arrows.

Lamia, smiling a devious smile, entered the room with her father. If Darius and Somnus had not been so dumbstruck in their complete admiration of her, they would now have understood why no man had yet asked her to be his wife. Her devious greed soon became apparent as she spoke:

> "Darius and Somnus, I am honored that you both seem to feel such strong love and admiration for me. Unfortunately, I cannot choose between you. My father and I have decided that it would be best to have a contest. Because you are both merchants and my family is a merchant family, we will have a contest of merchants. I will agree to marry the man who can demonstrate that he is the most successful.
>
> The contest will be this: at the end of each month for six months, you will both visit me and my father to report the amount of your business wealth and debts. At the end of the six months, we will see which business could pay off all its debts and have the most wealth left over. The owner of that business will be the winner. You may not invest any money in your business. You must do this strictly by operating the business.

One last requirement: the loser of this contest will agree to give up his entire business to my father. If you do not have the courage to agree to this, you cannot be in the contest, and you will never have my hand in marriage. . . ."

Of course, if Darius had been in his right mind he would never have agreed to such a ridiculous contest. Certainly, Lamia and her father wanted nothing more than to obtain the businesses of both men. In truth, Lamia cared little about any man and, like her father, was excited only by wealth and power. She would do what was necessary to obtain them.

Darius saw none of this, and as he and Somnus signed the document agreeing to the terms of the contest, Somnus turned and growled, "Darius, you are a boy trying to do a man's job." Lamia and her father smiled at this, but Darius did not see them. He was too much in love with Lamia to notice.

Darius Sees What the Contest Is Really About

Everyone in town thought Darius and Somnus were possibly the two greatest fools in the history of civilization, which even then was quite a while. There was much ridicule and laughter behind the backs of the two passionate competitors.

Darius was considered to be the greater of the two fools. Most people knew how much Dana cared for Darius. They knew that she was a sweet, intelligent, and faithful woman. This meant that Darius, instead of losing only his business, could lose both of the most valuable prizes in his life.

Lamia had said that the winner would be the man whose business could pay off all its debts and have the most wealth remaining. That sounded familiar to Darius. Then, he remembered that the owner's claim was how much the value of assets exceeded the amount of the debts.

Darius then realized that this was really a contest about which man could increase his owner's claim the fastest! "Oh, by the gods," he thought, "this is the same problem that I was trying to fix before!" Darius decided to go to Dana, the only person he trusted to help him.

Dana, with great difficulty, continued to work in the shop during the last two days, although she and Darius had not spoken. So strong was the power of Cupid's arrow on Darius, and so great was Darius' desire to win, that after work that day Darius asked Dana to help him.

He did not consider her pain when she learned what he had done. He did not consider how the laughter in the town made her feel. He did not consider that she looked pale or that her eyes were red with dark circles under them. The same Darius, who had always been so generous to others, could now only think of himself . . . such is the power of Cupid's arrows.

Darius said, "Dana, when we spoke last week, you said it would be necessary to identify how each transaction changes the picture of the business. You said it would be necessary to identify which of the changes affected the owner's claim, and to keep a record of these items."

"Yes."

"Dana, I am not sure I can identify all the transactions that affect the owner's claim. Also, I do not know how to keep a record of all of them. It is very important to me now that I increase my owner's claim as fast as possible."

Dana looked down and waited a long time before she quietly spoke. To Darius, it seemed as if Dana was having difficulty speaking. Then she said, "I am sorry, Darius, but I do not feel well. Please forgive me, but I would rather not discuss this matter again with you."

Darius Creates a Plan

Darius, in his heart, knew that Dana was a good person and that she had been good to him. He did not ask her anything more or try to speak to her again except for routine matters of the shop. But he had an idea: he remembered that fees from customers increase the owner's claim. Why not try to increase the fees by making more sales to more customers? Also, Darius thought it would be much easier to only keep a record of sales transactions rather than all the transactions.

Darius had several ideas for increasing sales. He decided to purchase brighter and more long-lasting paints. He would purchase some new and unusual colors and paint more pottery. This was more costly but he would have more customers. He would hire another employee to help him with the complicated designs of large wall paintings. Yes, making more sales to customers was the key!

The day of the first month's comparison with Somnus approached, and Darius was hopeful.

After the first month passed, Darius completed his record of the fees earned. He was very proud of his work. It showed each type of fee and looked like this:

Revenue	Month 1
Portrait fees	$ 500
Wall and fresco fees	900
Pottery fees	400
Total fees earned	$1,800

The following day, Darius would meet with Lamia and her father. This was the day that Darius and Somnus were going to show their progress after the first month. Darius felt the excitement of seeing Lamia again, and he felt especially good because his fees had been increasing. Darius excitedly began to prepare the statement of condition of his business.

Darius calculated the condition of his business and could not believe what he saw. He calculated the condition a second time. Then he compared the statement of condition at the end of last month to the statement of condition he had just completed. This is what Darius saw:

End of this month
Assets = Creditors' Claims + Owner's Claim
$8,800 = $7,500 $1,300

End of last month
Assets = Creditors' Claims + Owner's Claim
$9,300 = $7,400 $1,900

Darius sat in amazement. What had happened? How could his owner's claim have decreased by another $600? He went to bed that night with one hope—that Somnus had a worse month.

The next day, Darius was disappointed. As they were instructed, Darius and Somnus each presented a statement of the wealth and debts of their businesses. Somnus began to smile when he saw that he was winning.

Darius	
Total Wealth	$8,800
Gold	300
Due from customers	1,450
Supplies	1,700
Equipment	5,350
Total Debts	$7,500

Somnus	
Total Wealth	$25,300
Gold	4,300
Due from customers	950
Supplies	4,700
Equipment	15,350
Total Debts	$7,400

Darius tried to keep his wits. He noticed that neither Somnus nor Lamia nor Lamia's father knew how to calculate the condition of a business in the way that Darius knew how. They simply compared the wealth and the debts. When Darius saw this, he remembered something that he had learned from Hermes.

Immediately, Darius pointed out that Somnus had included his personal clothing and household furniture as part of the equipment of the business. Lamia and her father had to agree that this was incorrect. They reduced Somnus' business assets by the amount of the items that were personal. Somnus clenched his fists and glared at Darius.

Then Darius showed that Somnus had also included his shop as part of the equipment. Somnus, like Darius, rented his shop, so the shop did not belong to Somnus' business. After this was subtracted, the wealth of the two businesses was almost equal. Lamia and her father smiled at Somnus' rage. They really did not care who won. They knew that both businesses would soon be under their control.

The Second Month

Darius knew he had been lucky this time. Somnus would be more careful the next time. Darius tried harder than before for more fees. He and his assistant worked longer, used better paints, and painted better pottery. At the end of the second month, Darius calculated the total fees, and saw they were $940 greater than the first month:

Revenue	Month 1	Month 2
Portrait fees	$ 500	$ 840
Wall and fresco fees	900	1,100
Pottery fees	400	800
Total fees earned	$1,800	$2,740

Darius felt momentary relief, but when he prepared his statement of condition, this is what he saw:

End of Month 2
Assets = Creditors' Claims + Owner's Claim
$8,500 = $7,250 $1,250

The owner's claim and the assets had decreased again. The owner's claim was $50 less than the first month of the contest. At the two-month comparison, Darius watched Somnus smile with glee when the comparisons were made. Somnus did not make the same mistakes that he had made the last time.

Darius looked closely. Although Somnus did not think about calculating an owner's claim, Darius mentally calculated Somnus' owner's claim by subtracting $3,500 from $12,900. Somnus had a claim of $9,400. Then Darius anxiously looked back at his own claim again—only $1,250!

Darius	
Total Wealth	$8,500
Gold 250	
Due from customers 350	
Supplies 2,550	
Equipment 5,350	
Total Debts	$7,250

Somnus	
Total Wealth	$12,900
Gold 4,100	
Due from customers 1,100	
Supplies 2,150	
Equipment 5,550	
Total Debts	$3,500

When he returned to his shop, Darius knew that he had been much too confident in his plan. It was not working. The problem was that he had not yet fully explained the operational change in his owner's claim. He had not done what Dana had suggested when they worked together.

Darius had not bothered to keep a record of the assets used up in operations. Because it was easier, he had only been recording the operational increases caused by the fees. Only four months to go!

To get control, Darius knew now that he also needed to identify the decreases caused by operations. Darius was not sure that he could identify all the operational decreases, but now he had to try. He had no choice.

The Third Month

Darius discovered that keeping a record of all the operational decreases in his owner's claim was a great amount of extra work. There were so many of them! Even the name "assets used up in operations" was too long and too difficult to say. He started using the name "expenses" because assets were being expended . . . that is, used up.

To keep a record of expenses, Darius worked hard and his days were long. It was not easy to know exactly when there was an expense. It was clear to Darius when the business used up paints or canvas—that was an expense. (It helped to create value.) It was clear to him that when the business used up gold to pay an employee— that was an expense. It was less clear when he paid the rent, but then he remembered he could not do his work for customers without a shop to work in. So, paying the rent was an expense.

Paying the creditors puzzled Darius. After much thought, he decided that paying debts was not an expense, because this was only benefiting the creditors, not the customers. Paying debts did not use up assets as part of the process of creating something valuable for customers. The purpose of paying debts was to reduce a creditor's claim. With practice, Darius became better at identifying expenses.

At the end of the third month, Darius summarized the fees and the expenses with a new table:

Revenue	Month 2	Month 3
Portrait fees	$ 840	$ 850
Wall and fresco fees	1,100	1,500
Pottery fees	800	1,900
Total fees earned	$2,740	4,250
Expenses		4,500
Operational decrease in owner's claim		$ – 250

Darius now began to sense what was wrong. When he looked at the results of Month 3, he could see that his owner's claim was decreasing mostly because of operations. The operations used up assets as expenses faster than the operations received assets (the fees earned) from customers. For Month 3, operations used up $250 more in the value of the assets than was received from customers, which reduced the wealth of the business and the owner's claim.

Then Darius calculated the condition of his business and compared it to the condition at the end of last month. *Worse!* His owner's claim was down again!

End of Month 3
Assets = Creditors' Claims + Owner's Claim
$9,050 = $8,100 $950

End of Month 2
Assets = Creditors' Claims + Owner's Claim
$8,500 = $7,250 $1,250

Darius again looked at the owner's claim. The difference between $950 and $1,250 was a $300 decrease, not $250. Why the extra $50 decrease?

Darius felt his neck tighten and his head ache. He sensed that he could not try much harder. He already had worked very, very hard. He had kept a record of all sales. He had kept a record of all expenses. All this plus doing all his usual painting and design work! "Perhaps I am just too stupid to compete against Somnus," he thought. A feeling of sadness overcame him as he remembered all his wonderful dreams of a life together with beautiful and graceful Lamia.

On the next day, the meeting confirmed his fears. Again, Somnus was further ahead. Somnus' business had even paid off all its debts! Somnus loudly suggested that Darius quit the contest so he would not embarrass himself anymore. Lamia laughed and seemed not to notice Darius at all.

Darius	
Total Wealth	$9,050
Gold 100	
Due from customers 1,550	
Supplies 2,050	
Equipment 5,350	
Total Debts	$8,100

Somnus	
Total Wealth	$14,900
Gold 4,000	
Due from customers 1,200	
Supplies 2,700	
Equipment 7,000	
Total Debts	$0

The Fourth Month

Darius did not go to the shop the next day. Instead, he walked in the meadows around his house. He began to think about the real possibility of losing his business.

Darius did not go to work for the next two days. On the fourth day, when he returned to his shop, he had not shaved. Darius did not work on any new designs, and he did not do the thing that he loved the most—his painting.

Darius gave up recording the sales and the expenses. Although Darius had always liked to talk with his employees and customers, he seldom spoke now. For more than a week, he did no painting. He did nothing. Customers became angry waiting for their work. Two creditors, Aulis and Hela, came to Darius and told him that they were tired of waiting to be paid. They would not supply any more materials unless the business paid them more quickly.

All the employees, of course, observed this. Among them, Dana worried the most. Darius' foolish behavior had not stopped Dana from caring about what happened to him. Even though she had given up all hope for Darius' love, her noble character would not let him continue to suffer.

One day, she came to him in the shop and said, "Darius, I have not seen you do much painting lately. Are you thinking about new designs?"

"No," he said, "I am finished with that and I am finished with painting."

"Why is that?"

"Because I have discovered that I am probably too stupid to be any good at what I am trying to do. I think that my painting is poor and my ideas are poor. Even if I were a good painter, I am unable to be a businessman. It has taken me all this time to finally understand how operations decreased my owner's claim, and now I am too stupid to do anything more with this knowledge."

This shocked Dana. Darius had been a wonderful artist ever since he was a small child, and he loved painting more than anything in life. She decided to be bold. "Darius, I know all about this contest with Somnus. Everyone knows that one of you will lose his business." Darius opened his eyes wide when he heard her say this.

"I understand how taken you are with Lamia. But I know you well, Darius. There is something that you love even more than Lamia, and that is the joy you feel when you paint. Are you willing to give up painting because of her? Is her approval that important to you? Is she going to take your life away?" Darius stared at her with his mouth open.

"As for being stupid . . . well, Darius, do you not realize what you have just done? By identifying the fees earned and the expenses, you have explained all the operational changes to your owner's claim! This is powerful knowledge. Use it to change whatever is wrong! You are acting ridiculous, Darius. I will not watch you give up everything. Would you like me to help?"

"Help?" Darius mumbled. "Me? Now?"

"Darius," Dana said, putting her hand on his shoulder, "it is time to take what you have learned and really use it. We will figure out a way to make your owner's claim grow and then you can beat Somnus. But first help me put all this information together so we can understand what has happened." With Dana's encouragement, Darius began to think about his business again.

Over the next several hours, Dana and Darius designed a statement that explained all the changes in the owner's claim that they had found. (Their creation was so good that a similar statement is still used today.)

As a starting point, they wrote down the beginning and ending balances of the owner's claim for Month 3. This is what it looked like:

Statement of All Changes in Owner's Claim for Month 3		*Total decrease is $300!*
Prior balance, end of **Month 2**	$1,250	←
Current balance, end of **Month 3**	$ 950	←

Next, they prepared the statement showing the operational changes in the owner's claim because of fees and expenses. This was similar to what Darius had already prepared.

Statement of Operational Changes for Month 3	
Fees Earned	
Portraits	$ 850
Walls and frescoes	1,500
Pottery	1,900
Total fees earned	4,250
Total Expenses	4,500
Operational decrease	($250)

Then, in the statement of owner's claim, they entered the $250 operational decrease. Dana used brackets ( ) to show a minus amount, because it was easier to see than a minus sign of "–". Next, Dana wrote a "?" to show that a change was still unidentified.

Statement of All Changes in Owner's Claim for Month 3	
Prior balance, end of **Month 2**	$1,250
Less: Operational decrease	(250)
???	?
Current balance, end of **Month 3**	$950

Statement of Operational Changes for Month 3	
Fees Earned	
Portraits	$ 850
Walls and frescoes	1,500
Pottery	1,900
Total fees earned	4,250
Total Expenses	4,500
Operational decrease	($250)

Finally, Dana asked if there were any changes caused by investments and withdrawals. Darius had made no investments, but remembered that he had taken out $50 in withdrawals. This was the missing $50 dollar decrease! This completed all the changes in the owner's claim!

Statement of All Changes in Owner's Claim for Month 3	
Prior balance, end of **Month 2**	$1,250
Add: Owner's investments	–0–
Less: Operational decrease	(250)
Less: Owner's withdrawals	(50)
Current balance, end of **Month 3**	$950

Statement of Operational Changes for Month 3	
Fees Earned	
Portraits	$ 850
Walls and frescoes	1,500
Pottery	1,900
Total fees earned	4,250
Total Expenses	4,500
Operational decrease	($250)

The Mystery Is Solved

When they had finished, Dana clapped her hands. "Darius, look at what we have done! We have completely explained the entire change in your owner's claim with these two beautiful statements! The $300 decrease in your owner's claim was caused by just two kinds of increases and two kinds of decreases! Your investments and the fees from customers are the two increases. Withdrawals and expenses are the two decreases. The fees and expenses are from operations. We have solved the mystery!"

"This must be what Hermes had wanted," Darius said.

"Now comes the matter of beating Somnus," Dana answered. "Darius, I think I see what you need to do and it is rather important."

"What is that?" he asked.

"The expenses," she said. "Your troubles, I think, are caused by the operational decrease in your owner's claim. The expenses seem to be reducing your owner's claim faster than the fees from customers are increasing it."

"Yes, I think I understand that now."

"Good. But Darius, you have not yet detailed all the expenses as you have done with the fees. If you knew how much each of the individual expenses were, you could make decisions about changing or reducing them. I think we need to start keeping a record of *each kind* of expense. I can help you do this."

This is how Darius and Dana began keeping detailed records of the business operations. They began with the sales and expenses from the beginning of Month 4, and they continued recording for the remainder of the month. For Month 4, they had a much more detailed explanation of the operational change in the owner's claim. It looked like this:

Revenue	Month 3	Month 4
Portrait fees	$ 850	$ 1,200
Wall and fresco fees	1,500	2,750
Pottery fees	1,900	3,450
Total fees earned	4,250	7,400
Expenses	4,500	
Portrait materials and supplies		200
Walls/frescoes materials and supplies		1,250
Pottery materials and supplies		6,450
Rent		250
Other expenses		100
Operational decrease in owner's claim	$ (250)	$ (850)

The size of the decrease shocked Darius. He prepared the statement of condition at the end of Month 4. He could not believe what he saw.

End of Month 4
Assets = Creditors' Claims + Owner's Claim
$8,250 = $8,200 $50

Next, he prepared the statement that explained all the changes in his owner's claim.

Statement of All Changes in Owner's Claim for Month 4	
Prior balance, end of **Month 3**	$950
Less: Operational decrease	(850)
Less: Withdrawals	(50)
Current balance, end of **Month 4**	$50

Statement of Operational Changes for Month 4	
Fees Earned	
Portraits	$1,200
Walls and frescoes	2,750
Pottery	3,450
Total fees earned	7,400
Expenses	
Portrait materials/supplies	200
Walls/frescoes materials/supplies	1,250
Pottery materials/supplies	6,450
Rent	250
Other expenses	100
Total expenses	8,250
Operational decrease	($850)

As usual, Darius had not made any investments, so they omitted the line for investments.

"By the gods, I have only $50 of owner's claim left! I am practically finished!"

"No, you are not," Dana replied. "I think that now is your best opportunity. Tomorrow I will show you why I believe this, after you finish your meeting with Somnus and Lamia. Stay strong, Darius."

When Darius presented his wealth and debts at the end of the fourth month, he endured even more humiliation than usual. Somnus asked, "Darius, why do you not stop the contest to avoid further humiliation? You can leave town quietly." Both Somnus and Lamia burst into laughter when they saw Darius' presentation of wealth and debts. Darius remained silent as he clenched his jaw.

What Do You Think?

- What amount caused an increase in owner's claim? Where do you find it?

- What two amounts caused a decrease in owner's claim? Where do you find them?

- What business or financial advice would you offer to Darius now?

Total revenues of $7,400 caused the increase in owner's claim. It is on the Statement of Operational Changes. (An owner's investment would also have increased owner's claim, but Darius did not do this.)
Expenses of $8,250 decreased the owner's claim. Expenses are on the Statement of Operational Changes. A withdrawal of $50 also decreased the owner's claim. This is shown separately on the Statement of All Changes in Owner's Claim because it is not part of operations.

The Fifth Month—Important Business Decisions

Darius returned from the monthly meeting more angry and upset than usual. Dana immediately said, "All right, Darius, now is our time."

"I am ready to try anything," he said. "What was the opportunity that you spoke of yesterday?"

"Darius, you now have something very special—something that neither Somnus nor anyone else understands. You possess detailed information that tells you all the reasons why operations have decreased your owner's claim. To increase your claim, all you need to do now is use this information so you can make decisions that change the way you operate. Are you ready?"

"For anything."

"Good. I am certain that the answers you need are hiding in the two parts of operations—expenses and fees. There is one question for each part. First, the expenses: look closely at the total amount of each expense. Is the expense justified for the amount of value it creates? Second, the fees: are you charging the right price for each kind of work that you do?"

"I will need some time to think," he replied.

"Then think about these questions carefully tonight. We will discuss this again tomorrow."

Darius stayed in his shop that night. He lit many candles to keep his shop bright, and then thought intently about the two questions. One at a time, he thought about each expense that he saw on the statement of operations. For each expense, he asked himself, "*Is the expense justified* by the amount of value—that is, the fees—it helps my business get?"

The expenses of the pottery work amazed him, and as he began to think more about it, Darius realized that the special paints and glazes for pottery were always the most expensive supplies. Also, the waste was significant because pottery often baked improperly in the ovens and had to be thrown away.

The second question was, "Am I charging the right price for each kind of work?" For months, Darius had charged less than Somnus for everything: the portraits, the walls and frescoes, and the pottery. Darius hoped that selling for less would attract more customers, but this did not seem to attract many new customers, except for pottery painting.

After giving all of this much thought, Darius then made three business decisions:

First, he decided to increase some of his prices. He would charge the same as Somnus for walls and frescoes. Also, Darius decided to double his prices for portraits because they took so much time, and because he was a much better portrait painter than Somnus.

Second, Darius decided that he would try to reduce the cost of the wall and fresco designs.

Darius enjoyed his third decision most of all. Except for a few special customers, Darius decided to completely stop all the pottery painting!

Why? Darius realized that it would be impossible for pottery painting to be profitable. The pottery painting was slow and much more costly than he had ever realized. What was worse, he could never raise prices for pottery painting! Most customers refused to pay very much for the pottery painting because eventually pottery breaks and needs to be replaced. Except for a small number of wealthy customers, painting pottery would always cause large losses.

When he looked at the statement of operational changes for Month 4, Darius saw that pottery painting was the single biggest cause of his problems with the business. The pottery expenses of $6,450 were much greater than the pottery fees of $3,450. The pottery expenses simply could never create enough value!

The Perfect Trick

Then Darius had a wonderful idea, a trick that was worthy of Hermes himself! Darius decided to tell everyone that he was giving up pottery painting because Somnus was so much better. If the plan worked, then arrogant Somnus would eagerly take all of Darius' old pottery customers. In this way, Somnus would soon have all the same pottery expenses and begin to destroy his own business.

Darius realized that Somnus did not understand about the complete calculation of the condition of a business. He certainly had no idea about calculating the operational changes in the owner's claim. So, it would be a long, long time—if ever—before Somnus would find out what was wrong. The perfect trick!

On the next morning, when Darius and Dana discussed the decisions about increasing prices and trying to reduce the cost of wall and fresco designs, she agreed. She had reached those conclusions herself. And when Dana heard Darius' reasons for letting Somnus take over all the pottery painting in the village, she bubbled with excitement. "Why Darius, you are as clever as Hermes himself!" and she laughed so long that she had to sit on a bench as tears streamed from her eyes. Darius could not restrain his own smile.

On the second day of the fifth month of the contest, Darius raised his prices. He began telling most of his customers that he would no longer paint pottery for them because Somnus was too good. Somnus fell right into the trap. Soon he was working long hours for all his new pottery customers. He had to buy new equipment and hire an extra employee.

Darius could hardly wait until the end of the month.

It had started out as a difficult month, but it seemed to become easier to pay the creditors as the month progressed. Darius had high hopes as the time came to calculate the monthly statement of condition. Before he did this, Darius summarized his fees and expenses and compared them to Month 4.

Revenue	*Month 4*	*Month 5*	
Portrait fees	$ 1,200	$ 2,200	
Wall and fresco fees	2,750	3,250	
Pottery fees	3,450	–0–	←
Total fees earned	7,400	5,450	
Expenses			
Portrait materials and supplies	200	250	
Walls/frescoes materials and supplies	1,250	1,150	
Pottery materials and supplies	6,450	–0–	←
Rent	250	250	
Other expenses	100	100	
Operational change in owner's claim	$ (850)	$ 3,700	

When Darius saw the results of Month 5, satisfaction filled him like nourishment to a starving man. The operations had increased owner's equity by $3,700! The plan was beginning to work.

Next, he prepared the three necessary statements: the basic statement of condition and the two statements explaining the changes in the owner's claim.

End of Month 5
Assets = Creditors' Claims + Owner's Claim
$10,850 = $7,200 $3,650

Statement of All Changes in Owner's Claim for Month 5	
Prior balance, end of **Month 4**	$50
Add: Investments	–0–
Add: Operational decrease	3,700
Less: Withdrawals	(100)
Current balance, end of **Month 5**	$3,650

Statement of Operational Changes in Owner's Claim for Month 5	
Fees Earned	
Portraits	$2,200
Walls and frescoes	3,250
Pottery	–0–
Total fees earned	5,450
Expenses	
Portrait materials/supplies	250
Walls/frescoes materials/supplies	1,150
Pottery materials/supplies	–0–
Rent	250
Other expenses	100
Total expenses	1,750
Operational increase	$3,700

In the meeting at the end of the fifth month, Darius watched a different Somnus review wealth and debts for Lamia and her father. Somnus' assets had decreased and his debts had increased.

Darius	
Total Wealth	$10,850
Gold	1,900
Due from customers	1,550
Supplies	2,050
Equipment	5,350
Total Debts	$7,200

Somnus	
Total Wealth	$13,500
Gold	2,750
Due from customers	1,200
Supplies	2,550
Equipment	7,000
Total Debts	$3,900

Somnus kept staring at the paper and taking quick little breaths, which made him stammer. "Do not wor … wor … worry, Lamia, it is jus … jus … just … one mm … mm … month."

It was true that Somnus still had more wealth and fewer debts than Darius. It was also true that if this had been the last month of the contest, Somnus would win, because after paying all his debts Somnus would have $9,600 of wealth left over. Darius only had an owner's claim of $3,650. However, there was still one more month to go, and Darius was catching up.

The Final Month

As the sixth month began, Darius felt his determination surge like a rising river. Now he could chuckle to himself as he saw Somnus toiling at his shop every day, seldom resting, trying to complete all of his pottery painting work. Moreover, because Somnus now spent so much time on pottery painting, he began to lose some wall and fresco painting customers to Darius. Darius' decision now looked even better than before.

Dana also noticed the difference. Darius had both higher prices and new wall painting customers. Meanwhile Somnus, by painting so much pottery, was sinking into a hole that he was digging for himself. Dana felt that Darius had a chance to win when Lamia made the last comparison.

Dana was happy that Darius had a chance to save his business and that he was painting again. Every day she prayed for him to win. But Dana also knew that if Darius won, she would soon be out of his life. Lamia would see to that. The moment that Lamia selected Darius, Lamia would throw Dana out. Dana promised herself that no matter what, she would always be a friend to Darius; she would always give Darius the best advice that she knew. Her special smile would always belong to him.

The last day of Month 6 arrived. Darius calculated the fees and expenses for the sixth month and compared them to Month 5.

Revenue	Month 5	Month 6
Portrait fees	$2,200	$2,100
Wall and fresco fees	3,250	3,400
Pottery fees	–0–	–0–
Total fees earned	5,450	5,500
Expenses		
Portrait materials and supplies	250	300
Walls/frescoes materials and supplies	1,150	600
Pottery materials and supplies	–0–	–0–
Rent	250	250
Other expenses	100	50
Operational increase in owner's claim	$3,700	$4,300

Nervously, Darius calculated the condition of his owner's claim:

End of Month 6		
Assets = Creditors' Claims + Owner's Claim		
$14,900 =	$7,000	$7,900

Darius and Dana again prepared the statements explaining the changes in the owner's claim. However, what Darius really worried about now was the final balance of his owner's claim. It was the end of the six months and Darius' balance was $7,900. At the end of the previous month, Somnus had shown $9,600. Darius could only hope that the pottery losses were enough to bring Somnus down below $7,900.

That night, Darius slept restlessly, tossing and turning. He dreamed of Ammon, and Darius felt his old fears of losing the business. He dreamed of the old woman dressed in black and of the frightening visits by Hermes. He dreamed about his friends, the birthdays, and the wonderful feasts and good times. He dreamed about the beautiful Lamia and her father. In his dream they became great spiders, and he could hear their spider fangs clicking together and their spider feet brushing the ground as they hungrily approached him . . . and he awoke with a scream.

The day's first light illuminated the silver dew on every tree and flower and soon changed the silver into millions of glowing rainbow drops. As the minutes brightened, birds began sharing their melodies in a joyful chorus that proclaimed the fresh day. Darius made his final decision.

He bathed and ate a small breakfast. He picked up the paper on which he had written the business wealth and debts for Lamia and her father to examine and put it into his pocket.

He went directly to Dana's house. Ammon answered the door, and Darius said, "Ammon, I apologize if I am too early this morning. However, may I speak to your daughter?"

"Yes, Darius, one moment."

In a few minutes, Dana appeared. Darius looked at her directly and then said, "Dana, as you know, I am meeting with Lamia, her father, and Somnus this morning. I would like you to be there with me."

She stared at him. "Darius, you love Lamia. How can you ask me to do this?"

"Dana, trust me and be my friend one last time, please."

She was a true friend and, despite her uncertainty, she left with Darius. In another moment, Darius and Dana were walking on the road together. In less than an hour, they arrived at the home of Lamia and her father. Somnus arrived at almost the same time. Sullen and dark, he glared at them and said, "Now Darius, it is at last time for you to see who is the better man. It is time for you to disappear."

They were shown into the house, where Lamia and her father were waiting, smiling. Lamia's eyebrows arched and her eyes showed surprise when she saw Dana.

"Well, Dana, this is truly an unexpected pleasure. Did you come here to say good-bye?" Lamia and her father smiled hungrily. Lamia continued, "This is the moment, dear Darius and dear Somnus, I know you both have eagerly awaited. Now show me the statements you have prepared, and the winner will be my husband."

Darius handed his statement to Lamia. Somnus turned and glowered at Darius, to which Darius responded with a smile and a wink. Choking down his fury, Somnus shoved his statement into Lamia's outstretched hand.

"Gentlemen, gentlemen," she said, "let us now see which one of you shall enjoy the blessings of my companionship for the rest of your life." With that, she placed the two statements on a table so all could see:

Darius	
Total Wealth	$14,900
Gold	4,550
Due from customers	3,500
Supplies	1,500
Equipment	5,350
Total Debts	$7,000

Somnus	
Total Wealth	$15,500
Gold	1,100
Due from customers	2,700
Supplies	3,800
Equipment	7,900
Total Debts	$7,800

Lamia seemed to hesitate and consulted with her father. She turned and faced the three people in front of her. "Somnus, if we subtract the debts from the wealth, your business would have $7,700 of wealth remaining if it were to pay off all its debts today. Darius, I am surprised to say that your business would have $7,900 of wealth remaining if it were to do the same. Darius, you appear to be the winner."

Shaking, Somnus snarled, "Fraud!"

"No," Darius said, "you may check and verify everything, as I am sure Lamia will do."

Lamia now ignored Somnus and smiled directly at Darius. "Oh Darius, you are much the better man. You know, I never once doubted you. You have truly won my heart and you will at last be my husband." Then Lamia turned to a servant and said, "Show Dana the door. It is time for her to leave."

At the same moment, Somnus exploded into a rage, shrieking, "Fraud, fraud, you are a *fraud!*" Madly shaking, raving, Somnus screamed, "I . . . YOU . . . I challenge you, Darius, to a duel! . . . to the death . . . *the death!* . . . now, at this instant!"

Quick as cats, two of Lamia's servants were upon Somnus and forced him into a chair. After several minutes, Somnus began to calm and Darius spoke.

"First, Somnus, I regretfully decline your offer of a duel. It is not my intention to demonstrate your unworthiness twice in one day, and at the cost of your life."

Then Darius turned to Lamia. "Lamia, I have indeed won the contest. Regrettably, I must inform you that I decline your offer as well. You will not be my wife. However, as the winner, I will choose to keep my business for myself. I suggest that you and Somnus will be excellent for each other."

Darius reached over to Dana, and brought her nearest hand to his lips. "As for me, I have already won my prize, long before today."

Epilogue

And so that is what happened when the gods decided to let humankind learn about the condition of a business. Darius came to realize that despite all his troubles, he had received two wonderful gifts for which he always thanked the gods.

The first great gift was the ability to explain the condition of a business and why the condition changes, especially the change in the owner's claim. Darius, always generous, decided to share this knowledge with other merchants—yes, even with Somnus, who years later came to hold Darius in high esteem as his one true friend.

Darius told the other merchants that three statements are necessary: the first one, the basic statement of condition, is like a picture drawn at a point in time. The other two statements explain change, so they show what happened over a period of time. Darius made a list:

STATEMENT OF CONDITION

- a picture of the business at any point in time

STATEMENT OF CHANGES IN OWNER'S CLAIM

- summarizes all the changes in the owner's claim

STATEMENT OF OPERATIONAL CHANGES IN OWNER'S CLAIM

- explains in detail the changes in the owner's claim caused by operations. These have the most powerful effect on the owner's claim

Darius, always the artist, drew a diagram as an example for the other merchants to show them the three kinds of statements. In the diagram, Darius showed the condition of his business at the end of Month 3, Month 4, and Month 5 of the contest. Then he drew the two statements that showed change, explaining the changes in the owner's claim for Months 4 and 5.

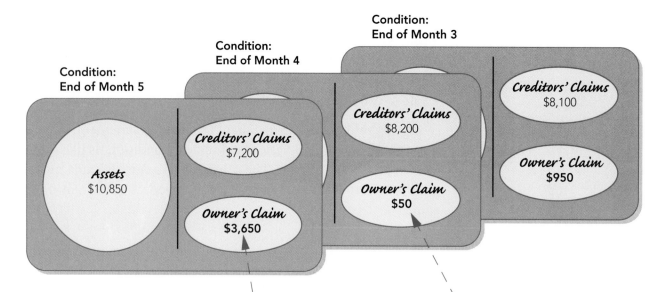

Condition:
End of Month 5

Condition:
End of Month 4

Condition:
End of Month 3

Assets
$10,850

Creditors' Claims
$7,200

Owner's Claim
$3,650

Creditors' Claims
$8,200

Owner's Claim
$50

Creditors' Claims
$8,100

Owner's Claim
$950

Month 5 *Statement of Changes* *in the Owner's Claim*			*Month 4* *Statement of Changes* *in the Owner's Claim*	
Beginning balance	$	**50**	Beginning balance	$ **950**
Add: Investments		–0–	**Add:** Investments	–0–
Less: Withdrawals		(100)	**Less:** Withdrawals	(50)
Operational increase		3,700	Operational decrease	(850)
Ending balance		**$3,650**	Ending balance	**$ 50**

Month 5 *Operational Changes* *in the Owner's Claim*		*Month 4* *Operational Changes* *in the Owner's Claim*	
Fees earned	$5,450	**Fees earned**	$7,400
Expenses		**Expenses**	
Portrait supplies	$ 250	Portrait supplies	$ 200
Wall/fresco supplies	1,150	Wall/fresco supplies	1,250
Rent	250	Pottery supplies	6,450
Other	100	Rent	250
Total expenses	1,750	Other	100
		Total expenses	8,250
Operational increase	$3,700	Operational decrease	$(850)

| LEARNING GOAL 8 | # Explain the Four Basic Changes in Owner's Equity |

Overview

Introduction

Because there are several different reasons for the changes in owner's equity, students who are just beginning their study of business and accounting sometimes forget or become confused by some of these changes. Owner's equity is so important—it is the owner's claim on business wealth—that its essential features are summarized for you in this learning goal.

There are four basic changes in owner's equity.

In Learning Goal 8, you will find:

The Features of Owner's Equity

Essential Features of Owner's Equity

It Is a Secondary Claim on Asset Value	Owner's equity is the owner's claim on the value of the business assets. However, when you are the owner, your owner's claim is secondary to the claim of the creditors. The owner's claim is calculated like this:

$$\text{Assets} - \text{Liabilities} = \text{Owner's Equity}$$

The Name to Use in a Specific Business	For any business (except a corporation), the owner's equity is identified by the word "capital" and the owner's name. For each individual business, the name of the owner of that business is written before the word "capital" to show whose claim it is.
Example	If your name is John Elton, then the owner's equity for your particular business would be called "John Elton, Capital."
Synonyms	Owner's equity is sometimes called **net worth** or **net assets.**

*"What do you mean . . .
'My claim is secondary'?"*

The Changes in Owner's Equity

All the Changes in Owner's Equity

The Causes of Change

There are actually six causes for increase or decrease in the owner's equity:

Cause	Increase or Decrease	Example
OWNER'S DIRECT ACTIONS		
■ *Investments*	Increase	You invest $5,000 of your own cash into your business.
■ *Withdrawals*	Decrease	You remove $5,000 cash from your business and use it personally.
OPERATIONAL CHANGES		
■ *Revenues*	Increase	The business sells $500 of services to a client.
■ *Expenses*	Decrease	The business uses up $100 of supplies.
OTHER CHANGES INCIDENTAL TO BEING IN BUSINESS		
■ *Gains*	Increase	The business sold some old equipment for $2,000 more than it cost.
■ *Losses*	Decrease	A fire burned down the warehouse.

The First Four Changes

The first four items—*investments, withdrawals, revenues,* and *expenses*—are by far the most important. These occur regularly in every business. These are the changes you will continue to study in this book.

The Last Two Changes

The last two items—*gains* and *losses*—are incidental occurrences that happen much less often than revenues and expenses. However, they have the same effect on owner's equity as revenues and expenses. For this reason, gains and losses will not be part of this discussion of owner's equity. Gains and losses are discussed again in the learning goals about corporations and in Volume 2.

continued ▶

All the Changes in Owner's Equity, *continued*

Illustration

The four basic causes of change in the owner's capital balance is illustrated below for an imaginary business in the years 2007 to 2009.

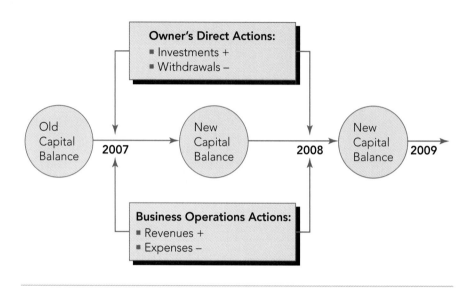

The Four Basic Changes

Owner's Investment

Owners investment is an *increase* in owner's capital caused by the owner contributing cash or other personal wealth into the business. These items become assets of the business, so this causes the total assets in the business to increase. As a result, the owner's equity increases. Using the equation:

$$A \uparrow = L + OE \uparrow$$

Note: Rarely, an owner may pay the debts of the business with his or her own personal funds. This is an owner investment that makes liabilities decrease instead of assets increase.

Owner's Withdrawals

Withdrawals (also called *drawing*) is a *decrease* in the owner's capital caused by the owner's withdrawal of cash or other assets out of the business for personal use. This causes the total assets to decrease, so the owner's claim decreases. Using the equation:

$$A \downarrow = L + OE \downarrow$$

The Four Basic Changes, *continued*

Revenue

Revenue is an *increase* in the owner's capital that results from making a sale of goods or services. The amount of the revenue is whatever the customer pays for the product or service. Owner's capital increases because the sale always causes either assets to increase or liabilities to decrease. Using the equation:

$$A \uparrow = L \quad + OE \uparrow$$

or

$$A \quad = L \downarrow + OE \uparrow$$

Expense

An expense is a *decrease* in the owner's capital caused by the business operations consuming resources. The amount of the expense is the cost of the asset or services consumed. The owner's capital decreases because an expense always causes either assets to decrease or liabilities to increase. Using the equation:

$$A \downarrow = L \quad + OE \downarrow$$

or

$$A \quad = L \uparrow + OE \downarrow$$

Summary of the Four Basic Changes

The table below summarizes the features of the four basic changes:

Increases or Decreases	Owner's Direct Actions	Operational Activity	Effect on Assets and Liabilities
Increases in owner's equity	Owner investments	Revenues	Assets $\uparrow$ **or** liabilities $\downarrow$
Decreases in owner's equity	Owner withdrawals	Expenses	Assets $\downarrow$ **or** liabilities $\uparrow$

Changes in a Corporation

For a corporation, the changes are practically identical, except that owners' investments in a corporation are called "paid-in capital" (or "contributed capital") and withdrawals are called dividends. (See Part VI, Learning Goals 28–31 for more detailed discussions of corporations.)

QUICK REVIEW

- For any business (except a corporation), use the owner's name followed by the word "capital" to describe the ownership claim.

- There are four basic changes in owner's equity:

  - *Changes caused by operations:* revenues and expenses

  - *Changes caused by the owner directly:* investments and withdrawals

- Revenues and investments are increases.

- Expenses and withdrawals are decreases.

VOCABULARY

Net assets: another name for owner's equity (page 188)

Net worth: another name for owner's equity (page 188)

Withdrawals: a decrease in the owner's capital caused by the owner's withdrawal of cash or other assets out of the business for personal use (page 190)

PRACTICE   Learning Goal 8

Solutions are in the disk at the back of the book and at: www.worthyjames.com

Learning Goal 8 is about explaining the four basic causes of change in the owner's equity. Use these questions and problems to practice what you have learned.

Reinforcement Problems

LG 8-1. Is it an expense? Is the transaction of *paying a liability* an expense? Give a brief, accurate answer in the space below.

_____

LG 8-2. A review of different items. Use this question to review all the specific kinds of assets, liabilities, and owner's equity items. On a separate piece of paper (so you can practice the problem again without seeing answers), place the correct letter next to each number.

a. Cash	h. Unearned revenue
b. Supplies	i. Revenue
c. Accounts receivable	j. Equipment
d. Note receivable	k. Withdrawal
e. Prepaid expense	l. Owner investment
f. Account payable	m. Expense
g. Note payable	n. Dividends

1. An increase in owner's equity caused by either an increase in assets or a decrease in liabilities as a result of performing services or selling products is called · · · · · · · ·.
2. Items such as paper, computer disks, binders, staples, solvents, and paper towels are called · · · · · · · ·.
3. An asset created when a sale is made to a customer "on account" (that is, no cash is received at the time of sale) is · · · · · · · ·.
4. A liability that is created on the books of the seller when a customer prepays before the service or product is provided to the customer is called · · · · · · · ·.
5. An asset that is created for the lender when a formal written promise to pay a certain amount is signed is called (a/an) · · · · · · · ·.
6. A liability that is created for the payor when a formal written promise to pay a certain amount is prepared and signed is called (a/an) · · · · · · · ·.
7. The owner transferring personal assets into a business is called · · · · · · · ·.
8. A decrease in owner's equity caused by a decrease in assets or an increase in liabilities resulting from the process of operating the business is (a/an) · · · · · · · ·.
9. An obligation to pay money (normally in 30–90 days) to a supplier is (a/an) · · · · · · · ·.
10. Currency that a business has on hand and the amounts in the checking and savings accounts that can be withdrawn on demand is called · · · · · · · ·.
11. A short-term asset created when a business pays for goods or services before it receives them or uses them up is (a/an) · · · · · · · ·.
12. The owner's withdrawal of assets from the business for his or her personal use is called (a/an) · · · · · · · ·.

PRACTICE   Learning Goal 8, continued

Solutions are in the disk at the back of the book and at: www.worthyjames.com

LG 8-3. **Practice with revenues affecting assets and liabilities.** Revenues always increase the owner's equity. The revenue transaction either causes an increase in assets or a decrease in liabilities. The purpose of this exercise is to have you identify whether a revenue is causing an increase in assets or a decrease in liabilities. (Just for fun, we've also included some examples that are not revenues. This is to remind you that not *all* increases in assets or decreases in liabilities are caused by revenues!)

Use a blank sheet of paper to complete the table. For each item, also draw an arrow indicating which part of the accounting equation is increasing and/or decreasing. Use the first two transactions as examples.

Transaction	Assets increased or liabilities decreased?	Revenue?	Why is it a revenue or not a revenue?	A	=	L	+	OE
a. An accountant performs $2,000 of accounting services and is paid in cash.	Yes (The asset Cash increases.)	Yes	Assets increase because services are performed for a customer, so it is a revenue transaction.	↑				↑
b. The accountant borrows $2,000 from her bank.	Yes (The asset Cash increases.)	No	Assets increase because of a loan, so it is not a revenue transaction.	↑		↑		
c. An accountant receives a $2,000 cash advance from a client as a prepayment for future services.			(Reminder: Use a separate sheet of paper to complete the table.)					
d. The accountant fully performs all the services for the client who prepaid her in (c) above.								
e. The accountant invests an additional $5,000 in her business.								
f. In September, the accountant performs $2,500 of services "on account."								

LG 8-3, *continued*

Transaction	Assets increased or liabilities decreased?	Revenue?	Why is it a revenue or not a revenue?	A	=	L	+	OE
g. The accountant collects $2,000 cash from the accounts receivable.								
h. A magazine publisher mails magazines to its subscribers who pre-paid subscriptions.								
i. A computer consultant is paid $1,000 immediately after finishing a job.								

LG 8-4. Why isn't it a revenue? A revenue increases assets or decrease liabilities. All of the following transactions either increase assets or decrease liabilities, but *none* of them are revenues. What critical attribute are they all missing that causes them *not* to be revenues?

- A business receives a $1,000 cash advance from a customer. (The asset Cash increases.)
- Supplies are purchased on account. (The asset Supplies increases.)
- Cash is collected from accounts receivable. (The asset Cash increases.)
- Accounts payable are paid. (The liability Accounts Payable decreases.)
- Owner invests $10,000 in the business. (The asset Cash increases.)

LG 8-5. Why isn't it an expense? An expense decreases assets or increases liabilities. All the following transactions either decrease assets or increase liabilities, but *none* of them are expenses. What critical attribute are they all missing that causes them *not* to be expenses?

- The owner withdraws $1,000 cash from the business. (The asset Cash decreases.)
- The business pays off a $200 account payable. (The asset Cash decreases.)
- The business borrows $10,000 from a bank. (The liability Notes Payable increases.)
- The business purchases $500 of supplies for cash. (The asset Cash decreases.)
- The business buys supplies on credit. (The liability Accounts Payable increases.)

LG 8-6. Practice with expenses affecting assets or liabilities. Expenses always decrease the owner's capital, and this can involve either a decrease in assets or an increase in liabilities. The purpose of this exercise is to have you identify whether an expense is causing a decrease in assets or an increase in liabilities. (For more fun, some of these items are *not* expenses.)

PRACTICE   Learning Goal 8, continued

Solutions are in the disk at the back of the book and at: www.worthyjames.com

LG 8-6, *continued*

Use a blank sheet of paper to complete the table. For each item, also draw an arrow indicating which part of the accounting equation is increasing and/or decreasing. Use the first two transactions as examples.

Transaction	Assets decreased or liabilities increased?	Expense?	Why is it an expense or not an expense?	A	=	L	+	OE
a. The business pays off a loan of $10,000.	Yes (The asset Cash decreases.)	No	Only creditors' equity is affected, not the owner's.	↓		↓		
b. $1,500 of supplies are used up.	Yes (The asset Supplies is used up.)	Yes	A direct using up of resources in operations.	↓				↓
c. A business pays off an account payable of $1,500.	**(Reminder: Use a separate sheet of paper to complete the table.)**							
d. A business pays employees $1,500 in wages as soon as they are earned.								
e. A business receives a $750 repair bill for this month's computer repair services. The bill is not paid immediately.								
f. The owner pays himself a "salary" and withdraws $1,000 in cash.								
g. A business pays this month's telephone bill of $300 as soon as it is received.								
h. A business owes its employees $15,000 in wages but will not pay them until next Monday.								
i. Next Monday, the business pays the wages to the employees.								

PRACTICE   **Learning Goal 8, continued**   *Solutions are in the disk at the back of the book and at: www.worthyjames.com*

LG 8-7. **Sometimes liabilities and expenses go together and sometimes they don't.** Use a blank sheet of paper to complete the table. The purpose of this exercise is to help remind you that when liabilities are created, it sometimes involves an expense and sometimes not. What matters is *why* the liability is being created. From the description of the transaction, indicate if there is an expense and the reason for your answer. Use the first transaction as an example.

Transaction	Expense?	Liabilities increased?	Did event happen as part of revenue-earning operations?
a. The business borrows $10,000 and records a liability to Fifth National Bank.	No	Yes (The liability Notes Payable increases.)	No (Borrowing money is not part of revenue-earning operations.)
b. The business owes its employees $8,500 for this week's wages and records it as a new liability by classifying it as Wages Payable.	(Reminder: Use a separate sheet of paper to complete the table.)		
c. The business receives a bill for this month's utilities.			
d. The business receives a bill for this month's accounting services.			
e. The business purchases $700 of supplies "on account."			
f. The $700 of supplies is consumed.			
g. The business purchases $4,000 of equipment on account.			
h. The business receives a $1,000 bill for this month's computer repair services.			
i. The business receives a $500 prepayment from a customer for services to be performed next month.			

PRACTICE   **Learning Goal 8, continued**   *Solutions are in the disk at the back of the book and at: www.worthyjames.com*

LG 8-8. Practice with the four kinds of changes to owner's equity. Use a blank sheet of paper to complete the table. Revenues and expenses and investments and withdrawals are the four basic kinds of changes in owner's equity, and they are always accompanied by changes in either the assets or the liabilities. In the following exercise, *all the transactions affect owner's equity.* In each transaction, indicate the type of change to owner's equity that is occurring, if the change is an increase or decrease, if an asset or a liability is affected, and whether that is an increase or decrease. Use the first transaction as an example.

Transaction affecting owner's equity	Type of change to owner's equity	Owner's equity increase or decrease?	Asset or liability affected?	Asset or liability increase or decrease?
a. An accountant prepares a tax return and collects $500 from a client.	Revenue	Increase	Asset (Cash)	Increase
b. An owner invests $10,000 cash in her business.	(Reminder: Use a separate sheet of paper to complete the table.)			
c. Office supplies are used up.				
d. A business receives a bill for consulting services payable on account.				
e. The same accountant as in (a) above prepares another tax return for $400 and sends the bill to the client.				
f. A real estate company receives and pays its current bill for advertising.				
g. A law firm receives its current bill from the telephone company but doesn't immediately pay it.				
h. An owner withdraws $500 worth of supplies from his business.				
i. An airline company provides a flight to a customer who purchased the ticket three months ago.				
j. The accountant receives a $950 bill for computer repair services for this month.				
k. An owner pays a debt of his business by writing a check on his personal checking account (not a good business practice).				

PRACTICE   Learning Goal 8, continued

Solutions are in the disk at the back of the book and at: www.worthyjames.com

LG 8-9. Practice with transactions that don't affect owner's equity. For each of the five transactions below, on a separate piece of paper (so you can practice the problem again without seeing answers), briefly and accurately explain the reason why they *don't* affect owner's equity.

a. Supplies are purchased on account.

b. A business receives a prepayment from a customer before services are provided.

c. A business pays an account payable.

d. A business borrows money.

e. A business collects cash from an account receivable.

INTERNET EXERCISES

Use the AICPA website. Go to the homepage of the American Institute of Certified Public Accountants (search AICPA). When you are on the homepage, click on the "Students" link, and then click on the "The Classroom" link. (Use bookmark/favorites to save the location in an "Accounting References" folder.)

a. What are the recommended courses a student should take if he or she is considering becoming a CPA? Would these courses have value in a business career if someone does not plan to be a CPA? Explain your reasons.
b. What is the 150-hour requirement? Is this something your state requires?
c. What are the essential skills and competencies of a CPA?
d. Return to the AICPA homepage. Explore three other links that seem interesting ("CPA links" can take you to your own state board of accountancy.) Summarize what you found on each link.

Your Questions?

It is *very* important to be aware of what you need to understand better. What do you need to understand better about this learning goal? On a separate piece of paper, write the questions that you want to discuss with your classmates, instructor, or supervisor. Try to be very specific about what is bothering you, such as explanations that you do not fully understand.

<table>
<tr><td>LEARNING GOAL 9</td><td># Analyze the Cumulative Effect of Transactions</td></tr>
</table>

Overview

Introduction

Until now, we have carefully analyzed the effect of each *individual* transaction on the condition of a business. In this learning goal, we use the accounting equation to analyze the **cumulative effect** of many transactions. One simple but useful way to do this is to calculate the total change in assets, liabilities, and owner's equity balances. Doing this gives a basic overview of what has happened to a business over a period of time.

There are many ways to summarize and analyze the cumulative effects of transactions. It is a very important subject. You will return to it again in Section IV on page 279 when you study how financial statements are specialized summaries of the cumulative effects of transactions.

"Cumulative Effect" Defined

The "cumulative" effect of transactions means whatever total change in assets, liabilities, and owner's equity occurs over some period of time and what balances result from these transactions.

Examples

- On January 1, the beginning balance of total assets was $100,000 and on December 31, the ending balance was $90,000. The total assets decreased by $10,000.
- If the beginning balance of owner's equity on October 1 is $35,500 and the owner's equity increased by $4,000, then the ending balance on October 31 is $39,500.
- If the ending balance of liabilities on June 30 was $20,000 and liabilities increased by $5,000 during June, then the beginning balance on June 1 must have been $15,000.

Use the Accounting Equation for the Analysis

It is most useful to analyze changes on all the parts that make up the condition of a company. For this reason, cumulative changes are usually expressed in the format of the accounting equation.

LEARNING GOAL 10

Explain the Accounting Process

In Learning Goal 10, you will find:

What Is Accounting and How Does It Work?

The Accounting System

What Is Accounting and How Does It Work?

Accounting

Overview

So far, you have spent a great deal of time learning the first step in the accounting process—analyzing events. Now you are ready to begin studying the next two steps in the accounting process:

- Processing transaction information
- Communicating financial information in reports

However, before we continue with these steps, it is important to be clear about the meaning of "accounting."

continued ▶

Accounting, *continued*

Definition of "Accounting"

Actually, there is no single, precise definition of accounting. However, one useful definition of accounting is as follows:

Accounting is a system of activities that analyzes, processes, communicates, and interprets financial data about a business or other entity. The objective of accounting is to provide financial information that is useful for decision making.

Examples

- The information system used by a college to record tuition receipts and operating expenses
- The work done by the people in the accounting department of a business to record transactions and prepare financial statements
- The system used by a church to record contributions and expenditures

The Accounting System

Three-Stage Process

Overview

An accounting system functions by a process of sequential steps. The process begins each time an event can potentially affect the financial condition of a business. If an event does affect the financial condition, the financial information from that event continues through each stage in the process that you see illustrated on page 219.

Process Illustrated

The illustration on page 219 shows the sequential stages of the accounting system as a process. The process begins with the analysis of a business event (Stage 1). This analysis identifies any event that is a transaction. If the event qualifies as a transaction, the data concerning that event will also pass through Stage 2 and Stage 3.

The Accounting Cycle

The steps that make up an accounting system are often referred to as the "accounting cycle." As you progress through this book and the first part of Volume 2, you will learn the detailed procedures of the accounting cycle.

Three-Stage Process, *continued*

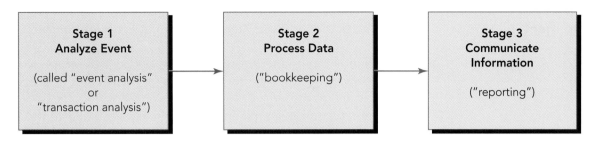

What Happens

- Test the event: Is there a change in the accounting equation?
- Identify:
  - Classification
  - Valuation
  - Timing
- If yes, go to stage 2. If no, stop.

What Happens

- Record transactions if:
  - Reliable data
  - Relevant data
- Summarize results.

What Happens

- Prepare financial reports and interpret them.

Stage 1: Analyze the Event (Transaction Analysis)

Overview

Analyzing an event is called *event analysis* or *transaction analysis*. Whatever you prefer to call it, to analyze an event for accounting purposes means to evaluate what happened to see if the accounting equation has been changed in some way. **Any possible change in the accounting equation must be identified three ways: By classification, by value, and by time (date) of occurrence.**

The good news is that you have already had a lot of basic practice with classification and valuation analysis in previous Learning Goals! You visualized and identified many kinds of changes in the accounting equation by analyzing the effect on assets, liabilities, and owner's equity.

Classification

Classification means identifying *what items* are increased or decreased in the accounting equation because of an event: assets, liabilities, or owner's equity. To do proper classification you need: (1) to understand the definition of these items so you can identify them and (2) to carefully visualize the transaction so you can identify all the items affected in the equation.

continued ▶

Stage 1: Analyze the Event (Transaction Analysis), *continued*

Valuation ("*Measurement*")	*Valuation* means determining the dollar values (economic values) to use for items in the equation. Valuation is also called **measurement**.

Valuation is important and sometimes quite controversial—accountants do not always agree on the correct values for many kinds of items!

We will return to this topic in Learning Goal 18 and again in Volume 2, but right now the **two essential points** you need to remember about valuation are:

1. Valuation means determining what dollar values should be used to record changes in the accounting equation.
2. Valuation is determined in two phases. First, an original transaction value is recorded when a transaction occurs. The value of an item when it is first recorded is usually clear and is what we have been discussing so far.

   Second, values of some of the recorded items may change at a later time. These changes can be caused by loss of future benefits, by price changes, and by other events. In many situations, these later value changes must also be recorded. In Volume 2, we discuss the principles and procedures for recording valuation changes.

Valuation Example

- **Initial value:** On June 12, our business purchased inventory. The invoice amount was $5,000. This is the value used to record the transaction.
- **Value change:** By December 31, the replacement cost of the inventory decreased to $3,000. For this asset, the value must be reduced to $3,000 in the accounting records.

Timing

Timing means identifying the correct date on which an event caused a change in the accounting equation. As you will see in this volume and especially in the next volume, event timing is especially important for correctly determining the net income or net loss for a business.

Why Event Analysis Is So Important

Correct event analysis is extremely important! This cannot be over-emphasized. If event analysis is incorrect, everything else—especially the financial reports, which many people depend on—will be incorrect. The resulting decisions based on those reports will be flawed, misleading, and potentially damaging. It is important for you to begin thinking about **cla**ssification, **va**luation, and **ti**ming whenever you think about transactions. (Think: "Mr. **Clavati**" to help you remember.) If analyzed incorrectly, these three elements can create confusion, and they can also be misused for financial manipulation and fraud.

Proper classification, valuation, and timing make up the heart of good accounting.

Stage 2: Process Data

Overview

After the event is analyzed and identified as a transaction that affects the accounting equation, the transaction data must be processed. The processing stage is usually referred to as **bookkeeping**. Bookkeeping consists primarily of recording and summarizing functions. In this volume and in the next volume, you will learn bookkeeping procedures. The next learning goal introduces you to some of these procedures.

Recording

Recording means formally entering the transaction data into the accounting books and records. Recording is also referred to as **recognition**. Recording (recognition) places the transaction data into the accounting system consistent with the results of the analysis from Step 1.

However, even though the event analysis in Step 1 is completed, two requirements must be met for recording to take place:

- The recorded data must be *reliable*. This means that the transaction data can be verified as authentic and that the data is unbiased.

- The data must be *relevant*. This means that the data will provide information that is useful and significant—it is not irrelevant or immaterial. Reliable and relevant data will ultimately result in reliable and relevant information in financial reports.

Summarizing

Summarizing means accumulating and organizing data in ways that make the recorded data more understandable and useful. Proper summarizing makes it possible to present and analyze data in financial reports. Summarizing also makes it possible for management to accurately use the data when dealing with customers, vendors, and other parties. When summarization happens, the data can be transformed into useful and usable *information*.

Stage 3: Communicate Information

Overview

The entire accounting process takes place with the ultimate goal of creating and presenting useful financial information about a business or other entity.

Financial Reports

Useful financial information is most often presented in the form of financial reports. Usually, at least four types of financial reports are prepared. You will begin to learn how to identify and prepare these reports beginning on page 277 in this volume and will continue into the next volume. In practice, these reports also contain footnotes, charts, graphs, tables, and other analysis to help the users of the reports.

Example of All Stages

The Event	On May 19, Ohlone Company purchases $250 of office supplies on account.

Analyze Event

- Classification: Does the event affect items in the accounting equation? Yes, the asset Office Supplies and the liability Accounts Payable are affected. We know this because we understand the definitions of the items in the accounting equation and because we carefully visualized the event to see in what ways the items might have been affected.

- Valuation: Office Supplies increases and Accounts Payable increases. The dollar value is given as $250. We are given this amount as the exchange value of the event. Thus, the amount is clear and there are no other values to consider.

- Timing: The date of the change in the equation (the purchase) is May 19.

Conclusion: This event is a transaction because the event causes changes in items in the accounting equation that we can classify, that are measurable in dollar value, and that happen at an identifiable date. The classification, valuation, and timing show us how to properly record the transaction.

Process Data

- Recording: The data from the transaction (accounts, values, date) are verified as reliable and relevant by examining documentation. The data is then recorded into the accounting books and records of Ohlone Company.

- Summarizing: At regular intervals, the data from this transaction with other accumulated data is totaled and reorganized using bookkeeping methods.

Communicate Information

Ohlone Company prepares monthly financial reports. Reports are prepared in specific ways that communicate the condition of the company as of the end of May and that explain the operations during May. The summarized data in the books and records of the company is the source of most of the information presented on the financial reports.

The Accounting Profession

Overview

Accountants are professional individuals who are academically trained and who are able to correctly apply the theory and the procedures to properly complete the entire accounting process. Because of their training, accountants are essential and indispensable people who implement the accounting process. Some accountants with advanced training obtain professional licenses.

The Accounting Profession, *continued*

Accountants with Special Certification

A *certified public accountant* (CPA) is a person who has passed a rigorous state examination to obtain a professional license to practice public accounting. CPAs have many financial skills; however, only a CPA can audit the financial statements of a company and express an opinion as to the fairness of the statements. CPAs are required to maintain a high level of independence and integrity. These qualities, in addition to the professional training, mean that CPAs perform essential roles in the accounting process. The main types of work in public accounting are:

- Auditing: CPAs who perform auditing services examine the books and records of a company and express a professional opinion as to the fairness of the company's financial statements.
- Taxation: CPAs who specialize in taxation prepare tax returns and offer tax planning advice. These accountants also represent clients when they are being examined by taxing authorities such as the Internal Revenue Service.
- Consulting services: This type of work is often called *management consulting*. It generally consists of designing accounting and other types of information systems but may also involve other specialized types of work.

A *certified management accountant* (CMA) is a person who analyzes the accounting process of a single company, with an emphasis on analyzing the procedures and operations. This is often called *managerial accounting*. A qualifying examination is required to obtain the CMA designation, and CMAs are also expected to maintain a high level of integrity. Areas of managerial accounting include:

- Accounting information system analysis
- Product cost analysis
- Budgeting
- General internal accounting and recording functions
- Internal auditing

Ethics in Accounting

Overview

Ethical behavior is an essential part of every action in the accounting process that we are discussing. The entire process would become completely meaningless if it consisted only of the application of technical knowledge, without the ultimate goal of providing honest and reliable financial information. Many people depend heavily on reliable financial information in many important ways. People who need financial and accounting information are called **stakeholders**. To meet the needs of stakeholders and to ensure the integrity of the accounting process, accountants have a special ethical responsibility.

continued ▶

Ethics in Accounting, *continued*

The Ethical Attitude

Ethics is the soul of good accounting. Ethical conduct means doing the right thing. Sometimes choices are clear because of existing rules or laws. At other times, choices can be difficult and complicated because it may not be exactly clear what is the right choice among various alternatives. However, in the end, the foundation of ethical conduct is always the same—the consistent *attitude* of always trying to do what one believes to be honest and right.

Important Ethical Standards

Professional accounting organizations have developed codes of conduct that members are expected to follow. Examples of these organizations are the American Institute of Certified Public Accountants (AICPA) and the Institute of Management Accountants (IMA).

Here are some important ethical standards from the AICPA code of conduct:

- **Integrity:** Basic honesty, never violating the trust of others
- **Objectivity:** Being impartial and fair to all parties
- **Independence:** Avoiding all relationships that impair objectivity
- **Due Care:** Properly applying all the necessary knowledge and skills

Guideline

The following table presents a guideline for ethical decision making when no clear rules, codes, or laws are available.

Step	Action
1	Recognize the moral issue of a potentially wrongful act that can result in loss, injury, or damage.
2	Review all the facts, including who is potentially involved.
3	List the alternative decisions.
4	Evaluate the possible outcomes of each alternative. ■ What decision does the most good and/or least harm? ■ Will everyone be treated fairly, regardless of the decision that is made?
5	Make a decision.
6	Thoughtfully appraise the results of your decision.

Ethics in Accounting, *continued*

Example

Thi Ngo, an accountant for Santa Clara Consulting Corporation, discovers that $20,000 of revenue was incorrectly recorded as consulting revenue. In fact, it was rental revenue from leasing some extra office space that the corporation had available for one year. Her supervisor tells Thi not to worry—there will be no effect on the net income of the company and the company does not want to worry investors with accounting technicalities. Thi knows that the revenue is not classified correctly but does not want to anger her supervisor and is uncertain about what to do.

- **Moral Issue:** Consulting is the main operation of the company not renting, and overstating consulting revenue could mislead people into believing that the business is more successful than it really is. People could make investment or employment decisions that might cause them to lose money or damage their careers if the business is actually less successful than it appears to be.
- **Review of Facts:** (a) $20,000 of rental revenue is incorrectly recorded as consulting revenue. (b) The affected parties are investors, lenders, suppliers, employees, corporate officers, and the responsible staff in the accounting department.
- **Alternatives:** (a) Do nothing. (b) Discuss again with the supervisor emphasizing the implications of the ethical issue. (c) Discuss with a higher authority within the company. (d) Make an anonymous report to top management, the auditors, or the board of directors. (e) Resign.
- **Possible Outcomes:** Doing nothing at a minimum establishes a pattern of unethical behavior. Worse outcomes are loss of business reputation and financial losses and job losses of stakeholders who relied on the information. Another discussion might annoy the supervisor but also might possibly help resolve the issue. A discussion with a higher authority may also help resolve the issue, although it would anger the supervisor even more, with possible consequences to Thi. Resigning immediately would mean loss of Thi's job without having attempted to solve the problem, although it would clearly avoid participation in an unethical action.
- **Decision:** The choice is not easy or obvious. Thi decides that the fair alternative that does the most good with the least harm is to first try another discussion with her supervisor, emphasizing the importance of the issue to the company and the investors. If the supervisor fails to act, Thi decides that she will look for a job with another company, while informing higher authorities within Santa Clara Corporation of the problem (as well as the auditors).

continued ▶

Ethics in Accounting, *continued*

Example

John Dobbs, the chief financial officer of Empire Company, has been very successful in all of his duties with the company. He has risen to the position of chief financial officer, and he is often considered to be a possible future candidate for the position of president of the company. John frequently accompanies the company president and other top managers on business trips. On these trips, John sees the company president spend hundreds and sometimes thousands of dollars on lavish or personal expenses such as very expensive hotels, luxury travel, personal sightseeing, and gifts for his wife and friends. John also knows that the company president records these items as business expenses and that he is reimbursed by company for all the expenditures.

- **Moral Issue:** The president is using his position of authority to defraud the company by submitting false expense reports.
- **Review of Facts:** The company is spending thousands of dollars on expenditures that have nothing to do with its operations and that are personal expenditures of the president. These expenditures can be documented or accurately estimated.
- **Alternatives:** (a) Do nothing. (b) Discuss his concerns with the president emphasizing the implications of the ethical issue. (c) Make an anonymous report to the auditors or the board of directors. (d) Resign.
- **Possible Outcomes:** Doing nothing means that the company will continue to be defrauded. Furthermore, the president is in a position of authority, and other managers may begin to imitate his actions. This could further weaken the company ethics and begin to create a widespread attitude resulting in actions (such as financial statement fraud) that can ultimately lead to dangerous consequences. On the other hand, John knows that his job is at risk if he openly reports this situation. John does not believe that he should resign because of the unethical actions of the president.
- **Decision:** John decides that the least damaging and most ethical action is to anonymously report the situation to the company's auditors and the board of directors. He will then watch to see if the situation improves.

Ethics in Accounting, *continued*

A Continuing Concern

Ethical behavior is *always* an ongoing concern in accounting. Lapses in the ethical behavior of just a few people can damage the good reputations of many people. Unethical behavior of a few can ultimately lead to the destruction of entire companies (for example, Arthur Andersen Company—formerly the largest CPA firm worldwide, and Enron, formerly the large energy company).

One of the most sensitive and controversial areas of ethical behavior is the proper reporting of results in financial statements. We will study financial statements in this volume and in greater depth in Volume 2.

Check Your Understanding

Write the completed sentences on a separate piece of paper.

Accounting is a three-stage process that provides financial information to decision makers who need this information. The first stage in the process is to · to identify transactions that cause changes in the accounting equation. In this stage, any change in the equation must be identified three ways. These three ways are · · · · · · · · · ·, · · · · · · · · · ·, and · · · · · · · · · · ("Mr. Clavati").

The second stage in the process requires you to ·. This means to first · provided that the data is · · · · · · · · · · and relevant. The second procedure in this stage requires you to ·, which is done by applying various bookkeeping methods.

The final stage in the process is to ·, which is usually done by preparing financial reports.

All of the stages above are essentially meaningless if they are manipulated or become unreliable. Therefore, the highest · · · · · · · · · attitude is required of accountants.

Answers

Accounting is a three-stage process that provides financial information to decision makers who need this information. The first stage in the process is to <u>analyze</u> <u>events</u> to identify transactions that cause changes in the accounting equation. In this stage, any change in the equation must be identified three ways. These three ways are <u>classification</u>, <u>valuation</u>, and <u>timing</u> ("Mr. Clavati").

The second stage in the process requires you to <u>process data</u>. This means to first record transactions provided that the data is <u>reliable</u> and relevant. The second procedure in this stage requires you to <u>summarize data</u>, which is done by applying various bookkeeping methods.

The final stage in the process is to <u>communicate information</u>, which is usually done by preparing financial reports.

All of the stages above are essentially meaningless if they are manipulated or become unreliable. Therefore, the highest <u>ethical</u> attitude is required of accountants.

QUICK REVIEW

- Accounting is a three-stage process consisting of event analysis (classification, valuation, and timing), processing data, and communicating information.

- The accounting process is implemented by accountants, people who are academically and professionally trained in theory and procedure. Accountants with special certification are CPAs and CMAs.

- High ethical standards are essential to accounting. These standards include integrity, objectivity, independence, and due care.

VOCABULARY

Accounting: a system of activities that has the objective of providing financial information that is useful for decision-making (page 218)

Bookkeeping: another name for the processing functions in the accounting process (page 221)

Measurement: another name for the valuation step in the accounting process (page 220)

Recognition: recording a transaction (page 221)

Stakeholders: people and organizations that use accounting information (page 223)

"It's up to you now Miller. The only thing that can save us is an accounting breakthrough."

PRACTICE   **Learning Goal 10**

Solutions are in the disk at the back of the book and at: www.worthyjames.com

Learning Goal 10 explains the accounting process. Use these questions to practice what you have just read. Select the best answer to each question.

Multiple Choice
Select the best answer.

1. Stage 3 of the accounting process, "communicate information" includes
   a. preparing and interpreting financial reports.
   b. recording transactions.
   c. analyzing the event.
   d. all of the above.

2. The people and organizations that use accounting information are often called
   a. internal users.
   b. external users.
   c. creditors.
   d. stakeholders.

3. For stage 1, "analyze the event," we have previously learned to analyze an event in three steps by asking: "Are assets affected? Are liabilities affected? Is owner's equity affected?" Now we refine our event analysis by analyzing these three essential elements of each step:
   a. classification, valuation, application
   b. classification, valuation, timing
   c. interpretation, valuation, summarization
   d. confirmation, recordation, recognition

4. The question "What items in the accounting equation are affected?" refers to analyzing which element of an event?
   a. classification
   b. valuation
   c. recognition
   d. interpretation

5. The question "What is the dollar amount of change in the items affected?" refers to analyzing which element of an event?
   a. classification
   b. valuation
   c. recognition
   d. interpretation

6. The question "When did the event happen?" refers to analyzing which element of an event?
   a. classification
   b. valuation
   c. timing
   d. interpretation

7. Event analysis is extremely important to the accounting process because
   a. incorrect event analysis will ultimately result in incorrect and misleading financial reports.
   b. the decision making based on the financial reports could be flawed, useless, or potentially damaging.
   c. both a and b.
   d. none of the above.

8. Stage 2 of the accounting process, "process data," includes
   a. recording transactions.
   b. summarizing the data.
   c. preparing financial statements.
   d. both a and b.

9. The most fundamental requirement for ethical behavior is
   a. attitude.
   b. independence.
   c. technical skills.
   d. consistency.

10. Basic honesty, never violating the trust of others, is which AICPA ethical standard?
    a. due care
    b. integrity
    c. independence
    d. objectivity

11. Being impartial and fair to all parties is which AICPA ethical standard?
    a. due care
    b. integrity
    c. independence
    d. objectivity

12. The first step in the ethical decision-making guideline is to
    a. review all the facts, including who is potentially involved.
    b. review possible outcomes that will do the most good, the least harm, and treat all parties fairly and impartially.
    c. recognize the moral issue of a potentially wrongful act.
    d. make a decision.

Reinforcement Problems

LG 10-1. **Practice event analysis.** Use a blank sheet of paper to complete the table. For each event on the following table, analyze the event to determine if it is a recordable transaction. If the event is a recordable transaction, enter the date that the transaction should be recognized in the T (timing) column. Write the name of the items affected in the C (classification) columns and the values to record in the V (valuation) columns. Also put a "+" in the V column if assets, liabilities, or owner's equity are increased and a "( )" around any value that is a decrease. Use the first item as an example.

PRACTICE   Learning Goal 10, continued

Solutions are in the disk at the back of the book and at: www.worthyjames.com

LG 10-1, *continued*

Event	T	Assets Affected?		Liabilities Affected?		Owner's Equity Affected?	
		C	V	C	V	C	V
a. On April 30, a count of supplies shows $400 of supplies used up.	April 30	Supplies	(400)			Supplies Expense	(400)
b. The owner invested $5,000 in his business on May 7.	(Reminder: Use a separate sheet of paper to complete the table.)						
c. $500 was collected from accounts receivable on October 12.							
d. On June 1, received $2,700 from a tenant for 3 months office rent beginning on June 1.							
e. On December 31, purchased $1,900 of supplies and will pay later.							
f. Provided $750 services to customer on December 31. Customer will pay later.							
g. On August 3, purchased $9,500 of equipment by paying $3,000 cash and signing a 2-month note payable.							
h. On January 5, received $300 bill from the telephone company for *telephone services up to December 31.*							
i. The owner wrote a $2,500 check to himself from the business checking account on November 23.							
j. It is now June 30, the end of the first month after item d above.							
k. On October 3, borrowed $6,500 on a new long-term note and used the money to pay off the note in item g.							

PRACTICE   Learning Goal 10, continued

Solutions are in the disk at the back of the book and at: www.worthyjames.com

LG 10-2. **Practice classification, valuation, and timing.** The table below contains a series of independent events. On a separate piece of paper, identify the classification, valuation, and timing for each event to determine if the event is a transaction and should therefore be recorded. Record revenues and expenses as increases and decreases to owner's equity. For classification of items, you can use ↑ for increase and ↓ for decrease. Identify any events that are not recordable transactions. Use the first item as an example.

Event	Classification	Valuation	Timing
a. On March 11, the owner invested $10,000 cash and $2,000 of supplies in her business.	Cash ↑ Supplies ↑ Owner's Equity ↑	$10,000 $ 2,000 $12,000	March 11
b. On December 31, a business counts the supplies inventory and determines that the amount of supplies have decreased by $900 during the last quarter. Financial statements are quarterly.	(Reminder: Use a separate sheet of paper to complete the table.)		
c. On September 4, a business performs $3,000 of services and sends the bill to the customer. No cash is received.			
d. On November 12, a business pays $5,000 cash to buy some computer equipment. The invoice is not received until November 23.			
e. On May 3, a commercial trade school receives a donation of 20 computers. Although the school can use the computers, it would be difficult to sell them because they are obsolete.			
f. On January 23, the local bank calls and offers to loan our business $25,000 no later than 7 days from today.			
g. A computer that had cost $1,500 suddenly stops functioning on June 23. It is not worth repairing.			
h. On October 27, $50,000 of merchandise inventory is destroyed by a fire.			
i. On November 23, a business hires a new employee at a salary of $80,000 per year.			
j. On July 16, the owner of business withdraws $5,000 cash from the business.			
k. On August 9, our business used a consulting service and incurred $2,000 of consulting expense. A bill arrived, but we will pay it later.			

PRACTICE   Learning Goal 10, continued

LG 10-3. We used the name "Mr. Clavati" as a memory tool to help remember something very important. What are we making sure that we remember?

INTERNET EXERCISES

Ethics—analyze cases. Go to the St. Louis University Emerson Center for Business Ethics page at http://ecbe.slu.edu/index.html. Select the Publications link and choose two cases that interest you. (Use bookmark/favorites to save the locations in an "Accounting References" folder.) For each case:

a. Use the ethics discussion and guidelines in this learning goal. Write down the case name, and analyze each case from an ethical perspective.
b. Make a decision or take a position. Write a paragraph to explain the facts and specify the reasons for your decision.

PRACTICE   **Learning Goal 10, continued**

Your Questions?

It is *very* important to be aware of what you need to understand better. What do you need to understand better about this learning goal? On a separate piece of paper, write the questions that you want to discuss with your classmates, instructor, or supervisor. Try to be very specific about what is bothering you, such as explanations that you do not fully understand.

| LEARNING GOAL 11 | # Begin to Record |

Overview

Introduction

In previous learning goals, you looked at the individual items in each transaction to analyze their effects on the condition of a business. For example, if you saw cash decrease and accounts payable decrease, you would conclude that total assets decreased and total liabilities decreased because a debt was paid. This classification and valuation analysis is important, and you will continue to practice it.

But analysis is of little use unless a permanent record is kept of the transactions. So now we begin to study the method for keeping a permanent record of transactions after we have analyzed them.

Concepts: Begin to Record

Get a Job!

Because you have progressed this far, I have decided that it is time for you to get a job. I want you to meet a friend of mine. His name is Jack "Flash" Davis, a professional guitar player who performs in his own band called "Flash." To supplement his performance income, Jack is opening a small guitar school in June, where he will give guitar lessons at all levels from beginner to master class. He needs accounting help, and I have recommended you to be the accountant for his guitar school.

To help you get started, I suggest that you keep a permanent record of all the increases and decreases for each item in the accounting equation. This can be done by setting up one column for each separate asset, liability, and owner's equity item. The increases and decreases are then shown in each column with a "+" or a "−." Using some imaginary transactions, such an approach would look like the table on page 236.

continued ▶

Concepts: Begin to Record, *continued*

	Assets			= Liabilities + Owner's Equity	
Transaction	Cash	Accounts Receivable	Supplies	Accounts Payable	Jack Davis, Capital
Owner's investment of cash	(+) $10,000				(+) $10,000
Purchase supplies	(−) 500		(+) 500		
Balance	9,500		500		10,000
Earned revenue "on account"		(+) 750			(+) 750
Balance	9,500	750	500		10,750
Collect receivable	(+) 750	(−) 750			
Balance	10,250	–0–	500		10,750
Withdraw cash	(−) 1,000				(−) 1,000
Balance	9,250		500		9,750
Use up supplies			(−) 100		(−) 100
Balance	9,250		400		9,650

. . . and so on, with each new transaction being added to or subtracted from the applicable columns, such that the equation always remains in balance.

Separate Columns for Increases and Decreases

One Column for Increase and One Column for Decrease

Another good way to record the changes in each of the equation items is to have separate increase columns and decrease columns for each item. The advantage of this method is that all the increases and decreases are easier to locate. What's more, this is the method that is used in practice and that you will later learn when studying accounts. Using the same transactions, the recording would look like the table on page 237.

Separate Columns for Increases and Decreases, *continued*

	Assets						=	Liabilities		+	Owner's Equity	
	Cash		Accounts Receivable		Supplies		Accounts Payable			Jack Davis, Capital		
Transaction	Increase	Decrease	Increase	Decrease	Increase	Decrease	Decrease	Increase		Decrease	Increase
Owner's investment of cash	$10,000										$10,000
Purchase supplies		500			500						
Balance	9,500				500						10,000
Earned revenue "on account"			750								750
Balance	9,500		750		500						10,750
Collect receivable	750			750							
Balance	10,250		–0–		500						10,750
Withdraw cash		1,000								1,000	
Balance	9,250				500						9,750
Use up supplies						100				100	
Balance	9,250				400						9,650

Same Balances as Before

We get exactly the same balances as before, except that now all the increases and decreases are easier to locate. We will use the two-column approach here so that you can get used to it. In this way, the increases and decreases for each item are split out into separate columns.

Use Accounting Customs

The custom in accounting is that "increase" columns for items on the left side of the equation (assets) are always placed to the left of each item name, and that "increase" columns for items on the right side of the equation are always placed to the right of each item name.

It is also the custom to show balances on the increase side because balances are positive numbers, just like increases. We will use these customary patterns. This will become clear as you follow the events.

Start Your Job and Enjoy . . .

Relax, take your time, and watch what happens to Jack.

TIP

To analyze, it might help you to visualize each transaction as explained in Section II. You can draw a picture or use the accounting equation.

continued ▶

Separate Columns for Increases and Decreases, *continued*

Here are the transactions for Jack's school for June, the first month of business:

A. Owner investment. Jack deposits $12,000 cash from personal funds into a business checking account.

Assets	=
$12,000	

Cash

Increase	Decrease	
$12,000		

B. Equipment purchased for cash. The business purchases some sound amplifiers and digital electronic equipment for $5,500 cash. (Notice that total assets don't change.)

Assets	=
$12,000	

	Cash				Equipment	
	Increase	Decrease			Increase	Decrease
A	$12,000					
B		$5,500			$5,500	
Balance	$6,500				$5,500	

C. Purchase supplies on credit. The business purchases $200 of office supplies "on account." Notice that total assets increase by $200, but so do creditors' claims (Accounts Payable).

Assets	=
$12,200	

	Cash			Supplies			Equipment	
	Increase	Decrease		Increase	Decrease		Increase	Decrease
A	$12,000							
B		$5,500					$5,500	
C				$200				
Balance	$6,500			$200			$5,500	

Notice that the custom is to always place balances on the "increase" side for each item because an increase means a positive number. Because the natural balance of any item is always a positive number, it makes sense to put a balance on the increase—the positive—side. For example, after two transactions, Cash has a balance of $6,500. Of course, this $6,500 balance is a positive number, so we place it on the positive side.

Separate Columns for Increases and Decreases, *continued*

Liabilities + Owner's Equity

$12,000

	Jack Davis, Capital		Operational Change in Owner's Equity	
	Decrease	Increase	Expense	Revenue
		$12,000		

Liabilities + Owner's Equity

$12,000

	Jack Davis, Capital		Operational Change in Owner's Equity	
	Decrease	Increase	Expense	Revenue
A		$12,000		
B				
Balance		$12,000		

Liabilities + Owner's Equity

$12,200

	Accounts Payable			Jack Davis, Capital		Operational Change in Owner's Equity	
	Decrease	Increase		Decrease	Increase	Expense	Revenue
A					$12,000		
B							
C		$200					
		$200			$12,000		

continued ▶

Separate Columns for Increases and Decreases, *continued*

D. **Revenue earned.** Jack teaches a beginners' class and receives $350 in cash from his students. (Notice that the revenue is an operational increase in owner's equity.)

	Assets	=
	$12,550	

	Cash			Supplies			Equipment	
	Increase	**Decrease**		**Increase**	**Decrease**		**Increase**	**Decrease**
A	$12,000							
B		$5,500					$5,500	
C				$200				
D	$350							
Balance	$6,850			$200			$5,500	

E. **Revenue earned.** Jack teaches a blues weekend master class at the university and receives $2,000 on account, plus $500 in cash. (Notice that three items are affected with this transaction.)

	Assets	=
	$15,050	

	Cash		Accounts Receivable		Supplies		Equipment	
	Increase	**Decrease**	**Increase**	**Decrease**	**Increase**	**Decrease**	**Increase**	**Decrease**
A	$12,000							
B		$5,500					$5,500	
C					$200			
D	$350							
E	$500		$2,000					
Balance	$7,350		$2,000		$200		$5,500	

You are in Jack's office and the door suddenly opens. Jack walks in with an angry look on his face. "Can you explain this to me?" he asks, his face red and his eyebrows menacingly tight. "I have only been in this business a few weeks and already I have lost almost $5,000!" You ask him how he found that out. "I invested $12,000 of my hard-earned money, and now the bank statement shows that I only have $7,350 left. That's how I know! That's almost a $5,000 loss in just a few weeks! You're the accountant. How did I have this loss and what happened to my money?" What do you think you should say to Jack?

Separate Columns for Increases and Decreases, *continued*

Liabilities + Owner's Equity

$12,550

	Accounts Payable			Jack Davis, Capital			Operational Change in Owner's Equity	
	Decrease	Increase		Decrease	Increase		Expense	Revenue
A					$12,000			
B								
C		$200						
D					$350			$350
		$200			$12,350			

Liabilities + Owner's Equity

$15,050

	Accounts Payable			Jack Davis, Capital			Operational Change in Owner's Equity	
	Decrease	Increase		Decrease	Increase		Expense	Revenue
A					$12,000			
B								
C		$200						
D					$350			$350
E					$2,500			$2,500
		$200			$14,850			

continued ▶

Separate Columns for Increases and Decreases, *continued*

First, you're silent for a moment, reflecting on Jack's questions. Then you open the lower desk drawer and pull out the manila folder that contains the accounting papers you have been using to record the changes in Jack's business. You see that Jack is right about the cash; your records do show a balance of $7,350.

The first thing that you say is, "OK, I've got all the data right here for you. Let's look at the cash." You show Jack that there have been four cash transactions: (Item A) a $12,000 increase from his investment; (Item B) a $5,500 decrease spent on equipment; (Item D) a $350 increase from the revenue for the beginner's class that he taught; and (Item E) a $500 increase from the master blues class revenue.

Jack says, "Well, OK, at least I can see what has happened to the cash, but how could I have had a loss so quickly?"

"Jack," you say, "I have some good news for you. You do not have a loss. You actually have net income—you know, a profit."

"How's that?"

You say, "How much did you invest?"

He answers, "$12,000."

"Jack, look at these records. They show that you have $15,050 in assets: $7,350 in cash, $2,000 in an accounts receivable, $200 in supplies, and $5,500 in equipment. If you subtract the $200 you owe on the account payable, that leaves you with $14,850 in owner's equity—you know, assets that you could claim. That's $2,850 more than you invested!"

Jack is quiet for a little while and then you hear him say, "Ah ... aaaaah, I think I see! When I have a profit or loss, that doesn't necessarily mean that it will all be just in cash. I have to count everything!"

You smile politely.

Separate Columns for Increases and Decreases, *continued*

Liabilities + Owner's Equity

$12,900

	Accounts Payable			Jack Davis, Capital				Operational Change in Owner's Equity	
	Decrease	Increase		Decrease	Increase			Expense	Revenue
A					$12,000				
B									
C		$200							
D					$350				$350
E					$2,500				$2,500
F		$170		$170				$170	
G	$200								
H				$150				$150	
I				$800				$800	
J									
K				$1,000				*	
		$170			$12,730				

* Withdrawals are not expenses, so withdrawals are not "operational" changes.

continued ▶

Separate Columns for Increases and Decreases, *continued*

> L. **Unearned revenue.** A student's parent pays an advance to the school in the amount of $250 cash for six weeks of lessons. (Receiving a customer advance payment creates a liability called "unearned revenue." No service has been provided yet, so there is an obligation to return the money until the revenue is actually earned.)

Assets   =

$13,150

	Cash		Accounts Receivable		Supplies		Equipment	
	Increase	Decrease	Increase	Decrease	Increase	Decrease	Increase	Decrease
A	$12,000							
B		$5,500					$5,500	
C					$200			
D	$350							
E	$500		$2,000					
F								
G		$200						
H						$150		
I		$800						
J	$750			$750				
K		$1,000						
L	$250							
Balance	$6,350		$1,250		$50		$5,500	

The day after you meet Jack in the parking lot with his $15,000 check, he walks into your office and says, "You know, now that things are going well, I have a loan application here that I'm working on to see if we can get some additional funds to expand our teaching facilities. The bank wants to see the financial statements of the business, and I need to show the best situation possible on the loan application. I want to make sure that we get that loan. I have an idea that I want you to use on the financial statements.

"When we get paid for lessons in advance, you have been showing the money we receive as a liability called 'unearned revenue.' This does not show up as revenue until later, when the lesson is given. I don't like this! After all, sooner or later we are going to give the lessons and earn the revenue anyway.

"I want you to show these receipts as revenue as soon as we get the money. I do not want you to show it as a liability. We will have a big advance coming in soon and this is a really good way to show a big increase in our profits right away."

Separate Columns for Increases and Decreases, *continued*

He looks you straight in the eye and says, "You know, this bank loan is going to be very important to both of us … to both of our jobs … do you understand what I mean?"

How do you respond to Jack? Is his proposal ethical?

Liabilities + Owner's Equity

$13,150

	Accounts Payable		Unearned Revenue		Jack Davis, Capital		Operational Change in Owner's Equity	
	Decrease	Increase	Decrease	Increase	Decrease	Increase	Expense	Revenue
A						$12,000		
B								
C		$200						
D						$350		$350
E						$2,500		$2,500
F		$170			$170		$170	
G	$200							
H						$150	$150	
I						$800	$800	
J								
K					$1,000			
L				$250				
		$170		$250		$12,730		

Jack is assuming that accounting rules can be changed to satisfy his own purposes and that he can force you to do what he wants. He is asking you to change an accounting method that you know is correct to one that is incorrect—for the sole purpose of misleading the bank by making the business look more profitable.

Only one safe and ethical course of action is open to you. First, you need to explain to Jack that you are obligated to follow a set of accounting principles. One of those principles requires that revenue can only be shown after it is fully earned and not before. The purpose of this is to provide reliable financial statements that do not make the business seem more profitable than it really is. You should also tell Jack that he will be much better off in the long run if the banker learns that the business financial statements are always accurate and that Jack is an ethical and trusted customer of the bank.

continued ▶

Separate Columns for Increases and Decreases, *continued*

Right now, Jack is not acting in an ethical way either to the bank or to you. By insisting that you do as he wishes, Jack puts you in a no-win situation because he is implying that if you don't cooperate, he will fire you. On the other hand, if you do cooperate, you put your own reputation and career at risk.

If Jack completely refuses to listen to you, you have no alternative but to respectfully and politely quit. As an accountant, your ethical conduct must set a standard for others. The financial statements you prepare must be reliable because so many people depend upon them. However difficult leaving may seem at the time, it is far better than developing a relationship in which Jack knows that he can always manipulate you. In a situation like this, your career and life will inevitably suffer as his demands become greater and greater every month.

This situation should be viewed as one of the occasional causes of job turnover in a field in which ethical requirements are unusually high.

> M. **Unearned revenue is earned.** Jack gives a $50 lesson to the student whose parents previously advanced the $250 for lessons. (Notice that when the revenue is earned, the liability is reduced. By performing $50 worth of services, Jack removed $50 of the liability and increased his own claim on the assets by $50.)

Assets   =

$13,150

	Cash Increase	Cash Decrease	Accounts Receivable Increase	Accounts Receivable Decrease	Supplies Increase	Supplies Decrease	Equipment Increase	Equipment Decrease
A	$12,000							
B		$5,500					$5,500	
C					$200			
D	$350							
E	$500		$2,000					
F								
G		$200						
H						$150		
I		$800						
J	$750			$750				
K		$1,000						
L	$250							
M								
Balance	$6,350		$1,250		$50		$5,500	

Separate Columns for Increases and Decreases, *continued*

Summary

What the Processing Has Accomplished So Far

- You have recorded all transactions in an organized way.
- You now have a permanent record of:
  - the individual transactions.
  - the current balance of each item in the accounting equation.

Notice that the "operational change in owner's equity" includes only revenues and expenses. The investment of $12,000 and the withdrawal of $1,000 did affect owner's equity because they were not part of the business operations. By separately identifying the operational changes, we can now see that the business operations increased the owner's equity, and therefore the owner's wealth, by $2,900 – $1,120 = $1,780. This means that the business was profitable—it has a "net income" of $1,780.

Liabilities + Owner's Equity

$13,150

	Accounts Payable		Unearned Revenue		Jack Davis, Capital		Operational Change in Owner's Equity	
	Decrease	Increase	Decrease	Increase	Decrease	Increase	Expense	Revenue
A						$12,000		
B								
C		$200						
D						$350		$350
E						$2,500		$2,500
F		$170			$170		$170	
G	$200							
H					$150		$150	
I					$800		$800	
J								
K					$1,000			
L				$250				
M			$50			$50		$50
		$170		$200		$12,780	$1,120	$2,900

Crossing the Line

How People Get Hurt

As we discussed in Learning Goal 10, high ethical standards in accounting are essential to ensure that financial statements are fair, reliable, and protect the many people who rely on them.

It is also true that a weakness in ethical judgment can have life-damaging consequences even for those normally good people who, as accounting employees, do not wish to harm anyone. This often occurs when an employee agrees to the demands of an unethical boss or manager or at a time when financial pressures become intense. The true story that follows describes what happened to just such an accountant.

Crossing the Line

By Susan Pulliam
The Wall Street Journal

Awaiting his court appearance to be charged with securities fraud, David Myers sat in a jail cell and counted the cinder blocks in the cell again and again to distract himself. In his pocket was a plastic red dog named Clifford, given to him by his young son. "He'll take care of you," the boy had said, according to his mother.

For Mr. Myers, the former controller of WorldCom Inc., the past four years have been a life-altering journey. It began when the prosperous businessman and father put aside his misgivings and agreed to go along with false accounting entries that eventually became part of an $11 billion fraud.

The scheme Mr. Myers participated in set off a chain of events that had a devastating impact on his company, his colleagues, and his family. The collapse of the telecommunications giant resulted in the loss of more than 17,000 jobs and billions of dollars in pensions and investments.

Hoping to win a lighter sentence, Mr. Myers, 47 years old, pleaded guilty and completely cooperated in the government's investigation. He helped prosecutors identify false numbers in WorldCom's financial filings from 2000 to 2002. That evidence, and his court testimony, helped convict WorldCom Chief Executive Officer Bernard Ebbers for his role in one of the largest financial frauds in corporate history.

As the U.S. government rolls through a historic wave of prosecutions of business fraud, Mr. Myers is one of the executives watching a successful life come unglued. He and his family are now preparing for his sentencing, set for June. Federal guidelines suggest he could serve more than 10 years in prison, though he is expected to receive a shorter sentence because of his cooperation.

"We don't know what is going to happen," says his wife, Lynn, 39. "I don't know if he's going to prison or for how long. I just want him home."

Raised in Jackson, Mississippi, Mr. Myers played basketball and was an honor student in high school. In 1993, Mr. Myers married his second wife, Lynn, an interior designer and onetime cheerleader, who is also a Jackson native. The couple settled into a suburban life working in the yard and having dinners with friends. They had a son, Jack, now 5. Mr. Myers joined WorldCom in 1995 as treasurer.

In January 2001, Mr. Myers and Buford Yates, an accountant who worked for him, met in the office of WorldCom's chief financial officer Scott Sullivan. Knowing that WorldCom would not meet (stock) analyst expectations for the coming quarter, the three agreed, at Mr. Sullivan's request, to reclassify some of the company's biggest expenses, according to Mr. Myers's testimony. This moved expenses off WorldCom's income statement, increasing the company's reported income.

"I didn't think that was the right thing to do, but I had been asked by Scott to do it and I was asking him [Mr. Yates] to do it," Mr. Myers testified.

In an illustration of how huge ethical lapses often begin with small steps, he justified his actions to himself, thinking WorldCom's business would soon improve, people close to the case say. But rather than being a temporary measure, the improper accounting continued. Mr. Myers helped direct false entries again and again. People close to Mr. Myers say he believed Mr. Sullivan's explanations that eventually the company's problems would be straightened out.

In the summer of 2001, Mr. Myers realized there was no end in sight to the company's woes. He became depressed. He considered quitting, but realized the scandal would follow him because of what he'd already done. On weekends, he withdrew, begging off on evenings out with friends, blaming the stress of work. He grew increasingly irritable and distant.

Mrs. Myers sought the advice of Buddy Stallings, a priest from their Episcopal church. "She was worried about their life," says Father Stallings. "She felt things were spiraling out of control." He told her that she and Mr. Myers shouldn't be afraid to make changes in their life.

One warm evening in 2001, Mrs. Myers stood by the lake outside their house. When Mr. Myers joined her, she began crying. "You're somewhere else," she recalls telling him. "We have a baby. You work all the time. Why not quit?" Mr. Myers, whose annual salary was about $240,000 before options, told her he wanted to earn enough to start his own business and that he didn't want to quit, out of loyalty to Mr. Sullivan, the chief financial officer.

But he didn't confide that he was also worried about the accounting at WorldCom. Mr. Myers's thoughts turned to suicide, according to investigators. He began entertaining the idea of staging his own fatal car accident. Over a period of weeks, Mr. Myers began driving his BMW faster and faster through a turn on a highway underpass between WorldCom's Clinton, Mississippi, headquarters and his home, according to a person close to the situation. Trying to determine the speed at which his car would completely lose control, Mr. Myers pushed the speedometer higher each time, reaching 115 miles an hour one night. Eventually Mr. Myers abandoned the idea.

Mrs. Myers says she urged her husband to see a doctor. He did, and began taking an antidepressant. His depression lifted. But he still didn't share the root of his troubles, Mrs. Myers says. "I knew something was wrong but I couldn't pull out of him what it was."

On a Sunday in June 2002, the phone rang at the Myers' house. Mr. Myers listened to a WorldCom employee who worked for Cynthia Cooper, head of internal audits. She was looking into accounting entries that she found suspicious. The employee said Ms. Cooper had focused on certain large expense items—ones that Mr. Myers knew would lead to his office.

Mr. Myers sat on the stairs at the back of his house, watching his wife and son play in the yard. He considered the enormity of the problem. He vowed to come clean if Ms. Cooper confronted him.

On June 17, 2002, Ms. Cooper entered Mr. Myers's office. She peppered him with questions, according to regulatory filings. Did he know about the entries? Was there any support for them? Were other companies doing the same thing?

Mr. Myers confessed. He calmly explained that he knew about the entries but there was no support for them. An auditor accompanying Ms. Cooper asked what he had planned to tell the Securities and Exchange Commission if officials asked about the bookkeeping. He said he hoped they wouldn't ask.

As the meeting broke up, Mr. Myers felt better than he had for months, as though a cloud over him had lifted, Mrs. Myers says he told her later. Inside WorldCom, panic erupted, as the company grappled with the explosive news that billions in profits had been manufactured through improper accounting. But initially, Mr. Myers was told by one WorldCom director that his job would probably be safe, people close to the situation say.

That changed a few days later, when Mr. Myers and Mr. Sullivan flew to Washington on the company plane for a meeting with the board's audit committee. The two men, seated at opposite ends of the plane, barely spoke. At one point, Mr. Sullivan offered Mr. Myers a chocolate-covered doughnut, telling him it was the only thing he could force himself to eat since the news broke. Mr. Myers declined.

It finally dawned on Mr. Myers that he was in trouble. He and Mr. Sullivan were excluded from a hastily called, closed-door meeting of WorldCom's management and board. When Mr. Myers attempted to talk to a World-Com lawyer, he was told that he should hire his own lawyer and stop confiding in the WorldCom legal staff, people close to Mr. Myers say. On his way out that day, another WorldCom lawyer wished him the best. Mr. Myers knew he was going to lose his job.

Later that evening, Mr. Myers, staying at an Embassy Suites hotel in Washington, got a call from a lawyer appointed for him by WorldCom, telling him no one would believe that Mr. Sullivan had pulled off the fraud alone. The board was offering him the chance to resign.

Mr. Myers, stricken, called his wife. He told her about his role in the bogus accounting entries. The usually restrained Mr. Myers cried as he asked what their friends and neighbors would say about him. Mrs. Myers, also crying, told him he was a good man and nothing would change that, she recalls. Mr. Myers later told her that he clung to those words in the weeks that followed.

The next morning, he flew home and faxed in his letter of resignation.

In the days that followed, Mr. and Mrs. Myers drew the blinds, pulled the car in the garage and went into hiding, people close to them say. Because he had acted on orders, Mr. Myers still didn't think he would face personal liability for the fraud, Mrs. Myers says. When two agents with the Federal Bureau of Investigation showed up at their door and flashed their badges, Mrs. Myers let them in.

"I was shocked, but I thought they were there to talk about Bernie and Scott," she says. "I didn't think we were in trouble." Mr. Myers led the agents to the sun porch. Mrs. Myers ran upstairs to call her father, a lawyer, who instructed her to tell Mr. Myers not to answer any questions without an attorney. As Mrs. Myers watched the agents drive away, she recalls thinking, "Oh my God, this is huge."

During a meeting with Richard Janis, the lawyer her husband later hired, Mrs. Myers recalls sobbing as he told them political pressure was high to make an example of WorldCom employees involved in the fraud. This was the first time she realized her husband might go to prison. "It was a helpless feeling," she says, realizing her husband could miss a big part of their son's childhood.

Mr. and Mrs. Myers moved to her parents' house in another part of Jackson to escape the media throng that had begun to gather at their own home. Once, when they saw a police car cruising the neighborhood, they froze, thinking the police might be looking for them, Mrs. Myers says. Mr. Myers began looking around when he took out the trash to see if anyone was watching him, Mrs. Myers says he told her.

On July 30, 2002, Mr. and Mrs. Myers prepared to go to New York, where he would be charged with securities fraud. Mrs. Myers cried as she kissed their son goodbye. "He didn't know why I was sad," she says. Jack, clutching a small plastic "Clifford" dog, handed the toy to his father, Mrs. Myers recalls. "That was his favorite toy and he gave it to David."

In New York, the couple met with Father Stallings, their former priest, who had relocated to a church on Staten Island. During a walk, Mr. Myers said he had been told he would have to turn over his shoelaces, belt, and tie when he turned himself in at the courthouse the next day. Father Stallings gave Mr. Myers a pair of loafers so he wouldn't have to remove any laces.

Afterward, he took the couple to the church and gave them communion. He thinks that gave Mr. Myers solace. "I believe it made a difference," he says.

The next day, Mr. Myers was fingerprinted in FBI offices in Manhattan and had his mug shot taken. He was led outside and handcuffed, in what is known as a "perp walk." Wearing a blue suit and a red tie, Mr. Myers appeared emotionless as he walked to a car waiting to take him to the federal courthouse. He wasn't allowed in the car for a few minutes, as an FBI agent sat inside with the door locked. Cameras flashed. The agent unlocked the door and Mr. Myers was let in.

Before returning home, the Myers visited the World Trade Center site and Mr. Myers placed the plastic toy dog on an informal memorial there.

On September 25, 2002, Mr. Myers was the first of four WorldCom managers to plead guilty to securities fraud. Standing under an umbrella, his lawyer said, "Myers was a reluctant participant in the events that have led us here. . . . He recognizes that as a corporate officer, those facts do not relieve him of his own responsibility in this matter."

The Myers returned to Jackson and tried to pick up their lives. Mr. Myers began volunteering as a bookkeeper at their church and worked on an archaeology dig nearby. Once, while on a treadmill at his gym, he looked up and saw his own image in handcuffs on television. He put his head down and moved faster, Mrs. Myers says he told her. Driving around Jackson, he often thought he was recognized at stoplights, she says.

With the support of friends, the Myers slowly began to emerge from their isolation. They received more than 200 letters from people who sympathized with their situation, Mrs. Myers says.

A turning point for Mr. Myers came in June 2003, when he borrowed a bicycle and signed up to help chaperone a 500-mile bike ride with a group of youngsters, including some from troubled homes. Mr. Myers struggled to make the long rides each day. Often alone, he contemplated the future and his past actions, Mrs. Myers says. He strained to climb one particularly steep hill—and the exhilaration of riding down the other side made him believe good times still lay ahead, she says.

He returned home more optimistic. He bought a necklace with a cross on it at the gift shop of a Jackson church and began wearing it daily. Their priest reminded him everyone makes mistakes but it's how a person deals with them that matters, Mrs. Myers says.

Anticipating a prison sentence, Mr. Myers began preparing. The family moved to a smaller house that shared a backyard with the couple's best friends. He started a real-estate company with Mr. Yates, the accountant who worked for him and also pleaded guilty to securities fraud. They hoped the company, which buys residential real estate, would produce profits to help tide their wives over if Mr. Myers and Mr. Yates were sent to prison.

Mr. Myers's work as a witness for the government increased. In December 2003, he spent most of a weekend in a New York hotel room, poring over WorldCom documents. Every five hours, he would take a break, walking across the street to grab some pizza and a soda. That Sunday, he handed prosecutors a computer disk detailing every false number he recognized in WorldCom's financial statements from 2000 to 2002.

Around that time, prosecutors were working to win a plea agreement from Mr. Sullivan, the former chief financial officer. Ultimately, they hoped to get Mr. Sullivan to testify against Mr. Ebbers, the former chief executive.

On March 2, 2004, Mr. Sullivan pleaded guilty to three counts of securities fraud—and agreed to testify against Mr. Ebbers. In testimony, Mr. Sullivan said that one of the reasons he decided to plead guilty was Mr. Myers's statements to investigators about him. The same day, Mr. Ebbers was indicted on fraud charges.

In January, Mr. Myers stood in the witness room at the courthouse in Manhattan, waiting to testify against Mr. Ebbers. Looking out the window at St. Andrew's church, he noticed an ornate cross on the rear peak of the roof, similar to the one he wears around his neck. As his testimony proceeded over the next several days, he often looked out at the cross at St. Andrew's, while holding the one around his neck, Mrs. Myers says.

On February 3, the day after Mr. Myers completed his testimony, the couple returned to Jackson. Their son was sleeping, and Mrs. Myers laid down beside him. He woke up and asked where his father was. He raced to the bedroom and jumped into bed with Mr. Myers, crying "my daddy," Mrs. Myers recalls.

Mrs. Myers says she hasn't told Jack his father may have to spend time in prison. "He doesn't understand what's going on," she says. "He loves his daddy. What do you say when daddy doesn't come home?"

PRACTICE   Learning Goal 11

Learning Goal 11 is about beginning to record transactions. Use these questions and problems to practice what you have learned.

Reinforcement Problems

LG 11-1. Record transactions.

a. On a separate piece of paper, use the column recording format from Learning Goal 11, record the following transactions, and total the columns. Identify revenues and expenses and withdrawals next to the column for owner's equity. (You can also make copies of the transaction recording paper template in the disk at the back of the book.)

b. Calculate the net income or loss of the business.

(1) Edgar Mendoza invested $15,000 cash to begin his new business, Computer Training Services.

(2) The business paid $1,200 to purchase office equipment.

(3) The business used $210 cash to purchase some supplies.

(4) The business received an advance payment of $3,300 from a corporate customer.

(5) The business paid $1,100 rent expense for the office.

(6) The business provided $800 of training services to a client who paid in cash.

(7) The business received a $750 bill for legal services that was not immediately paid. (Legal service is the resource consumed.)

(8) The business purchased an additional $250 of supplies on account.

(9) The business used $120 of supplies. (Supplies are the resources consumed.)

(10) The business provided $1,500 of training service on account.

(11) Edgar Mendoza withdrew $900 from the business for his personal use.

(12) The business paid the legal bill (7) in full.

(13) The business received a $550 advertising bill that was not immediately paid. (Advertising service is the resource consumed.)

(14) The business provided $1,650 of training service. The client paid $1,000 cash and will pay the balance later.

(15) The client in transaction (10) above paid the account balance in full.

(16) The business provided $2,000 of services to client in (4) above who made the advance payment.

(17) The business collected $250 from a customer on account.

(18) The business paid the advertising bill (13) in full.

LG 11-2. Following is a schedule showing the balances (**Bal**) of the assets and equities of Sugar Eclair's Gym and Aerobics Club at the end of August. Record the September transactions as they happen. Space has been provided to add new assets or equities to the schedule. After you record each transaction, retotal the assets and equities, carry the new balances down, and then enter the totals of the assets and equities at the top of the next section to prove that the equation still balances. You may omit $ signs.

(Note: Make a copy of these pages so you can try this problem more than once. Leave these pages blank. You can also make copies of the transaction recording paper in the disk at the back of the book.)

If any transaction involves an expense or a revenue, keep a separate record of expenses and revenues after you record their effects on owner's equity. Calculate the net income or loss for the period of September.

a. *Example:* Supplies of $100 are purchased for cash.

Assets   **=**

$40,020

	Cash		Accounts Receivable				Gym Supplies		Gym Equipment	
	Increase	Decrease	Increase	Decrease			Increase	Decrease	Increase	Decrease
(Bal)	10,300		4,100				620		25,000	
A		100					100			
(New Bal.)	10,200		4,100				720		25,000	

b. The club collects $2,000 cash from the accounts receivable.

Assets   **=**

$40,020

	Cash		Accounts Receivable				Gym Supplies		Gym Equipment	
	Increase	Decrease	Increase	Decrease			Increase	Decrease	Increase	Decrease
(Bal)	10,200		4,100				720		25,000	
B										
(New Bal.)										

PRACTICE   **Learning Goal 11, continued**   *Solutions are in the disk at the back of the book and at: www.worthyjames.com*

Liabilities + Owner's Equity

$40,020

Accounts Payable						Sugar Eclair, Capital			Exp.		Rev.
Decrease	Increase					Decrease	Increase				
	200						39,820				
	200						39,820				

Liabilities + Owner's Equity

$40,020

Accounts Payable						Sugar Eclair, Capital			Exp.		Rev.
Decrease	Increase					Decrease	Increase				
	200						39,820				

LG 11-2, *continued*

c. The club prepays a nine-month fire insurance policy for $1,500.

	Assets									=
	$_____									

	Cash		Accounts Receivable				Gym Supplies		Gym Equipment	
	Increase	Decrease	Increase	Decrease			Increase	Decrease	Increase	Decrease
(Bal)										
C										
(New Bal.)										

d. The club receives member dues of $5,300 for the current month.

	Assets									=
	$_____									

	Cash		Accounts Receivable				Gym Supplies		Gym Equipment	
	Increase	Decrease	Increase	Decrease			Increase	Decrease	Increase	Decrease
(Bal)										
D										
(New Bal.)										

e. The club sends out bills to members for dues of $2,900 for the current month.

	Assets									=
	$_____									

	Cash		Accounts Receivable				Gym Supplies		Gym Equipment	
	Increase	Decrease	Increase	Decrease			Increase	Decrease	Increase	Decrease
(Bal)										
E										
(New Bal.)										

PRACTICE   Learning Goal 11, continued

Solutions are in the disk at the back of the book and at: www.worthyjames.com

Liabilities + Owner's Equity

$_____

Accounts Payable						Sugar Eclair, Capital			Exp.	Rev.
Decrease	Increase					Decrease	Increase			

Liabilities + Owner's Equity

$_____

Accounts Payable						Sugar Eclair, Capital			Exp.	Rev.
Decrease	Increase					Decrease	Increase			

Liabilities + Owner's Equity

$_____

Accounts Payable						Sugar Eclair, Capital			Exp.	Rev.
Decrease	Increase					Decrease	Increase			

LG 11-2, *continued*

f. The club receives and pays the utilities bill of $550.

Assets										=
$_____										

	Cash		Accounts Receivable				Gym Supplies		Gym Equipment	
	Increase	Decrease	Increase	Decrease			Increase	Decrease	Increase	Decrease
(Bal)										
F										
(New Bal.)										

g. The club receives but does not pay the telephone bill of $185.

Assets										=
$_____										

	Cash		Accounts Receivable				Gym Supplies		Gym Equipment	
	Increase	Decrease	Increase	Decrease			Increase	Decrease	Increase	Decrease
(Bal)										
G										
(New Bal.)										

h. The club pays $200 of the accounts payable.

Assets										=
$_____										

	Cash		Accounts Receivable				Gym Supplies		Gym Equipment	
	Increase	Decrease	Increase	Decrease			Increase	Decrease	Increase	Decrease
(Bal)										
H										
(New Bal.)										

Liabilities + Owner's Equity

$_____

Accounts Payable						Sugar Eclair, Capital				
Decrease	Increase					Decrease	Increase		Exp.	Rev.

Liabilities + Owner's Equity

$_____

Accounts Payable						Sugar Eclair, Capital				
Decrease	Increase					Decrease	Increase		Exp.	Rev.

Liabilities + Owner's Equity

$_____

Accounts Payable						Sugar Eclair, Capital				
Decrease	Increase					Decrease	Increase		Exp.	Rev.

LG 11-2, *continued*

i. The club borrows $50,000 from the 5th National Bank and signs a 15-year note.

	Assets										=

$_____

	Cash		Accounts Receivable				Gym Supplies		Gym Equipment	
	Increase	Decrease	Increase	Decrease			Increase	Decrease	Increase	Decrease
(Bal)										
I										
(New Bal.)										

j. Cash of $590 is received from members who prepay a conference room rental fee.

Assets   **=**

$_____

	Cash		Accounts Receivable				Gym Supplies		Gym Equipment	
	Increase	Decrease	Increase	Decrease			Increase	Decrease	Increase	Decrease
(Bal)										
J										
(New Bal.)										

k. Sugar withdraws $2,000 from the business for personal living expenses.

Assets   **=**

$_____

	Cash		Accounts Receivable				Gym Supplies		Gym Equipment	
	Increase	Decrease	Increase	Decrease			Increase	Decrease	Increase	Decrease
(Bal)										
K										
(New Bal.)										

Liabilities + Owner's Equity

$_____

Accounts Payable					Sugar Eclair, Capital			Exp.	Rev.
Decrease	Increase				Decrease	Increase			

Liabilities + Owner's Equity

$_____

Accounts Payable					Sugar Eclair, Capital			Exp.	Rev.
Decrease	Increase				Decrease	Increase			

Liabilities + Owner's Equity

$_____

Accounts Payable					Sugar Eclair, Capital			Exp.	Rev.
Decrease	Increase				Decrease	Increase			

Solutions are in the disk at the back of the book and at: www.worthyjames.com

PRACTICE   **Learning Goal 11, continued**

LG 11-2, *continued*

l. The business purchases $500 of supplies and $1,000 of equipment on credit.

	Cash		Accounts Receivable				Gym Supplies		Gym Equipment	
	Increase	Decrease	Increase	Decrease			Increase	Decrease	Increase	Decrease
(Bal)										
L										
(New Bal.)										

Assets $\_\_\_\_\_$ =

m. Air conditioning repairs are required for $900. The bill will be paid later.

Assets $\_\_\_\_\_$ =

	Cash		Accounts Receivable				Gym Supplies		Gym Equipment	
	Increase	Decrease	Increase	Decrease			Increase	Decrease	Increase	Decrease
(Bal)										
M										
(New Bal.)										

n. Sugar spends the $2,000 she withdrew for new furniture for her home.

Assets $\_\_\_\_\_$ =

	Cash		Accounts Receivable				Gym Supplies		Gym Equipment	
	Increase	Decrease	Increase	Decrease			Increase	Decrease	Increase	Decrease
(Bal)										
N										
(New Bal.)										

- What are the total revenues that the club received during September? _____

- What are the total expenses of the club during September? _____

- Calculate the club's net income or loss during September. _____

Liabilities + Owner's Equity

$_____

Accounts Payable					Sugar Eclair, Capital				
Decrease	Increase				Decrease	Increase		Exp.	Rev.

Liabilities + Owner's Equity

$_____

Accounts Payable					Sugar Eclair, Capital				
Decrease	Increase				Decrease	Increase		Exp.	Rev.

Liabilities + Owner's Equity

$_____

Accounts Payable					Sugar Eclair, Capital				
Decrease	Increase				Decrease	Increase		Exp.	Rev.

LG 11-3. On a separate sheet of paper, use the information for items a through n, below, to record which specific items increase or decrease as a result of each event. Write in the name of the item affected in the "increase" or "decrease" columns below. Use the first item as an example.

	Assets		=	Liabilities	+	Owner's Equity	
	Increase	Decrease		Decrease	Increase	Decrease	Increase
a. A business collects $1,000 of accounts receivable from a customer.	Cash	Accts. Rec.					
b. A business pays a bill to a vendor.	(Reminder: Use a separate sheet of paper to complete the table.)						
c. A business purchases supplies on account.							
d. A business makes a sale on account.							
e. A business uses up some supplies.							
f. A business buys a $5,000 computer, pays $1,000 cash, and signs a note.							
g. A business receives an advance payment from a customer.							
h. The owner removes some cash and supplies from her business.							
i. A business prepays rent for three months in the amount of $1,500.							
j. The owner buys a new car for herself.							
k. A business pays the wages to its employees.							
l. One month has passed since the rent was prepaid in item i, above.							
m. A business receives a bill from the telephone company.							
n. The business performs services for the customer who prepaid in item g, above.							
o. A business that incurred a liability pays the liability.							
p. A customer pays a business for an amount owed.							

PRACTICE   Learning Goal 11, continued

Instructor-Assigned Problems

If you are using this book in a class, these review problems may be assigned by your instructor for homework, group assignments, class work, or other activities. Only your instructor has the solutions.

IA-6.

a. Using the column recording format from Learning Goal 11, record the following transactions and total the columns. Identify revenues and expenses and withdrawals next to the column for owner's equity. (Column recording paper for this format is available in the appendix or you can print them out from the disk at the back of this book.)

b. Calculate the net income or loss of the business.

   (1) David Aldrich invested $15,000 cash to begin his new business, Aldrich Internet Consulting.
   (2) The business used $300 cash to purchase some supplies.
   (3) The business paid $3,000 to purchase office equipment.
   (4) The business purchased an additional $400 of supplies on account.
   (5) The business received an advance payment of $2,700 from a client for future services.
   (6) The business used $150 of supplies.
   (7) The business provided $1,200 of consulting services to a client who immediately paid in cash.
   (8) The business paid $1,900 rent expense for the office.
   (9) The business provided $2,500 of consulting service on account.
   (10) David Aldrich withdrew $1,000 from the business for his personal use.
   (11) The business received a $650 telephone bill that was not immediately paid.
   (12) The business provided $900 of consulting service. The client paid $700 cash and will pay the balance later.
   (13) The client in transaction (9) above paid the account balance in full.
   (14) The business provided $850 of services to client in (5) above who made the advance payment.
   (15) The business used $100 of supplies.
   (16) The business received a $750 bill for legal services that was not immediately paid.
   (17) The business paid the telephone bill (11) in full.

IA-7.

a. Using the column recording format from Learning Goal 11, record the following transactions and total the columns. Identify revenues and expenses and withdrawals next to the column for owner's equity. (Column recording paper for this format is available in the appendix or you can print them out from the disk at the back of this book.)

b. Calculate the net income or loss of the business.

   (1) Jennifer Chang invested $42,000 cash to begin her new business, Chang Book Design Services.
   (2) The business paid $3,000 to purchase $2,500 of computer equipment and $500 of supplies.
   (3) The business purchased an additional $340 of supplies on account.
   (4) The business received an advance payment of $4,000 from a client for future design services.
   (5) The business used $270 of supplies.
   (6) The business provided $1,900 of consulting service on account.
   (7) The business provided $3,100 of consulting services to a client who immediately paid in cash.

PRACTICE   Learning Goal 11, continued

IA-7, *continued*

  (8) The business paid $2,400 rent expense for the office.

  (9) Jennifer Chang withdrew $2,500 from the business for her personal use.

(10) The business received a $1,590 advertising bill that was not immediately paid.

(11) The business provided $2,100 of design services. The client paid $400 cash and will pay the balance later.

(12) The business received a call from a publisher confirming the intention to contract for $3,500 of design services.

(13) The client in transaction (6) above paid the account balance in full.

(14) The business provided $2,700 of services to client in (4) above who made the advance payment.

(15) The business received a $600 bill for accounting services, which was not immediately paid.

(16) The business received a $980 bill for Internet advertising services that was not immediately paid.

(17) The business paid the advertising bill (10) in full.

IA-8. **Ethical analysis.** Review the article called "Crossing the Line" on page 256 of this learning goal.

a. Considering the transaction elements of classification, valuation, and timing, which element did the fraud primarily affect?

b. Apply the ethical decision guideline from Learning Goal 10 as if you were the controller and Mr. Sullivan asked you to make the changes in how expenses were recorded. In your answer, show each step in the decision process.

c. In your opinion, what factors may have affected Mr. Myers' initial decision to accept what Mr. Sullivan wanted him to do?

d. Consider the situation of Cynthia Cooper, the internal auditor. What obligations, conflicts, and personal pressures do you think affected her? Are special qualities required of auditors? Research the story of Cynthia Cooper at WorldCom, Inc.

INTERNET EXERCISES

Ethics—analyze cases. Go to the AICPA home page and click on the "Antifraud Resource Center" link. Then click on the link to "Fraud and Ethics Case Studies and Commentaries for Business and Industry." Scroll down until you find the list of cases. Scan the cases and select two that interest you. For each case:

a. Write down the case name and use the ethics discussion and guidelines in Learning Goal 10 to analyze each case from an ethical perspective. Then make a decision or take a position.

b. Compare your decision to the official commentary. Do you agree? Explain your reasons.

Your Questions?

It is *very* important to be aware of what you need to understand better. What do you need to understand better about this learning goal? On a separate piece of paper, write the questions that you want to discuss with your classmates, instructor, or supervisor. Try to be very specific about what is bothering you, such as explanations that you do not fully understand.

The Essential Financial Statements

| LEARNING GOAL 12 | # Describe the Financial Statements |

Review and Preview

Review

In the prior learning goal, you practiced Stages 1 and 2 of the accounting process: you analyzed events and, if the events qualified as transactions, you recorded them.

In This Learning Goal . . .

This learning goal introduces you to Stage 3 in the accounting process: communicating what has happened to a business. Communication in accounting is done by summarizing the recorded events into financial statements.

In Learning Goal 12, you will find:

Financial Statements and What They Do

Financial Statements Are Summaries

What Are Financial Statements?

Financial statements are well-organized summaries of all the transactions that have already been recorded.

What Financial Statements Do

Because financial statements are well-organized summaries, they can *communicate* important financial information about a business to the people and organizations (the stakeholders) who make decisions concerning the business. This clarified overview would be impossible by only looking at individual transactions one at a time.

The Types of Financial Statements

Four General-Purpose Financial Statements

Four general-purpose financial statements are normally prepared to provide information to stakeholders:

- The balance sheet (explains the basic statement of financial condition)
- The income statement (explains certain changes in the balance sheet)
- The statement of owner's equity (explains certain changes in the balance sheet)
- The statement of cash flows (explains certain changes in the balance sheet)

These statements are called "general purpose" because they are prepared for general use by any **stakeholder**—an owner, a manager, an investor, a lender, or anyone else.

Note: An individual financial statement is sometimes called a "report."

continued ▶

"So . . . tell me all about financial statements."

The Types of Financial Statements, *continued*

Special-Purpose Financial Statements	Accountants can also prepare special-purpose reports. These reports usually focus on the business operations in great detail, such as analysis of costs and profitability of services and products. They are intended only for owners and managers for use within a business. This kind of work is called ***managerial accounting***.
The Annual Report	Large companies present the four general-purpose reports at the end of each year's operations in a single document called the ***annual report***.

Features of the Annual Report

Frequency	Annual.
Financial Statements	The four general-purpose financial statements are in the annual report: balance sheet, income statement, statement of owner's equity, and statement of cash flows.
Full Disclosure	Annual reports must contain very detailed footnotes, graphs, charts, and tables that explain the numbers in the financial statements.
	The importance of full and understandable disclosure cannot be overemphasized, as was dramatically revealed as the 21st century began with the surprise bankruptcies of very large companies such as Enron, WorldCom, and Global Crossing. Because their financial statements gave the impression that the companies were all viable "going concerns," the bankruptcies surprised many stakeholders and resulted in large financial losses, numerous fraud allegations, and the subsequent collapse of a major accounting firm, Arthur Andersen Company.
	These events revealed the weaknesses in the existing disclosure rules. In 2002, as a result, the United States Congress created the ***Public Company Accounting Oversight Board***, also called the PCAOB. The PCAOB now independently supervises the full-disclosure and auditing standards that accountants must apply to large corporations whose stocks are publicly traded.
Example of Failure to Disclose	Using complex accounting methods, Enron Corporation created numerous partnerships with other parties. However, Enron never disclosed the business purpose of these transactions (often there was none—only to hide losses or remove debt) or that a share of property sale gains would go to senior Enron officers.

Features of the Annual Report, *continued*

Audited	The financial statements in the annual report are audited by Certified Public Accountants, so the financial statements must conform to generally accepted accounting principles. (This is not true of unaudited interim reports.)
MD & A	Annual reports also contain management's opinion about the past and future performance of the company. This is called "management discussion and analysis" or simply *MD & A*. The MD & A must include an explanation of liquidity (cash position), sources of capital invested in or loaned to the company, and the operating results. The MD & A must also discuss the management's opinion about the future performance of the company.

The Qualities of Information

How Good Is Information in the Financial Statements?

It Must Be Useful!	If you want to use a financial report to make a financial decision next week, do you want the report to contain numbers that are only guesses? Do you want information about the cost of eggs in Boston in 1909? Do you want information that was calculated using one method one month and a different method the next month? Of course not—none of this would be useful to you. The highest authority in accounting, the Financial Accounting Standards Board, has stated that the most important quality of the information on financial statements is that it must be *useful*.
Various Qualities Required	If you study more advanced accounting, you will discover a surprising number of separate qualities that are needed to make financial information useful. The most essential of these important qualities are shown below.

Four Important Qualities

The Two Most Important Qualities

The table below shows the two most important qualities of financial information: Reliability and relevance.

Quality Name	What It Means	Example	Nonexample
■ *Reliability*	Information must be free of material error. The information can be verified.	The balance sheet shows that the cash balance of Kline Company is $15,500. Auditors verified this by examining the bank account, which showed $15,501.32.	The Kline Company president reports that the value of some company land is $500,000 because that is what she thinks is correct.
■ *Relevance*	The information is important enough to make a differ-ence in a decision, if it were not available.	The loan officer at the bank discovers that the liabilities of Lin Company are $250,000, twice the amount of last year. The loan officer changes her mind about approving a loan.	On one occasion, Lin Company was late making a pay-ment to a creditor. The amount was $100. This information has no effect on the loan officer's decision.

Two Other Important Qualities

- *Consistency:* The information on the financial statements should be determined by using the same method of accounting, consistently applied.
- *Comparability:* The result of consistency should be that financial state-ments are comparable both over time and between different companies. Unfortunately, GAAP rules do not always do a good job of making infor-mation comparable between different companies.

TIP

Comparability can be a problem because consistency is not required between companies; that is, different companies can use different cal-culation methods.

QUICK REVIEW

- Financial statements are well-organized summaries of information already recorded. Financial statements (reports) communicate important information to stakeholders.

- The four general-purpose reports are:

  - Balance sheet
  - Income statement
  - Statement of owner's equity
  - Statement of cash flows

- Annual reports are prepared by large companies and contain financial reports, footnotes, and MD & A.

- The most important quality of financial statements is that they must be useful. To be useful, financial statements must have the essential qualities of reliability, relevance, consistency, and comparability.

VOCABULARY

Annual report: a document, usually prepared by a large corporation, that contains audited financial statements, footnotes, and management discussion and analysis (page 280)

Comparability: the quality of information that makes it comparable between companies and over time (page 282)

Consistency: the quality of information that is prepared using the same methods and procedures (page 282)

Managerial accounting: a kind of accounting that focuses on the detailed information needs of a specific company, rather than on the general public (page 280)

MD & A: "management discussion and analysis" found in annual reports (page 281)

Public Company Accounting Oversight Board (PCAOB): a federal government organization that supervises the disclosure and auditing standards that accountants must apply to corporations whose stock is publicly traded (page 280)

Relevance: the quality of information that makes it significant or important (page 282)

Reliability: the quality of information that makes it free from material error or bias (page 282)

Stakeholder: an individual or organization that has a personal, financial, or other interest in the condition of a business (page 279)

Learning Goal 12 describes the four general-purpose financial statements. Use these questions to practice what you have just read. Select the best answer to each question.

Multiple Choice
Select the best answer.

1. The most fundamental requirement for accounting information is that it
   a. must be accurate.
   b. must be useful.
   c. is prepared at least annually.
   d. is relevant.

2. Financial statement information that can be verified and is free of material error describes the information quality of
   a. relevance.
   b. comparability.
   c. reliability.
   d. consistency.

3. Information that is important enough to make a difference in a decision if it is not available describes the quality of
   a. relevance.
   b. comparability.
   c. reliability.
   d. consistency.

4. Due to the collapse of major corporations such as Enron, WorldCom, and Global Crossing, the United States Congress in 2002 created the · · · · · · · ·, which independently supervises the full-disclosure and auditing standards that must be used by CPA firms when auditing large (publicly traded) companies.
   a. Securities and Exchange Commission (SEC)
   b. American Auditing Board
   c. Public Company Accounting Oversight Board (PCAOB)
   d. Chartered Accountants Oversight Board

5. MD & A is a required management presentation that is always part of a(n)
   a. income statement.
   b. balance sheet.
   c. tax return.
   d. annual report.

6. Which of the following is *not* a feature of an annual report?
   a. balance sheet, income statement, statement of owner's (or stockholders') equity, and statement of cash flows that have been audited
   b. MD & A
   c. tax return
   d. footnotes, graphs, and tables

7. The kind of accounting that focuses on the detailed internal information needs of a company is
   a. managerial accounting.
   b. internal auditing.
   c. tax accounting.
   d. fund accounting.

PRACTICE   **Learning Goal 12, continued**

Solutions are in the disk at the back of the book and at: www.worthyjames.com

8. Which of the following is considered to be a "general purpose" financial statement?
   a. balance sheet
   b. income statement
   c. statement of cash flows
   d. all of the above

9. Information on financial statements that is determined by using the same accounting methods and procedures each reporting period has the quality of
   a. consistency.
   b. reliability.
   c. relevance.
   d. comparability.

10. If you are looking at the financial statements of several companies which you are analyzing for the purpose of making an investment, an additional quality of information on the financial statements that is important to you is
    a. consistency.
    b. reliability.
    c. relevance.
    d. comparability.

11. If the management of a company knows that a large bank loan is coming due and will require full payment in the near future, the requirement that this information be made available as part of the financial statements is called
    a. consistency.
    b. full disclosure.
    c. relevance.
    d. reliability.

12. Full financial statements disclosure consists primarily of
    a. charts and graphs.
    b. footnotes.
    c. tables.
    d. all of the above.

INTERNET EXERCISES

Finding and analyzing websites of CPA firms. Do an Internet search and locate ten to fifteen CPA firms in your local area. (Suggestion: Try www.cpafirms.com as one source. Use bookmark/favorites to save the web links in an "Accounting References" folder.) List the firm names.

   a. What services are most frequently offered? Which are the most unusual?
   b. Can you find descriptions of these services at the firms' websites? If so, briefly describe the services for each firm, naming the firm.
   c. Which services would be most useful to an individual, a small business, and a large business?

Your Questions?

It is *very* important to be aware of what you need to understand better. What do you need to understand better about this learning goal? On a separate piece of paper, write the questions that you want to discuss with your classmates, instructor, or supervisor. Try to be very specific about what is bothering you, such as explanations that you do not fully understand.

LEARNING GOAL 13

Identify and Prepare an Income Statement

Overview

Preparation Sequence

When all the financial statements are being prepared, the income statement is normally prepared first. This and the next three learning goals explain each of the financial statements in the order in which they are normally prepared: income statement (Learning Goal 13), statement of owner's equity (Learning Goal 14), balance sheet (Learning Goal 15), and statement of cash flows (Learning Goal 16).

Introduction

What the Income Statement Shows

The *income statement* shows the change in owner's equity that was caused by the business operations. *Remember:* "Operations" means the process of creating and selling desired resources.

The Income Statement Formula

The basic formula for the income statement is: $R - E = NI$ (or NL), where:

- R means total revenues.
- E means total expenses.
- NI and NL mean net income and net loss.

Reason for the Income Statement

Revenues and expenses are the *most powerful* force of change on the condition of the business.

All the efforts that go into operating the business show up in the amount of revenues and expenses. Revenues and expenses are of great interest to all users of financial statements. Financial statement users want to identify and analyze the individual amounts of revenues and expenses. To provide this detail, the types of revenues and expenses are identified individually on a separate statement—the income statement.

In Learning Goal 13, you will find:

What It Is and the Four Steps to Prepare It

What It Is and the Four Steps to Prepare It

Features of the Income Statement

Time Period	Unlike the balance sheet, the income statement is for a *period of time*.
Why a Period of Time?	The date of an income statement shows a period of time because the income statement shows change, and *change happens over time*. This could be a month, a quarter, a year, etc. Notice in the example below for Jack's Guitar School that the date is "for the *month ended* June 30, 2008." Therefore, this is the operational change in owner's equity that happened during June.
Individual Sections	The basic income statement has one section for revenues and another section for expenses.
Synonyms	Other names for the income statement are:

- *Statement of earnings*
- *Operating statement/statement of operations*
- *Profit and loss statement*
- **P & L statement**

Note: The financial statements shown in this learning goal are introductory examples. Larger and more complex examples are presented in Volume 2 and in the discussion of corporations later in this book.

continued ▶

Features of the Income Statement, *continued*

Example

Jack's Guitar School
Income Statement
For the Month Ended June 30, 2008

Revenues		
Instruction fees		$2,900
Expenses		
Rent expense	$800	
Supplies expense	150	
Utilities expense	100	
Telephone expense	70	
Total expenses		1,120
Net income		$1,780

Check Your Understanding

Write the completed sentences on a separate piece of paper. The answers are below.

The date of an income statement is for a · · · · · · · · of · · · · · · · · because the income statement shows · · · · · · · · . This is different than a balance sheet, which shows the condition of the business at a · · · · · · · · in time.

What the income statement explains is the · · · · · · · · · · · · · · · · in owner's equity. This is caused by · · · · · · · · and · · · · · · · · .

Answers

The date of an income statement is for a period of time because the income statement shows change. This is different than a balance sheet, which shows the condition of the business at a point in time.

What the income statement explains is the operational change in owner's equity. This is caused by revenues and expenses.

Four Steps in Preparing an Income Statement

Summary of Steps

The following pages show you how to prepare an income statement in four basic steps. Here is a summary of the steps:

1. Write the title.
2. List the revenues (type and amount).
3. List the expenses (type and amount).
4. Calculate and enter net income (or loss) and enter it on the statement.

STEP 1	
Action	**Rule**
Write the title.	The title is always prepared in the following order: 1. Name of company 2. Name of statement 3. Time period

Example

> **Jack's Guitar School**
> **Income Statement**
> **For the Month Ended June 30, 2008**

STEP 2	
Action	**Rule**
List the revenues (type and amount).	■ If there are separate types of revenues, the total of each type is always shown. ■ If there are more than one type, show the largest total first. ■ The total of revenues is shown above the expenses.

Source of the Numbers

The numbers for this income statement come from the totals of the revenue and expense transactions that are recorded for Jack's Guitar School (see page 255).

continued ▶

Four Steps in Preparing an Income Statement, *continued*

STEP 3	
Action	**Rule**
List the expenses (type and amount).	■ If there are separate types of expenses, the total of each type is always shown (examples are wages expense, supplies expense, etc.). ■ The total of expenses is shown below the revenues.

Note: Expenses can be listed in different ways, but we will put the *largest expenses first*. Listing expenses this way makes it easy to quickly see the expenses that reduced the net income the most.

Example of Steps 2 and 3

Jack's Guitar School
Income Statement
For the Month Ended June 30, 2008

Revenues		
Instruction fees		$2,900
Expenses		
Rent expense	$800	
Supplies expense	150	
Utilities expense	100	
Telephone expense	70	
Total expenses		1,120

STEP 4	
Action	**Rule**
Calculate and enter net income (or loss).	■ **Net income** or **net loss** is always calculated by subtracting total expenses from total revenues. (The completed statement is on page 288.)

Rule for Dollar Signs

A dollar sign ($) is placed next to the top number in any column of numbers. A dollar sign is also placed next to the final total—the number above the double line.

QUICK REVIEW

The income statement			
Also called: ■ Operating statement ■ P & L statement ■ Profit and loss statement ■ Statement of earnings ■ Statement of operations			
explains . . .			
the *operational* changes in *owner's equity*			
and contains . . .			
■ Revenues ■ Expenses			

VOCABULARY

Income statement: a report that explains the operational changes in owner's equity for a specific period of time (page 286)

Net income: when revenues exceed expenses (page 290)

Net loss: when expenses exceed revenues (page 290)

Operating statement: another name for the income statement (page 287)

P & L statement: another name for the income statement (page 287)

Profit and loss statement: another name for the income statement (page 287)

Statement of earnings: another name for the income statement (page 287)

Statement of operations: another name for the income statement (page 287)

PRACTICE   Learning Goal 13

Solutions are in the disk at the back of the book and at: www.worthyjames.com

Learning Goal 13 concerns the identification and preparation of the income statement. Use these three problems to practice the material you just read.

Reinforcement Problems

LG 13-1. **Prepare an income statement.** On July 1, 2008, David Running-Elk begins his new orthopedic medical practice with an investment of $37,000, which he has obtained from his friends and relatives. As of the end of the first month of operation, the bookkeeper has determined the balances for the items below. On a separate sheet of paper, use the correct items to prepare an income statement for David Running-Elk, M.D., for the month of July.

Accounts Payable	$ 1,100	Rent Expense	$ 1,500	Note Payable	$ 9,000
Unearned Revenue	$ 500	Drawings	$ 1,000	Accounts Receivable	$ 3,100
Supplies	$ 700	Fees Earned	$ 4,250	Interest Expense	$ 300
Cash	$ 8,500	Equipment	$35,000	Prepaid Insurance	$ 750
Wages Expense	$ 850	Utilities Expense	$ 150		

LG 13-2. **Missing information—prepare an income statement.** An analysis of the owner's equity of the De Anza Operating Company shows the following items for the year ended December 31, 2008.

Rent Expense	$12,000	Supplies Expense	?	Owner Withdrawals	$5,000
Service Revenue Earned	?	Wages Expense	$7,500	Utilities Expense	$2,000
Advertising Expense	$3,000				

Other information: The net income for the year was $10,000. On January 1, the company had $3,000 of supplies and on December 31, the company had $5,000 of supplies. During the year, the company purchased $4,000 of supplies.

Required: On a separate sheet of paper, prepare an income statement for the De Anza Operating Company. Show calculations separately and in good form.

LG 13-3. **Business operations.** You know that the income statement explains the effect of business operations on the owner's equity. Operations affect the owner's equity because of two transaction types. What are the two types of transactions?

a.

b.

Your Questions?

It is *very* important to be aware of what you need to understand better. What do you need to understand better about this learning goal? On a separate piece of paper, write the questions that you want to discuss with your classmates, instructor, or supervisor. Try to be very specific about what is bothering you, such as explanations that you do not fully understand.

| LEARNING GOAL 14 | # Identify and Prepare a Statement of Owner's Equity |

Review

What It Shows

The **statement of owner's equity** explains *all* the changes in owner's equity for a specific period of time. The statement of owner's equity combines the *operational* change in owner's equity from the income statement *with the rest of the changes* in owner's equity. The rest of the changes are:

1. Owner's investments
2. Owner's withdrawals

The Owner's Equity Statement Formula

The formula for the statement of owner's equity consists of three parts: beginning balance + (current changes) = ending balance.

Three possible current changes are:

1. Net income or net loss (+/−)
2. Owner's investment (+)
3. Owner's withdrawals (−)

Net Income Combines Two Effects

Question: We previously said that four transaction types can affect owner's equity: revenues, expenses, investments, and withdrawals. Why do we see only three current changes on the statement of owner's equity?

Answer: Two of the changes—revenues and expenses—are combined into one number—net income (or net loss)—from the income statement.

In Learning Goal 14, you will find:

What It Is and the Four Steps to Prepare It

What It Is and the Four Steps to Prepare It

Features of the Statement of Owner's Equity

Date	Like the income statement, the statement of owner's equity is for a *period of time* because it is a statement that shows change.
Same Final Balance as Shown on the Balance Sheet	The final balance on the statement of owner's equity is the same balance of owner's equity as on the balance sheet (which we discuss in the next learning goal). The statement of owner's equity is simply itemizing the current changes to arrive at the final balance of owner's equity.
Synonym	The statement of owner's equity is sometimes called the **capital statement**.
Example	*Note:* Beginning balance is zero because this is a new business.

Jack's Guitar School
Statement of Owner's Equity
For the Month Ended June 30, 2008

Jack Davis, Capital, June 1	$ 0
Add: Owner investment	12,000
Net income	1,780
	13,780
Less: Drawings	1,000
Jack Davis, Capital, June 30	$12,780

Write the completed sentences on a separate piece of paper. The answers are below.

The statement of owner's equity is for a · · · · · · · · of time and summarizes · · · · · · · · the changes in owner's equity. The statement has three parts: (1) the · · · · · · · · balance of owner's equity, (2) the · · · · · · · · · · · · · · · · ·, and (3) the · · · · · · · · balance. The ending balance of owner's equity must be the same number as the owner's equity that appears on the · · · · · · · · · · · · · · · · ·.

Answers

The statement of owner's equity is for a period of time and summarizes all the changes in owner's equity. The statement has three parts: (1) the beginning balance of owner's equity, (2) the current changes, and (3) the ending balance. The ending balance of owner's equity must be the same number as the owner's equity that appears on the balance sheet.

Four Steps in Preparing the Statement of Owner's Equity

Summary of Steps

The following pages show you how to prepare a statement of owner's equity in four basic steps. Here is a summary of the steps:

1. Write the title.
2. Enter the beginning balance (with description).
3. Enter the current changes (with descriptions).
4. Calculate the ending balance (with description) and verify it.

STEP 1	
Action	**Rule**
Write the title.	The title is always prepared in the following order: 1. Name of company 2. Name of statement 3. Time period

continued ▶

Four Steps in Preparing the Statement of Owner's Equity, *continued*

Example

> **Jack's Guitar School**
> **Statement of Owner's Equity**
> **For the Month Ended June 30, 2008**

STEP 2	
Action	**Rule**
Enter the beginning balance (with description).	The beginning balance is always: ■ The ending balance from the *prior* statement of owner's equity or balance sheet, or . . . ■ For a new business, the beginning balance of owner's equity is zero.

STEP 3	
Action	**Rule**
Enter the current changes (with descriptions).	The possible current changes are: ■ Net income (or loss) from the income statement ■ Owner investments ■ Owner withdrawals

Four Steps in Preparing the Statement of Owner's Equity, *continued*

Example	The beginning balance and current changes for Jack's Guitar School are shown below.

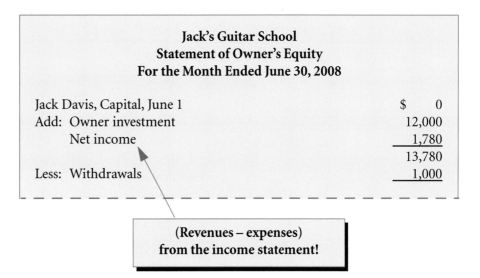

Jack's Guitar School
Statement of Owner's Equity
For the Month Ended June 30, 2008

Jack Davis, Capital, June 1	$ 0
Add: Owner investment	12,000
Net income	1,780
	13,780
Less: Withdrawals	1,000

(Revenues – expenses)
from the income statement!

STEP 4	
Action	**Rule**
Calculate the ending balance (with description) and verify it.	▪ The ending balance is calculated by adding/subtracting the three possible current changes to the beginning balance. ▪ The ending balance is verified by checking that it is the same amount as the owner's equity showing on the balance sheet.

Example	An example of the completed statement of owner's equity for Jack's Guitar School is on page 294.

QUICK REVIEW

(Prepare first) The income statement	(Prepare second) The statement of owner's equity		
Also called: ■ Operating statement ■ P & L statement ■ Profit and loss statement ■ Statement of earnings ■ Statement of operations	Also called: ■ Capital statement		
explains . . .	explains . . .		
The *operational* changes in *owner's equity*	*All* the changes in *owner's equity*		
and contains . . .	and contains . . .		
■ Revenues ■ Expenses	■ Net income (loss) ■ Investments ■ Withdrawals		

VOCABULARY

Capital statement: another name for the statement of owner's equity (page 294)

Statement of owner's equity: the financial statement that explains all the changes in owner's equity (page 293)

PRACTICE   Learning Goal 14

Solutions are in the disk at the back of the book and at: www.worthyjames.com

Learning Goal 14 concerns the identification and preparation of the statement of owner's equity. Use these two problems to practice the material you just read.

Reinforcement Problems

LG 14-1. **Prepare a statement of owner's equity.** On July 1, 2008, David Running-Elk began his new orthopedic medical practice with an investment of $37,000, which he has (obtained) from his friends and relatives. As of the end of the first month of operation, the bookkeeper has determined the balances for the items below. On a separate sheet of paper, use the correct items to prepare a statement of owner's equity for David Running-Elk, M.D., for the month of July. Remember that you can use the information on the income statement that you already prepared in the Practice for Learning Goal 13 (see page 292, Reinforcement Problem LG 13-1).

Accounts Payable	$ 1,100	Fees Earned	$ 4,250
Unearned Revenue	$ 500	Equipment	$35,000
Supplies	$ 700	Utilities Expense	$ 150
Cash	$ 8,500	Note Payable	$ 9,000
Wages Expense	$ 850	Accounts Receivable	$ 3,100
Rent Expense	$ 1,500	Interest Expense	$ 300
Drawings	$ 1,000	Prepaid Insurance	$ 750

LG 14-2. **Missing information—prepare a statement of owner's equity.** Lucy Palangian, the owner of West Valley Company, wants you (her assistant) to prepare a statement of owner's equity and to determine the net income or loss for the year ended December 31, 2008. Unfortunately, there is no detailed information that shows individual revenue or expense transactions.

Luckily, Ms. Palangian does remember that she invested $15,000 in the business this year and withdrew $5,300 for personal expenses. The balance of owner's equity on January 1, 2008 was $3,800. On December 31, total assets are $41,000 and total liabilities are $37,000.

Required: On a separate sheet of paper, prepare a statement of owner's equity. Then tell the owner the net income or loss for the year. Show any calculations clearly and in good form.

Your Questions?

It is *very* important to be aware of what you need to understand better. What do you need to understand better about this learning goal? On a separate piece of paper, write the questions that you want to discuss with your classmates, instructor, or supervisor. Try to be very specific about what is bothering you, such as explanations that you do not fully understand.

LEARNING GOAL 15

Identify and Prepare a Balance Sheet

In Learning Goal 15, you will find:

What It Is and the Four Steps to Prepare It

Features of the Balance Sheet

What It Shows

The **balance sheet** is like a flash picture—it shows assets and claims on assets at a moment in time. In other words, a balance sheet shows the business wealth and claims on the wealth at a point in time. Notice that in the example on page 301 for Jack's Guitar School, the date is a point in time—June 30—meaning at the end of the business day on June 30. The date is not for a period of time, like "the month of June."

It Balances

The total claims on assets equal the total assets. In the example, the total assets are $13,150. The creditors' claims of $370 + the owner's claim of $12,780 = $13,150.

Individual Sections

The assets, liabilities, and owner's equity are each presented in their own sections, and the total is calculated for each section.

Format: Report Form and Account Form

The side-by-side presentation of assets and equities in the example is called the **account form** of the balance sheet. Sometimes the form of the balance sheet varies slightly, with all assets shown at the top of the report and the liabilities and owner's equity shown below the assets. Such a format is called the **report form**.

Features of the Balance Sheet, *continued*

Synonym

The balance sheet is sometimes called the ***statement of position*** or the ***statement of condition***.

Source of the Information

The asset and liability amounts come from the ending balances of the individual accounting equation items for Jack's Guitar School (see pages 254 and 255). The owner's equity is the ending balance that was calculated in the statement of owner's equity.

TIP

See it as a photograph. Try to remember the balance sheet as a "flash photograph" of the business at a moment in time.

Example: Completed Balance Sheet (Account Form)

Jack's Guitar School
Balance Sheet
June 30, 2008

Assets		Liabilities	
Cash	$6,350	Accounts payable	$ 170
Accounts receivable	1,250	Unearned revenues	200
Supplies	50	Total liabilities	370
Equipment	5,500		
		Owner's Equity	
		Jack Davis, Capital	12,780
		Total liabilities	
Total assets	$13,150	and owner's equity	$13,150

This must also be the ending balance on the statement of owner's equity (page 294).

continued ▶

Write the completed sentences on a separate piece of paper. The answers are below.

The balance sheet is also called the statement of · · · · · · · · or the statement of · · · · · · · ·.
The balance sheet is like a flash · · · · · · · · of business wealth and · · · · · · · · on · · · · · · · ·. The source
of the asset and liability information for a balance sheet is the · · · · · · · · balances of the individual
accounting equation items.

Answers

The balance sheet is also called the statement of position or the statement of condition. The balance sheet is like a flash picture of business wealth and claims on wealth. The source of the asset and liability information for a balance sheet is the ending balances of the individual accounting equation items.

Four Steps in Preparing a Balance Sheet

Summary of Steps

The following pages show you how to prepare a balance sheet in four basic steps. Here is a summary of the steps:

1. Write the title.
2. Enter the asset and liability names, amounts, and totals.
3. Enter the owner's equity and verify it.
4. Total the liabilities and owner's equity and compare to asset total.

STEP 1	
Action	**Rule**
Write the title.	The title is always prepared in the following order: 1. Name of company 2. Name of statement 3. Date *(NOT a time period)*

Jack's Guitar School   **Balance Sheet**   **June 30, 2008**

Four Steps in Preparing a Balance Sheet, *continued*

STEP 2	
Action	**Rule**
Enter the asset and liability names, amounts, and totals.	**Assets:** ■ Assets are listed in order of liquidity. *Liquidity* means how quickly an asset can be turned into cash or used instead of spending cash. The most liquid asset is cash, so it is written first. The next most liquid asset is accounts receivable, and so on. (This takes a little practice, but after working some problems, you will soon be doing it perfectly.) ■ Assets must be totaled. A <u>double line</u> indicates a total. **Liabilities:** ■ Liabilities are listed in the order in which they will probably require payment. There is no exact order here, but accounts payable are often written first. ■ Liabilities must be totaled. A double line is not used.

Jack's Guitar School
Balance Sheet
June 30, 2008

Assets		Liabilities	
Cash	$ 6,350	Accounts payable	$170
Accounts receivable	1,250	Unearned revenues	200
Supplies	50	Total liabilities	370
Equipment	5,500		
		Owner's Equity	
Total assets	$13,150		

continued ▶

Four Steps in Preparing a Balance Sheet, *continued*

STEP 3	
Action	**Rule**
Enter the owner's equity and verify it.	▪ Use the ending balance on the statement of owner's equity to find the amount of owner's equity. ▪ Owner's equity must be labeled by writing the owner's name followed by the word "capital." ▪ Owner's equity is *verified* by subtracting total liabilities from total assets.

STEP 4	
Action	**Rule**
Total the liabilities and owner's equity and compare to asset total.	▪ The total of the liabilities and the owner's equity is always shown. It must be equal to the total assets.

Example

The completed balance sheet for Jack's Guitar School is on page 301. Notice that total assets of $13,150 minus total liabilities of $370 verify owner's equity of $12,780.

Rule for Dollar Signs ($)

A dollar sign ($) is placed next to the top number in any column of numbers. A dollar sign is also placed next to the final total—the number above the <u>double line</u>.

Note: Some preparers of financial statements omit dollar signs entirely because they believe that it is understood that all amounts are in U.S. dollars. (Do not do this without checking with your instructor or supervisor.)

The Four General-Purpose Financial Statements

One Condition Statement and Three Change Statements Compared

The table below compares the features and functions of the condition statement (balance sheet) and the three change statements.

The Condition Statement is . . .	The Change Statements are . . .		
The balance sheet	The income statement	The statement of owner's equity	The statement of cash flows
Also called: ■ Statement of position ■ Statement of condition	Also called: ■ Operating statement ■ P & L statement ■ Profit and loss statement ■ Statement of earnings ■ Statement of operations	Also called: ■ Capital statement ■ Statement of stock-holders' equity (corporation)	Also called: ■ Cash flows statement ■ Statement of changes in cash position
shows . . .	explains . . .	explains . . .	explains . . .
Wealth and claims on wealth at a point in time	The *operational* changes in *owner's equity*	*All* the changes in *owner's equity*	All the changes in the cash balance
and contains . . .	and contains . . .	and contains . . .	and contains . . .
■ Assets (wealth) ■ Liabilities (claim) ■ Owner's equity (claim)	■ Revenues ■ Expenses	■ Net income (– loss) ■ Investments ■ Withdrawals	■ Operating activities ■ Investing activities ■ Financing activities
and is structured . . .	and is structured . . .	and is structured . . .	and is structured . . .
A = L + OE	R – E = Net Income (or Loss)	Beginning balance + net income (loss) + investments – drawings = ending balance	Beginning balance + operating activities + investing activities + financing activities = ending balance

What Are the Connections Between the Statements?

Each Balance Sheet Is Linked to the Next One

As you can see in the table above, each change statement explains changes in certain key parts of the balance sheet—the owner's equity and the cash balances. You could say that the change statements form "links" between one balance sheet and the next.

continued ▶

What Are the Connections Between the Statements? *continued*

*Example: Two
Balance Sheets*

Suppose that you prepared the balance sheet for a company as of June 30 and later prepared another balance sheet for that company as of July 31:

*Explain the Changes
in the Owner's Equity
and Cash*

- You want to explain why the owner's equity is different on the July 31 balance sheet than on the June 30 balance sheet.
- You also want to explain why the cash balance on the July 31 balance sheet is different than on the June 30 balance sheet. How can the changes in these items be explained? By preparing the statements that show change: the income statement, statement of owner's equity, and statement of cash flows.

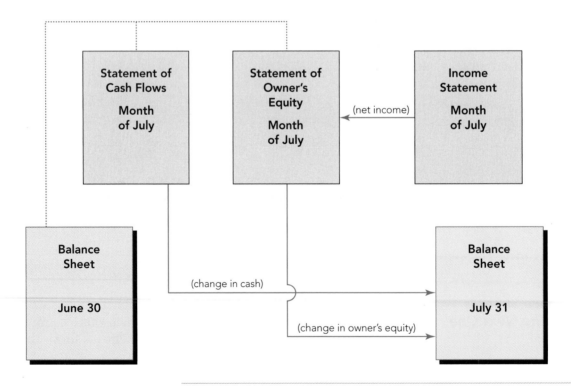

What Are the Connections Between the Statements? *continued*

Prior Balance Sheet Provides the Beginning Balances

The line from the June 30 balance sheet to the statement of cash flows and to the statement of owner's equity means the following:

- The beginning cash balance on the statement of cash flows, before any July transactions, comes from the June 30 balance sheet.
- The beginning owner's equity balance on the statement of owner's equity, before any July transactions, also comes from the June 30 balance sheet.

Current Period Transactions Complete the Links

The link to the July 31 balance sheet by each change statement is completed like this:

- All the current period July transactions that affect cash are summarized on the statement of cash flows, which explains the ending cash balance on the July 31 balance sheet.
- All the current period July transactions that affect owner's equity are summarized on the statement of owner's equity and the income statement. Together they explain the July 31 owner's equity on the balance sheet.

The ending balances showing on the statement of cash flows and on the statement of owner's equity correspond exactly to the same balances on the July 31 balance sheet. The statement of cash flows and the statement of owner's equity now link the June 30 and the July 31 balance sheet balances of cash and owner's equity.

Articulation

Whenever any change statement is connected to another financial statement, this connection is called "articulation."

Examples of the Connections

Jack's Guitar School July Results

Imagine that you have also recorded the July transactions and prepared the July financial statements for Jack's Guitar School, for which you followed the June transactions in Learning Goal 11. Without actually looking at any specific July transactions, assume that an overview of the results is what you see on page 318, with the cash and owner's equity balances shown to you.

continued ▶

Examples of the Connections, *continued*

	Prior Balance Sheet June 30			(July changes) Transactions		Current Balance Sheet July 31		
	Assets		**Liabilities**			**Assets**		**Liabilities**
Cash	$6,350	*xxx*	$$$$	→	*Cash*	$22,300	*xxx*	$$$$
xxx	$$$$	*xxx*	$$$$		*xxx*	$$$$	*xxx*	$$$$
xxx	$$$$	*xxx*	$$$$		*xxx*	$$$$	*xxx*	$$$$
xxx	$$$$	*Owner's Equity*	$12,780	→	*xxx*	$$$$	*Owner's Equity*	$17,420
Totals	**$13,150**		**$13,150**	→		**$32,520**		**$32,520**

July Changes

You can see that the July transactions are the reasons for changes in the balance sheet amounts. The new balance sheet as of July 31 is clearly different than the previous one. Specifically, we are most interested in the changes in cash and owner's equity.

The cash balance has changed from $6,350 on June 30 to $22,300 on July 31. The owner's equity balance has changed from $12,780 on June 30 to $17,420 on July 31.

Page 320 shows an illustration of the July 31 balance sheet, along with the three change statements *that explain the changes* in cash and owner's equity balances *during July*. These change statements are the "links" between the June 30 and July 31 balance sheet totals of cash and owner's equity.

Cash Transaction Examples

Suppose that during July:

- The business spent $500 cash to purchase supplies. This transaction reduced the cash balance on the balance sheet and was a use of cash in the "Operating activities" explanation on the July statement of cash flows.
- The business spent $4,200 to buy equipment. This transaction reduced the cash balance on the balance sheet, and was a use of cash in "Investing activities" on the July statement of cash flows.
- The business collected $800 from a customer. This increased cash on the balance sheet (and decreased accounts receivable). This increase in cash is shown as a source of cash from "Operating activities" on the statement of cash flows.

Examples of the Connections, *continued*

Owner's Equity Transaction Examples	Suppose that during July:

- The business sold $1,500 of teaching services to a customer on account. This transaction increased accounts receivable on the balance sheet and is explained on the July income statement as "Revenue," which increased owner's equity.
- The business used up $200 of supplies in the operations. This transaction decreased the asset supplies and is explained on the July income statement as "Expense," which decreased owner's equity.
- The total revenues exceeded the total expenses by $2,940. This net income was the overall increase to owner's equity from operations and is detailed on the July income statement. The net amount also appears on the July statement of owner's equity.

More Than One Change Statement Affected

Sometimes a transaction may affect both cash and owner's equity.

Examples:

- An owner's cash investment will increase both cash and owner's equity on the balance sheet. Therefore, the transaction will be explained on both the statement of owner's equity and the statement of cash flows.
- Paying cash for an expense item is a decrease to cash on the balance sheet. It is also an expense. Therefore, this type of transaction will be part of the income statement and the statement of cash flows.

continued

Examples of the Connections, *continued*

July Statement of Cash Flows

(The July Changes in Cash)

Operating activities:

Collection from customers	$33,000
Less: Expense payments	(14,550)
Net cash from operating activities	$18,450

Investing activities:

Purchase of equipment	(4,200)

Financing activities:

Owner investments less drawing	1,700
Net change in cash	15,950
Beginning cash balance **July 1, 2008**	6,350
Ending cash balance **July 31, 2008**	**$22,300**

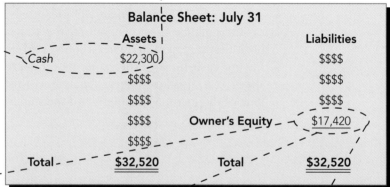

Balance Sheet: July 31

Assets		Liabilities	
Cash	$22,300		$$$$
	$$$$		$$$$
	$$$$		$$$$
	$$$$	Owner's Equity	$17,420
	$$$$		
Total	**$32,520**	Total	**$32,520**

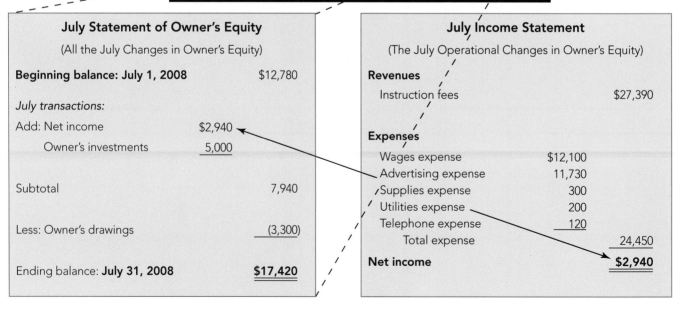

July Statement of Owner's Equity

(All the July Changes in Owner's Equity)

Beginning balance: July 1, 2008	$12,780

July transactions:

Add: Net income	$2,940	
Owner's investments	5,000	
Subtotal		7,940
Less: Owner's drawings		(3,300)
Ending balance: July 31, 2008		**$17,420**

July Income Statement

(The July Operational Changes in Owner's Equity)

Revenues		
Instruction fees		$27,390

Expenses		
Wages expense	$12,100	
Advertising expense	11,730	
Supplies expense	300	
Utilities expense	200	
Telephone expense	120	
Total expense		24,450
Net income		**$2,940**

Check Your Understanding

Write the completed sentences on a separate piece of paper.

1. The statement that shows the financial condition (wealth and claims on wealth) at a point in time is called the ·. Three change statements explain the changes in owner's equity and cash between two balance sheets. The first change statement explains the change in owner's equity caused by operations. This statement is called the ·. The net result of this statement flows into the ·, which explains all the changes in · · · · · · · · · · · · · · · · · · ·. The final statement change statement is the statement of · · · · · · · · · · · · · · · · · ·, which explains the changes in the · · · · · · · · · balance.

2. **Show how transactions affect the financial statements**

   a. Place the dollar amount of each transaction in the correct location(s) in the table below to show how each financial statement is affected by each transaction. To show negative amounts on the balance sheet, statement of owner's equity, and statement of cash flows, place amounts in parentheses ( ).
   b. Use the balance sheet asset and liability column totals to verify the correct final balance of owner's equity. Enter an amount in the balance sheet owner's equity column only as a total after you compute the final balance from the columns for the statement of owner's equity (item 14).
   c. Total the income statement columns to verify the amount of net income.
   d. Total the statement of cash flow columns to calculate the net change in the cash balance.

   (1) The owner invests $25,000 in his new business.
   (2) A $300 electric bill arrives and is paid.
   (3) The business performs $3,500 of services for a client, and client will pay later.
   (4) A client makes an advance payment of $2,000.
   (5) An advertising bill for $900 arrives and will be paid later.
   (6) $1,450 of supplies are purchased, and the bill will be paid later.
   (7) The business performs the services for the client who made the advance payment.
   (8) The owner withdraws $1,500 cash.
   (9) The business collects $2,000 from accounts receivable.
   (10) $300 of supplies are used.
   (11) Employee wages for this month are $2,900. Employees will be paid next week.
   (12) The employee wages in (11) are paid.
   (13) At the end of the period the net income is determined to be $1,100
   (14) The final balance of owner's equity is calculated from the statement of owner's equity, and this amount is placed on the balance sheet.

continued ▶

	Balance Sheet			Income Statement		Statement of Owner's Equity		Statement of Cash Flows	
	Asset	Liability	Owner's Equity	Revenue	Expense	Net Income/ Investment	(Net Loss/ Withdrawal)	Source of Cash	(Use of Cash)

Suggestion: Make copies of this page so you can use the problem more than once.

Answers

1. The statement that shows the financial condition (wealth) and claims on wealth at a point in time is called the balance sheet. Three change statements explain the changes in owner's equity and cash between two balance sheets. The first change statement explains the change in owner's equity caused by operations. This statement is called the income statement. The net result of this statement flows into the statement of owner's equity, which explains all the changes in owner's equity. The final statement is the statement of cash flows, which explains the changes in the cash balance.

2.

	Balance Sheet			Income Statement		Statement of Owner's Equity		Statement of Cash Flows	
	Asset	Liability	Owner's Equity	Revenue	Expense	Net Income/Investment	(Net Loss/Withdrawal)	Source of Cash	(Use of Cash)
(1)	$25,000					$25,000		$25,000	
(2)	(300)				$300				($300)
(3)	3,500			$3,500					
(4)	2,000	$2,000						2,000	
(5)		900			900				
(6)	1,450	1,450							
(7)		(2,000)		2,000					
(8)	(1,500)						($1,500)		(1,500)
(9)	2,000							2,000	
	(2,000)								
(10)	(300)				300				
(11)		2,900			2,900				
(12)	(2,900)	(2,900)							(2,900)
(13)						1,100			
(14)			$24,600						
	$26,950	$2,350	$24,600	$5,500	$4,400			$29,000	($4,700)

- The owner's equity is: $26,950 − $2,350 = $24,600. On the statement of owner's equity:
  $25,000 + $1,100 − $1,500 = $24,600
- The net income is: $5,500 − $4,400 = $1,100
- The change in cash is: $29,000 − $4,700 = $24,300 increase.

Detailed Examples of Owner's Equity Connections

Overview

The diagram on page 316 illustrates how two balance sheets are linked together. The statement of cash flows explains the change in cash. The income statement and statement of owner's equity together explain the change in the owner's equity.

In this section we focus on the details of how the income statement and statement of owner's equity explain the change in owner's equity. We will see how items on the income statement and statement of owner's equity affect the balance sheet. To do this, we examine one transaction at a time.

Balance Sheet Effects of Income Statement Items

The four basic types of changes in owner's equity—revenues and expenses (which are shown on the income statement) and investments and withdrawals (which are shown on the statement of owner's equity)—always affect either some asset or some liability on the balance sheet. To begin, we look at specific income statement transactions. The typical balance sheet effects are:

■ **Revenues increase owner's equity and . . .**

• Increase cash, or
• Increase accounts receivable, or
• Decrease unearned revenue (a liability).

■ **Expenses decrease owner's equity and . . .**

• Decrease cash, or
• Decrease other assets, or
• Increase accounts payable and other short-term liabilities.

Note: Technically, a revenue or expense can affect any asset or any liability. For example, a customer could pay us in gold nuggets or by reducing a long-term debt we owe to him. However, these other types of transactions are unusual and infrequent. For now we will focus on what we expect to see most often.

Our Example

We now look at a very simplified balance sheet of an imaginary company called Uncle Billy's Courier Service. To focus on the idea of how statements are connected, we look at transactions that happen over the period of just one day, December 23. For this example, you will see the changes recorded directly onto the financial statements.

Note: Individual transactions are not normally recorded directly onto financial statements. We are doing it here just for illustration. Also, to save space, descriptions are abbreviated.

Detailed Examples of Owner's Equity Connections, *continued*

Expense Decreases Cash

The first expense transaction of the day is a $2,000 cash payment to the landlord for the office rent. This is an operational transaction that appears as Rent Expense on the income statement and also causes cash to decrease. On the balance sheet, this asset decrease is not connected with any other asset or liability, so the owner's equity also decreases by $2,000 to $19,500.

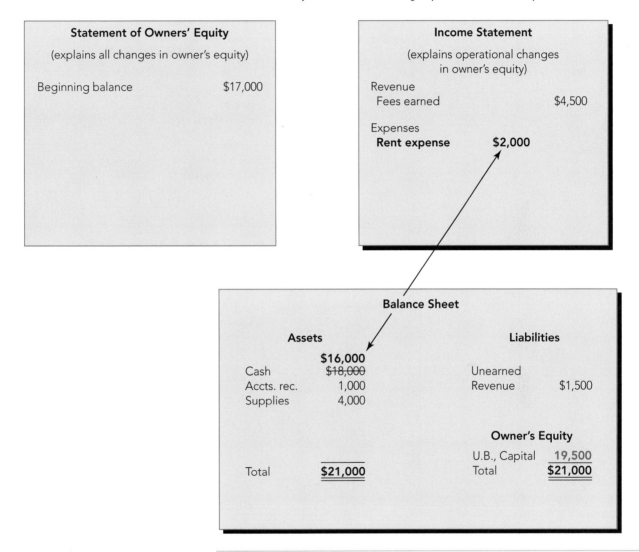

Using the Equation

The equation would show the changes as:

$$\downarrow A = L + \downarrow OE$$

continued ▶

Detailed Examples of Owner's Equity Connections, *continued*

Expense Decreases Other Assets

The next expense of the day for Uncle Billy's Courier Service happens when the business uses up $1,000 of the office supplies to prepare some packages for delivery. The decrease in Supplies is an operational transaction that appears as Supplies Expense on the income statement. On the balance sheet, this asset decrease is not connected with any other asset or liability, so the owner's equity also decreases by $1,000 to $18,500.

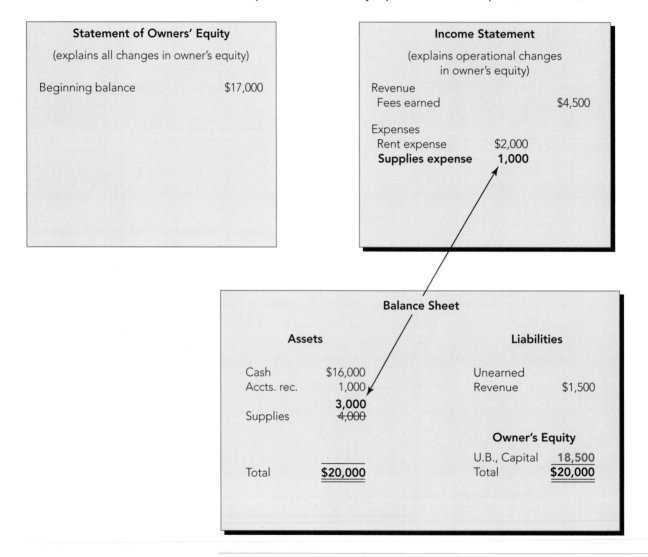

Statement of Owners' Equity

(explains all changes in owner's equity)

Beginning balance	$17,000

Income Statement

(explains operational changes in owner's equity)

Revenue		
Fees earned		$4,500
Expenses		
Rent expense	$2,000	
Supplies expense	**1,000**	

Balance Sheet

Assets			Liabilities	
Cash	$16,000		Unearned	
Accts. rec.	1,000		Revenue	$1,500
	3,000			
Supplies	~~4,000~~			
			Owner's Equity	
			U.B., Capital	18,500
Total	$20,000		Total	$20,000

Using the Equation

The equation would show the changes as:

$$\downarrow A = L + \downarrow OE$$

Detailed Examples of Owner's Equity Connections, *continued*

Owner's Withdrawal Decreases Cash

Finally, suppose that in the afternoon (quite a busy day), Uncle Billy decides that he needs $1,000 for personal reasons and withdraws the money from his business. On the balance sheet, this reduces cash and causes a decrease in the owner's equity, U.B., Capital.

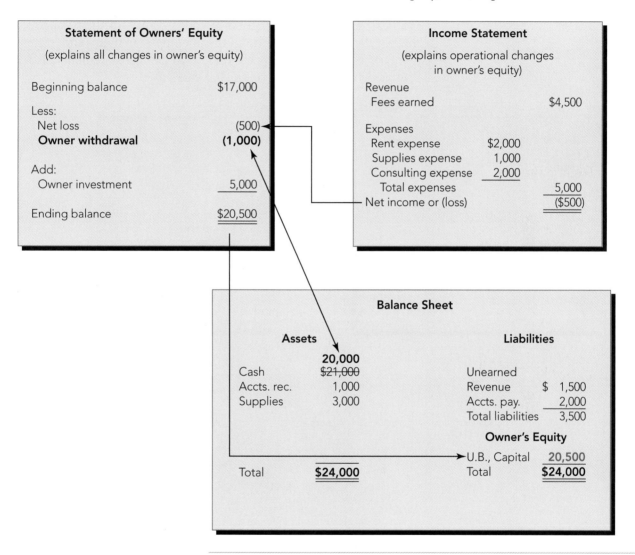

Using the Equation

The equation would show the changes as:

$$\downarrow A = L + \downarrow OE$$

continued ▶

Detailed Examples of Owner's Equity Connections, *continued*

Final Result

The result of the owner's investment and withdrawal actions is a $4,000 net increase in owner's equity to a final balance of $20,500. You can verify this on the balance sheet by subtracting the total liabilities of $3,500 from the total assets of $24,000.

You can see how the $20,500 of owner's equity on the balance sheet has been fully explained by both the income statement and statement of owner's equity. The items on these two change statements also affected both assets and liabilities on the balance sheet.

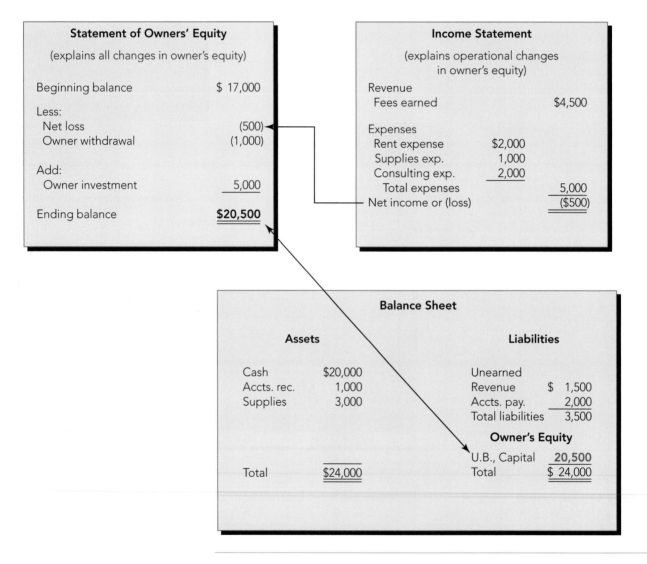

Detailed Examples of Owner's Equity Connections, *continued*

Summary

What you have seen are accurate, but simplified, examples of how individual owner's equity transactions connect three financial statements. But keep in mind that in "real life":

- Individual transaction data are never entered directly onto financial statements, as we did here. Instead, the data are first recorded and classified in special accounting records over a period of time. Then the data are summarized, and the summary totals are placed on the financial statements. In the next section, you will begin to do this for yourself.

- Financial statements are never prepared "moment by moment" for each individual transaction as we did here. This would be impossible and totally unnecessary (actually, crazy). Financial statements are normally prepared at useful intervals such as monthly, quarterly, or annually.

However, you would be perfectly correct to say that the summary totals used on financial statements consist of many individual transactions, and some of them are owner's equity transactions that form connections between the statements, as you have seen here.

Analyze, Don't Just Memorize

Occasionally students ask me this question: "Will you please just draw a picture of an income statement, statement of owner's equity, and balance sheet and then draw lines to show all the kinds of transactions that create links between the statements? Then we can memorize how all the items connect the statements."

I would love to do that. However, a really complete and accurate picture would be very confusing. There are so many different potential transactions connecting these statements that the picture would have lines going everywhere. It would look like a spaghetti dinner!

A much better idea is this:

1. *Learn the relationships between the statements.* This is what we have just finished doing. The illustration on page 320 and the table on the next page summarize these relationships.

2. *Learn to analyze each transaction.* This is what we did in Learning Goal 11. If you can analyze a transaction, you will be much clearer about its effects on the financial statements. You will not have to do much memorizing.

continued ▶

Detailed Examples of Owner's Equity Connections, *continued*

Summary Table

The following table summarizes how owner's equity transactions shown on the income statement and statement of owner's equity affect the balance sheet.

Change Statement		Balance Sheet	
Income Statement	**Statement of Owner's Equity**	**Effect**	**Example**
OWNER'S EQUITY IS INCREASED			
Revenue	Owner Investment	Assets ↑ or Liabilities ↓	■ Cash or A/R received when services are performed. (Revenue) ■ Owner invests cash in the business. (Owner investment) ■ Unearned revenue decreases when services are performed. (Revenue) ■ Owner personally pays business debts. (Owner investment)
OWNER'S EQUITY IS DECREASED			
Expense	Owner Withdrawal	Assets ↓ or Liabilities ↑	■ Cash is used to pay for repairs when completed. (Expense) ■ Supplies are used up. (Expense) ■ Owner takes cash from the business. (Owner withdrawal) ■ Repairs are done but will be paid later. (Expense) ■ Business incurs debt, but owner keeps the money. (Withdrawal—rare)

Could Other Change Statements be Created?

Sure! In addition to only explaining the changes in owner's equity or cash, you could design a statement to explain the changes in any other balance sheet item, such as Accounts Receivable, Inventory, Notes Payable, and so on. In fact, many companies keep informal internal records analyzing the changes in many balance sheet items (for example, Accounts Receivable and Inventory). However, these records are not prepared as formal financial statements because of time, cost, and other considerations.

Detailed Examples of Owner's Equity Connections, *continued*

TIP

Which statement should you prepare first? It is best to prepare the financial statements in the following order:

1. *Income statement*—because net income is used in the statement of owner's equity
2. *Statement of owner's equity*—because the ending balance of owner's equity is the owner's equity on the balance sheet
3. *Balance sheet*—because balance sheets are needed to prepare the statement of cash flows
4. *Statement of cash flows*

QUICK REVIEW

- There are four general-purpose financial statements:

  - Income statement
  - Statement of owner's equity
  - Balance sheet
  - Statement of cash flows

- The balance sheet is a statement of condition at a point in time. The other statements are all "change" statements. They summarize the kinds of transactions that caused changes in either the cash balance or the owner's equity balance on the balance sheet.

- Because the change statements explain the differences between two balance sheets, the change statements can be viewed as the "links" between one balance sheet and the next.

- The connection between a change statement and any other financial statement is called "articulation."

- The kinds of transactions that create connections from a prior capital balance to the next capital balance are:

  - Revenues
  - Expenses
  - Investments
  - Withdrawals

PRACTICE   **Learning Goal 17**   *Solutions are in the disk at the back of the book and at: www.worthyjames.com*

Learning Goal 17 is about comparing, contrasting, and connecting financial statements. Use these questions and problems to practice what you have learned.

Multiple Choice
Select the best answer.

1. If revenue of $1,000 is earned and received in cash, then
   a. assets will increase and revenue will appear on the statement of owner's equity.
   b. assets will decrease and revenue will appear on the statement of owner's equity.
   c. assets will decrease and expense will appear on the statement of owner's equity.
   d. assets will increase and revenue will appear on the income statement.
2. If the owner withdraws $1,000 in cash, then
   a. assets will decrease and expense will appear on the statement of owner's equity.
   b. assets will decrease and revenue will appear on the statement of owner's equity.
   c. assets will decrease and drawing will appear on the statement of owner's equity.
   d. assets will decrease and drawing will appear on the income statement.
3. An income statement
   a. details all the changes in owner's equity.
   b. shows total assets, liabilities, and owner's equity.
   c. shows the revenues and expenses at a specific date.
   d. none of the above.
4. If a telephone expense of $500 appears on the income statement, then
   a. assets have decreased and expenses will appear on the statement of owner's equity.
   b. either assets have increased and/or liabilities have decreased.
   c. either assets have decreased and/or liabilities have increased.
   d. none of the above.
5. If Service Fees Earned of $10,000 appears on the income statement, then
   a. assets have increased and expenses will decrease on the income statement.
   b. either assets have increased and/or liabilities have decreased.
   c. either assets have decreased and/or liabilities have increased.
   d. none of the above.
6. Four kinds of transactions affect owner's equity, but the statement of owner's equity only shows three change items: (1) net income/(loss); (2) owner's investments; and (3) owner's drawings. This is because
   a. owner's drawings need to be considered as an expense.
   b. owner's investments are never counted as a change.
   c. showing four changes would be an overstatement.
   d. the revenues and expenses are combined into one number.
7. If accounts receivable have increased by $1,500, then most likely
   a. the owner has invested in the business.
   b. revenue has been earned.
   c. expenses have been incurred.
   d. none of the above.

8. One balance sheet prepared on March 31 is linked by the other financial statements to the next balance sheet prepared on April 30 because
   a. the statement of cash flows for April explains the difference between the two cash balances.
   b. revenues and expenses on the April income statement affect the owner's equity on the balance sheet.
   c. the drawings and owner investments on the April statement of owner's equity affect the owner's equity on the balance sheet.
   d. all of the above.

9. The Mikado Tea Shop income statement for the month of October shows a net loss of $14,000. There were no withdrawals or investments. Which of the following is *not* true?
   a. The statement of owner's equity will show a decrease item of $14,000.
   b. Total assets on the balance sheet have decreased and/or total liabilities have increased.
   c. Expenses have exceeded revenues.
   d. The change in the cash balance can be determined from this information.

10. The statement of cash flows is primarily
    a. a statement of condition.
    b. a statement of equity.
    c. a statement of change.
    d. none of the above.

11. The three types of activities that change the cash balance are
    a. operating, investing, and withdrawing.
    b. operating, recording, and financing.
    c. operating, investing, and financing.
    d. none of the above.

12. You are interested in investing in a company. Which financial statement(s) would you use to analyze the profitability of the company?
    a. statement of owner's equity or statement of cash flows
    b. statement of owner's equity and income statement
    c. income statement
    d. balance sheet

13. You are a supplier of auto parts. Kansas City Company wants to make a large purchase from you on account, with payment in 30 days. Which financial statement(s) would you use to find out how much debt Kansas City Company already has coming due in the near future and how much available cash it has?
    a. statement of cash flows
    b. statement of owner's equity and income statement
    c. income statement
    d. balance sheet

14. Financial statements are usually prepared in the following order:
    a. balance sheet, income statement, statement of cash flows, owner's equity statement
    b. income statement, balance sheet, statement of cash flows, owner's equity statement
    c. income statement, owner's equity statement, balance sheet, statement of cash flows
    d. The order varies among accountants.

15. On an income statement, the net loss is $7,000 and total expenses are $50,000. Total revenue
    a. is $43,000.
    b. is $57,000.
    c. is greater than $57,000.
    d. cannot be determined with this information.

16. On the statement of owner's equity for Pettigrew Company, the ending balance of owner's equity is $90,000, the net loss was $10,000, owner's drawings were $12,000, and the owner's investment was $5,000. What is the beginning balance of owner's equity?
    a. $107,000
    b. $100,000
    c. $73,000
    d. none of the above

17. During the month of October, total assets of Macon Company increased by $50,000 and total liabilities increased by $30,000. If the owner had invested $5,000 but did not withdraw anything, the income statement will show
    a. a net income of $15,000.
    b. a net income of $20,000.
    c. a net loss of $20,000.
    d. a net income of $80,000.

18. A balance sheet is often called a(n)
    a. statement of cash flows.
    b. P & L statement.
    c. statement of position.
    d. operating statement.

19. The financial statements that show change in a business are
    a. the balance sheet, the income statement, and the statement of owner's equity.
    b. the balance sheet, the income statement, and the statement of cash flows.
    c. the income statement, statement of owner's equity, and the statement of cash flows.
    d. the income statement and the balance sheet.

20. Which financial statement is similar to a "flash photograph" of a business?
    a. the balance sheet
    b. the income statement
    c. the statement of cash flows
    d. the statement of owner's equity

Discussion Questions and Brief Exercises for Learning Goals 12–17

1. What is the correct format for writing a title to a financial statement?

2. Explain how the date should be written for each of these financial statements: income statement, statement of owner's equity, and balance sheet. Give examples for the year that ends on December 31, 2008.

3. What are the two categories of items that appear on an income statement? Explain what they mean.

4. What are the three categories of items that appear on a balance sheet? Explain what they mean.

5. What is the purpose of an income statement? What does it explain?

6. What is the purpose of a statement of owner's equity? What does it explain?

7. What is the purpose of a balance sheet? What does it explain?

8. What is the purpose of a statement of cash flows? What does it explain?

9. Your study group partner Rasheed Marshall is preparing for an exam in another accounting class. He wants to make sure that he understands how the income statement, statement of owner's equity, and balance sheet relate to each other, and if some of the numbers on one statement appear on other statements. What would you say to him in the study group?

10. Fall River Consulting Services Company finished a job for a client, who paid the company $5,000 as soon as the job was completed. What are the two effects on the income statement, the two effects on the statement of owner's equity, and the two effects on the balance sheet?

11. Lowell Internet Services Company used up $900 of supplies in its operations during the month of June. What are the two effects on the income statement, the two effects on the statement of owner's equity, and the two effects on the balance sheet?

12. On September 30, month-end, the owner's equity on the balance sheet of Worcester Company was $250,000. The statement of owner's equity showed a September 1 balance of $259,000. The owner withdrew $15,000 cash during the month but made no investments. What is the net income that should appear on the income statement?

13. Which of the following would be a "change statement"? Which would be a "condition statement"? (1) balance sheet, (2) income statement, (3) statement of cash flows, (4) or statement of owner's equity.

14. Identify four important qualities of information on financial statements. Which two are most important?

PRACTICE   Learning Goal 17, continued

Solutions are in the disk at the back of the book and at: www.worthyjames.com

Reinforcement Problems

LG 17-1. Which statement is it on? Use a blank sheet of paper to complete the table. The following table shows items that occur in the four financial statements. Place a "✓" in the correct space to identify which financial statement the item appears on. The financial statements are for the month ending May 31 and the condition as of May 31 of the Bill Jones Company. Use the first item as an example.

Item	Balance Sheet	Income Statement	Statement of Owner's Equity	Statement of Cash Flows
Office Supplies	✓			
Service Revenue	(Reminder: Use a separate sheet of paper to complete the table.)			
Accounts Payable				
Net Loss				
Withdrawals (Drawing)				
Financing Activities				
Bill Jones, Capital—May 31				
Wages Expense				
Net Income				
Accounts Receivable				
Operating Activities				
Investing Activities				
Rent Expense				
Bill Jones, Capital—May 1				
Unearned Revenue				
Wages Payable				
Cash				
Prepaid Rent Expense				

LG 17-2. Identifying where items appear on the financial statements. Use a blank sheet of paper to complete the table. Place a "✓" in the correct box to indicate where on either the income statement or the balance sheet an item appears. Use the first item as an example.

	Income Statement		Balance Sheet		
	Revenue	Expense	Asset	Liability	Capital
a. Cash			✓		
b. Accounts Payable	(Reminder: Use a separate sheet of paper to complete the table.)				
c. Interest Revenue					
d. Interest Receivable					
e. Fees Earned					
f. Unearned Revenue					
g. Notes Receivable					
h. Wages Payable					
i. Office Supplies					
j. Office Equipment					
k. Office Supplies Expense					
l. Prepaid Insurance					
m. Dee Markowitz, Capital					

LG 17-3. Review: Identify which transactions affect owner's equity. Use a separate sheet of paper to complete the table. In the table below, indicate whether each transaction increases owner's equity (**+**), decreases owner's equity (**–**), or has no effect on owner's equity (**NE**). Use the first transaction as an example.

Transaction	Effect
a. The owner invests $7,500 in his business.	+
b. The business earns service revenue and receives $500 cash.	(Reminder: Use a separate sheet of paper to complete the table.)
c. The business buys $100 of office supplies on account.	
d. The business buys $2,000 of equipment for cash.	
e. The business pays rent expense of $1,500.	
f. The business earns service revenue for $1,000 on account (accounts receivable).	
g. The business pays the $100 account payable for the purchases of supplies.	
h. The owner withdraws $200 cash.	
i. The business collects $1,000 cash from the account receivable.	

PRACTICE   Learning Goal 17, continued

Solutions are in the disk at the back of the book and at: www.worthyjames.com

LG 17-4. Explain the effects of transactions on financial statements.

  a. Place the dollar amount of each transaction in the correct location(s) in the table on page 347 to show how each financial statement will be affected by each transaction. To show negative amounts on the balance sheet, statement of owner's equity, and statement of cash flows, place amounts in parentheses ( ).

  b. Total the balance sheet asset and liability columns to verify the correct final balance of owner's equity. Use the owner's equity column in the balance sheet only after you compute the final balance from the statement of owner's equity (item 16).

  c. Total the income statement columns to verify the amount of net income.

  d. Total the statement of cash flow columns to calculate the net change in the cash balance.

Suggestion: You may want to practice this problem more than once. Make a copy of the table on page 347 or use the blank worksheet template in the disk at the back of the book.

Transactions:

  (1) The owner invests $40,000 cash in her new business.
  (2) $1,800 of supplies were purchased and the bill will be paid later.
  (3) The business paid $1,100 for a one-year insurance policy.
  (4) The business performed $3,300 of services for a client on account.
  (5) A client makes an advance payment of $2,850.
  (6) The business performed $1,650 of services for a client, and the client paid cash.
  (7) The business received a $700 bill for repairs expense. The bill will be paid later.
  (8) A $200 bill for telephone expense is received and is paid immediately.
  (9) $820 of supplies are used up.
  (10) The owner withdraws $2,100 cash.
  (11) The business collects $1,700 from customers on account.
  (12) The business performed services and earned 40% of the advance payment received in (5).
  (13) The repair bill in (7) is paid.
  (14) Employee wages for the month are $3,100 and are not paid immediately.
  (15) At the end of the period, the net income is determined to be $1,270.
  (16) The final balance of owner's equity is calculated from the statement of owner's equity, and this amount is placed on the balance sheet.

LG 17-4, *continued*

	Balance Sheet			Income Statement		Statement of Owner's Equity		Statement of Cash Flows	
	Asset	Liability	Owner's Equity	Revenue	Expense	Net Income/ Investment	(Net Loss/ Withdrawal)	Source of Cash	(Use of Cash)
(1)									
(2)									
(3)									
(4)									
(5)									
(6)									
(7)									
(8)									
(9)									
(10)									
(11)									
(12)									
(13)									
(14)									
(15)									
(16)									

LG 17-5. **You be the teacher—grade the financial statements!** You have just given a weekly quiz and asked the students to prepare financial statements for the month of November 2008. Here is a paper from one of your students who has just taken the quiz. Each mistake is minus one point. The three statements together are worth 30 points. Grade the exam. What score would you give? (Mistakes are from actual exams.)

Moorpark Repair Services
Balance Sheet
November 30, 2008

Assets		Debts	
Cash	$10,540	Accounts payable	$ 2,000
Equipment	$15,440	Wages payable	$540
Supplies	$95	Total	$ 2,540
Accounts receivable	$1,050		
		Owner's Equity	
		Diane Smith, Capitol	$24,485
Total	$27,385	Total liabilities and owner's equity	$27,385

Moorpark Repair Services
Income Statement
November 30, 2008

Revenues		
Service revenues	$44,200	
Unearned revenues	3,500	
Total revenues		47,700
Expenses		
Wages expense	$24,100	
Rent expense	4,950	
Prepaid expenses	4,100	
Telephone expenses	290	
Total expenses		33,440
Profit		$14,260

Moorpark Repair Services
Statement of Owner's Equity
For the Period Ending November 30, 2008

Diane Smith, Capital, November 1		$ 6,325
Add: Owner investment	$ 5,000	
Net income	14,620	
		19,620
Less: Withdrawals		1,000
Diane Smith, Capital, November 30		$24,945

LG 17-6. Calculate missing financial statement balances using information from other financial statements. For each of the four separate businesses below, calculate the missing amounts for 2008 on a separate piece of paper.

	Mheta Tarsal Medical School	Lynne Guinni Cooking College	Pop Flies Baseball Clinic	Manuel Dexterity Acting Academy
JANUARY 1, 2008				
Assets	$ 75,000	$100,000	g. _____	$120,000
Liabilities	$ 15,000	$ 20,000	$ 15,000	j. _____
Owner's Equity	a. _____	d. _____	h. _____	k. _____
DECEMBER 31, 2008				
Assets	$120,000	$112,000	$ 51,000	l. _____
Liabilities	$ 40,000	e. _____	$ 1,000	$ 50,000
Owner's Equity	b. _____	f. _____	i. _____	$ 22,000
CHANGE IN OWNER'S EQUITY DURING 2008				
Owner Investment	c. _____	$ 12,000	$ –0–	$ 10,000
Revenues	$ 52,000	$ 82,000	$ 49,000	$ 98,000
Expenses	$ 35,000	$ 71,000	$ 22,000	$178,000
Withdrawals	$ 5,000	$ 3,000	$ 8,000	$ –0–

LG 17-7. Prepare financial statements. Using the information below for the Wendy Monahan Real Estate Company, prepare an income statement and statement of owner's equity for the year ended December 31, 200X, and a report form balance sheet as of December 31, 200X.

Computer Equipment	$9,000	Service Revenue	$221,800
Unearned Revenue	3,200	Wages Payable	7,500
Office Furniture	5,750	Rent Expense	24,000
Notes Payable	25,000	Prepaid Insurance	3,660
Insurance Expense	780	Wages Expense	108,000
Land	185,200	Wendy Monahan, Withdrawals	55,000
Accounts Payable	24,220	Interest Expense	2,100
Office Supplies	2,000	Accounts Receivable	47,500
Cash	37,100	Telephone Expense	2,450
Travel Expense	650		
Wendy Monahan Capital, January 1	183,470	During the year the owner made an $18,000 investment in the business.	

LG 17-8. Prepare financial statements—use them for a decision. Robert Jimenez started his real estate sales business on January 1, 2008 with an investment of $10,000. At year-end on December 31, 2008, Robert gives you a listing of the assets and liabilities as well as the revenues and expenses for the year. Robert withdrew $17,000 during the year. On a separate piece of paper, prepare an income statement and statement of owner's equity for the year ended December 31, 2008, and a balance sheet as of December 31, 2008 in good form.

Robert wants to take the financial statements to his bank to apply for a business loan, but he isn't sure what the loan officer will think of them. Based on the information in the financial statements, do you think that Robert's business will be able to borrow money? How much do you think you would lend Robert if you were the banker?

Cash	$38,000	Unearned Fees Revenue	$3,800
Notes Payable	10,000	Travel Expense	2,050
Accounts Receivable	12,000	Accounts Payable	1,150
Fees Earned	84,000	Utilities Expense	1,000
Prepaid Insurance Expense	2,500	Insurance Expense	3,000
Rent Expense	18,400	Equipment	15,000

LG 17-9. Prepare financial statements and determine missing item on the statement of owner's equity. Listed below are amounts of various financial statement items for the Sanderson Ecology Services Company. From the amounts listed, prepare an income statement and a statement of owner's equity for the year ended December 31, 2008 and a balance sheet as of year-end. Dave Sanderson opened the firm with an investment of $250,000 on January 1. He cannot remember the amount of his drawings. Please tell him.

Service Fees	$122,500	Cash	$199,300
Wages Expense	104,300	Accounts Receivable	43,080
Rent Expense	16,500	Supplies	3,800
Utilities Expense	1,400	Office Equipment	25,600
Supplies Expense	750	Prepaid Insurance	1,500
Advertising Expense	3,300	Accounts Payable	23,750
Travel Expense	8,150	Unearned Service Fees	12,300

9. Paseo Rancho Castilla Company owns several stores that all together cost $800,000. A buyer calls the company and offers $1,000,000 for the three stores. The company hires an appraiser who says the stores are worth $1,300,000. Based on this information, the company
    a. should make no changes to its balance sheet.
    b. should change the assets to $1,300,000.
    c. should change the assets to $1,000,000.
    d. none of the above.

10. Which of the following qualitative characteristics are most essential to financial statements?
    a. relevance
    b. reliability
    c. both (a) and (b)
    d. none of the above

11. "Underlying Assumptions" refers to
    a. the specific GAAP rules that accountants use in their daily practice of accounting.
    b. limitations in the way GAAP is properly applied.
    c. the annual decisions by the FASB.
    d. the conditions that must exist in any enterprise if GAAP accounting is to be applied.

12. An American company and a French company both show approximately $1,000,000 of net income.
    a. The true increase in the owners' wealth would be the same for both companies.
    b. The net income of the French company is probably incorrect.
    c. The net income of the French company probably cannot be measured according to GAAP rules.
    d. GAAP rules probably apply to both companies.

13. A cost is
    a. the amount of money spent on something.
    b. the amount of resources given up to acquire something.
    c. an expense.
    d. a decrease in owner's equity.

14. FASB refers to
    a. the Financial Assets Securities Board.
    b. the Financial Accounting Standards Board.
    c. the Financial Auditing Standards Board.
    d. none of the above.

15. An example of a stakeholder would be
    a. the owner.
    b. the customer.
    c. the financial analyst.
    d. all of the above.

16. "Operating guidelines" refers to
    a. broad GAAP and specific GAAP.
    b. assumptions, constraints, and GAAP.
    c. when to identify and record expenses.
    d. all of the above.

17. A generally accepted accounting principle is
    a. a standard or rule that guides accountants on how to do something.
    b. a required condition that must exist for accounting to function.
    c. an objective of financial reporting.
    d. a limitation on the way certain rules can be applied.

18. New Orleans Enterprises buys $10,000 of equipment. The equipment normally sells for $14,000, but New Orleans Company does not record this amount. This is an example of the
    a. matching principle.
    b. going-concern principle.
    c. full disclosure principle.
    d. cost principle.

19. Shreveport Company signed a contract to sell $50,000 of merchandise to a customer. The merchandise has been identified and packaged, and it is ready to ship. The accountant for the company records $50,000 of revenue. This is an error in applying which basic accounting principle?
    a. the revenue recognition principle
    b. the matching principle
    c. the reliability principle
    d. the cost principle

20. Baton Rouge partnership bought some equipment last month. The accountant cannot find an invoice, so she calls the seller. The seller of the equipment tells her that the equipment sold for $25,000. The accountant does not use this information right away. Instead, she locates a canceled check. This is an example of applying which accounting principle?
    a. the revenue recognition principle
    b. the matching principle
    c. the reliability principle
    d. the cost principle

21. The primary reason that the cost principle is used is because it
    a. results in reliable numbers.
    b. keeps the balance sheet at current values.
    c. ensures that net income will be correctly reported.
    d. does not prematurely report income.

22. The primary reason that the matching principle is used is because it
    a. results in reliable numbers.
    b. keeps the balance sheet at current values.
    c. ensures that expenses are recorded in the correct periods.
    d. does not prematurely report income.

Discussion Questions and Brief Exercises for Learning Goal 18

1. What does "GAAP" stand for? What does GAAP refer to?

2. Describe the two general categories of GAAP.

3. Where does GAAP come from?

4. What are the three objectives of financial reporting? Give some examples of how financial reporting meets these objectives.

5. What is the cost principle? Identify the two rules that are applied for this principle. What are the advantages and disadvantages of the cost principle?

6. At what value would you record each of the following transactions?

   ▪ Equipment is purchased for $900. The next day the buyer discovers that another dealer is selling the same equipment for $750. A month later the equipment is being sold for $1,200.
   ▪ A city donates land to a corporation so it will relocate to the area.

CUMULATIVE TEST   Learning Goals 10–18, continued

27. After a transaction is analyzed, the recording process requires that
    a. every item in the accounting equation must show some change.
    b. every item affected by the transaction must show either an increase or decrease.
    c. every item affected by the transaction must show either an increase or decrease, and a new balance.
    d. none of the above.
28. Which of the following is true?
    a. The financial information in the balance sheet, income statement, and statement of owner's equity is for a specific period of time and explains changes.
    b. The financial information in the balance sheet, income statement, and statement of owner's equity is for a specific point in time and shows condition.
    c. The financial information in the balance sheet is for a specific date, and the information in the income statement and statement of owner's equity is for a specific period of time.
    d. The financial information in the income statement is for a specific date, and the information in the balance sheet and statement of owner's equity is for a specific period of time.
29. The revenue recognition principle
    a. requires that revenue be recorded only when it is earned.
    b. requires that revenue must be recorded as soon as the cash is received.
    c. is an example of a narrow or specific GAAP principle rather than a broad one.
    d. is an example of articulation between financial statements.
30. The ultimate objective described by the conceptual framework is to
    a. simplify financial statements.
    b. provide useful information that improves decision making.
    c. increase the reliability of audits.
    d. minimize taxes that are paid by businesses.
31. The balance sheet of Lehigh Company included the following balances:

    Cash ?   Accounts receivable $3,000
    Accounts payable $18,000   Land $35,000
    Supplies $1,000   Robert Fair, capital ?
    Unearned revenue $4,000

    If the balance of Robert Fair, Capital was $55,000 then what was the balance of cash?
    a. $34,000   c. $55,000
    b. $16,000   d. none of the above
32. Which of the following items does not belong on the income statement?
    a. insurance expense   c. miscellaneous expense
    b. service revenue earned   d. accounts payable
33. Which of the following items does not belong on the statement of owner's equity?
    a. net income   c. service revenue earned
    b. net loss   d. prior period ending balance of owner's equity

34. Richard Gillis Company had these balances at the dates indicated:

Cash (March 1) $?

Cash (March 31) $10,000

Accounts Receivable (March 1) $5,000

Accounts Receivable (March 31) $3,000

Supplies (March 1) $1,000

Supplies (March 31) $1,500

Accounts Payable (March 1) $2,000

Accounts Payable (March 31) $2,500

Richard Gillis, Capital (March 1) $?

Richard Gillis, Capital (March 31) $?

Gillis Company had a net loss of $5,000 during March and no withdrawals, but the owner invested $2,000 during March. The correct owner's equity balances for March 1 and March 31 are

a. March 1: $6,000   March 31: $14,500

b. March 1: $12,000   March 31: $15,000

c. March 1: $9,000   March 31: $12,000

d. March 1: $15,000   March 31: $12,000

35. Which financial statement shows the liabilities?

a. income statement   c. both (a) and (b)

b. balance sheet   d. statement of owner's equity

36. The key part of the analysis step in the accounting process is

a. classification.   c. timing.

b. valuation.   d. all of the above.

CUMULATIVE TEST SOLUTIONS   Learning Goals 10–18

Multiple Choice

1. c   2. d   Supplies increase by $3,000 and Accounts Payable increase by $3,000.
3. c   These are the two most important qualitative characteristics that make information useful, although there are other characteristics as well.   4. a
5. a   Using the income statement formula, Revenues – Expenses = Net income/(loss): Revenues – 15,000 = –10,000. Therefore, Revenues = 5,000.
6. d   ($20,200 – $7,900 = $12,300 decrease)
7. c   Using the formula for the statement of owner's equity, which explains all the changes in the capital balance: beginning balance + net income/(loss) + investments – withdrawals = ending balance. Therefore: 31,800 + **X** + 0 – 15,000 = 10,000. X = –6,800 (a net loss).
8. d   For (a), the item is the ending balance of owner's equity; for (b), the item is net income/(loss); for (c), the item is the ending cash balance.
9. d   10. b   11. a   12. b   13. c   14. a
15. d   The balance sheet shows assets, liabilities, and owner's equity.
16. c   Only the annual report conforms to GAAP and has management discussion and analysis.
17. a   18. a   Using up assets in operations is an expense, and this decreases the owner's claim.
19. b   20. c   Same transactions and ending balances—the beginning balances must be the same! For any item you can always use the formula: beginning balance + increases – decreases = ending balance, and then solve for the missing item. Beginning balance + 4,600 – 1,350 = 11,200. Beginning balance = 7,950.
21. a   22. d   23. c   Cash is an asset and would be on the balance sheet. *Unearned* revenue is a liability and would be on the balance sheet. *Prepaid* insurance expense is an asset and would be on the balance sheet. Liabilities would be on the balance sheet.
24. b   You can visualize the statement of owner's equity, or you can use the formula for the statement of owner's equity, which is faster. To visualize beginning balance: $12,500 *plus* owner's investments of $2,000 *plus* net income of ? (or minus net loss of ?) *less* owner's drawing of $1,000 equals the ending balance of $10,000. Putting the data into a familiar format may be easier, like this:

Beginning balance	$12,500
Add: Owner's investment	2,000
Net income (or loss)	?
Less: Owner's drawing	1,000
Ending balance	$10,000

Or, you can use a formula:
$12,500 + $2,000 + **X** – $1,000 = $10,000.
X = –$3,500 (a net loss).

25. d   26. c   If total assets increase but total liabilities do not change, owner's equity must have gone up. Only three possible items on the statement of owner's equity can explain the change: net income/(loss), investments, and drawing. Loss and drawing did not occur.
27. c   28. c   29. a   30. b
31. d   Total equities are: $55,000 + $4,000 + $18,000 = $77,000. Therefore, $77,000 – $1,000 – $3,000 – $35,000 = $38,000 cash balance.
32. d   33. c
34. d   First, determine the March 31 owner's capital and then use the formula for the statement of owner's equity, which explains all the changes in owner's equity, to work back to the beginning balance. This question should remind you that both the income statement and statement of owner's equity link the owner's equity balances between balance sheets. March 31: Total assets $14,500 – $2,500 liabilities = $12,000 owner's equity. Using the formula in the statement of owner's equity: **X** – $5,000 + $2,000 = $12,000. X = $15,000 beginning balance of owner's equity.
35. b   36. d

HELP TABLE — Identify Your Strengths and Weaknesses

The questions in this test cover the nine learning goals of Sections III and IV. After you have circled the number of each question that you missed, look at the table below.

Go to the first learning goal category in the table: "Explain the Accounting Process." The second column in the table shows which questions on the test covered this learning goal. Look on the test to see if you circled numbers 1, 17, 19, or 36. How many did you miss? Write this number in the "How Many Missed?" column. Repeat this process for each of the remaining learning goal categories in the table.

If you *miss* **two** *or more questions* for any learning goal, you need more practice in that learning goal and you need to *review*. The last column shows you where to read and practice so you can improve your score.

Some learning goal categories have more questions because you need to be especially well prepared in these areas. More questions means your performance must be better.

Learning Goal	Questions	How many missed?	Material begins on . . .
SECTION III			
10. Explain the Accounting Process	1, 17, 19, 36		page 217
11. Begin to Record	2, 18, 20, 27		page 235
SECTION IV			
12. Describe the Financial Statements	3, 16, 21		page 278
13. Identify and Prepare an Income Statement*	5, 14, 23, 32		page 286
14. Identify and Prepare a Statement of Owner's Equity*	7, 13, 24, 33		page 293
15. Identify and Prepare a Balance Sheet*	4, 15, 22, 31		page 300
16. Identify the Statement of Cash Flows	6, 12, 25		page 307
17. Compare, Contrast, and Connect All the Financial Statements	8, 11, 26, 28, 34, 35		page 314
18. Describe the Conceptual Framework of Accounting	9, 10, 29, 30		page 355

* For Learning Goals 13, 14, and 15, you should also practice preparing a balance sheet, an income statement, and a statement of owner's equity on a blank piece of paper. Use problems in any book for which you also have a solution. (You do not have to prepare a statement of cash flows, but you should be able to identify one and understand what it does.)

Using a Basic Accounting System

OVERVIEW

What this section does	This section shows you how to use a traditional accounting system.
Use this section if . . .	. . . you want to learn about a traditional accounting system. This includes debits and credits, journals, ledgers, trial balance, and the accounting cycle.
Do not use this section if . . .	. . . you are not clear about how to analyze a transaction (see Section II starting on page 76), or
	. . . debits and credits have already given you a lot of trouble. Study Section III first (starting on page 216), and then return to this section.

LEARNING GOALS

LEARNING GOALS

| LEARNING GOAL 19 | # Explain the Five Kinds of Information |

Overview

Introduction

In this section, you are introduced to the basic components of a traditional, general-purpose accounting system. The ultimate purpose of every accounting system is to provide useful information to decision makers. To do this, five particular kinds of information arrangements are always necessary.

These five kinds of information arrangements are what every general-purpose accounting system must supply to users. Everything that you learn in the rest of this book is a part of these five information arrangements. Learning Goal 19 introduces you to these five arrangements.

Note: If you need to know more about accounting systems, we expand our discussion of accounting systems in Volume 2.

In Learning Goal 19, you will find:

Review

Describe Financial Condition

*Visualizing the
Financial Condition
of a Business*

In Section I through Section III, you learned how to see the basic financial condition of all businesses. The condition of any business can be shown as a picture that is based on the accounting equation. This equation is: Assets = Liabilities + Owner's Equity. The financial picture of any business looks like this:

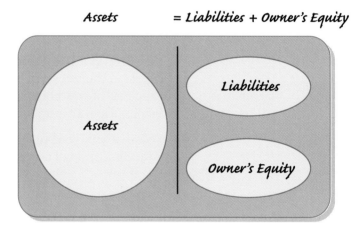

What the picture and the equation both show is that the value of the assets, which is the wealth of a business, is claimed first by creditors and then by the owner.

In Section III, you learned how to record changes in the picture. You learned that we can show the *changes*, called "transactions," in the condition of a business directly in the picture or in the equation. For example, if we wanted to show a business buying $5,000 of equipment by paying $1,000 cash and signing a $4,000 promissory note, we could show:

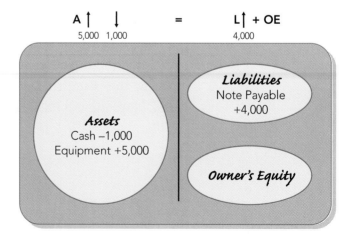

Describe Financial Condition, *continued*

Use a Table to Show Changes

However, a more efficient way to show the changes (transactions) is to use the accounting equation to create a table. We use the table to record all the changes in the individual items in the equation. We can create separate columns for all the items in the accounting equation and record the changes directly in the columns. For example, suppose the Nevada Company has recorded all its transactions in this way for the week beginning May 2. You could prepare a table like this:

	Assets				= Liabilities + Owner's Equity	
Week of May 2	Cash	Accounts Receivable	Supplies	Equipment	Note Payable	C. Goldman, Capital
5/2 Balance	17,300	4,500	900	12,000	10,000	24,700
5/4 Collection	+800	−800				
5/5 Revenue		+1,000				+1,000
5/7 Buy supplies	−400		+400			
5/7 Revenue	+2,000					+2,000

On May 8, the Nevada Company recorded the purchase of $5,000 of equipment by paying $1,000 cash and signing a $4,000 note payable. It would look like this:

	Assets				= Liabilities + Owner's Equity	
Week of May 2	Cash	Accounts Receivable	Supplies	Equipment	Note Payable	C. Goldman, Capital
5/2 Balance	17,300	4,500	900	12,000	10,000	24,700
5/4 Collection	+800	−800				
5/5 Revenue		+1,000				+1,000
5/7 Buy supplies	−400		+400			
5/7 Revenue	+2,000					+2,000
5/8 Buy equipment	*−1,000*			*+5,000*	*+4,000*	
5/8 Balance	18,700	4,700	1,300	17,000	14,000	27,700

continued ▶

Describe Financial Condition, *continued*

An Improvement: Separate Columns for Increases and Decreases

Finally, we decided that we could improve this method by using a separate increase and decrease column for each item. Separate increase and decrease columns make it much easier to see all the increases and decreases for each element in the accounting equation. No "+" or "−" signs are required. Also, this is what is actually done in practice and what we practiced in Learning Goal 11.

Because assets are on the left side of the equation, we agree to make left-side columns positive for assets. Because liabilities and owner's equity are on the right side of the equation, we agree to make right-side columns positive for liabilities and owner's equity. This is the usual accounting custom.

If we omit the explanation column to save space, the Nevada Company record of transactions will now look like this (beginning and ending balances are on May 2 and May 8):

	Assets								=	Liabilities + Owner's Equity			
	Cash		Accounts Receivable		Supplies		Equipment			Note Payable		C. Goldman, Capital	
	Increase	Decrease	Increase	Decrease	Increase	Decrease	Increase	Decrease		Decrease	Increase	Decrease	Increase
5/2	bal. **17,300**		bal. **4,500**		bal. **900**		bal. **12,000**				bal. **10,000**		bal. **24,700**
5/4	800			800									
5/5			1,000										1,000
5/7		400			400								
5/7	2,000												2,000
5/8		1,000					5,000				4,000		
5/8	bal. **18,700**		bal. **4,700**		bal. **1,300**		bal. **17,000**				bal. **14,000**		bal. **27,700**

The Five Data Arrangements

Overview

Transaction Data Are Important

Transaction data are important. The data are the source of all financial information. Transaction data explain and verify changes in the business.

The way data are organized and presented can make a tremendous difference in the efficiency of a business. Therefore, data must be organized to show in the clearest possible way the kind of information that a business will need.

Even when we use computers to electronically process information, the human brain still needs to see the final results presented in a clear, easy-to-use, and well-organized way.

Five Data Arrangements Are Necessary

Accountants, after many years of practice, discovered that transaction data must be arranged in a way that meets five basic information requirements. Look again at the table on page 388 showing the transactions of the Nevada Company. The information is arranged in a way that meets the five requirements presented below.

1. Find a Transaction by Date

Chronological Listing

To easily locate a transaction by date, there must be a *chronological listing of the transactions* as they happened. The earliest transactions are shown first, and the more recent ones follow. From May 2 on, you can follow the sequence of events and easily locate a transaction by date.

Example

Suppose that you want to find all transactions that happened on May 7. Look at the date column on the left side. It is easy to follow it down until you come to May 7 (5/7). It turns out that there were two transactions on May 7. You can now examine the details of each transaction.

2. See All Parts of a Transaction

**All Parts Are
Easy to See**

After you locate a transaction, it is easy to see *all the individual items in each transaction*. This is because all parts of the transaction appear on the same line.

Example

In the May 8 transaction, the company purchased $5,000 of equipment using some cash and borrowing the balance. If you look on the line for May 8, you can easily see all three items that are affected: Cash decreased by $1,000, Equipment increased by $5,000, and Notes Payable increased by $4,000.

3. See if the Equation Stays in Balance

**Increases and
Decreases in
Each Transaction**

You can easily prove that each transaction keeps the equation in balance. If you look on any line with a transaction, you can quickly see that the increases and decreases in the equation items keep the equation in balance.

Example

In the May 8 transaction, Cash decreased by $1,000 and Equipment increased by $5,000. This is a net $4,000 increase in total assets. On the right side of the equation for May 8, you can see that the liabilities increased by $4,000. The equation remains in balance.

4. See the Historical Detail of Each Item

**A Record of All
Increases and Decreases**

There is a permanent record of both *the increases and decreases in every item*.

4. See the Historical Detail of Each Item, *continued*

Example	You can select any item in the equation. Suppose you want to know the changes in the cash account for the week beginning May 2. You can see that there was an increase of $800, a decrease of $400, an increase of $2,000, and a decrease of $1,000. Each increase and decrease is always shown separately.

> *Note:* If you want to explain why the cash changed with a particular transaction, you can examine the parts of any transaction in which you are interested. You could also add an explanation column.

5. Determine the Balance of Each Item

Calculate the Balance Whenever You Want	You can easily find the *balance of each item* in the equation. A balance can be calculated at any time.

Examples

- Suppose you want to know the balance of Supplies on May 8. Look on the May 8 date line. Under Supplies, the balance shows as $1,300.
- Suppose you want to know how much cash you had on May 6. Just take the beginning balance ($17,300), add any increases through May 6 ($800), and subtract the decreases through May 6 (none). The cash balance on May 6 is $18,100.

". . . and I'm telling you, we want FIVE kinds of data arrangements."

Check Your Understanding

Write the completed sentences on a separate piece of paper. The answers are on page 393.

Transaction data must be arranged in a way that meets five basic information requirements. First, transactions are recorded in · · · · · · · · order. Second, it must be easy to see all the · · · · · · · of each transaction. Third, it must be easy to verify that the transaction keeps the accounting · · · · · · · · in · · · · · · · ·. Fourth, there must be a permanent historical record of all the · · · · · · · · and · · · · · · · · of each item. Fifth, it must be easy to find the · · · · · · · · of each item.

What data arrangement is needed? *For each situation in the table below, mark the correct box to indicate which information arrangement(s) is (are) required in each situation.*

	Five Basic Information Arrangements				
Situation	*1* *Find a transaction by date*	*2* *See all parts of a transaction*	*3* *See if the equation stays in balance*	*4* *See the historical detail of each item*	*5* *Determine the balance of each item*
1. The owner wants to know how much cash the business has today.	**(Reminder: Use a separate sheet of paper to complete the table.)**				
2. A tax auditor wants to know for what purpose a large check was written.					
3. The manager wants to know if the property tax payments were made before December 10 to avoid a late payment penalty.					
4. A customer is disputing the balance we are showing in our account receivable from him.					
5. Our business has purchased another business. It is a complex transaction with many changes to the accounting equation.					
6. Before deciding on a loan, the bank wants to know the amount of debt that our business has.					
7. The owner wants to know if the May 3 cash deposit was from a revenue or from a customer advance payment.					

Answers

Situation	**Five Basic Information Arrangements**				
	1 *Find a transaction by date*	2 *See all parts of a transaction*	3 *See if the equation stays in balance*	4 *See the historical detail of each item*	5 *Determine the balance of each item*
1. The owner wants to know how much cash the business has today.					✓
2. A tax auditor wants to know for what purpose a large check was written.	✓	✓			
3. The manager wants to know if the property tax payments were made before December 10 to avoid a late payment penalty.	✓	✓			
4. A customer is disputing the balance we are showing in our account receivable from him.				✓	✓
5. Our business has purchased another business. It is a complex transaction with many changes to the accounting equation.		✓	✓		
6. Before deciding on a loan, the bank wants to know the amount of debt that our business has.					✓
7. The owner wants to know if the May 3 cash deposit was from a revenue or from a customer advance payment.	✓	✓			

Transaction data must be arranged in a way that meets five basic information requirements. First, transactions are recorded in chronological order. Second, it must be easy to see all the parts of each transaction. Third, it must be easy to verify that the transaction keeps the accounting equation in balance. Fourth, there must be a permanent historical record of all the increases and decreases of each item. Fifth, it must be easy to find the balance of each item.

LEARNING GOAL 20 — Explain the Use of Accounts

Overview

Introduction

At the most basic level, an accounting system is simply a way of recording increases and decreases. Why? Because the financial condition of every business is described by the accounting equation $A = L + OE$, and there are only two possible ways that the items in the equation can change: either increase or decrease.

The means of keeping a record of all increases and decreases of each item in the accounting equation is the "account." This learning goal explains the account.

In Learning Goal 20, you will find:

The Account and How It Is Used

The Account and How It Is Used

Example

Example of Recording Increases and Decreases

Look again at the last table that we used to record the transactions for the Nevada Company (see page 387). This table uses separate increase and decrease columns for all the items in the accounting equation. For each item, notice that the increase and decrease columns form a "T."

For example, the cash item in the accounting equation of Nevada Company for the week beginning May 2 shows the following entries:

Cash

	Increase	Decrease
5/2 beginning balance	17,300	
	800	400
	2,000	
		1,000
5/8 ending balance	18,700	

An item can change in only two possible ways—either increase or decrease. By putting an increase column on one side and a decrease column on the other side, a T is formed. All the increases are shown on one side, and the decreases are shown on the other side. The ending balance of 18,700 is calculated by subtracting the total of the decrease side (1,400 on the right side) from the total of the positive (increase) side (20,100 on the left side).

The Account

Definition

Each one of these increase/decrease T arrangements is called an account. An **account** is a detailed, historical record that shows all the increases and all the decreases, and balance, of a specific item in the accounting equation.

continued

The Account, *continued*

The T Account	The simplest form of an account is called a ***T account*** (see example on page 395). It shows only the most basic information: name, increases, decreases and balance. (Later on, we will add other useful information and expand the account.)
Entry	Each recording on the left side or right side of an account is called an ***entry***.
Footing	Because an account keeps a record of all increases and all decreases, an account can also show a balance. The balance of an account is called a ***footing***, and to total an account is ***to foot*** it.

Examples

Refer back to the last table for the Nevada Company on page 387.

- Cash, Accounts Receivable, Supplies, and Equipment are asset accounts.
- Note Payable is a liability account.
- C. Goldman, Capital is an owner's equity account.

The Cash account shows four entries: two increases and two decreases. The footing (the balance) of the Cash account on May 8 is $18,700.

Two Information Requirements Are Fulfilled

An account fulfills two of the five information requirements. The two requirements are:

- An account keeps a record of all increases and decreases of a specific item in the accounting equation (the "historical detail").
- An account shows the balance of a specific item in the accounting equation.

Write the completed sentences on a separate piece of paper. The answers are below.

An account is a detailed historical record of all the · · · · · · · · and all the · · · · · · · · of a specific item in the accounting equation. An account can show the · · · · · · · · of the item at any desired time.

Answers

An account is a detailed historical record of all the increases and all the decreases of a specific item in the accounting equation. An account can show the balance of the item at any desired time.

Rules for Increasing and Decreasing the Accounts

Concept

The essential concept behind all the rules for recording increases and decreases in the accounts is:

- We agree that one side of an account will be the positive side. This is called the **"normal"** or **"natural" side** of the account, and it is used for increases.
- Therefore, the other side of the account will be the negative side— for recording decreases.

It is actually this simple.

Positive Sides

Over many years, accountants have agreed on the positive sides:

- For accounts in the left side accounting equation (assets), the left side of an account shall be the positive side. ("Left goes with left.")
- For accounts in the right side accounting equation (liabilities and owner's capital), the right side of an account shall be the positive side. ("Right goes with right.")

continued ▶

Rules for Increasing and Decreasing the Accounts, *continued*

Examples

The following illustration and table show you how this rule affects each type of account, when recording changes:

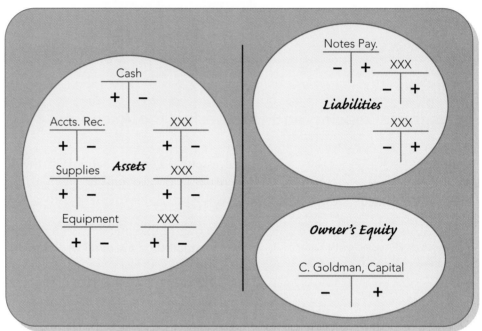

Change	Assets	Liabilities	Owner's Capital
Positive (increase)	Left side	Right side	Right side
Negative (decrease)	Right side	Left side	Left side

Nothing Magic Here!

There is nothing magic or mysterious about this method. We could just as easily agree that the natural positive location should be the top part of an account and decreases should be on the bottom part of an account. To keep a record of increases and decreases that the human brain can see, all we need are two separate locations in each account. Most people find left and right to be easiest, probably because the accounting equation is divided into left and right parts.

<table>
<tr><td>**LEARNING GOAL 21**</td><td></td></tr>
</table>

| **LEARNING GOAL 21** | # Use the Owner's Capital Accounts |

In Learning Goal 21, you will find:

The Parts of Owner's Equity

Overview of Owner's Equity

The Individual Owner's Equity Accounts

In practice, the owner's equity account is subdivided to show the specific kinds of changes that affect owner's equity.

Revenues, expenses, owner drawing, and owner investment are the recurring changes that affect the owner's capital. The first three of these changes—revenues, expenses, and owner drawing—happen frequently and need to be carefully monitored. Therefore, in practice, the owner's capital is subdivided by creating individual accounts for revenues, expenses, and owner drawing.

Rule

Because owner's equity is on the right side of the accounting equation, all increases to owner's equity and the specific accounts that increase owner's equity are recorded on the right side of an account. Decreases are left-side entries.

continued ▶

Overview of Owner's Equity, *continued*

Capital Account Expanded

In the diagram below, the owner's capital is expanded to show the individual owner equity accounts. These separate accounts are a subdivision of the owner's capital. Because investments do not happen frequently and are therefore easy to follow, they are recorded directly into the owner's capital account.

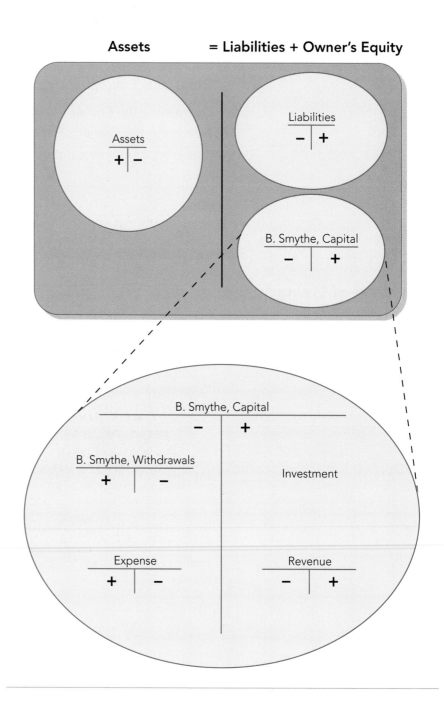

PRACTICE   Learning Goal 21, continued

Solutions are in the disk at the back of the book and at: www.worthyjames.com

Reinforcement Problems

LG 21-1. Explain concepts about owner's capital accounts.

a. Why is the natural positive side ("normal side") of the owner's capital the right side of the account?

b. Why is the owner's capital subdivided into separate accounts for revenue, expense, and drawing, in addition to the owner's capital account?

c. Why is the natural positive side ("normal side") of an expense account or drawing account the left side?

d. The more an expense or drawing account increases, the more the total owner's capital decreases. Why?

e. Why is the natural positive side ("normal side") of a revenue account the right side?

LG 21-2. Negative balance in owner's capital? We know that assets and liabilities cannot really have negative balances, although sometimes assets such as Cash or Accounts Receivable might be temporarily shown with negative balances as a shortcut. However, can the owner's capital account ever have a negative balance? Why?

LG 21-3. Practice using owner's equity accounts. Each of the following statements describes a separate transaction. Below, blank T accounts are arranged under the accounting equation. For each statement, do the following: Using a separate piece of paper, draw the accounts, write the names of the accounts that are affected above the T accounts, and then make entries for the dollar amounts into the accounts. (*Remember:* The entries must keep the equation in balance!)

a. On October 1, David Jefferson invests $15,000 to start a new business called Jefferson Consulting Services.

b. On October 5, the business spends $5,000 cash to purchase $4,000 of computer equipment and $1,000 of office supplies from a vendor.

c. On October 7, the business uses up $500 of supplies in performing a consulting job for a client.

d. On October 20, the business receives a $200 bill from the electric company. The bill will be paid early next month.

e. On October 28, the business completes a consulting job, and the client pays $1,500 cash.

f. On October 31, David Jefferson withdraws $750 cash from his business.

LG 21-3, *continued*

Assets	=	Liabilities	+	Owner's Equity

LG 21-4. Practice using owner's equity accounts. Draw the T accounts that you see below on a separate piece of paper. Using the T accounts and the transaction items listed below, enter the debits and credits in the correct T accounts. Identify each transaction by placing the letter of the transaction next to the debits and credits for the transaction. When you are finished with all the transactions, calculate the account balances and enter them on the correct sides of the accounts. Then calculate the net income or loss of the business.

a. Howard Laguna invested $10,000 in his business.
b. The business paid $2,000 for the current month's rent expense.
c. The business received a bill for advertising in the local paper, $700. The bill was not paid immediately.
d. The business purchased $300 of supplies on account.
e. The business performed services for a client on account, $3,900.
f. The business used $150 of supplies.
g. The business performed services for a client and received $1,500 cash.
h. The business received the utility bill for $90 but did not pay it immediately.
i. The business paid employee wages of $1,600.
j. Howard Laguna withdrew $1,000 cash from the business.

Cash	Accounts Receivable	Supplies	Accounts Payable

LG 21-4, *continued*

Howard Laguna, Capital

Wages Expense	Travel Expense	Advertising Expense		Service Revenue

Utilities Expense	Rent Expense	Howard Laguna, Withdrawals

LG 21-5. Practice using owner's equity accounts. Draw the T accounts that you see below on a separate piece of paper. Using the T accounts and the transaction items listed below, enter the debits and credits in the correct T accounts. Identify each transaction by placing the letter of the transaction next to the debits and credits for the transaction. When you are finished with all the transactions, calculate the account balances and enter them on the correct sides of the accounts. Then calculate the net income or loss of the business.

  a. Anne Quincy invested $20,000 cash and $500 of supplies in her business.
  b. The business paid $3,500 for the current month's advertising expense.
  c. The business received an advance payment of $5,000 from a customer.
  d. The business performed services for a client on account, $1,300.
  e. The business purchased $700 of supplies on account.
  f. The business performed services for a client and received $900 cash.
  g. The business received a repair service bill of $375 but did not pay it immediately.
  h. The business paid employee wages of $3,000.
  i. The business used $400 of supplies.
  j. The business performed services and earned $3,000 of the unearned revenue.
  k. Anne Quincy withdrew $5,000 cash from the business.
  l. Received a $500 bill for monthly utilities but did not pay bill immediately.
  m. Paid for $300 of additional repairs.

PRACTICE   Learning Goal 21, continued

Solutions are in the disk at the back of the book and at: www.worthyjames.com

LG 21-5, *continued*

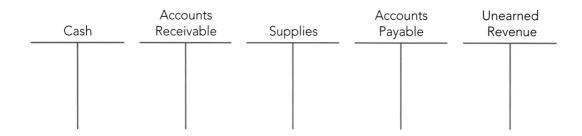

Anne Quincy, Capital

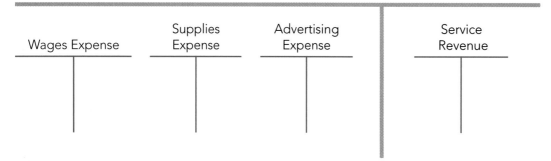

| LEARNING GOAL 22 | # "Debits on the left, credits on the right!" |

In Learning Goal 22, you will find:

The Words "Debit" and "Credit"

Debit and Credit Rules Applied to All Account Types

The Words "Debit" and "Credit"

What Debit and Credit Really Mean

Introduction

Every occupation has its own special terminology. Two of the accounting terms that most people have heard at one time or another are the terms *debit* and *credit*. Even though these words only refer to the left and right sides of an account, there seems to be much confusion and even anxiety about the meaning of these two words.

The truth is really quite simple. Accounting was first developed in Italy during the 1400s. At that time, educated businesspeople spoke Latin. The root word of the Latin term for "left" was "debere." The root word for "right" was "credere." Today, those words have changed into "debit" and "credit" in English, but the meaning is still the same—left and right. The word "debit" is often abbreviated as *Dr.,* and the word "credit" is often abbreviated as "*Cr.*"

Rule

- Instead of saying "left side," say "debit."
- Instead of saying "right side," say "credit."

continued ▶

What Debit and Credit Really Mean, *continued*

Do Not Make These Mistakes!

People who should know better (financial writers, TV broadcasters, and even some nonaccounting teachers) often use debit and credit terminology in completely mistaken ways. They think that the words debit and credit mean things like good or bad, or always increase, always decrease, etc. Ignore these people. The words debit and credit *refer only to* **location**—left or right.

The words debit and credit *do not mean* "good" or "bad" or "favorable" or "unfavorable" or "always increase" or "always decrease" or "gain" or "loss" or anything else!

Debit means "left" and credit means "right." And that is all.

Debit and Credit Rules Applied to All Account Types

Apply Debits and Credits to the Accounts

Introduction

If you have already practiced recording transactions in other learning goals, you will be happy to know that applying debit and credit to accounts does not really involve doing anything much different. *All you need to do is remember to say "debit" instead of "left," and "credit" instead of "right." The rules for increasing and decreasing accounts are* **still the same**.

> *Note:* To **charge** an account means to debit it. There is no alternative word for credit.

The Recording Rules

If you have not yet studied the basic recording rules, they are repeated here:

- **Increases:** Any account that is a *left-side* account in the accounting equation (assets) is increased with a *left-side entry* (debit). Any account that is a *right-side* account in the accounting equation (liabilities and owner's capital) is increased with a *right-side entry* (credit).

- **Decreases:** Learn increases first. Decreases are then recorded on the opposite side from increases. (So, assets are decreased with credits, and liabilities and owner's capital are decreased with debits.)

If you are not completely comfortable with these rules, you can study them in Learning Goal 11.

Apply Debits and Credits to the Accounts, *continued*

Rules Illustrated

The expanded illustration below shows the rules for recording all transaction types.

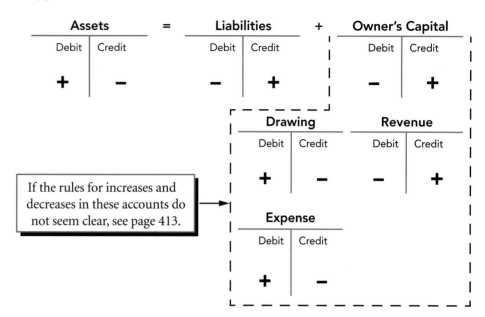

If the rules for increases and decreases in these accounts do not seem clear, see page 413.

Debit and Credit Rules for the Six Basic Account Types

Summary

The table below shows a summary of the rules for debits and credits for each of the six basic account types in the accounting equation. This is exactly the same information that you see in the illustration above.

Assets   =   Liabilities +   Owner's Equity

	Assets	Liabilities	Owner's Capital	Revenue	Expense	Drawing
Debit (left)	Increase (and natural positive balance)	Decrease	Decrease	Decrease	Increase (and natural positive balance)	Increase (and natural positive balance)
Credit (right)	Decrease	Increase (and natural positive balance)	Increase (and natural positive balance)	Increase (and natural positive balance)	Decrease	Decrease

To know if a debit or credit will be an increase or a decrease, you have to specify the type of account. Items on the left side of the equation are increased with debits. Items on the right side (liabilities and owner's equity) are increased with credits. Decreases are the opposite.

continued ▶

Debit and Credit Rules for the Six Basic Account Types, *continued*

Examples

Philadelphia Company performs $3,000 of consulting services and mails a bill to the client. The book-keeper debits Accounts Receivable for $3,000 and credits Fees Earned for $3,000.

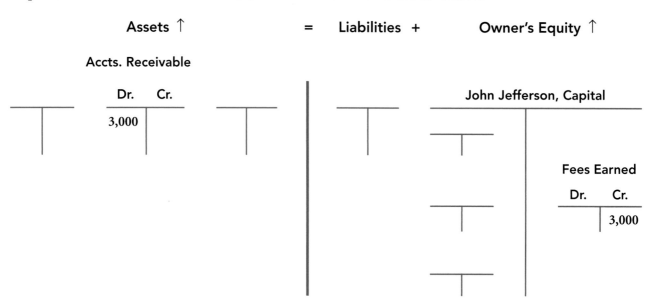

Allegheny Company spends $5,000 cash to purchase $4,000 of computer equipment and $1,000 of office supplies. The bookkeeper records the transaction with a debit to Supplies for $1,000, a debit to Equipment for $4,000, and a credit to Cash for $5,000.

Assets ↓ ↑   =   Liabilities +   Owner's Equity

Cash		Supplies		Equipment				David Jefferson, Capital
Dr.	Cr.	Dr.	Cr.	Dr.	Cr.			
	5,000	1,000		4,000				

QUICK REVIEW

- The words "debit" and "credit" refer only to location. Debit means left and credit means right. They do not have any other meaning.

- The rules for increasing and decreasing accounts are:

- Accounts in the left side of the equation are increased with left-side entries, and accounts in the right side of the equation are increased with right-side entries.
- Remember increases first; then decreases are on the opposite sides.

VOCABULARY

Charge: to debit an account (page 428)

Credit: a right-side entry or the right side of an account (page 427)

Cr.: the abbreviation for the word "credit" (page 427)

Debit: a left-side entry or the left side of an account (page 427)

Dr.: the abbreviation for the word "debit" (page 427)

"They will love it! 'Debit' for left and 'credit' for right!"

PRACTICE   Learning Goal 22

Solutions are in the disk at the back of the book and at: www.worthyjames.com

Learning Goal 22 is about using debit and credit terminology when recording transactions. Answer the questions and problems below to practice what you have just read.

Multiple Choice
Select the best answer.

1. Which of the following is *not* true?
   a. Items on the left side of the accounting equation are increased with debits, and items on the right side are increased with credits.
   b. Items on the left side of the accounting equation are decreased with credits, and items on the right side are decreased with debits.
   c. Both sides of the accounting equation are decreased with debits and increased with credits.
   d. Both (a) and (b).
2. The correct meaning of the words "debit" and "credit" is
   a. debit means increase and credit means decrease.
   b. debit means decrease and credit means increase.
   c. they can be interpreted as either "favorable" or "unfavorable" or as "give" and "take," depending on the transaction involved.
   d. none of the above.
3. Albuquerque Company receives a bill for advertising services, which will be paid next week. The company will have to
   a. debit Owner's Capital and credit Cash.
   b. debit Advertising Expense and credit Accounts Payable.
   c. debit Advertising Expense and credit Cash.
   d. wait until payment is made.
4. How are decreases to accounts distinguished from increases?
   a. Decreases are always on the side opposite from the side for increases.
   b. Decreases are always right-side (credit) entries.
   c. Decreases are always left-side (debit) entries.
   d. Decreases are always shown with a minus sign.
5. If the Santa Fe Art Shoppe collected $500 of cash from Accounts Receivable, it would have to
   a. debit Accounts Receivable $500 and credit Cash $500.
   b. debit Cash $500 and credit Accounts Receivable $500.
   c. debit Cash $500 and credit Owner's Equity $500.
   d. none of the above.
6. An account that is increased with a credit is
   a. Cash.
   b. Equipment.
   c. Accounts Payable.
   d. both (a) and (b).
7. The Luna Voc Tour Company purchased $100 of supplies on account. It should
   a. debit Supplies $100 and credit Cash $100.
   b. debit Supplies $100 and credit Owner's Equity $100.
   c. debit Supplies $100 and debit Cash $100.
   d. debit Supplies $100 and credit Accounts Payable $100.
8. Which of the following is *not* true?
   a. Debits increase assets.
   b. Credits decrease assets.
   c. Credits increase liabilities.
   d. Credits decrease liabilities.

9. A credit to Accounts Payable is
   a. an increase to Accounts Payable.
   b. a decrease to Accounts Payable.
   c. an unfavorable entry.
   d. both (a) and (c).

10. A credit to Unearned Revenue is
   a. an increase to a revenue.
   b. an increase to a liability.
   c. an increase to an asset.
   d. none of the above.

11. Las Cruces Enterprises shows a Service Revenue account with a credit balance of $44,200. Accounts Payable has a normal balance of $11,000, owner's drawing has a normal balance of $5,000, and expenses total $37,100 normal balance. Las Cruces has
   a. a net loss of $8,900.
   b. a net loss of $3,900.
   c. a net income of $2,100.
   d. a net income of $7,100.

12. Debits record
   a. decreases in liabilities and assets.
   b. decreases in assets and increases in liabilities.
   c. decreases in liabilities and increases in assets.
   d. increases in liabilities and assets.

13. Accounts payable was debited and cash was credited. Which of the following best describes what happened?
   a. The company borrowed cash.
   b. The company used cash to pay accounts payable that was owing.
   c. The company reduced accounts payable by earning income.
   d. The company is owed money for services rendered.

14. Cash is credited and supplies is debited. Which of the following best describes what happened?
   a. The company bought some supplies.
   b. The company used up some supplies.
   c. The company sold some supplies to another business, which owes the cash.
   d. The company sold some supplies and received the cash.

15. Cash is debited and unearned revenue is credited. Which of the following best describes what happened?
   a. The company is owed cash for services rendered to a customer.
   b. The company receives cash for services provided.
   c. The company receives cash for services not yet performed.
   d. None of the above.

16. Cash is debited and accounts receivable is credited. Which of the following best describes what happened?
   a. The company collects cash owing from a customer(s).
   b. The company collects cash prior to rendering services.
   c. The company borrows cash and owes the money to the creditor.
   d. None of the above.

17. Equipment is debited and notes payable is credited. Which of the following best describes what happened?
   a. The company sold equipment and is owed the money by the buyer.
   b. The company purchased equipment for cash.
   c. The owner personally purchased equipment and then contributed it to the company.
   d. None of the above.

PRACTICE   **Learning Goal 22, continued**   *Solutions are in the disk at the back of the book and at: www.worthyjames.com*

Reinforcement Problems

LG 22-1. Identify the natural positive side ("Normal Side"). For each of the accounts listed below, indicate if the account has a natural debit or credit balance.

Account
a. Supplies
b. Accounts Payable
c. Service Revenue
d. Cash
e. R. Penland, Drawing
f. R. Penland, Capital
g. Accounts Receivable
h. Rent Expense
i. Prepaid Rent
j. Equipment
k. Unearned Revenue
l. Notes Payable

LG 22-2. Explain how to use debits and credits. For each item below, correctly complete the sentence on a separate piece of paper.

a. Debits are increases when . . .
b. Debits are decreases when . . .
c. Credits are increases when . . .
d. Credits are decreases when . . .

LG 22-3. The six elements of the accounting equation: Identify the debit and credit rules. On a separate piece of paper, draw a table like the one below. Complete the following table by writing the word "increase" or "decrease" in the spaces in each column of the six elements in the accounting equation. **Write the increases first.** At the bottom of each column, also write "Dr." or "Cr." to identify which side of an account for each element shows the natural positive balance (the "normal balance").

	Assets	Liabilities	Owner's Capital	Revenue	Expense	Drawing
Debit	. . . .	. . . .	. . . .	. . . .	. . . .	. . . .
Credit	. . . .	. . . .	. . . .	. . . .	. . . .	. . . .
Natural Positive Balance?	. . . .	. . . .	. . . .	. . . .	. . . .	. . . .

LG 22-4. You be the teacher—Debits and credits explained. As an accounting teacher, I always get lots of questions when the subject of debits and credits is introduced for the first time. However, this semester I will be away at a conference on the day that we begin the introduction to debits and credits. Instead of canceling class, I am asking you for some help—you be the new teacher today—and answer these (actual) questions from students:

a. "Why doesn't it work so that 'debit' always means increase?"

b. "Why doesn't it work so that 'credit' always means decrease?"

c. "Expenses are part of owner's equity, which is on the opposite side of the equation from assets. So why are assets and expenses both increased with debits?"

d. "How do I figure out how to use debits and credits for increases and decreases?"

LG 22-5. Record debit and credit entries into accounts. In each of the transactions listed below, draw T accounts on a separate piece of paper to record transactions. Before recording each transaction, complete the "analysis" and "apply the rule" sections. The first transaction is presented as an example.

Note: Remember that you can visualize each transaction by either drawing a picture of the condition of the business or by using the accounting equation. Then place T accounts in the picture or under the equation.

LG 22-5, *continued*

Example: Annapolis Enterprises pays $550 to purchase office supplies.

Analysis (account type, account name, and increase or decrease):
The *asset Supplies increases* by $550. The *asset Cash decreases* by $550.

Apply the rule (debits and credits):
Assets are decreased with credits: credit Cash $550.
Assets are increased with debits: debit Supplies $550.

Record in T account:

Cash		Supplies	
	550	550	

---

a. Essex Company receives $1,000 from a customer before the services are provided.

Analysis (account type, account name, and increase or decrease):

Apply the rule (debits and credits):

Record in T account:

---

b. Montgomery Enterprises receives a $200 electric bill. The bill is not paid immediately.

Analysis (account type, account name, and increase or decrease):

Apply the rule (debits and credits):

Record in T account:

PRACTICE

Learning Goal 22, continued

Solutions are in the disk at the back of the book and at: www.worthyjames.com

LG 22-5, *continued*

c. Prince Georges Company finishes consulting services for a client and sends the client a bill for $5,000.

> **Analysis (account type, account name, and increase or decrease):**
>
> **Apply the rule (debits and credits):**
>
> **Record in T account:**

d. Cecil Company prepays six months of fire insurance for $2,500.

> **Analysis (account type, account name, and increase or decrease):**
>
> **Apply the rule (debits and credits):**
>
> **Record in T account:**

e. James Lafayette, owner of Anchorage Company, invests $9,000 in his business.

> **Analysis (account type, account name, and increase or decrease):**
>
> **Apply the rule (debits and credits):**
>
> **Record in T account:**

LG 22-5, *continued*

f. Soldotna Company pays a $1,000 account payable.

Analysis (account type, account name, and increase or decrease):

Apply the rule (debits and credits):

Record in T account:

g. Nome Commercial Company purchases $10,000 of equipment, paying $3,000 cash and signing a note payable for the balance.

Analysis (account type, account name, and increase or decrease):

Apply the rule (debits and credits):

Record in T account:

LG 22-6. **More practice with debits and credits—Use T accounts to record transactions.** Listed below are the individual transactions from the example of Jack's Guitar School in Learning Goal 11.

- Draw T accounts or print T accounts from the disk at the back of the book. Write the name of each account above the account: Cash, Accounts Receivable, Supplies, Equipment, Accounts Payable, Unearned Revenue, Jack Davis–Drawing, Jack Davis–Capital, Teaching Revenue, Utilities Expense, Telephone Expense, Supplies Expense, Rent Expense
- For each transaction, enter the debits and credits in the accounts.
- Total each of the accounts and enter the account balances in the proper locations.
- After you have finished the exercise and checked the answer, return to Learning Goal 11, page 235 and compare your entries and accounts to the example. Can you see that the basic rule for increasing and decreasing is still the same? The only difference is that now we will call the entries by the names "debit" and "credit." (And we have subdivided the capital account into separate accounts for revenues, expenses, and drawing.)

LG 22-6, *continued*

Transactions:

(a) Jack deposits $12,000 cash from personal funds into a business checking account.

(b) The business purchases some sound amplifiers and digital electronic equipment for $5,500 cash.

(c) The business purchases $200 of office supplies "on account."

(d) Jack teaches a beginners' class and receives $350 in cash from his students.

(e) Jack teaches a blues weekend master class at the university and receives $2,000 on account plus $500 in cash.

(f) The school received a utility bill for $100 and a telephone bill for $70 that are not paid immediately.

(g) Jack (the school) pays the $200 account payable owing on the supplies.

(h) You check the supplies to find that only $50 of supplies remain. ($150 has been used.)

(i) The school pays $800 for rent expense for the month.

(j) The music school collects $750 of the open account receivable from the university.

(k) Jack withdraws $1,000 cash from the business for his personal use. He calls it a "salary."

(l) A student's parent pays an advance to the school of $250 cash for six weeks of lessons.

(m) Jack gives a $50 lesson to the student whose parents previously advanced the $250 for lessons.

LG 22-7. Record transactions into T accounts. On a separate piece of paper, draw T accounts in the format you see below. Record the transactions shown below into T accounts.

- Write the accounting equation A = L + OE across the top of a blank sheet of paper, leaving ample space between each part of the equation. (You will have more space if you turn the paper so the long side is horizontal.)
- Under each part of the equation, draw as many blank T accounts as you need to record the transactions shown below. Refer to the example below.
- Record each transaction with debits and credits in the appropriate T accounts. Write each account's name above the account as needed. Identify the entries of each transaction with the letter of the transaction.
- After all transactions are recorded, enter the final balance of each T account on the appropriate normal side of the account.
- Calculate the net income or net loss for the period.

Example:

A   =   L   +   OE

LG 22-7, *continued*

Transactions:

(a) Anne Alvarez, the owner of Brownsville Real Estate Company, invested $35,000 in her new business.
(b) The business purchased supplies for $460 on account.
(c) Purchased office equipment for $4,500 cash.
(d) Performed services (commission revenue) for $3,900 on account.
(e) Paid the current month's rent, $2,400.
(f) Received a $5,000 advance payment from a client wishing to locate new business offices.
(g) Received a $510 bill for newspaper advertising services, which was not paid immediately.
(h) Performed services for $4,100 and received $3,000 cash, with the balance on account.
(i) Received a $190 bill from the telephone company. The bill was not paid immediately.
(j) Purchased land for $11,000 by paying $2,500 cash and signing a note payable for the balance.
(k) Made a $250 payment on account.
(l) Collected $1,200 from a customer on account.
(m) Performed $2,000 of services for the client who had made the advance payment.
(n) Anne Alvarez withdrew $2,500 cash from the business for personal use.
(o) Paid $1,000 for Internet advertising.

Instructor-Assigned Problems

If you are using this book in a class, these review problems may be assigned by your instructor for homework, group assignments, class work, or other activities. Only your instructor has the solutions.

IA-11. Record the transactions shown below into T accounts.

- Write the accounting equation A = L + OE across the top of a blank sheet of paper, leaving ample space between each part of the equation. (You will have more space if you turn the paper so the long side is horizontal.)
- Under each part of the equation, draw as many blank T accounts as you need to record the transactions shown below. Refer to the example shown in the instructions for LG 22-7.
- Record each transaction with debits and credits in the appropriate T accounts. Write each account's name above the account as needed. Identify the entries of each transaction with the letter of the transaction.
- After all transactions are recorded, enter the final balance of each T account on the appropriate normal side of the account.
- Calculate the net income or net loss for the period.

Transactions:

(a) Dorothy Tang invested $40,000 in her new business, Orlando Business Travel Services.
(b) The business purchased office supplies for $285 on account.
(c) The business purchased computer equipment for $7,500 cash.
(d) The business performed travel planning services for $2,700 on account.
(e) The business paid $1,500 for the monthly Internet website expense.
(f) The business received a $6,000 advance payment from a corporate client.
(g) The business paid the current month's office rent, $4,100.
(h) Dorothy Tang withdrew $1,000 cash from the business for personal use.
(i) The business performed services for $4,000 and received $3,000 cash, with the balance to be paid on account.

PRACTICE   Learning Goal 22, continued

IA-11, *continued*

(j) The business received a $2,470 bill for advertising in a business publication. The bill was not paid immediately.

(k) The business purchased new office furniture for $15,000 by paying $5,750 cash and signing a note payable for the balance.

(l) The business made a $400 payment on account.

(m) The business collected $900 from a customer on account.

(n) The business performed $1,900 of services for the client who had made the advance payment.

(o) The business received a $700 bill for other Internet expenses, which was not paid immediately.

IA-12. Record the transactions shown below into T accounts.

- Write the accounting equation A = L + OE across the top of a blank sheet of paper, leaving ample space between each part of the equation. (You will have more space if you turn the paper so the long side is horizontal.)
- Under each part of the equation, draw as many blank T accounts as you need to record the transactions shown below. Refer to the example shown in the instructions for LG 22-7.
- Record each transaction with debits and credits in the appropriate T accounts. Write each account's name above the account as needed. Identify the entries of each transaction with the letter of the transaction.
- After all transactions are recorded, enter the final balance of each T account on the appropriate normal side of the account.
- Calculate the net income or net loss for the period.

Transactions:

(a) Jackson Green invested $70,000 in his new business, Detroit Printing Services.

(b) The business purchased paper supplies for $5,800 on account.

(c) The business purchased computer equipment for $3,700 cash.

(d) The business purchased $60,000 of printing equipment by paying $40,000 cash and signing a note payable.

(e) The business paid $1,500 for the current month's rent.

(f) The business performed brochure printing services for $3,600 on account.

(g) The business received a $770 bill for printing equipment repairs. The bill was not paid immediately.

(h) The business performed printing services for $11,200 and received $5,000 cash, with the balance owing from the customer.

(i) The business received a $520 bill from the utilities company that was not paid immediately.

(j) The business signed a printing contract and received a $7,500 advance payment from a large client.

(k) The business paid the utility bill in (i) above.

(l) The business collected $900 from a customer on account.

(m) The business received a $1,450 bill for equipment repairs. The bill was paid immediately.

(n) The business performed $3,800 of services for the client who had made the advance payment.

(o) Jackson Green withdrew $2,000 cash from the business for personal use.

(p) A physical count of paper supplies showed that $3,500 of supplies had been used up.

Your Questions?

It is *very* important to be aware of what you need to understand better. What do you need to understand better about this learning goal? On a separate piece of paper, write the questions that you want to discuss with your classmates, instructor, or supervisor. Try to be very specific about what is bothering you, such as explanations that you do not fully understand.

LEARNING GOAL 23

Use a Ledger

Overview

Introduction

In the prior three learning goals, you learned about accounts and that individual accounts fulfill items #4 and #5 of the five information requirements (page 385). In this learning goal, you will learn how the accounts are arranged to save space and make it easy to add new accounts.

Our Present Arrangement

So far, we have used a table to record transactions and to meet the five information requirements.

	Assets								=	Liabilities + Owner's Equity			
	Cash		Accounts Receivable		Supplies		Equipment			Note Payable		C. Goldman, Capital	
	Increase	Decrease	Increase	Decrease	Increase	Decrease	Increase	Decrease		Decrease	Increase	Decrease	Increase
5/2	bal. 17,300		bal. 4,500		bal. 900		bal. 12,000				bal. 10,000		bal. 24,700
5/4	800			800									
5/5			1,000										1,000
5/7		400			400								
5/7	2,000												2,000
5/8		1,000					5,000				4,000		
5/8	bal. 18,700		bal. 4,700		bal. 1,300		bal. 17,000				bal. 14,000		bal. 27,700

The Table Is Not Practical

Unfortunately, there is one serious problem in the way we are recording transactions in tables, SPACE! Even though we nicely satisfy all five requirements, we will quickly run out of space for accounts. Because we are placing the accounts across a page, we are limited by the width of a page. Already we will need to show the owner's various capital sub-accounts, and this may include several different revenues and many individual expenses. We will also have additional assets and liabilities. Even if we go across two pages we will never have enough space! However, remain calm . . . you only have to read the next page to find the solution to the problem.

Separate Books for Different Purposes

Two Books: The Journal and the Ledger

To solve the space problem and still satisfy all five information requirements, accountants have found that they need to enter the transaction information into *two* separate kinds of records. These records are usually kept in two separate books, called a journal and a ledger. In a computerized system, they are shown as two separate files.

Journal Defined

A *journal* is like a daily diary that keeps a list of all the transactions as they happen.

We will discuss the journal in depth in the next learning goal, starting on page 449.

The General Ledger

Ledger Defined

A *ledger* is a book that contains individual accounts. The general-purpose kind of ledger that we study here is also called the ***general ledger*** because it contains all the accounts. The accounts in a ledger are sometimes called ***ledger accounts***. A ledger fulfills two information requirements because with a ledger you can see:

- A record of all the increases and decreases in each account
- The balance of each account

The Structure of the Ledger

A ledger solves the space problem by placing each account on its own page. The accounts as individual pages are then placed into the book (the ledger). We can have as many accounts as we want. The book is designed so that the back can be separated and new pages can be added. So, any time we need a new account, we can just add another page! The diagram on the next page illustrates this idea.

continued

The General Ledger, *continued*

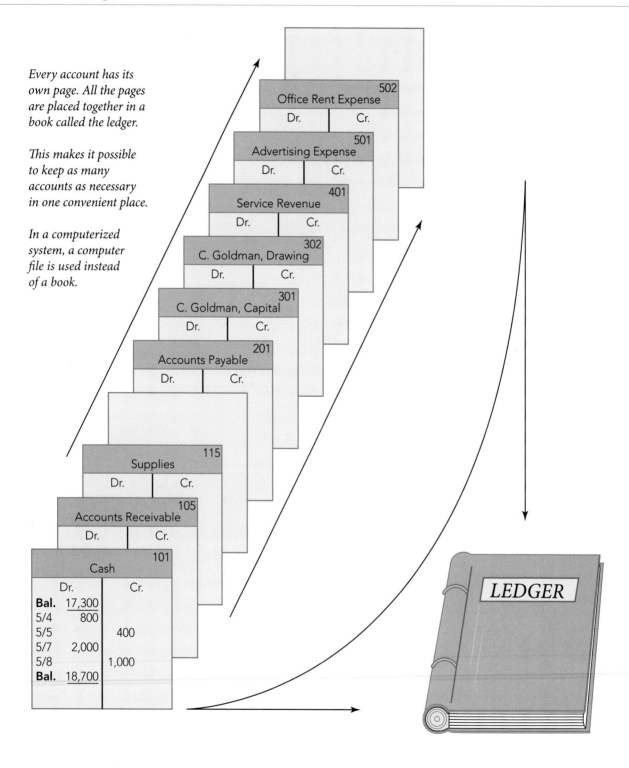

Every account has its own page. All the pages are placed together in a book called the ledger.

This makes it possible to keep as many accounts as necessary in one convenient place.

In a computerized system, a computer file is used instead of a book.

The General Ledger, *continued*

How Many Accounts?

How many accounts a business needs depends upon the size and the nature of a particular business, what kinds of transactions it usually has, and how much detail the owners and managers want to know about the operations.

Account Identification Numbers

In the upper-right corner of each account in the illustration on page 444, you will notice a number. Each account has its own permanent identification number. These are called **account numbers**.

Rule for Assigning Account Numbers

The account numbers are assigned to accounts in the approximate ordering sequence that the accounts normally appear on the financial statements.

- The balance sheet accounts are assigned the first numbers, in the same order that they will appear on the balance sheet. For example, assets are shown first, beginning with cash, then liabilities, and finally the owner's capital account.
- The drawing account is numbered next.
- The revenue accounts are next.
- Expense accounts are numbered last.

Rule for Placing Accounts in the Ledger

Account pages are placed in the ledger in the same sequence as their account numbers.

Note: In a computerized system, ledger accounts also appear in the same sequence.

The Chart of Accounts

The names of all the accounts and the numbers assigned to them can be found in a listing called the **chart of accounts**. The chart of accounts is usually located on the first page of a ledger.

Gaps in the Numbering Sequence

You can see that there are large gaps of unused numbers in the sequence of numbers assigned to the accounts. This is done intentionally. The gaps are for numbers that might be needed later when new accounts are added. For example, the number 111 might be used later if Nevada Company wanted to create an account called "Cleaning Supplies."

continued ▶

The General Ledger, *continued*

Example: Chart of Accounts

Although there is no one format for every chart of accounts, here is an example of how the chart of accounts might look for the Nevada Company:

Nevada Company
Chart of Accounts

Asset Accounts: Numbers 101–199
- #101   Cash
- #105   Accounts Receivable
- #115   Supplies
- #140   Office Equipment
- #160   Building
- #170   Land

Liability Accounts: Numbers 201–299
- #201   Accounts Payable
- #205   Wages Payable
- #210   Unearned Revenue

Owner's Capital Accounts: Numbers 301–399
- #301   C. Goldman, Capital
- #302   C. Goldman, Drawing

Revenue Accounts: Numbers 401–499
- #401   Service Revenue
- #405   Interest Earned

Expense Accounts: Numbers 501–599
- #501   Advertising Expense
- #502   Office Rent Expense
- #507   Equipment Rent Expense
- #510   Wages Expense
- #515   Utilities Expense
- #520   Supplies Expense
- #525   Insurance Expense
- #550   Miscellaneous Expense

TIP

Can you determine what type of entity a business is (proprietorship, partnership, or corporation) just by looking at the chart of accounts? Yes you can! Simply look at the capital accounts. A proprietorship is what you see above. A partnership shows the names of two or more partners, and a corporation shows the names of capital accounts discussed in Learning Goal 29.

QUICK REVIEW

A ledger . . .	
meets these two information requirements . . .	*arranges data by . . .*
<ul><li>keeps a historical record of *all the increases* and *all the decreases* in each account.</li><li>shows the *balance* of each account at any time.</li></ul>	<ul><li>accounts, which are all placed in a single book or file.</li><li>keeping numbered accounts in numerical sequence.</li></ul>

VOCABULARY

Account numbers: unique identification numbers assigned to accounts (page 445)

Chart of accounts: a listing of account names and identification numbers (page 445)

General ledger: a book or computer file that contains all the ledger accounts (page 443)

Journal: a chronological record of transactions (page 443)

Ledger: a book or computer file that contains accounts (page 443)

Ledger accounts: accounts which are found in a ledger (page 443)

Learning Goal 23 is about the purpose and function of a ledger. Use these questions to practice what you have just read.

Multiple Choice
Select the best answer.

1. A ledger is
   a. an individual record of increases and decreases of a particular item in the accounting equation.
   b. a book or a file that contains all the accounts of a business.
   c. a chronological record of transaction data.
   d. both (b) and (c).
2. The purpose of a ledger is to
   a. maintain normal balances in accounts.
   b. prove that debits equal credits.
   c. maintain a detailed record of all the increases and decreases and balances in each account.
   d. serve as a source of business transaction documentation.
3. An account number will always be found
   a. in a record of transactions.
   b. on a ledger account.
   c. in the part of the ledger called the "chart of accounts."
   d. both (b) and (c).
4. Which kind of account would you normally expect to see last in a ledger?
   a. Revenues
   b. Liabilities
   c. Assets
   d. Expenses
5. Accounts are usually placed into a ledger in what order?
   a. in the sequence of their account numbers
   b. by size
   c. alphabetically
   d. by type of account
6. If you have only the number of an account, and want to find out the account name, the best plan is to
   a. look through the ledger until you find the account with the correct number.
   b. look in the chart of accounts.
   c. look in the journal.
   d. speak with the accountant who recorded the transactions.
7. Information in the ledger is arranged by
   a. account.
   b. transaction.
   c. size (largest to smallest).
   d. chronological order.
8. A ledger fulfills which of the following information needs?
   a. You can easily see all parts of each transaction and the balance of each account.
   b. You can see that the accounting equation stays in balance with each transaction.
   c. You can see a historical record of the increases and decreases in each account and the account balance.
   d. You can easily see all parts of each transaction and a historical record of each account.

LEARNING GOAL 24

Use a Journal

In Learning Goal 24, you will find:

The Purpose and Structure of a General Journal

Overview

Introduction

A *journal* is like a daily transaction diary. A journal is where transaction information is first recorded in an accounting system. This transaction information comes from business documents.

Accountants have discovered that it is actually more efficient to first record the transaction information into a journal. For that reason, the journal is often called the *book of original entry*. After transaction information is entered into the journal, the same information is then recorded into the ledger accounts.

Both the journal and the ledger contain exactly the same information. However, each book *arranges* the information differently to meet different information needs.

continued ▶

Overview, *continued*

<table>
<tr>
<td>A Journal Meets Three
Information Needs</td>
<td>A journal arranges data to meet information needs #1, #2, and #3 (see page 389). With a journal, you can:

<ul>
<li>find a transaction by date</li>
<li>see all the accounts affected by each transaction</li>
<li>see if the accounting equation stays in balance with each transaction</li>
</ul>
</td>
</tr>
<tr>
<td>General Journal</td>
<td>Most businesses have more than one kind of journal. However, we will study the most common kind of journal that all businesses use. This is an all-purpose journal called the general journal. Recording information into a journal is called journalizing.</td>
</tr>
</table>

The Structure of a General Journal

<table>
<tr>
<td>Why the Journal
Is Different</td>
<td>Like a ledger, a journal is a book with individual pages. However, the journal is different because it arranges the transaction information differently. In a journal, the journal pages record all of the complete transactions in the order in which they happen. This is different from a ledger, which uses each page to record information about only one account.</td>
</tr>
<tr>
<td>Example</td>
<td>In the example below, you see the top part of a journal page. On the page are two transactions of the Jill Hirata Company for the week of June 5.</td>
</tr>
</table>

Date	Account	Dr.	Cr.
2008 June 5	Cash Jill Hirata, Capital Owner made investment to start business	10,000	 10,000
June 7	Supplies Accounts Payable Purchase supplies on account	500	 500

Notice that these three information requirements are met:

- Transactions can be located by date because they are recorded chronologically (in order of occurrence).
- You can see each complete transaction.
- All the accounts in each separate transaction are easily identified and it's easy to check if debits equal credits.

Recording Transactions in a General Journal

How Transactions Are Recorded in a General Journal

Using the Example Above . . .

We can use the transaction on the previous page for June 5 to see how an entry should be recorded into a journal.

Rule for Date

Date: The date that is entered is always the date of the transaction, not the date that it is being recorded, which may be later.

Date	Account	Dr.	Cr.
2008 June 5			

Rules for Recording the Debits

- Debits are always recorded first.
- Use the *exact name* of the account that needs to be debited. Do not put something like "cash investment" because there is no account by that name.
- Write the name of the account next to the left margin.
- If there is more than one account to debit, write the name of the next account to be debited on the next line. There is no particular order for entering account names.

Dollar amount: Write the dollar amount being debited into the debit (Dr.) column on the same line as the name of the account. Dollar signs are not used.

Date	Account	Dr.	Cr.
2008 June 5	Cash	10,000	

continued ▶

How Transactions Are Recorded in a General Journal, *continued*

Rules for Recording the Credits

- Credit entries are recorded after all debits are recorded.
- Use the *exact name* of the account that needs to be credited. Do not put something like "increase in capital" because there is no account by that name.
- It is customary to *indent the name of a credited account,* so it is easy to identify.
- If there is more than one account to credit, write the name of next account to be credited on the next line. There is no particular order for entering account names.

Dollar amount: Write the dollar amount being credited into the credit (Cr.) column on the same line as the name of the account.

Date	Account	Dr.	Cr.
2008 June 5	Cash	10,000	
	Jill Hirata, Capital		**10,000**

Check Equality

Check to see that the dollar value of debits equals the dollar value of the credits. In this example, it is pretty obvious. In bigger journal entries with multiple debits and credits, however, it is not always so easy to see. If debits do not equal credits, the transaction being recorded will cause the accounting equation to be out of balance.

Equality OK!

Date	Account	Dr.	Cr.
2008 June 5	Cash	10,000	
	Jill Hirata, Capital		10,000

Explanation Is a Good Idea

Check with your teacher or supervisor to find out if an explanation is required. However, it is usually a good idea to write an explanation. This is especially true in complicated or unusual transactions where you should also *identify the source of the information.* Weeks, months, or years later, when someone asks you for an explanation (like the IRS), you will thank yourself for being so careful.

T Account Analysis, *continued*

Step 2: Determine the dollar amounts of changes (valuation).

- The asset Cash decreases $500.
- The liability Accounts Payable decreases $500.

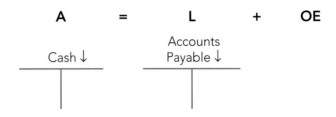

Step 3: Use the debit and credit rules to enter the amounts.

Items on the left side of the equation are decreased with right-side entries (credits). Items on the right side of the equation are decreased with left-side entries (debits). Therefore, credit Cash $500, and debit Accounts Payable $500.

To record this transaction in the general journal, the rule is all debits first and all credits second:

April 3	Accounts Payable	500	
	Cash		500
	Paid vendor on account.		

continued ▶

T Account Analysis, *continued*

Example #2

In a previous period, Humbolt Company received a $900 advance payment from a customer. During the current accounting period, Humbolt performed $750 of services for this customer.

Step 1: Show the T accounts affected (classification).

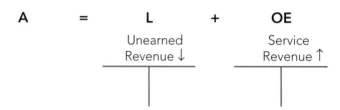

$$A \quad = \quad L \quad + \quad OE$$

Unearned Revenue ↓   Service Revenue ↑

Step 2: Determine the dollar amounts of changes (valuation).

- The liability Unearned Revenue decreases $750.
- Service Revenue increases $750.

$$A \quad = \quad L \quad + \quad OE$$

Unearned Revenue ↓   Service Revenue ↑

Step 3: Use the debit and credit rules to enter the amounts.

Items on the right side of the equation are decreased with left-side entries (debits). Items on the right side of the equation are increased with right-side entries (credits). Therefore, debit Unearned Revenue $750, and credit Service Revenue $750.

$$A \quad = \quad L \quad + \quad OE$$

Unearned Revenue ↓   Service Revenue ↑

750   750

T Account Analysis, *continued*

To record this transaction as a general journal entry, the rule is all debits first and all credits second:

Sept. 28	Unearned Revenue	750	
	Service Revenue		750

Performed services and earned previously unearned revenue.

Example #3

On June 12, Appalachian Enterprises purchased $15,000 of equipment from Penn Company by paying $7,000 cash down and signing an $8,000 promissory note for the balance.

Step 1: Show the T accounts affected (classification).

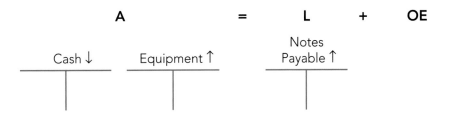

Step 2: Determine the dollar amounts of changes (valuation).

- The asset Cash decreases $7,000.
- The asset Equipment increases $15,000.
- The liability Notes Payable increases $8,000.

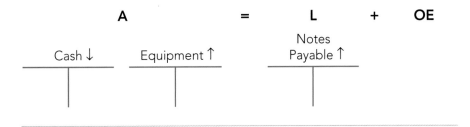

continued ▶

T Account Analysis, *continued*

Step 3: Use the debit and credit rules to enter the amounts.

Items on the left side of the equation are increased with left-side entries (debits) and are decreased with right-side entries (credits). Items on the right side of the equation are increased with right-side entries (credits). Therefore, debit Equipment $15,000, and credit Cash $7,000. Credit Notes Payable $8,000.

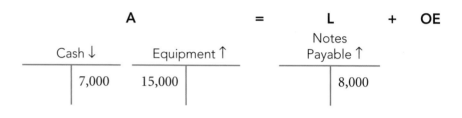

		A		**=**	**L**	**+**	**OE**

Cash ↓	Equipment ↑	Notes Payable ↑
7,000	15,000	8,000

To record this transaction in the general journal, the rule is all debits first and all credits (in any order) second:

June 12	Equipment	15,000	
	Cash		7,000
	Notes Payable		8,000
	Purchased equipment from Penn Company		

TIP   Any entry with more than two accounts is called a ***compound entry***.

Example #4

On January 29, Hattiesburg Corporation made the January loan payment of $3,800 to County Bank. $2,700 of the payment was for interest on the loan, and the rest was for a payment on the loan principal.

Step 1: Show the T accounts affected (classification).

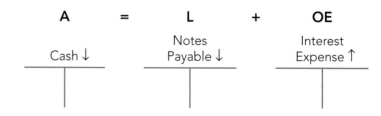

A	**=**	**L**	**+**	**OE**

Cash ↓	Notes Payable ↓	Interest Expense ↑

T Account Analysis, *continued*

Step 2: Determine the dollar amounts of changes (valuation).

- The asset Cash decreases $3,800.
- The expense Interest Expense increases $2,700. (Remember, an increase in an expense is really a reduction in the owner's equity.)
- The liability Notes Payable decreases $1,100.

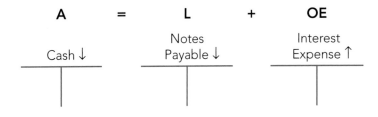

Step 3: Use the debit and credit rules to enter the amounts.

Items on the left side of the equation are decreased with right-side entries (credits). Items on the right side of the equation are decreased with left-side entries (debits). Therefore, credit Cash $3,800, debit Notes Payable $1,100, and debit Interest Expense $2,700. (The interest expense is a decrease in the owner's equity.)

		A	=	L	+	OE
				Notes		Interest
		Cash ↓		Payable ↓		Expense ↑
		3,800		1,100		2,700

To record this transaction as a general journal entry, the rule is all debits (in any order) first and all credits second:

Jan. 29	Interest Expense		2,700	
	Notes Payable		1,100	
	Cash			3,800
	Made January loan payment to County Bank			

continued ▶

T Account Analysis, *continued*

Example #5

On May 8, Belhaven Company collected $3,500 from customers on account.

Step 1: Show the T accounts affected (classification).

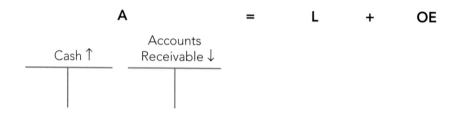

Step 2: Determine the dollar amounts of changes (valuation).

- The asset Cash increases $3,500.
- The asset Accounts Receivable decreases $3,500.

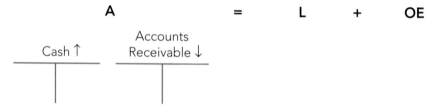

Items on the left side of the equation are increased with left-side entries (debits). Items on the left side of the equation are decreased with right-side entries (credits). Therefore, debit Cash $3,500, and credit Accounts Receivable $3,500.

Step 3: Use the debit and credit rules to enter the amounts.

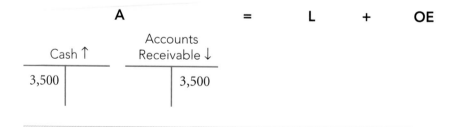

PRACTICE   Learning Goal 24, continued

LG 24-4, *continued*

Sept. 10: Received a $2,000 payment from a client for services to begin on October 1.
Sept. 12: Performed $3,100 of services on account for a client
Sept. 18: Received an $800 bill for computer repair services. The bill was not paid immediately.
Sept. 21: Collected an account receivable in the amount of $750.
Sept. 26: Received a bill for Internet maintenance services, $350. The bill was not paid immediately.
Sept. 30: Emily Heath withdrew $2,500 cash from the business for her personal use.

Date	Account	Dr.	Cr.
Sept.			
1	Cash	17,000	
	Emily Heath, Capital		17,000
1	Insurance Expense	1,200	
	Cash		1,200
2	Office Supplies Expense	800	
	Office Furniture	4,000	
	Accounts Payable		4,800
3	Cash	3,100	
	Service Revenue		3,100
4	Cash	20,000	
	Accounts Payable		20,000
6	Rent Expense	1,800	
	Cash		1,800
7	Wages Expense	750	
	Wages Payable		750
7	Cleaning Service Expense	15	
	Cash		15
8	Accounts Payable	6,000	
	Cash	4,000	
	Computer		10,000

LG 24-4, *continued*

Date	Account	Dr.	Cr.
Sept.			
10	Cash	2,000	
	Service Revenue		2,000
12	Accounts Receivable	3,100	
	Service Revenue		3,100
21	Cash	750	
	Service Revenue		750
30	Salary Expense	2,500	
	Cash		2,500

LG 24-5. Prepare general journal entries. The general journal that you see below contains explanations but no journal entries. On a separate piece of paper, using the explanations, prepare the correct journal entries.

Date	Account	Dr.	Cr.
2008			
Feb. 8			
	Ken Peters invested $25,000 cash to begin his new business, Du Page		
	Delivery Enterprises.		
9			
	Prepaid 1 year of insurance for $1,500.		
10			
	Purchased office supplies from Jolliet Company, $250 on account.		

LG 24-5, *continued*

Date	Account	Dr.	Cr.
12			
	Paid $1,000 and signed a $2,000 note payable for an office computer.		
14			
	Ken Peters invested an additional $5,000 cash in the business, plus a van worth		
	$15,000. With the van is a note payable of $7,000.		
15			
	Billed Morraine Valley Company for services, $575 on account.		
17			
	Paid $200 owing to Jolliet Company from February 10.		
20			
	Used up $200 of supplies.		
24			
	Wrote $520 check to Sunshine Day Care for owner's child-care expense.		
27			
	Collected $300 from Morraine Valley Company on account.		

Solutions are in the disk at the back of the book and at: www.worthyjames.com

PRACTICE   **Learning Goal 24, continued**

LG 24-6. **Write explanations to journal entries.** After you have practiced enough journal entries, you should be able to look at a journal entry and know what has happened. This exercise helps you practice this skill. The general journal below contains journal entries without explanations. On a separate piece of paper, write a brief, complete, and accurate explanation for each journal entry.

Date	Account	Dr.	Cr.
2008			
July 11	Accounts Payable, Grants Pass Company	1,000	
	Cash		1,000
12	Andrea Sheaffer, Drawing	750	
	Cash		750
14	Supplies Expense	190	
	Supplies		190
15	Cash	3,500	
	Accounts Receivable, Portland Enterprises		3,500
17	Accounts Receivable, Gresham Corporation	4,100	
	Fees Earned		4,100
20	Computer Equipment	10,300	
	Cash		2,500
	Notes Payable		7,800

LG 24-6, *continued*

Date	Account	Dr.	Cr.
22	Cash	850	
	Unearned Revenue		850
24	Rent Expense	1,500	
	Prepaid Rent		1,500
25	Land	145,000	
	Building	90,000	
	Cash		50,000
	Notes Payable		185,000
27	Repairs Expense	175	
	Accounts Payable		175

LG 24-7. **Reconstruct journal entries from ledger accounts.** You know that in the normal recording procedure, journal entries are always prepared first, before transferring data into the ledger accounts. However, in this exercise we will test your understanding by working backwards from ledger accounts. Using the information in the T accounts shown below, prepare the general journal entries for the month of May and include explanations. (Make copies of blank journal paper from the disk at the back of the book.)

Solutions are in the disk at the back of the book and at: www.worthyjames.com

PRACTICE   Learning Goal 24, continued

LG 24-7, *continued*

Ledger (partial)

Cash				Accounts Receivable				Supplies				Prepaid Rent		
May 5			900	May 6			330	May 7	250			May 18		700
6	330			15	500			17	250					
10	750													
12			450											
17			1,050											

Equipment				Accounts Payable				Notes Payable		
May 17	2,800			May 7			250	May 17		2,000
				10			1,500			
				12	450					

Service Revenue				Wages Expense				Advertising Expense				Rent Expense		
May 10			750	May 5	900			May 10	1,500			May 18	700	
15			500											

LG 24-8. **Prepare general journal entries; review classification, valuation, and timing.** For the events described below for the Santa Cruz Office Locator Service in June 2008, prepare the necessary general journal entries. Before you write a journal entry, on a separate page identify the correct classification, valuation, and timing using the following format as an example:

Classification	Valuation	Timing
Cash	25,000	June 1
David Washington, Capital	25,000	

When entering values that are decreases, enter the amounts in parentheses, "( )".

You may omit explanations in this exercise. (For journal paper, you can make general journal copies from the general journal template in the disk at the back of this book.) When doing this exercise, use T account analysis whenever you feel it is necessary to help visualize the transaction.

June 1: David Washington transferred $25,000 from his personal bank account into his business bank account with the name of Santa Cruz Office Locator Service.

June 2: The business purchased $500 of office supplies and $2,700 of furniture from Aptos Office Supply Company. The purchase was on account.

June 2: Hired a secretary for the office to be paid at the rate of $14 per hour.

LG 24-8, *continued*

June 3: Borrowed $15,000 from Santa Cruz City Bank.

June 5: Performed services for a client and received $2,250 cash.

June 6: Paid for cleaning services, $150.

June 8: Purchased $7,000 of computer equipment by paying $3,000 cash and signing a note payable for the balance owing. Although the actual cost of the computer equipment was $7,000 paid by Santa Cruz Office Locator Service, the equipment is listed for sale by a different supplier for $6,800.

June 10: Received a $3,000 advance payment from Capitola Company with instructions to locate various kinds of office space meeting the Company's specifications.

June 12: Performed $2,500 of services on account for Corralitos Company by locating office space.

June 15: Paid secretary's wages, $1,120.

June 15: Paid $1,000 to Aptos Office Supply Company on account.

June 15: Paid the June rent, $1,500.

June 18: Received an $800 bill for advertising in the local paper. The bill was not paid immediately. The transaction was recorded on June 30.

June 22: Performed locating services on account for Moss Landing Internet Company, $750.

June 25: Received a partial collection from Corralitos Company, $1,000 (June 12 above).

June 28: Received a bill for Internet maintenance services, $500. The bill was not paid immediately.

June 29: Located the office space meeting the specifications for Capitola Company. The total bill to Capitola Company was $5,000 (see June 10).

June 30: A count of the office supplies purchased on June 2 shows that one-fourth of the supplies have been used up.

June 30: Paid $750 to Santa Cruz Bank. $500 of the payment was for interest on the loan, and the balance was applied to the amount owing on the note payable.

June 30: David Washington withdrew $2,000 cash for personal use.

July 3: Received a bill from the telephone company for June services up to June 30, $210. The bill was not paid immediately.

LG 24-9. **Review: Distinguish between the journal and the ledger.** Using a separate piece of paper, complete the following table to contrast the essential features of a journal and a ledger.

	A journal . . .	A ledger . . .
meets these information needs . . .	(Reminder: Use a separate sheet of paper to complete the table.)	
and does not meet these information needs . . .		
and the data is primarily arranged by . . .		

PRACTICE   Learning Goal 24, continued

INTERNET EXERCISES

Take a tour of the history of accounting. Do an Internet search to learn about the history of accounting. (Use bookmark/favorites to save the locations of links you use in an "Accounting References" folder.)

  a. What are the earliest records of accounting activity?
  b. What was the beginning of what later evolved into modern accounting? When and where did this beginning primarily take place? Why did it take place?
  c. What person is often referred to as the "father of modern accounting"? Why does he get credit for this?
  d. What connection do Britain and the industrial revolution have to the accounting profession as we know it today?
  e. In the United States, what effect did the stock market crash of 1929 and the resulting great depression of the 1930s have on the American accounting profession and financial reporting?
  f. Did the 2002 establishment of the Public Company Accounting Oversight Board (PCAOB) affect any long-standing privileges of American accountants? In what way? What happened to cause this?

Your Questions?

It is *very* important to be aware of what you need to understand better. What do you need to understand better about this learning goal? On a separate piece of paper, write the questions that you want to discuss with your classmates, instructor, or supervisor. Try to be very specific about what is bothering you, such as explanations that you do not fully understand.

Use a Basic Accounting System

In Learning Goal 24, you will find:

Practical Forms of the General Journal and the Ledger Account

A More Realistic Journal

Two Improvements

Only two improvements are needed to make our journal realistic and fully usable. The following page shows the general journal for David's tiny little Bodyguard Service for the first week of operations after all the transactions are recorded. Notice the two improvements in the journal.

Journal Page Number: Every journal has page numbers. The "J1" that you see in the upper right corner of the journal means page 1 of the general journal. (Sometimes the letters "G" or "GJ" are used instead.)

"Posting Reference" Column: The new column that is titled "Post. Ref." is only used during the posting procedure (which will be explained later). When data is transferred from the journal to a ledger account, that account's identification number is entered in the "Post. Ref." column. (Sometimes the "Posting Reference" column is titled "LP" for ledger page, or "folio.")

continued ▶

A More Realistic Journal, *continued*

GENERAL JOURNAL				J1
Date	Account Titles and Explanation	Post. Ref.	Debit	Credit
2008				
June 1	Cash		20	
	David Lilliput, Capital			20
	Owner made investment to start business			
2	Office Supplies		5	
	Office Equipment		20	
	Accounts Payable			25
	Purchase supplies and equipment from London Company			
3	Cash		7	
	Unearned Revenue			7
	Advance payment from Houyhnhnm Company			
4	Supplies Expense		3	
	Office Supplies			3
	Office supplies used up for the Swift report			
5	Accounts Receivable		5	
	Security Service Revenue			5
	Security services for Shadow Company			
6	Accounts Payable		3	
	Cash			3
	Payment on Accounts Payable—London Company			

PRACTICE   Learning Goal 25, continued

Discussion Questions and Brief Exercises for Learning Goals 23–25

1. What is a ledger and what is its purpose?

2. What is a journal and what is its purpose?

3. Explain the difference between a journal and a ledger. What are the advantages of using each?

4. What is a debit and what is a credit? What is a debit balance and what is a credit balance?

5. Does the use of debits and credits change the rules for increasing and decreasing the accounts?

6. The meaning of "double entry" in an accounting system is that every transaction must be recorded twice. Correct? Explain what you think.

7. Anne Soleimani, a beginning accounting student in your study group, believes that debits are favorable and credits are unfavorable. Mark Reese, also in your study group, disagrees. He believes that debits are unfavorable and credits are favorable. Who do you agree with? Why?

8. Your friend Julia Chen is concerned about taking her first accounting test this week because she can never remember if debit means increase or decrease and if credit means increase or decrease. Can you explain this and help her relax?

9. Describe the process for entering transaction information into an accounting system.

10. Answer the following about general journal entries: (a) What date should be used? (b) What should you record first, debits or credits? (c) What do you write in the "account" column of the journal? (d) Should you make an entry in the "Post. Ref." column when you make the journal entry? (e) After you make the journal entry, what should you always check?

11. If you look in a ledger account, how can you tell where the entries in the account came from?

12. If you look in a journal, how do you know if the information was also entered in the ledger?

13. What is a chart of accounts? How is it organized and where can you usually find it?

14. Suppose that you decided not to use a journal. Instead, you record transaction information directly into the ledger accounts because this saves time. Could this be done? What would be the result?

Reinforcement Problems

LG 25-1. Complete the posting. Return to the journal (J1) beginning on page 487 in the "Completed transactions" discussion. Using the journal, and the ledger accounts following the journal, complete the posting for the June 5, 6, 7, and 8 transactions.

LG 25-2. Practice posting from a completed journal. The general journal shown below has not been posted yet. Complete the posting of the journal information into the ledger accounts. (For ledger account paper, you can print out copies from the disk at the back of the book.) Before you begin the posting, enter account numbers on the ledger accounts using the chart of accounts that you see below.

PRACTICE   Learning Goal 25, continued

LG 25-2, *continued*

Assets:		Revenue:	
101	Cash	401	Service Revenue
110	Accounts Receivable		
120	Supplies	**Expenses:**	
150	Furniture	510	Wages Expense
160	Computer Equipment	515	Rent Expense
		525	Advertising Expense
Liabilities:		530	Maintenance Expense
202	Accounts Payable	535	Cleaning Expense
220	Notes Payable	550	Interest Expense
230	Unearned Revenue		
Owner's Equity:			
302	David Washington, Capital		
310	David Washington, Withdrawals		

Page 8

Date		Account	Ref.	Dr.	Cr.
2008					
June					
	1	Cash		25,000	
		David Washington, Capital			25,000
	2	Supplies		500	
		Furniture		2,700	
		Accounts Payable			3,200
	3	Cash		15,000	
		Notes Payable			15,000
	5	Cash		2,250	
		Service Revenue			2,250
	6	Cleaning Expense		150	
		Cash			150
	8	Computer Equipment		7,000	
		Cash			3,000
		Notes Payable			4,000
	10	Cash		5,000	
		Unearned Revenue			5,000

PRACTICE   **Learning Goal 25, continued**

Solutions are in the disk at the back of the book and at: www.worthyjames.com

LG 25-2, *continued*

Page 9

Date	Account	Ref.	Dr.	Cr.
12	Accounts Receivable		2,500	
	Service Revenue			2,500
15	Wages Expense		1,120	
	Cash			1,120
15	Accounts Payable		1,000	
	Cash			1,000
15	Rent Expense		1,500	
	Cash			1,500
18	Advertising Expense		800	
	Accounts Payable			800
22	Accounts Receivable		750	
	Service Revenue			750
25	Cash		1,000	
	Accounts Receivable			1,000
28	Maintenance Expense		500	
	Accounts Payable			500
30	Interest Expense		500	
	Notes Payable		250	
	Cash			750
30	Withdrawals		2,000	
	Cash			2,000

PRACTICE   Learning Goal 25, continued

LG 25-3. Record transactions in a general journal and post to a ledger. John Covina is an electrical contractor who opened his new business called Covina Electrical Contracting on September 2, 2008. The business installs electrical systems in both business and residential buildings. Using the information below, do the following:

1. Record the September transactions into the general journal. (Before journalizing use T account analysis whenever you feel it is necessary to visualize a transaction.)
2. Post the journal information into the ledger accounts. Before you begin the posting, enter account names and numbers on the ledger accounts using the chart of accounts that you see below.
3. When you finish recording all transactions, verify that each ledger account shows a current balance. (For journal paper and for ledger account paper, you can make copies from the general journal and ledger templates from the disk at the back of the book.)

Covina Electrical Contracting Chart of Accounts			
Assets:		**Revenues:**	
Cash	103	Service Revenue	410
Accounts Receivable	110		
Office Supplies	120	**Expenses:**	
Electrical Supplies	125	Rent Expense	505
Prepaid Insurance	150	Wages Expense	510
Equipment: Office	170	Auto & Gas Expense	520
Tools	180	Insurance Expense	530
		Advertising Expense	535
Liabilities:		Utilities Expense	540
Accounts Payable	203	Office Supplies Expense	545
Unearned Revenue	210	Electrical Supplies Expense	550
Wages Payable	215	Legal Expense	560
Notes Payable	250	Accounting Expense	570
		Interest Expense	590
Owner's Equity:			
J. Covina, Capital	305		
J. Covina, Withdrawals	310		

LG 25-3, *continued*

Transactions:

Sept. 2: John Covina invested $100,000 cash plus office equipment valued at $10,000 to open his new business, Covina Electrical Contracting.

Sept. 2: The business paid $6,000 for one year of insurance in advance.

Sept. 3: Performed $7,500 of electrical installation services; the client immediately paid $2,000 cash.

Sept. 7: Purchased $1,000 of office supplies on account.

Sept. 12: Purchased tools for $7,800 and electrical supplies for $4,200 by paying $5,000 cash and signing note payable for the balance.

Sept. 14: Collected $3,000 on account.

Sept. 15: Installed electrical systems for computer servers and billed the customer $6,100.

Sept. 16: Received a utilities bill in the amount of $315 and a gasoline bill for $190.

Sept. 17: Paid $390 for office supplies.

Sept. 22: (Begin journal page 2.) Paid office rent, $2,200.

Sept. 23: Received an advance payment of $12,000 for 6 months of electrical maintenance services from a local business.

Sept. 24: Paid $720 owing on accounts payable.

Sept. 27: John Covina withdrew $2,000 from the business for personal use.

Sept. 29: A count of supplies showed that $175 of office supplies and $2,900 of electrical supplies had been consumed.

Sept. 30: Recorded $4,100 of wages expense as owing but unpaid.

Sept. 30: Recorded one month of the prepaid insurance being used up in the amount of $500.

Sept. 30: Performed $5,000 of services for the client in the September 23 transaction.

LG 25-4. **Record transactions in general journal and post to ledger.** Rita Markstein is an employee benefits specialist who opened her new business called Markstein Consulting on June 3, 2008. The business provides consulting services to large businesses that want to create employee benefit plans. Using the information below, do the following:

1. Record the June transactions into the general journal. (Before journalizing use T account analysis whenever you feel it is necessary to visualize a transaction.)
2. Post the journal information into the ledger accounts. Before you begin the posting, enter account names and numbers on the ledger accounts using the chart of accounts that you see below.
3. When you finish recording all transactions, verify that each ledger account shows a current balance. (For journal paper and for ledger account paper, you can make copies from the disk at the back of this book.)

Solutions are in the disk at the back of the book and at: www.worthyjames.com

PRACTICE   Learning Goal 25, continued

LG 25-4, *continued*

Markstein Consulting Chart of Accounts			
Assets:		*Revenues:*	
Cash	101	Consulting Revenue	405
Accounts Receivable	108		
Office Supplies.....................	115	*Expenses:*	
Prepaid Insurance	150	Rent Expense	502
Prepaid Travel	155	Wages Expense	508
Office Equipment	170	Auto & Gas Expense	512
Office Furniture	180	Insurance Expense	516
		Advertising Expense	520
Liabilities:		Utilities Expense	524
Accounts Payable..................	205	Office Supplies Expense	528
Unearned Revenue	210	Travel Expense	532
Wages Payable	220	Legal & Accounting Expense	536
Notes Payable	280	Interest Expense	540
		Internet Expense	544
Owner's Equity:			
R. Markstein, Capital	303		
R. Markstein, Withdrawals...........	304		

Transactions:

June 2: To open her new business, Markstein Consulting, Rita Markstein invested $25,000 cash, $800 of office supplies, and office furniture with a value of $4,000.

June 2: The business paid $3,000 in advance for one year of insurance and also paid $1,800 for airline tickets, which will be used in August.

June 3: Received a bill for legal services in the amount of $2,500.

June 3: Performed $5,200 of consulting services; the client immediately paid $1,000 cash.

June 7: Purchased $930 of office supplies on account.

June 9: Purchased computers (office equipment) for $12,000 by paying $8,000 cash and signing a note payable for the balance.

June 14: Collected $2,500 from Accounts Receivable.

June 16: Received a utilities bill in the amount of $420 and a bill for Internet Services of $700.

June 17: Paid office rent, $2,750.

June 21: (Begin journal page 2.) Received an advance payment of $4,000 for 12 months of consulting services from Argyle Corporation.

June 24: Paid $925 owing on accounts payable.

June 25: Rita Markstein withdrew $1,000 from the business for her personal use.

June 27: Completed a consulting engagement and billed Dunwoody Corporation $5,000.

June 29: A count of supplies showed that $245 of office supplies had been used.

June 30: Recorded $3,800 of wages expense as owing but unpaid.

June 30: Recorded one month of the prepaid insurance being used up in the amount of $250.

June 30: Completed $750 of services for Argyle Corporation in the June 21 transaction.

Instructor-Assigned Problems

If you are using this book in a class, these review problems may be assigned by your instructor for homework, group assignments, class work, or other activities. Only your instructor has the solutions.

IA-13. **Record transactions in a general journal and post to a ledger.** On October 5, 2008, Armando Rubio, a psychologist, began his new family therapy practice called Family Therapy Resources. Using the information below, do the following:

1. Record the October transactions into the general journal. (Before journalizing use T account analysis whenever you feel it is necessary to visualize a transaction.)
2. Post the journal information into the ledger accounts. Before you begin the posting, enter account names and numbers on the ledger accounts using the chart of accounts that you see below.
3. When you finish recording all transactions, verify that each ledger account shows a current balance. (For journal paper and for ledger account paper, you can make copies from the disk at the back of the book.)

Family Therapy Resources
Chart of Accounts

Assets:		*Revenues:*	
Cash	102	Counseling Revenue	405
Accounts Receivable	106		
Office Supplies	110	*Expenses:*	
Prepaid Insurance	150	Rent Expense	503
Prepaid Subscriptions	155	Wages Expense	508
Office Equipment	175	Travel Expense	513
Office Furniture	185	Insurance Expense	521
		Professional Journals Expense	526
Liabilities:		Utilities Expense	531
Accounts Payable	202	Office Supplies Expense	536
Unearned Revenue	208	Continuing Education Expense	541
Wages Payable	210	Legal & Accounting Expense	546
Notes Payable	275	Interest Expense	590
Owner's Equity:			
A. Rubio, Capital	305		
A. Rubio, Withdrawals	310		

PRACTICE   Learning Goal 25, continued

IA-13, *continued*

Transactions:

October 5: To open his new business, Dr. Rubio invested $50,000 cash and office furniture with a value of $10,000.

October 6: The business paid $12,000 in advance for one year of insurance beginning in October and paid $1,500 for 12 months of professional journals subscriptions that will begin in November.

October 7: Received a bill for accounting services in the amount of $1,700. Immediately paid $500 of the bill.

October 9: During October 2–7 provided counseling services in the amount of $8,100, receiving $2,000 of cash payments. The balance was billed on account.

October 10: Purchased $1,175 of office supplies on account.

October 11: Purchased computers and software (office equipment) for $15,000 and office furniture for $5,000 by paying the vendor $10,000 cash and signing a note payable for the balance.

October 14: Collected $1,900 from Accounts Receivable.

October 17: Received a utilities bill in the amount of $385 and a bill for continuing education classes in the amount of $1,500.

October 18: Paid for monthly office rent, $2,750.

October 19: Received an advance payment from Sardis Corporation of $15,000 for counseling services to be provided to employees requesting such services.

October 24: Paid $1,800 owing on accounts payable.

October 25: Dr. Rubio withdrew $750 from the business for his personal use.

October 27: Made a loan payment of $800, of which $640 was interest expense, the balance being a payment on the note payable.

October 28: (Begin journal page 2.) A count of supplies showed that $445 of office supplies had been used.

October 29: Recorded $4,500 of office wages expense as owing but unpaid.

October 30: Recorded one month of the prepaid insurance being used up in the amount of $1,000.

October 30: Completed $1,950 of services for Sardis Corporation in the October 19 transaction.

October 31: During October 8–31 provided other counseling services in the amount of $14,500, receiving $5,000 of cash payments. The balance was billed on account.

IA-14. **Record transactions in a general journal and post to a ledger.** On July 2, 2008, Dennis Kim, a licensed insurance agent and Certified Financial Planner, started a new insurance agency called Kim Insurance Agency. Using the information below, do the following:

1. Record the July transactions into the general journal. (Before journalizing use T account analysis whenever you feel it is necessary to visualize a transaction.)
2. Post the journal information into the ledger accounts. Before you begin the posting, enter account names and numbers on the ledger accounts using the chart of accounts that you see below.
3. When you finish recording all transactions, verify that each ledger account shows a current balance. (For journal paper and for ledger account paper, you can make copies from the disk at the back of this book.)

PRACTICE   Learning Goal 25, continued

IA-14, *continued*

Kim Insurance Agency Chart of Accounts			
Assets:		**Revenues:**	
Cash	105	Insurance Revenue	410
Accounts Receivable	110	Financial Planning Revenue	420
Office Supplies	120		
Prepaid Rent	140	**Expenses:**	
Prepaid Insurance	145	Rent Expense	505
Office Equipment	175	Wages Expense	508
Office Furniture	185	Advertising Expense	511
		Insurance Expense	514
Liabilities:		Internet Expense	517
Accounts Payable	210	Utilities Expense	520
Unearned Revenue	220	Office Supplies Expense	523
Wages Payable	225	Continuing Education Expense	526
Notes Payable	280	Legal & Accounting Expense	529
		Interest Expense	550
Owner's Equity:			
D. Kim, Capital	302		
D. Kim, Withdrawals	303		

Transactions:

July 2: To open his new business, Dennis Kim invested $30,000 cash.

July 6: The business paid $9,000 in advance for one year of liability insurance beginning in July.

July 7: Completed a financial plan for the client and billed the client $1,800.

July 7: Paid $1,500 for rent for the month of July plus another $3,000 for August and September.

July 10: Purchased $500 of office supplies on account.

July 11: Purchased computers and software (office equipment) for $18,000 and office furniture for $4,500 by paying the vendor $8,000 cash and signing a note payable for the balance.

July 14: Collected $1,000 from Accounts Receivable.

July 17: Received a utilities bill in the amount of $280.

July 18: Received cash commissions for insurance policies sold, $3,800.

July 18: Received an $800 bill for Internet service maintenance and a bill for continuing education classes in the amount of $2,100.

July 19: Received a $20,000 advance payment from Bellevue Corporation for financial planning services to be provided to the company employees.

July 24: Paid $1,600 owing on accounts payable.

July 25: Dennis Kim withdrew $750 from the business for his personal use.

July 27: Made a loan payment of $500, of which $430 was interest expense, the balance being a payment on the note payable.

July 28: (Begin journal page 2.) Completed $2,500 of financial planning services and billed the client, who immediately paid $1,000 and will pay the balance later.

July 30: A count of supplies showed that $210 of office supplies had been used.

July 31: Completed $2,000 of services for Bellevue Corporation from the July 19 transaction.

July 31: Recorded $750 of prepaid liability insurance being used for July.

PRACTICE   **Learning Goal 25, continued**

Cumulative Problems for Comprehensive Practice

Learning Goals 24 and 25 complete your introduction to the use of the general journal and general ledger. For comprehensive practice in the use of the general journal, general ledger, and the preparation of financial statements, two cumulative problems are included at the end of Learning Goal 26. These extended problems contain a variety of transactions.

Your Questions?

It is *very* important to be aware of what you need to understand better. What do you need to understand better about this learning goal? On a separate piece of paper, write the questions that you want to discuss with your classmates, instructor, or supervisor. Try to be very specific about what is bothering you, such as explanations that you do not fully understand.

LEARNING GOAL 26	# The Trial Balance—Prepare It and Use It Two Ways

In Learning Goal 26, you will find:

What Is a Trial Balance?

What Is a Trial Balance?

The Trial Balance

Trial Balance Defined

A *trial balance* is a listing of all the ledger account names with their balances. The account names are listed in a column. Next to the name of each account is *the balance of that account* as either a debit or credit. Accounts with zero balances are not usually included. The next page shows an example.

"What is a trial balance?"

continued ▶

The Trial Balance, *continued*

The East Lake Street Company
Trial Balance
June 30, 2008

Account Name	Dr.	Cr.
Cash	$ 7,580	
Accounts receivable.	4,207	
Office supplies	533	
Accounts payable.		$ 2,500
Wages payable		750
Cindy Walczak, capital		8,220
Cindy Walczak, drawing	500	
Fees earned.		5,550
Rent expense	1,200	
Supplies expense	300	
Wages expense	2,700	
Total	**$17,020**	**$17,020**

When Is It Prepared?

A trial balance can be prepared at any time, but it is usually prepared at the end of an accounting period, just before the financial statements are prepared.

Where does the Information Come From?

The amounts listed in the trial balances are the non-zero ending balances of all the individual ledger accounts. Therefore, the source of the information is the general ledger.

The Two Functions of the Trial Balance

The trial balance:

- *tests* whether or not the total of all the debit balance accounts equals the total of all the credit balance accounts. This proves that both sides of the accounting equation are equal, which is necessary in double-entry accounting.
- is the *source of the financial statements.* If all the account balances in the trial balance are correct, we can prepare a balance sheet, income statement, and statement of owner's equity from the trial balance. All the accounts with balances are in the trial balance.

Example of Preparing a Trial Balance

Example   On page 506, you will find all the completed ledger accounts for David's tiny little Bodyguard Service for the entire month of June, as of June 30. Using these accounts, you can prepare a trial balance like this:

Step	Action	Example
1	Prepare the trial balance headings. Be sure the date is correct. *Note:* The trial balance is a point in time, not a period of time.	**David's tiny little Bodyguard Service** **Trial Balance** **June 30, 2008** **Account Title** **Dr.** **Cr.**
2	Beginning with the first account in the ledger, list the names of the accounts and their balances in the same order that they appear in the ledger. Do not list any zero-balance accounts.	**David's tiny little Bodyguard Service** **Trial Balance** **June 30, 2008** **Account Title** **Dr.** **Cr.** Cash . . . . 15 Accounts receivable. . . . . 7 Prepaid insurance . . . . 10 Office equipment . . . . 20 Accounts payable. . . . . 25 Unearned revenue . . . . 4 David Lilliput, capital . . . . 20 David Lilliput, drawing. . . . . 3 Security service revenue . . . . 30 Advertising expense . . . . 3 Rent expense . . . . 9 Accounting expense . . . . 2 Insurance expense. 4 Utilities expense. . . . . 1 Supplies expense 5

continued ▶

Example of Preparing a Trial Balance, *continued*

LEDGER					

CASH   ACCT. NO. 101

Date	Explan.	Post. Ref.	Debit	Credit	Balance
2008					
June 1		J1	20		20
3		J1	7		27
6		J1		3	24
7		J1		10	14
7		J1	15		29
15		J2		9	20
23		J3		2	18
25		J3		4	14
27		J3		1	13
28		J3	5		18
30		J3		3	15

ACCOUNTS RECEIVABLE   ACCT. NO. 105

Date	Explan.	Post. Ref.	Debit	Credit	Balance
2008					
June 5		J1	5		5
28		J3		5	–0–
30		J3	7		7

OFFICE SUPPLIES   ACCT. NO. 110

Date	Explan.	Post. Ref.	Debit	Credit	Balance
2008					
June 2		J1	5		5
4		J1		3	2
11		J2		2	–0–

PREPAID INSURANCE   ACCT. NO. 115

Date	Explan.	Post. Ref.	Debit	Credit	Balance
2008					
June 7		J1	10		10

OFFICE EQUIPMENT   ACCT. NO. 140

Date	Explan.	Post. Ref.	Debit	Credit	Balance
2008					
June 2		J1	20		20

ACCOUNTS PAYABLE   ACCT. NO. 201

Date	Explan.	Post. Ref.	Debit	Credit	Balance
2008					
June 2		J1		25	25
6		J1	3		22
12		J2		3	25

UNEARNED REVENUE   ACCT. NO. 210

Date	Explan.	Post. Ref.	Debit	Credit	Balance
2008					
June 3		J1		7	7
8		J1	3		4

DAVID LILLIPUT, CAPITAL   ACCT. NO. 301

Date	Explan.	Post. Ref.	Debit	Credit	Balance
2008					
June 1		J1		20	20

DAVID LILLIPUT, DRAWING   ACCT. NO. 302

Date	Explan.	Post. Ref.	Debit	Credit	Balance
2008					
June 30		J3	3		3

SECURITY SERVICE REVENUE   ACCT. NO. 401

Date	Explan.	Post. Ref.	Debit	Credit	Balance
2008					
June 5		J1		5	5
7		J1		15	20
8		J1		3	23
30		J3		7	30

ADVERTISING EXPENSE   ACCT. NO. 501

Date	Explan.	Post. Ref.	Debit	Credit	Balance
2008					
June 12		J2	3		3

RENT EXPENSE   ACCT. NO. 505

Date	Explan.	Post. Ref.	Debit	Credit	Balance
2008					
June 15		J2	9		9

ACCOUNTING EXPENSE   ACCT. NO. 510

Date	Explan.	Post. Ref.	Debit	Credit	Balance
2008					
June 23		J3	2		2

INSURANCE EXPENSE   ACCT. NO. 520

Date	Explan.	Post. Ref.	Debit	Credit	Balance
2008					
June 25		J3	4		4

UTILITIES EXPENSE   ACCT. NO. 525

Date	Explan.	Post. Ref.	Debit	Credit	Balance
2008					
June 27		J3	1		1

SUPPLIES EXPENSE   ACCT. NO. 530

Date	Explan.	Post. Ref.	Debit	Credit	Balance
2008					
June 4		J1	3		3
11		J2	2		5

Example of Preparing a Trial Balance, *continued*

Step	Action	Example
3	Add the trial balance columns and compare the totals.	**David's tiny little Bodyguard Service** **Trial Balance** **June 30, 2008**

Account Title	Dr.	Cr.
Cash.	$15	
Accounts receivable	7	
Prepaid insurance	10	
Office equipment	20	
Accounts payable		$25
Unearned revenue		4
David Lilliput, capital		20
David Lilliput, drawing	3	
Security service revenue		30
Advertising expense.	3	
Rent expense.	9	
Accounting expense.	2	
Insurance expense	4	
Utilities expense	1	
Supplies expense	5	
Total	**$79**	**$79**

Step	Content
4	If the totals are equal and you know that the individual account balances are correct, you can use the trial balance to prepare the financial statements. ■ *Income statement:* Use the revenue and expense accounts. ■ *Statement of owner's equity:* Use the owner's capital account, the drawing account, and the net income (or loss) from the income statement. ■ *Balance sheet:* Use the asset and liability accounts and the final balance of owner's capital from the statement of owner's equity.

Prepare Financial Statements from the Trial Balance

Example

The financial statements below were prepared from the June 30 trial balance of David's tiny little Bodyguard Service on page 507.

David's tiny little Bodyguard Service
Income Statement
For the Month Ended June 30, 2008

Revenues		
Security service revenue		$30
Expenses		
Rent expense	$9	
Supplies expense	5	
Insurance expense	4	
Advertising expense	3	
Accounting expense	2	
Utilities expense	1	
Total expenses		24
Net income		$ 6

David's tiny little Bodyguard Service
Statement of Owner's Equity
For the Month Ended June 30, 2008

David Lilliput, capital, June 1	$ 0
Add: Owner investment	20
Net income	6
	26
Less: Drawings	(3)
David Lilliput, capital, June 30	$23

David's tiny little Bodyguard Service
Balance Sheet
June 30, 2008

Assets		Liabilities	
Cash	$15	Accounts payable	$25
Accounts receivable	7	Unearned revenue	4
Prepaid insurance	10	Total liabilities	29
Office equipment	20		
		Owner's Equity	
		David Lilliput, capital	23
Total assets	$52	Total liabilities and owner's equity	$52

Prepare Financial Statements from the Trial Balance, *continued*

TIP

To find out if the owner made an investment, you will need to look into the ledger account for the owner's capital. For example, by just looking at the $20 of David Lilliput, Capital on the trial balance, you cannot be sure if it includes any current investment or is the beginning balance. This makes a difference, because any owner's investments must be disclosed separately on the statement of owner's equity.

Locating Errors in the Trial Balance

How to Locate Errors

What if the totals are not equal? In a manual accounting system, locating errors in the trial balance can be a slow process. In a faulty computerized accounting system that requires a programming fix, the process of finding the source of an error in the trial balance can be even more difficult. Here is how to proceed: *work backwards from the trial balance.*

Step	Action	Possible Errors
1	Examine the trial balance. *Note:* Check the difference between the totals:	■ Columns were added incorrectly. ■ An account balance was omitted. ■ A balance was placed into the wrong column. ■ Amounts were written down incorrectly. If the difference between the totals is evenly divisible by 9, a transposition (like 51 instead of 15) or a slide (like 10 instead of 100) may be the only problem. If the difference is evenly divisible by 2, an amount written in the wrong column may be the only problem. Look for exactly half the difference.
2	Check the individual ledger accounts.	■ The balance of an account was calculated incorrectly. ■ The balance is shown incorrectly (debit instead of credit, or credit instead of debit).
3	Check the posting.	■ Debit was posted as a credit, or credit posted as a debit. ■ The same amount was posted more than once. ■ Part of a transaction posting was omitted. ■ A wrong amount was posted.
4	Check the journalizing.	■ Debits did not equal credits when a transaction was journalized.

continued ▶

Locating Errors in the Trial Balance, *continued*

What the Trial Balance DOES NOT Detect!	A correct trial balance proves that the total debits equal the total credits. However, the trial balance does not detect these kinds of errors:

- Any transaction that was not journalized
- Any transaction that was not posted
- Journal entries that balance, but use wrong amounts or wrong accounts
- Multiple journalizing or posting of the same transaction
- In a computerized system, failing to choose the correct default settings

All of these errors can occur, and the trial balance will still balance! These errors must be corrected before the financial statements are prepared and given to investors, lenders, and other stakeholders. You will learn how to deal with some of these problems in the second book in this series (Volume 2) when we discuss adjusting and correcting entries.

NO Debits or Credits on Financial Statements

Even though the trial balance uses debits and credits, *financial statements never have debits and credits.* This is because most people who use financial statements do not understand debits and credits.

QUICK REVIEW

- The trial balance is a listing of all accounts and their ending balances. (Accounts with zero balances are not usually included.)

- A trial balance can be prepared at any time, but normally it is prepared at the end of an accounting period, just before the financial statements are prepared.

- A trial balance serves two important functions:

  - It proves that the accounting equation is in balance for all the ledger accounts. The total of all debit balances must equal the total of all credit balances.

- It is the source of the account balances used on the income statement, statement of owner's equity, and balance sheet.

- The trial balance does not identify errors in which the accounting equation still balances.

- Never use debits or credits on financial statements.

PRACTICE   Learning Goal 26

Solutions are in the disk at the back of the book and at: www.worthyjames.com

Learning Goal 26 is about learning to prepare a trial balance and the two ways of using the trial balance. Use these questions and problems to practice what you have learned.

Multiple Choice
Select the best answer.

1. A trial balance is prepared
   a. usually just before financial statements are prepared.
   b. at any time the accountant desires to verify that the books are in balance.
   c. using the ending balances in all nonzero accounts.
   d. all the above.
2. A trial balance is used
   a. to test if all the debit account balances equal the total credit account balances.
   b. as the source of information that is used to prepare financial statements.
   c. as a financial statement.
   d. both (a) and (b).
3. A trial balance would help in detecting which error?
   a. A journal entry that was not posted
   b. A journal entry that was posted twice
   c. A journal entry that was posted to the wrong accounts
   d. None of the above
4. If a trial balance does not balance, it could mean that
   a. a ledger account was added incorrectly.
   b. a journal entry was posted twice.
   c. a journal entry was posted to the wrong accounts.
   d. none of the above.
5. If a $700 credit to Accounts Receivable was posted as a $700 credit to Cash, on the trial balance
   a. total debits will exceed total credits by $700.
   b. total credits will exceed total debits by $700.
   c. the trial balance will be completely unaffected.
   d. none of the above.
6. If a $500 debit to Cash was posted as a $50 debit to Cash, on the trial balance
   a. the cash is understated by $500.
   b. total debits will exceed total credits by $450.
   c. total credits will exceed total debits by $450.
   d. the cash is overstated by $500.
7. If $250 of supplies are consumed, but this is journalized and posted as a $250 debit to Supplies Expense and a $25 credit to Supplies, on the trial balance
   a. total debits will be overstated.
   b. total debits will exceed total credits.
   c. total credits will exceed total debits.
   d. total credits will be overstated.
8. Debits and credits are
   a. used only on the balance sheet.
   b. used only on the income statement.
   c. never used on any financial statements.
   d. are optional on financial statements.

Reinforcement Problems

LG 26-1. Prepare a trial balance. Listed below in random order are various ledger accounts with balances for the Overland Park Company, as of December 31, 2008. On a separate piece of paper, prepare a trial balance in good form. Account numbers are in parentheses ( ).

(#150) Land: $35,780
(#115) Supplies: 425
(#130) Prepaid Insurance: 800
(#101) Cash: 4,281
(#515) Wages Expense: 3,500
(#415) Interest Earned: 125

(#201) Wages Payable: $1,500
(#401) Service Revenue: 8,400
(#510) Utility Expense: 202
(#505) Rent Expense: 800
(#301) R. Wills, Draw: 1,000

(#215) Unearned Revenue: $1,250
(#520) Repairs Expense: 1,315
(#110) Accounts Receivable: 7,227
(#300) R. Wills, Capital: 54,555
(#140) Equipment: 10,500

LG 26-2. You be the teacher—Grade the financial statement (report form balance sheet). You have just given a weekly quiz that requires your students to prepare financial statements from a trial balance. Shown below is a report form balance sheet prepared by one of your students. Preparation of a correct balance sheet is worth 10 points. Identify the mistakes and grade this balance sheet. How many points would you give? (Mistakes are from actual exams.)

Wayne Grey-Eagle Company
Balance Sheet

	Dr.	Cr.
Assets:		
Cash	$21,500	
Accounts receivable	7,150	
Office supplies	325	
Prepaid rent	2,800	
Equipment	15,900	
Total assets	47,675	
Liabilities and Owner's Equity		
Liabilities:		
Wages payable		3,300
Accounts payable		4,470
Notes payable		22,500
Total liabilities		30,270
Owner's Equity:		
Wayne Grey-Eagle, capital, January 1		17,925
Wayne Grey-Eagle, drawing		(5,000)
Net income		4,480
Wayne Grey-Eagle, capital, January 31		17,405
Total	$47,675	$47,675

LG 26-3. Prepare a trial balance. The ledger account activity of Pham Company has been condensed into the T accounts that you see below. Using the T accounts, prepare a trial balance in good form as of June 30, 2008.

Cash		Accounts Receivable		Office Supplies		Computer Supplies		Prepaid Rent	
90,000	6,000	5,500	3,000	1,000	440	4,200	2,400	6,000	500
2,000	5,000	6,100	500	390					
3,000	390	1,000							
7,000	2,200								
	720								
	2,000								

Office Equipment		Computer Equipment		Accounts Payable		Unearned Revenue		Wages Payable	
10,000		17,800		720	1,000	5,000	12,000		4,100
					505				

Notes Payable		Hoan Pham, Capital		Hoan Pham, Withdrawals		Service Revenue		Rent Expense	
	7,000		106,000	2,000			7,500	2,200	
							6,100		
							5,000		

Wages Expense		Travel Expense		Insurance Expense		Supplies Expense		Internet Expense	
4,100		190		500		440		175	
								3,040	

PRACTICE   **Learning Goal 26, continued**   *Solutions are in the disk at the back of the book and at: www.worthyjames.com*

LG 26-4. **Prepare financial statements from a trial balance; analyze the business.** Your friend Frank Wade is an expert mechanical engineer. Early this year, he started a new engineering design and consulting business, Wade Engineering, in which he invested all the cash that the business needed to begin the consulting operations.

The first year of operations has just ended, and Frank meets you for lunch. During lunch, he tells you that he is looking for a partner to invest an additional $25,000 cash in the business. He would make you an equal partner for only the investment. You would not have to do any work in the business. He says that he has been quite busy with many clients and has not done any financial work himself. He did, however, hire a reliable bookkeeper who prepared the trial balance, which he lets you keep to review. Frank is hoping for an answer from you within the next 7 to 10 days.

Wade Engineering
Trial Balance
December 31, 2008

Account Name	Dr.	Cr.
Cash	$ 3,100	
Accounts receivable	17,100	
Office supplies	1,100	
Design supplies	1,200	
Prepaid rent	650	
Office equipment	3,500	
Design equipment	14,700	
Wages payable		$ 4,900
Accounts payable		2,900
Frank Wade, capital		25,000
Frank Wade, drawing	4,400	
Design fees		27,800
Interest earned		100
Rent expense	1,400	
Wages expense	12,500	
Utilities expense	380	
Supplies expense (Office)	140	
Supplies expense (Design)	530	
Total	$60,700	$60,700

Instructions:

■ **Prepare financial statements.** On a separate piece of paper, prepare the balance sheet, the income statement, and the statement of owner's equity for the year ended December 31, 2008. Prove the amount of Frank's original investment when you prepare the financial statements.

■ **Analyze the statements and make a decision.** After you have prepared the three financial statements, you realize that you would also like to have a statement of cash flows to analyze, but you have not yet learned to prepare one. Fortunately, you have a friend in a more advanced accounting class who can prepare this statement, which you see on the next page.

LG 26-4, *continued*

Wade Engineering
Statement of Cash Flows
For the Year Ending December 31, 2008

Cash flows from **operating** activities:

Receipts:			
Cash collections from customers			$10,700
Interest earned			100
Payments:			
Rent expense		$2,050	
Utilities expense		380	
Wages expense		7,600	
Supplies expense		70	
Total cash payments			10,100
Net cash provided by operating activities			700
Cash used in **investing** activities:			
Purchase of equipment			(18,200)
Cash flows from **financing** activities:			
Owner investment		25,000	
Less: withdrawals		(4,400)	
Net cash provided by financing activities			20,600
Net increase in cash			3,100
Cash balance January 3, 2008			–0–
Cash balance December 31, 2008			$ 3,100

Now that you have all four financial statements available, answer the following questions to help you decide if you should invest.

a. The income statement shows the change in the company's wealth that resulted from operating the business. Was there an increase or decrease in total wealth as a result of operations? How much?

b. The statement of cash flows shows the sources and uses of cash for the business. Frank Wade claims he actually invested $25,000 cash to start the business. If the beginning cash balance was zero, and Frank invested $25,000, then why is the December 31 cash balance only $3,100?

c. How much cash did the business obtain from its operations?

LG 26-4, *continued*

d. Look at the fees earned on the income statement, and look at the statement of cash flows. What do you think of the ability of the business to collect cash from its customers?

e. What was the biggest use of cash during the year? Is it likely to happen again next year?

f. Take a close look at the balance sheet. What do you think about the company's ability to pay current liabilities when they come due? What are the immediate sources of cash? Why do you think Frank wants an answer from you in the next 7 to 10 days?

g. What might cause a company to show on the income statement that it increased its wealth from operations, and yet on the statement of cash flows show that it did not receive the same amount of cash from operations?

h. Every business always has **two** *abiding and overriding issues* that dictate its ability to survive. From the questions so far, can you guess what these two survival issues are?

i. So what do you think? Are you going to invest $25,000 to be an equal partner and not have to work in the business? What are your reasons?

LG 26-5. **Cumulative problem: Journalize, post to ledger, prepare trial balance, prepare financial statements from trial balance.** Mary Antonelli is a landscape designer who opened her new business called Antonelli Landscape Services, on May 1, 2008. The business provides both landscape design and gardening maintenance services to its customers. Using the information below, do the following:

a. Record the May transactions into the general journal. Skip a line between transactions as shown in the book. Explanations are not required. (Before journalizing use T account analysis whenever you feel it is necessary.)

b. Post the journal information into the ledger accounts. Before you begin the posting, enter account names and numbers on the ledger accounts using the chart of accounts that you see below.

c. After all transactions are recorded and posted, prepare a trial balance as of May 30, 2008.

d. Prepare an income statement and statement of owner's equity for the month ending May 31, 2008, and an account form balance sheet as of May 31, 2008.

LG 26-5, *continued*

(For journal paper and for ledger account paper, you can make copies from the disk at the back of this book.)

Antonelli Landscape Services
Chart of Accounts

Assets:

Cash	102	
Accounts Receivable	115	
Office Supplies	125	
Gardening Supplies	135	
Prepaid Rent	150	
Equipment: Office	180	
Equipment: Automotive	185	
Equipment: Gardening	190	

Liabilities:

Accounts Payable	202
Unearned Revenue	230
Notes Payable	250

Owner's Equity:

M. Antonelli, Capital	302
M. Antonelli, Withdrawals	305

Revenues:

Design Revenue	405
Maintenance Revenue	410

Expenses:

Rent Expense	505
Wages Expense	510
Auto & Gas Expense	515
Insurance Expense	520
Advertising Expense	525
Utilities Expense	530
Office Supplies Expense	535
Gardening Supplies Expense	540
Interest Expense	570

Transactions:

May 1: Mary Antonelli invested $90,000 cash plus office equipment valued at $12,000 to open her new business, Antonelli Landscape Services.

May 2: Paid $6,000 for four months' office rent in advance, as required by the leasing company.

May 3: Received a bill for current month insurance charges, $150.

May 4: Paid $250 for office supplies.

May 5: Purchased $1,100 of garden supplies on account.

May 5: Prepared landscape design plans for a new home. Billed the client $5,500.

May 8: Purchased a small truck for $35,000 by signing a $20,000 note payable; paid the balance in cash.

May 11: Paid for advertising in a local newspaper, $1,000.

May 14: Received an advance payment of $12,000 for 6 months of landscape maintenance services for the local city hall and city offices location.

LG 26-5, *continued*

May 15: Purchased gardening supplies for $2,800 and gardening equipment for $5,000 by signing a note payable.

May 15: Prepared landscape design services for a new company and received $7,500 cash.

May 18: (Begin journal page 2.) Paid the May 3 insurance bill in full and paid $800 of the May 5 garden supplies bill.

May 19: Received a bill for gasoline purchased, $280.

May 21: Performed landscape maintenance services and billed the client $250.

May 25: Received a utilities bill in the amount of $170.

May 26: Made a monthly payment to the bank in the amount of $1,800 of which $1,400 is interest, with the balance applied to the amount owing on the note payable.

May 27: Mary Antonelli withdrew $2,000 from the business for personal use.

May 28: Collected $3,000 on account from a customer.

May 30: Recorded one month of the prepaid rent being used up in the amount of $1,500.

May 30: A count of the supplies showed that $100 of the office supplies and $840 of the gardening supplies had been used up.

May 30: One-half month revenue in the amount of $1,000 of the unearned revenue has been earned for services provided to the city during the current month.

May 31: Paid wages for the month in the amount of $8,500.

May 31: Received a bill for advertising in the local paper, $950.

LG 26-6. **Cumulative problem: Journalize, post to ledger, prepare trial balance, prepare financial statements from trial balance.** Consolidated Eco-Tour Service Company is about to begin operations after the owner on June 30 made an initial investment in the business and obtained a loan. The company will provide guided tours through the desert Southwest to show the beauty of the area and to teach the importance of protecting the fragile environment for future generations. Consolidated has prepared an initial trial balance and will prepare monthly financial statements. Using the information below:

a. Enter the June 30 balances in affected ledger accounts and write "bal." in the explanation column.

b. Record the July transactions into the general journal. Skip a line between transactions as shown in the book. Explanations are not required. (Before journalizing use T account analysis as you think necessary.)

c. Post the journal information into the ledger accounts. Before you begin the posting, enter account names and numbers on the ledger accounts using the chart of accounts that you see below.

d. After all transactions are recorded and posted, prepare a trial balance as of July 31, 2008.

e. Prepare an income statement and statement of owner's equity for the month ending July 31, 2008, and a report form balance sheet as of July 31, 2008.

LG 26-6, *continued*

(For journal paper and for ledger account paper, you can make copies from the disk at the back of this book.)

Consolidated Eco-Tour Service Company
Trial Balance
June 30, 2008

Account

Cash	$280,000	
Supplies	1,200	
Office equipment	15,000	
Notes payable		$100,000
J. Dunston, capital		196,200
Totals	$296,200	$296,200

Consolidated Eco-Tour Service Company
Chart of Accounts

Assets:
Cash	101
Accounts Receivable	115
Supplies	125
Prepaid Insurance	130
Equipment: Office	150
Equipment: Automotive	160
Building	170
Land	180

Liabilities:
Accounts Payable	205
Unearned Revenue	220
Notes Payable	230

Owner's Equity:
J. Dunston, Capital	301
J. Dunston, Withdrawals	305

Revenues:
Tour Revenue	410
Snack Revenue	420

Expenses:
Wages Expense	510
Gasoline Expense	520
Maintenance Expense	525
Insurance Expense	530
Advertising Expense	535
Utilities Expense	540
Supplies Expense	550
Interest Expense	590

PRACTICE   **Learning Goal 26, continued**   *Solutions are in the disk at the back of the book and at: www.worthyjames.com*

LG 26-6, *continued*

Transactions:

July 2: Purchased two vans for $85,000 paying $30,000 cash down and signing a note payable for the balance.

July 3: Prepaid six months of insurance $2,400.

July 5: Purchased $800 of supplies on account.

July 6: Received a bill for advertising services, $4,500.

July 6: Purchased land and building by paying $150,000 cash. The building is valued at $110,000.

July 7: Provided Mojave desert tour for customers and received $1,500.

July 9: Received an advance payment of $8,000 from a school for a canyon tour to be provided later.

July 12: Provided Mojave desert tour on account for local hotel. Billed the hotel $2,700.

July 13: Conducted Grand Canyon tour for Japanese tourists and received $4,200.

July 15: Paid drivers' wages of $3,800.

July 16: Paid amount owing on July 5 supplies bill.

July 18: Paid $2,000 of the amount owing on the July 6 advertising bill.

July 19: (Begin journal page 2) Provided Painted Desert tour for retired Canadian tour group on account. Billed the Canadian travel agency $3,700.

July 24: Received the gasoline credit card bill for $1,800. The bill showed the following purchases: Gasoline, $500; van maintenance, $1,200; towing insurance, $100. The total is credited to Accounts Payable.

July 27: Received a utilities bill in the amount of $210.

July 28: Made a monthly payment to the bank in the amount of $2,500 of which $1,900 is interest, with the balance applied to the amount owing on the note payable.

July 29: Conducted Bryce Canyon tour for the school that had made the advance payment on July 9.

July 30: Paid drivers' wages of $5,500.

July 30: Received payment in full from hotel for July 12 tour.

July 31: Recorded one month of the prepaid insurance being used up in the amount of $400.

July 31: A count of the supplies showed that $300 of the supplies had been used up.

July 31: J. Dunston withdrew $1,500 cash from the business for personal use.

July 31: Records indicate that the business received $700 from customers for food and snacks.

Your Questions?

It is *very* important to be aware of what you need to understand better. What do you need to understand better about this learning goal? On a separate piece of paper, write the questions that you want to discuss with your classmates, instructor, or supervisor. Try to be very specific about what is bothering you, such as explanations that you do not fully understand.

LEARNING GOAL 27 # Explain the Accounting Cycle

The Accounting Cycle

Definition

Accounting activity occurs in a recurring, sequential kind of pattern. The recurring, sequential pattern of accounting activity is known as the *accounting cycle*.

The main elements of the cycle are analyzing, processing, and communicating.

What You Have Learned so Far

The parts of the cycle that you have learned to perform so far are:

Analyze: Business events are analyzed for classification, valuation, and timing to see if they have affected the accounting equation. Any event that changes the accounting equation is called a *transaction* and must be recorded.

Process: Processing refers to recording and organizing data. (Sometimes this is called *recognition*.) This consists of journalizing, posting, summarizing, adjusting, and correcting procedures. So far, you have learned:

- recording (journalizing) transactions
- posting
- preparing a trial balance

You will learn more about the remaining steps in processing in the next book in this series (Volume 2).

Communicate: Communication refers to the preparation of financial reports and disclosures and interpretations. So far, you have practiced preparing three reports: the income statement, the statement of owner's equity, and the balance sheet.

Some Variations

Not every business and not every accountant is exactly the same. So, you can expect some small variations in the exact steps of the cycle. However, a useful overview of the cycle is on page 523 for you to study.

continued

The Accounting Cycle, *continued*

Manual Accounting Compared to Computerized Accounting

The accounting cycle is essentially the same for both a computerized and manual accounting system. A computerized system automates some specific mechanical procedures and saves time. This is especially true about the way transaction data is processed in a computerized system.

However, computers can never perform the analysis part of the cycle. Analysis is your most important skill. Computers are also very poor communicators.

You need to have a clear understanding of all the steps in the accounting cycle. Just because a computer is doing much of the work, *this does not mean that you do not need to understand what is happening.* You do!

For these reasons, it can be a good idea to practice with and understand how a *manual accounting system* functions. This is because . . .

- many people learn and remember better by practicing manually for the first time,
- most parts of a computerized system are essentially the same as a manual system, and
- you may actually be involved in using a manual accounting system.

The Accounting Cycle, *continued*

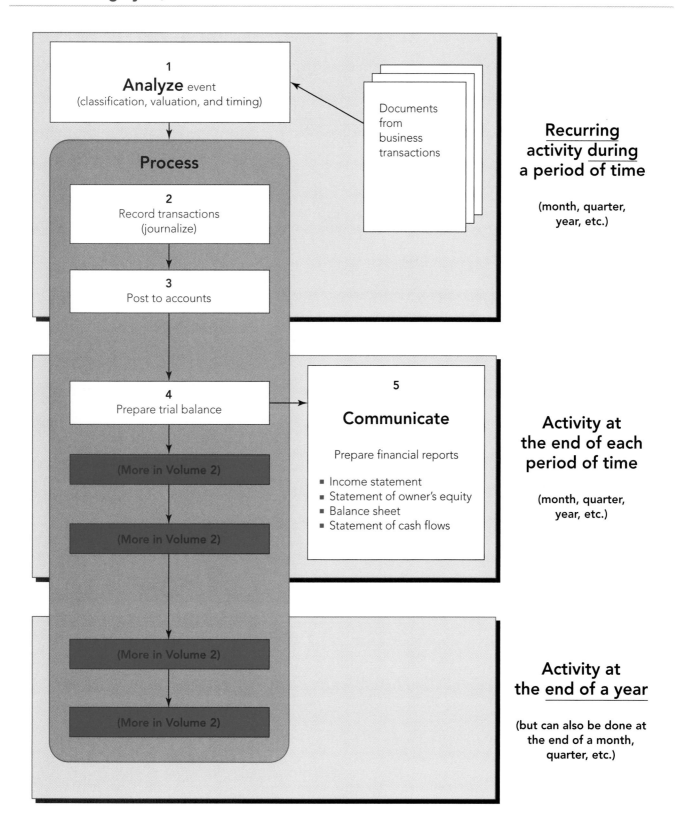

1
Analyze event
(classification, valuation, and timing)

Documents
from
business
transactions

**Recurring
activity during
a period of time**

(month, quarter,
year, etc.)

Process

2
Record transactions
(journalize)

3
Post to accounts

4
Prepare trial balance

(More in Volume 2)

(More in Volume 2)

5

Communicate

Prepare financial reports

- Income statement
- Statement of owner's equity
- Balance sheet
- Statement of cash flows

**Activity at
the end of each
period of time**

(month, quarter,
year, etc.)

(More in Volume 2)

(More in Volume 2)

**Activity at
the end of a year**

(but can also be done at
the end of a month,
quarter, etc.)

PRACTICE   Learning Goal 27

Learning Goal 27 is about the accounting cycle. Use these questions and problems to practice what you have just read.

Multiple Choice
Select the best answer.

1. The accounting cycle consists of these steps in this order:
   a. analyze, journalize, and post
   b. analyze, process, and communicate
   c. communicate, analyze, journalize, and post
   d. none of the above
2. Recording, posting, and preparing a trial balance are all part of
   a. communicating.
   b. analyzing.
   c. transactions.
   d. processing.
3. Preparing financial statements is the most important part of
   a. communicating.
   b. analyzing.
   c. transactions.
   d. processing.
4. Analyzing, journalizing, and posting are activities that happen
   a. on a recurring basis throughout a period of time.
   b. only at the end of a designated period of time.
   c. usually at the end of a year.
   d. none of the above.
5. Preparing financial statements is an activity that usually happens
   a. on a recurring basis throughout a period of time.
   b. only at the end of a designated period of time.
   c. usually at the end of a year.
   d. none of the above.

Reinforcement Problem

LG 27-1. The illustration below is a diagram of the five steps in the accounting cycle that you
have learned up to this point. On a separate piece of paper, copy the illustration and fill in
each of the five empty parts of the illustration by writing in a description for the five steps
that you have learned.

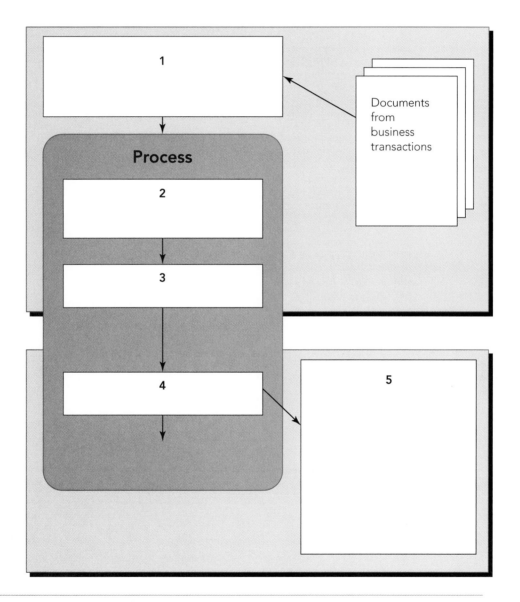

Your Questions?

It is *very* important to be aware of what you need to understand better. What do you need
to understand better about this learning goal? On a separate piece of paper, write the
questions that you want to discuss with your classmates, instructor, or supervisor. Try to
be very specific about what is bothering you, such as explanations that you do not fully
understand.

CUMULATIVE VOCABULARY REVIEW

This is a vocabulary review for Learning Goals 19 through 27. Match each description with the term that it describes. The answer for each term is in the right column. *Suggestion:* Cover the answers in the right column as you test your vocabulary.

Term	Description	Answers
1. Footing	a. A listing of all nonzero ledger account names and balances.	1 h
2. Debit	b. A right-side entry or balance.	2 n
3. Journalize	c. A simple form of an account used for analysis.	3 l
4. Accounting cycle	d. A journal.	4 j
5. Posting	e. An entry consisting of three or more accounts.	5 o
6. Account	f. An abbreviation for "debit."	6 k
7. Journal	g. To debit.	7 m
8. Cr.	h. The balance or total of a column of numbers.	8 p
9. To charge	i. A book or computer file containing all the accounts of a business.	9 g
10. Dr.	j. Analyze, process, and communicate.	10 f
11. General ledger	k. An historical record of all changes in an item in the accounting equation.	11 i
12. Book of original entry	l. To record a transaction in a journal.	12 d
13. Compound entry	m. A chronological recording of transactions, like a diary.	13 e
14. Trial balance	n. A left-side entry or balance.	14 a
15. Ledger account	o. Transferring information from a journal into a ledger.	15 q
16. T account	p. An abbreviation for "credit."	16 c
17. Credit	q. An account showing debit, credit, balance, date, explanation, and posting reference.	17 b

CUMULATIVE TEST   Learning Goals 19–27

Solutions are on page 532

Time Limit: 55 Minutes

Instructions

*Select the best answer to each question. Do **not** look back in the book when taking the test. (If you need to do this, you are not ready.) After you finish the test, refer to the answers and circle the number of each question that you missed. Then go to the **Help Table** (on page 533) to identify your strong and weak knowledge areas by individual learning goal.*

Multiple Choice
On the line provided, enter the letter of the best answer for each question.

1. Which one of the following is *not* one of the five basic data arrangements?
   a. seeing the balance of any item in the accounting equation
   b. seeing the audit trail posting reference of an entry in a ledger account
   c. seeing all the parts of a transaction together in one place
   d. keeping an historical record of all increases and decreases for each item in the accounting equation

2. The natural positive balance (normal balance) of an account is
   a. the minimum balance that must always be maintained in an account.
   b. always located on the side of the account used for increases.
   c. always located on the side of the account used for decreases.
   d. always calculated by excluding the beginning balance of the account.

3. Owner's equity accounts that will be increased by a debit would be
   a. revenues and expenses.   c. expenses and drawing.
   b. capital and revenue.   d. revenue and drawing.

4. To record a decrease in an account, use
   a. debits.
   b. credits.
   c. credits, if the normal balance is debit, and debits if the normal balance is credit.
   d. credits, if the normal balance is credit, and debits if the normal balance is debit.

5. All the accounts of a business are grouped together in a book or file called the
   a. ledger.   c. trial balance.
   b. journal.   d. accounting system.

6. The general journal does *not* do which of the following?
   a. provide a chronological record of all transactions
   b. show all the accounts involved in each transaction together
   c. show the balance of each account
   d. help locate recording errors by showing debits and credits together for each transaction

7. You are looking at the Accounts Payable account in the ledger, and you see an entry in the "Posting Reference" column (sometimes called the "LP" or "Folio" column). This entry
   a. refers to the account number of that account.
   b. refers to a page number in the journal.
   c. refers to the sequential number of the journal entry.
   d. refers to the date of the original transaction.

8. "Posting" means that transaction information is transferred from the
   a. journal to the trial balance.   c. ledger to the journal.
   b. ledger to the trial balance.   d. journal to the ledger.

9. A trial balance is
   a. a listing of accounts and their balances, usually prepared at any point in time.
   b. a listing of the names of accounts with their account numbers, prepared before a new account is added.
   c. a listing of nonzero accounts and their balances, usually prepared at the end of an accounting period.
   d. another name for the book of accounts.

10. Which of the following account types should show a normal credit balance?
    a. asset, liability, and expense
    c. liability, revenue, and owner's capital
    b. asset, revenue, and liability
    d. liability, expense, and drawing

11. The usual sequence in the recording of transaction data is
    a. analyze the event, post into the ledger, journalize, prepare the trial balance.
    b. journalize the transaction, analyze the event, prepare a trial balance, post into the ledger.
    c. analyze the event, journalize, post into the ledger, prepare a trial balance.
    d. analyze the event, journalize, post into the ledger.

12. Use the journal entry below to answer the next question.

Date	Account Titles and Explanation	Post. Ref.	Debit	Credit
2008				
August 3	Supplies		220	
	Accounts Payable			220

This journal entry is recording
a. the purchase of supplies.
c. the using up of supplies.
b. the payment of a liability.
d. an owner investment of personal supplies into the business.

13. A manager needs to know how much merchandise inventory the company has available. This is an example of needing to use which kind of data arrangement?
    a. a chronological record of transactions
    b. an historical record of all increases and decreases for each item in the accounting equation
    c. the balance of any item in the accounting equation
    d. all the accounts involved in each individual transaction

14. An account is
    a. an historical record of transactions, like a diary.
    b. a listing of all balances for each asset, liability, or owner's equity item in the equation.
    c. a description of recordable business events.
    d. an historical record of all changes and the balance of an asset, liability, or owner's equity item.

15. Increases in the owner's capital are usually the result of
    a. debits to revenue accounts and debits to expense accounts.
    b. credits to revenue accounts and debits to the capital account.
    c. debits to expense accounts and debits to revenue accounts.
    d. none of the above.

16. Use the illustration to answer the next question.

Accounts Receivable	
bal. 2,000	
15,000	10,000

The best explanation of what happened in this account is
a. credits increased the account by $15,000, resulting in a $7,000 credit balance.
b. credits decreased the account by $10,000 and debits increased the account by $15,000, resulting in a $7,000 credit balance.
c. credits decreased the account by $10,000 and debits increased the account by $15,000, resulting in a $5,000 debit balance.
d. credits decreased the account by $10,000 and debits increased the account by $15,000, resulting in a $7,000 debit balance.

17. If you want to know the amount of the accounts payable owing as of today, you would look in
a. the journal.   c. the book of original entry.
b. the ledger.   d. the trial balance.

18. Which of the following journal entries has been recorded correctly?

a.

Cash		500
Wages Expense	500	

b.

Equipment	3,700	
Cash		1,650
Notes Payable		1,950

c.

Supplies Expense	500	
Telephone Expense	900	
Accounts Payable		1,400

d. None of the above.

19. Tempe Service Company shows a normal accounts payable balance of $10,500 on December 31. During December, there were payments to creditors of $11,900 and new purchases on account of $10,700. The balance of accounts payable on December 1 was a
a. credit balance of $1,200.   c. credit balance of $11,700.
b. debit balance of $11,700.   d. credit balance of $9,300.

20. Which error would *not* cause the total credits in a trial balance to be greater than the total debits?
a. Cash sales of $5,000 recorded in the journal is accidentally posted twice into the ledger by debiting Land $5,000 and crediting Notes Payable $5,000.
b. A journal entry recording cash collections from customers of $200 is posted as a debit to the Cash account in the ledger for $200 and as a credit to Accounts Receivable for $2,000.
c. The account balance of Accounts Receivable is a normal balance of $950, and is entered in the trial balance "Credit" column for $950.
d. None of the above.

21. A journal entry that consists of three or more accounts is called a
    a. complex entry.   c. compound entry.
    b. simple entry.   d. group entry.

22. A partner of the Burlington and Champlain partnership wants to know why the Notes Payable account shows increases of $20,000 during September. This is an example of needing which kind of accounting data arrangement?
    a. a chronological record of transactions
    b. an historical record of all increases and decreases for each item in the accounting equation
    c. the balance of any item in the accounting equation
    d. all the accounts involved in each individual transaction

23. Which of the following is *not* true about the words "debit" and "credit"?
    a. Debits are increases and credits are decreases.
    b. Debits and credits can describe the balance of an account.
    c. Debits and credits can describe increases and decreases in an account.
    d. The left side of an account is called the debit side, and the right side is called the credit side.

24. The usual sequence of accounts in the ledger is
    a. assets, expenses, owner's capital, revenues, drawing.
    b. revenues, expenses, drawing, assets, liabilities.
    c. liabilities, assets, revenues, drawing, expenses.
    d. assets, liabilities, owner's capital, revenues, expenses.

25. Which of the following is *not* true?
    a. Assets are increased by credits.   c. Revenues are increased by credits.
    b. Liabilities are decreased by debits.   d. Expenses are increased by debits.

26. The trial balance would not detect which error?
    a. recording revenue on account by debiting Service Revenue and debiting Accounts Receivable
    b. incorrectly totaling the balance in a ledger account
    c. debiting Cash and forgetting to credit Accounts Receivable
    d. forgetting to post an entire transaction already recorded in the journal

27. The correct general journal entry to record the purchase of supplies for cash would include
    a. a debit to Cash recorded just above the credit to Supplies.
    b. a debit to Cash recorded just below the credit to Supplies.
    c. a credit to Supplies recorded just below the debit to Cash.
    d. a debit to Supplies recorded just above the credit to Cash.

28. The ending balance of any account can be calculated as
    a. the total debits, minus the total credits.
    b. the beginning balance, minus the total credits, plus the total debits.
    c. the beginning balance, plus the total increases, minus the total decreases.
    d. the beginning balance, plus the total credits, minus the total debits.

29. The Concord Company shows revenues with credit balances totaling $38,000, total debits to Accounts Receivable of $10,000, expenses with debit balances totaling $42,000, and debits to the drawing account totaling $5,000. The company had a
    a. net income of $6,000.   c. net loss of $4,000.
    b. net income of $1,000.   d. net loss of $9,000.

30. In October, the Supplies account of Dover Company has a normal beginning balance of $7,300, total debits of $12,950, and a normal ending balance of $14,400. What was the October Supplies Expense?
    a. $5,850   c. $12,950
    b. $1,450   d. none of the above

31. If you want to find the ledger account number for Rent Expense, you would look in
  a. the chart of accounts.   c. the ledger.
  b. the journal.   d. none of the above.

32. The correct general journal entry to record fees earned on account includes
  a. a debit to Cash recorded just above the credit to a revenue.
  b. a credit to a revenue recorded just below the debit to Accounts Receivable.
  c. a debit to a revenue recorded just below the credit to Accounts Receivable.
  d. a credit to Accounts Receivable recorded just below the debit to a revenue.

33. Which of the following is correct?
  a. Information is first entered in a journal, and then entered in the chart of accounts.
  b. Information is first entered in a journal, which will have ledger account numbers after the information is transferred to the ledger.
  c. The journal and the ledger contain exactly the same information.
  d. Both (b) and (c) are correct.

34. Financial statements are prepared from the
  a. general journal.   c. trial balance.
  b. general ledger.   d. none of the above.

35. Which of these accounts is *not* a subdivision of the owner's capital?
  a. revenues   c. drawing
  b. liabilities   d. expenses

Use this table for the next two questions:

	Assets	Liabilities	Owner's Capital	Revenue	Expense	Drawing
Debit	1	2	3			
Credit			4	5	6	

36. The boxes labeled "1," "2," and "3" in the table above should contain the words
  a. decrease, increase, increase.   c. decrease, decrease, increase.
  b. increase, decrease, increase.   d. increase, decrease, decrease.

37. The boxes labeled "4," "5," and "6" in the table above should contain the words
  a. increase, increase, decrease.   c. decrease, decrease, decrease.
  b. increase, decrease, increase.   d. decrease, decrease, increase.

38. An auditor is examining the Cash ledger account. She wants to verify the account balance by locating and checking the transactions that affected the account. The auditor should:
  a. use posting references in the ledger account to locate transactions in the journal.
  b. scan the journal to locate relevant transactions.
  c. use the posting references in the ledger account to locate accounts in the chart of accounts.
  d. search documents that contain the same debit and credit amounts in the Cash account.

CUMULATIVE TEST SOLUTIONS   Learning Goals 19–27

Multiple Choice

1. b **2.** b **3.** c Because expenses and drawing are reducing the owner's capital.

4. c *Remember:* decreases are simply the side opposite from increases. **5.** a **6.** c

7. b An entry in the ledger should always be traceable to the page of the journal where it originated. **8.** d **9.** c **10.** c **11.** c **12.** a **13.** c **14.** d

15. d The correct answer is credits to revenue accounts and credits to the owner's capital account.

16. d This is an asset account, so credits decrease it and debits increase it.

17. b Because the ledger contains all the accounts and their balances.

18. c (a) is wrong because the credits have been recorded before the debits. (b) is wrong for two reasons: first, the names of the accounts being credited are not indented; second, the total credits add up to 3,600 but the debit is for 3,700.

19. c When calculating a missing amount in an account, *you have two good choices:* (1) you can use the formula that applies to all accounts: **beginning balance + increases – decreases = ending balance** or (2) you can set up a T account, plug in the information that you know, and look for the missing amount. If you use the first approach, then: $X + 10{,}700 – 11{,}900 = 10{,}500$. Therefore, $X = 11{,}700$. The natural positive balance (normal balance) of accounts payable is a credit balance. Using the T account method:

Accounts Payable

	?
10,700	11,900
	10,500

20. a Even though mistakes were made in the entry (a), total debits equal total credits. In entry (b), credits will exceed debits by $1,800. In (c), a $950 debit is entered as a $950 credit, making the credits in the trial balance exceed debits by $1,900.

21. c **22.** a A journal would contain the transactions that explain the increases.

23. a **24.** d **25.** a

26. d Forgetting to post an entry does not cause total debits and credits to be unequal in the ledger accounts. All the other situations will cause the total debits and credits in the ledger to be unequal. In (a), there are two debits and no credits. In (b), the incorrect total will cause total debits and credits in the ledger to be unequal. In (c), there is a debit but no credit.

27. d *Always try to visualize the entry.* Write it down if you need to:

Supplies	xxx	
Cash		xxx

28. c Debits and credits do not mean increase or decrease, only left and right.

29. c The formula for net income (or loss) is: **Revenues – Expenses = Net Income (or loss)**. Therefore, $38{,}000 – $42{,}000 = –$4{,}000$. The debits to the accounts receivable are already included as part of the total revenue. Drawings are not expenses and do not affect the net income.

30. a Supplies expense means the amount of supplies used up. You need to calculate the decrease in the Supplies account. So, this is like #19.

   (a) You can use the formula for an account: **beginning balance + increases – decreases = ending balance**. Because Supplies is an asset account, debits are increases, therefore: $7{,}300 + 12{,}950 – X = 14{,}400$. This gives: $–X = –5{,}850$. So, $X = 5{,}850$.

   (b) *Using the T account approach:*

Supplies

7,300	
12,950	?
14,400	

31. a **32.** b *Always try to visualize the entry.* Write it down if you need to:

Accounts Receivable	xxx	
Fees Earned		xxx

33. d **34.** c **35.** b **36.** d **37.** a **38.** a

HELP TABLE

Identify Your Strengths and Weaknesses

The questions in this test cover the nine learning goals of Section V. After you have circled the number of each question that you missed, look at the table below.

Go to the first learning goal category in the table: "Explain the Five Kinds of Information." The second column in the table shows which questions on the test covered this learning goal. Look on the test to see if you circled numbers 1, 13, or 22. How many did you miss? Write this number in the "How Many Missed?" column. Repeat this process for each of the remaining learning goal categories in the table.

If you *miss **two** or more questions* for any learning goal, you are too weak in that learning goal and you need to *review*. The last column shows you where to read and practice so you can improve your score.

Some learning goal categories have more questions because you need to be especially well prepared in these areas. More questions means your performance must be better.

Learning Goal	Questions	How many missed?	Material begins on . . .
Section V			
19. Explain the Five Kinds of Information	1, 13, 22		page 385
20. Explain the Use of Accounts	2, 14, 16, 19, 28, 30		page 394
21. Use the Owner's Capital Accounts	3, 15, 29, 35		page 411
22. "Debits on the left, credits on the right!"	4, 10, 23, 25, 36, 37		page 427
23. Use a Ledger	5, 17, 24, 31		page 442
24. Use a Journal	6, 12, 18, 21, 27, 32		page 449
25. Use a Basic Accounting System	7, 8, 33, 38		page 479
26. The Trial Balance—Prepare It and Use It Two Ways*	9, 20, 26, 34		page 503
27. Explain the Accounting Cycle	11		page 521

* For Learning Goal 26, you should also practice preparing a balance sheet, an income statement, and a statement of owner's equity on a blank piece of paper from the information on a trial balance. Use problems in any book for which you also have a solution.

VI Corporations

What this section does

This section provides you with a comprehensive introduction to fundamental corporate concepts. Additionally, to maintain a single and unified presentation of the topic, the discussion continues beyond the basic concepts to more in-depth subjects of corporate accounting procedures and financial reporting.

How to use this section	If you want . . .	then read . . .
	. . . only an introduction to the corporate concept and form of business . . .	Learning Goal 28.
	. . . an introduction to basic corporate accounting concepts and procedures . . .	Learning Goals 28 and 29.
	. . . an in-depth introduction to corporate accounting and financial reporting, including some challenging cumulative problems . . .	all of Section VI.

Suggestion

It is not necessary to complete this section to continue to Volume 2. You can study the principles and procedures in Volume 2 and later return here as appropriate for your own goals.

LEARNING GOALS

LEARNING GOAL 28	# Describe the Corporate Entity

Introduction

Because of their ability to obtain large amounts of money by selling ownership shares to the public, corporations (called **publicly traded** corporations) have become a successful and dominating economic force in American and international business operations. The corporation as a business entity was introduced in Learning Goal 5 when we analyzed the major types of business entities. The discussion that follows provides more detailed information about corporations.

In Learning Goal 28, you will find:

The Corporation

Issuing Stock

The Corporation Defined

Definition

A **corporation** is an entity that is created by law and has the specific qualities that are described below.

Separate Legal Person

Because a corporation is created by law, it is a "legal person," different and separate from any living "natural person." As a legal person, a corporation acts independently, in its own name. For example, a corporation buys, sells, enters into binding contracts, pays taxes, sues, and can be sued. None of these actions are legally binding on the owners (stockholders) of the corporation who purchase shares of stock. Also, as a separate legal person, a corporation has a continuous existence that is not affected by changes in ownership.

The Corporation Defined, *continued*

Stockholder Limited Liability	Because the acts of corporations do not bind the stockholders (owners), creditors can look only to corporate assets to satisfy claims. Therefore, the assets of individual stockholders are generally protected from corporate creditors, even if a corporation becomes bankrupt. The result is that a stockholder ordinarily has limited personal liability and can lose no more than the amount of the investment in a company's stock.

> *Note:* There are a few exceptions. Especially, if an owner, officer, or director performs a fraudulent or illegal act in the name of a corporation. Such an individual may have personal liability.

Ownership	The ownership of a corporation is divided into units. These units are called shares of stock (often called capital stock), and owners are called stockholders or shareholders. Shares of capital stock are the means of identifying ownership in a corporation. There are different kinds of stock, and we will discuss this in more detail a little later.

Transfer of Ownership	Stock shares are the personal property of the owner and can be transferred by the owner. This can be done by selling the stock or by an exchange, gift, or other methods. The transfer of the stock does not require the consent of any other stockholders, and the transfer will have no effect on the activities of the business. The stock is said to be **negotiable**. (Notice how this is different from a partnership, in which transfer of ownership usually requires approval of other partners and terminates the existing partnership.)

> *Note:* Some limited exceptions may defer the time of transfer. This often involves new issues for what is called *restricted stock*.

No Mutual Agency	"Mutual agency" means that all the owners of a business can act as agents of the business. Therefore, the acts of any owner will be binding on the business and affect all the other owners. This is what happens in partnerships. There is no mutual agency for corporations. An individual can act as a corporate agent only if the corporation has approved that individual to act as an agent. Officers, directors, and employees of a corporation are generally considered to be agents.

continued ▶

The Corporation Defined, *continued*

Centralized Management Authority	Stockholders are the owners of a corporation. Stockholders indirectly control the management of a corporation by electing a board of directors that acts as the central management authority. The ***board of directors*** is a group of responsible individuals who vote on corporate policy, supervise management, and safeguard the interests of the stockholders. In larger businesses, the board of directors delegates many management duties by hiring professional corporate officers and managers.

Often, members of the board of directors are also stockholders of the same corporation. In particular, in small corporations with just one or a few stockholders, the stockholders will also be members of the board of directors. |
| ***Double Taxation*** | A corporation is a separate "person" for legal purposes. Therefore, a corporation pays taxes on its income. (This is unlike a proprietorship or partnership in which an owner's share of income is reported as part of his or her personal taxable income.)

In addition to a corporation paying tax on its income, when cash from that income is distributed to stockholders in the form of dividends, the stockholders also pay tax on the dividends. For this reason, it is said that the same stream of corporate income is taxed twice—once at the corporate level and again at the individual level. (*Exception:* Certain tax elections can eliminate double taxation for small corporations.) |

The Corporate People

Overview	Although a corporation can exist legally on paper, real people are needed to create, organize, manage, and own the corporation. The following discussion summarizes who these people are and what they do. These people are the:

- Incorporator
- Stockholders
- Directors
- Officers and managers |

The Corporate People, *continued*

Incorporator

The ***incorporator*** is the person who chooses a corporate name and completes the application process to create the corporation. This application contains the articles of incorporation. The incorporator completes and signs the articles of incorporation and files the application with the official—usually the secretary of state—of the state that will approve the creation of the corporation. By law, the incorporator has a fiduciary responsibility to provide full disclosure and act independently and honestly. Incorporators are often stockholders.

> *Note:* A *fiduciary* responsibility is one that requires honesty, trustworthiness, and competence.

Stockholders

Stockholders are the owners of a corporation. The number of shares of stock that a stockholder owns determines the stockholder's proportionate (percentage) ownership. Stockholders have the following basic rights (unless otherwise restricted):

- Share proportionately in profits and losses
- Share proportionately in voting for matters requiring stockholder approval
- Share proportionately in the remaining assets when a business liquidates (goes out of business)

Directors

A director is an individual elected by stockholders to a position on the board of directors. The directors meet and vote on corporate policy and supervise the management on behalf of the stockholders. By law, directors also have a ***fiduciary duty*** to safeguard the financial condition of the corporation and the stockholders' investments and to act honestly and in good faith.

Officers and Managers

Officers and managers are employees who are responsible for the day-to-day management and operations. Officers are the president, often called the ***chief executive officer*** (or ***CEO***), vice president of finance, who is usually the ***chief financial officer*** (or ***CFO***), other vice presidents, secretary, and other designated officers. Like directors, officers have a fiduciary duty to act honestly and in good faith. Also, the CEO and CFO of publicly traded companies are personally liable for the accuracy of financial statements. The relationships above are summarized below in an ***organization chart***.

Often the most powerful and influential individual in a company is the chairman of the board of directors.

continued ▶

The Corporate People, *continued*

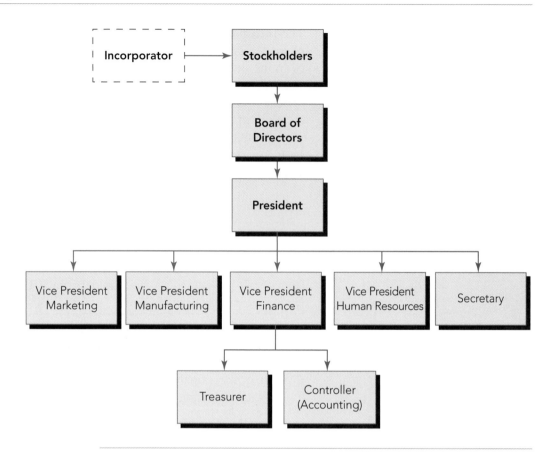

Small Corporations

In a small corporation with one or just a few stockholders, the same individuals generally can be the incorporator, stockholder(s), directors, and officers. For example, if Jane decides to form a corporation for her new computer repair business, she can be the incorporator, the only stockholder, the only board member, and the only officer.

VOCABULARY

Callable preferred stock: preferred stock that can be purchased from stockholders by the issuing corporation at a fixed price (page 570)

Capital stock: another term for the total par or stated value of issued stock (page 567)

Convertible preferred stock: preferred stock that is convertible into common stock (page 569)

Cumulative dividend: a feature of preferred stock requiring that all dividends declared must be paid for preferred dividends in arrears plus current preferred dividend before common stockholders can receive a dividend (page 568)

Date of record: the date by which stock ownership must be officially recorded for the owner to receive a dividend (page 565)

Declaration date: the date that a board of directors approves a dividend (page 565)

Dilution: a reduction in the percentage ownership of existing stockholders in a class of stock (also a reduction in earnings per share—see Learning Goal 31) (page 560)

Dividends: non-liquidating distributions of assets from a corporation to its stockholders (page 558)

Dividends in arrears: dividends not declared on cumulative preferred stock (page 568)

Ex-dividend date: the date before which a stock must be purchased to allow enough time for the buyer's name to be officially recorded to receive a dividend—usually two business days before the date of record (page 565)

Legal capital: a minimum amount of paid-in capital that must be maintained for the protection of creditors and that can never be paid to stockholders until the corporation is liquidated and creditors are paid in full (page 554)

Limited liability: investor personal liability that is limited to the part of the investment that is legal capital (page 555)

Liquidating dividend: a dividend that exceeds the balance in retained earnings (page 564)

No-par stock: stock without a par value (page 555)

Organization Expense (also Organization Cost): the account names used to record the costs of organizing and forming a corporation (page 562)

Paid-in capital: the part of stockholders' equity that comes from investments in the corporation, primarily by stockholders (page 553)

Paid-in capital in excess of par (or excess of stated value): paid-in capital that represents non-legal capital (page 556)

Par value: a minimal amount per share that is paid in and establishes a stockholder's limit of liability (page 555)

Payment date: the date a dividend is paid (page 565)

Participating preferred stock: a preferred stock that receives additional dividends, based on a formula, after the common stockholders are paid (page 570)

Preemptive right: the right of existing stockholders to maintain the same percentage ownership in the same class of stock (page 560)

Preferred stock: a type of stock that gives its owners dividend and liquidation preferences over common stockholders (page 556)

Residual claim: the owners' right to share in assets only after the creditors are paid (page 560)

Retained earnings: the part of the stockholders' equity claim that comes from the cumulative amount of net income since the business was formed, *less* net losses, dividends, and certain stockholders' equity transactions (page 557)

Secret reserves: under-valued assets received for stock (page 562)

Start-up costs: a name that refers to the costs related to organizing and forming a corporation or any other business (page 562)

Stockholders' equity: the owners' equity of a corporation (page 552)

Stock premium: another term for paid-in capital in excess of par (page 556)

Watered stock: stock that is issued for over-valued assets (page 562)

PRACTICE   **Learning Goal 29**

Solutions are in the disk at the back of the book and at: www.worthyjames.com

This learning goal is about owners' equity of a corporation. Use these questions and problems to practice what you have just read.

Multiple Choice
Select the best answer.

1. How is stockholders' equity categorized on a balance sheet?
   a. by claims on wealth: liabilities and capital
   b. by type of stock: preferred stock and common stock
   c. by sources of capital: paid-in capital and retained earnings
   d. by dividend preference
2. Par value and stated value
   a. provide a limited and fixed amount of protection for creditors.
   b. are the same as legal capital, which prohibits negative retained earnings.
   c. are good indicators of the true value of stock.
   d. must be used with all types of stock, by state law.
3. Stockholders' equity shows total paid-in capital of $500,000 from common stock and retained earnings of $230,000. The paid-in capital in excess of par on common stock is $450,000. What is the total par value?
   a. $50,000
   b. $450,000
   c. $500,000
   d. $730,000
4. The true amount of legal capital
   a. should always be clearly presented in stockholders' equity.
   b. may not always be able to be shown in stockholders' equity.
   c. always depends on the amount of par value.
   d. none of the above
5. The basic type of stock issued by every corporation is
   a. preferred stock.
   b. common stock.
   c. par value stock.
   d. capital stock.
6. Corporations may issue preferred stock and different classes of stock because
   a. state laws limit the number of shares of any particular class or type of stock.
   b. GAAP limits the number of shares of any particular class or type of stock.
   c. corporations are trying to obtain the most money possible by appealing to different investors.
   d. different classes of stock will provide additional protection to creditors.
7. Retained earnings
   a. cannot be negative.
   b. is part of total paid-in capital.
   c. should be included as part of legal capital.
   d. none of the above
8. Huntsville, Inc. issued 20,000 shares of $.10 par value common stock at $8 per share. The journal entry should include
   a. a debit to Cash of $160,000 and a credit to Common Stock of $160,000.
   b. a debit to Cash of $2,000 and a credit to Common Stock of $2,000.
   c. a debit to Cash of $160,000 and a credit to Common Stock of $2,000.
   d. none of the above

9. Montgomery Corporation has issued 10,000 shares of 4%, $50 par value preferred stock that was sold at par. The company also has issued 100,000 shares of $.01 par value common stock that has a paid-in capital in excess of par of $171,000 dollars. The retained earnings is $720,000. What is the total stockholders' equity?
    a. $720,000
    b. $891,000
    c. $1,391,000
    d. none of the above

10. Stock is issued for
    a. cash.
    b. non-cash assets, such as equipment.
    c. services.
    d. all of the above

11. Ashland Company became a corporation and issued 2,000 shares of $1 par value stock to the attorney who provided legal services for the incorporation and who agreed to accept the shares instead of billing $10,000 for the value of her services. The journal entries should include
    a. a debit to Organization Expense of $2,000.
    b. a credit to Common Stock of $8,000.
    c. a debit to Organization Expense of $10,000 and a credit to paid-in capital in excess of par of $8,000.
    d. a debit to Organization Expense of $10,000 and a credit to Common Stock of $10,000.

12. To receive a dividend, stock must be purchased before the
    a. declaration date.
    b. date of record.
    c. ex-dividend date.
    d. payment date.

13. A dividend becomes a liability on the
    a. declaration date.
    b. date of record.
    c. ex-dividend date.
    d. payment date.

14. The annual amount of dividend that a corporation should pay on 20,000 shares of 6%, $100 par value preferred stock is
    a. $12,000.
    b. $120,000.
    c. $2,000,000.
    d. none of the above

15. Siskiyou Corporation has issued 5,000 shares of $5, $50 par preferred stock and 100,000 shares of $.10 par common stock. The board of directors declared a $200,000 annual dividend. How much will the common stockholders receive?
    a. $10,000
    b. $175,000
    c. $200,000
    d. none of the above

16. Klamath Falls, Inc. has issued 7,000 shares of 4%, $100 par cumulative preferred stock and 200,000 shares of $.01 stated value common stock. The preferred stock is 2 years in arrears, not including the current year. The board of directors declared a $250,000 dividend for the current year. How much will the common shareholders receive?
    a. $166,000
    b. $194,000
    c. $250,000
    d. none of the above

17. For which of the following rights does preferred stock generally *not* have preference over common stock?
    a. dividends
    b. preference in liquidation
    c. voting
    d. none of the above

18. No-par stock
    a. shows the legal capital as the stockholders' equity balances of "Common Stock" or "Preferred Stock."
    b. is recorded as Paid-in Capital in Excess of Par for common or preferred stock.
    c. always has a minimum stated value.
    d. none of the above

19. Which of the following does *not* correctly describe legal capital? Legal capital
    a. equals the amounts shown as "Common Stock" or "Preferred Stock" in stockholders' equity.
    b. is the minimum amount of permanent capital a corporation must maintain.
    c. is intended to provide protection to a corporation's creditors.
    d. all of the above

20. The maximum number of shares of stock that a corporation can issue is called
    a. Paid-in Capital in Excess of Par.
    b. legal capital shares.
    c. authorized shares.
    d. issued shares.

21. Organization costs of a corporation are
    a. recorded as an expense when incurred.
    b. recorded as an asset when incurred.
    c. not recorded.
    d. recorded at a value determined by the board of directors.

22. What is the correct description of the shares of stock that a corporation has sold?
    a. issued stock
    b. outstanding stock
    c. authorized stock
    d. par-value stock

23. What are the basic categories of stockholders' equity?
    a. legal capital and par value
    b. paid-in capital and retained earnings
    c. common stock and preferred stock
    d. paid-in capital, retained earnings, and legal capital

24. Capital maintenance requirements
    a. are established at the time stock is issued.
    b. are usually less than par or stated value amounts.
    c. are usually greater than par or stated value amounts.
    d. usually include the balance of retained earnings.

25. Retained earnings
    a. are part of paid-in capital.
    b. are the cumulative amount of undistributed income minus losses.
    c. do include losses incurred.
    d. cannot have a negative balance.

Discussion Questions and Brief Exercises

1. What is the difference between legal capital and par value? Describe the features of par value.

2. What is the difference between paid-in capital and retained earnings?

3. How much can an investor lose as a result of investing in a corporation? How much is an investor's personal liability to creditors?

4. Wakefield Corporation has issued 10,000 shares of $100 par, 5% cumulative preferred stock. Calculate the preferred dividend payable for each of the following situations. Explain your calculations.
   a. The current annual dividend is declared.
   b. The current quarterly dividend is declared.
   c. The dividends are 2 years in arrears, and the current quarterly dividend is declared.

5. Providence, Inc. has declared a dividend payable on April 20 to stockholders of record of on March 31. What do these dates signify? By what date would an investor normally have to purchase the stock to receive the dividend?

6. Warwick Corporation has issued callable $100 par, $4, cumulative preferred stock that was sold at $101 and is callable at a price of $104. 10,000 shares are issued. How much would Warwick Corporation pay to call the stock under each of the following situations? Explain your calculations.
   a. 5,000 shares are called, and the most recent quarterly dividend has been paid.
   b. 5,000 shares are called, and the most recent quarterly dividend has not been paid.
   c. 5,000 shares are called, the preferred stock is 2 years in arrears, not counting the current quarterly dividend, which has not been paid.

7. Why is preferred stock called "preferred"? What are the typical differences between preferred stock and common stock?

8. Why do corporations issue preferred stock? Why do corporations issue different classes of stock?

9. What different items of paid-in capital were presented in this learning goal? Describe the items.

10. Pawtucket Corporation has issued 12,000 shares of convertible $75 par, 5%, cumulative preferred stock, issued at $77 per share. Each share of preferred is convertible into 3 shares of $1 par common. Prepare the general journal entry if 4,000 shares are converted to common stock by preferred stockholders. Is there a gain or loss? Does total stockholders' equity change?

11. What are the meanings of the following dates: date of declaration, date of record, ex-dividend date, and payment date? On which dates are journal entries necessary?

12. What are the meanings of "cumulative," "callable," and "convertible" as they relate to preferred stock?

13. When stock is issued for non-cash assets, what is the procedure for determining the value of the transaction (the amount of the increase in paid-in capital)?

Solutions are in the disk at the back of the book and at: www.worthyjames.com

PRACTICE   Learning Goal 29, continued

14. Identify each item below as either a preferred stock characteristic or a common stock characteristic.
    a. usually non-voting
    b. dividends with the greatest variability
    c. can be callable
    d. usually receives assets before other classes of stock in liquidation
    e. will be the most profitable if the business is very profitable
    f. can be convertible
    g. often has a claim on unpaid dividends from previous years

15. If you are an investor considering the purchase of a common stock, which value will be the most important in your decision: par value or market value?

16. Raymer Corporation began business on January 3, 2006. It issued 250,000 shares of no-par common stock and 10,000 shares of $100 par value, 6%, cumulative preferred stock on January 3. In 2006, the company paid no dividends. In 2007, the board of directors declared a $125,000 dividend for the year. In 2008, the board of directors declared a $150,000 dividend. What was the total amount of dividends received by the preferred and common stockholders each year?

17. What are the two methods for protecting creditors that are imposed by state laws?

18. When a corporation is liquidated, what will be the likely results for stockholders? How valuable is the preferred stock liquidating preference in these situations?

19. Assume that a corporation receives stock subscriptions for 100,000 shares of $.10 par value common stock. The share price is $12 per share, and the subscription agreement requires a 40% down payment. How much cash will be received when the subscriptions are received? How much cash will be received after the subscriptions are fully paid by all investors? How and when is stockholders' equity affected by the subscription and the issuance of stock?

20. What three requirements must be fulfilled for a corporation to pay dividends?

21. What is dilution?

Reinforcement Problems

LG 29-1. **Prepare stockholders' equity, calculate dividend.** Shown below are selected December 31, 200X year-end account balances for Springfield Corporation.

a. Use the account balances to prepare the stockholders' equity section of the balance sheet.
b. Calculate the total annual dividend for the preferred stock.

Account	Balance	Account	Balance
Paid-in Capital in Excess of Par, Common Stock	$650,000	Retained earnings	$985,000
Common Stock, $.10 par value, 100,000 shares issued	10,000	Preferred Stock, $50 par value, 4%, 5,000 shares issued	250,000

Solutions are in the disk at the back of the book and at: www.worthyjames.com

PRACTICE   Learning Goal 29, continued

LG 29-2. Prepare stockholders' equity, analyze results. Shown below are selected December 31, 200X year-end account balances for St. Louis Company, Incorporated.

- Use the account balances to prepare the stockholders' equity section of the balance sheet.
- Calculate the average selling price per share of the preferred stock and the common stock.
- Can you make any conclusions about the results of the company's operations?
- Calculate the total annual dividend for the preferred stock.

Account	Balance	Account	Balance
Paid-in Capital in Excess of Par, Common Stock..................	$3,150,000	Retained earnings..............	($785,000)
Common Stock, $.05 par value, 300,000 shares issued.............	?	Preferred Stock, $100 par value, $6, 10,000 shares issued............	1,000,000
Paid-in-Capital in Excess of Par, Preferred Stock.................	108,000		

LG 29-3. Prepare journal entries. Racine Enterprises incorporated its business and completed the transactions that you see below.

a. Journalize the transactions. (For journal paper, you can make general journal copies from the disk at the back of this book.)
b. Analyze the transactions. Who do you think got the best deal on the issuance of the common stock—the legal and accounting firms or the equipment supplier? How did you determine this?

Oct. 10   Sold 500,000 shares of $.10 par value common stock to an underwriter for $11 per share, less a 7% deduction for the underwriter's commission. The underwriter will not offer the shares for sale to the public until November 1, when they will begin to trade on stock exchanges.

   19   Received bills from the law firm and the CPA firm that completed the business incorporation. The legal and accounting costs were $125,000 based on normal hourly rates; however, the law firm and CPA firm agreed to accept a total of 15,000 shares of common stock instead of cash. As of this date, the stock is not yet trading on stock exchanges.

   25   The company exchanged 12,000 shares of common stock to an equipment supply company for manufacturing equipment that had a standard invoice price of $175,000 among all vendors.

Nov. 12   Sold 2,500 shares of preferred stock for $253,750 to investors without the use of an underwriter. The preferred stock is cumulative, $100 par value, with a 4% annual dividend. (Shares of company stock began trading regularly on November 1.)

LG 29-4. **Prepare journal entries.** Madison Corporation concluded the selected transactions that you see below during 2008 and 2009.

a. Journalize the transactions. (For journal paper, you can make general journal copies from the disk at the back of this book.)

2008
Jan. 3   The board of directors declared a $100,000 annual cash dividend to stockholders of record as of January 10. Madison Corporation has 7,500 shares of $100 par, 3% preferred stock outstanding and 100,000 shares of $.01 par common stock outstanding.
   17   Paid the cash dividends.
   30   Issued 10,000 shares of a new Class B no par, $2.50 preferred stock. The new preferred stock was sold at a price of $51 per share.
Jan. 27 Issued an additional 50,000 shares of common stock at a price of $22 per share.

2009
Jan. 12 The board of directors declared a $50,000 annual cash dividend to stockholders of record as January 19.
   31   Paid the cash dividends.

LG 29-5. **Prepare journal entries and stockholders' equity.** Akron, Inc. completed the selected transactions that you see below during 2008.

a. Journalize the transactions. (For journal paper, you can make general journal copies from the disk at the back of this book.)
b. Prepare a stockholders' equity section of the balance sheet as of December 31, 2008.

July 8   The board of directors declared a $250,000 quarterly cash dividend to stockholders of record as of July 15. Akron, Inc. has 25,000 shares of $100 par, 5% preferred stock outstanding that were sold at par and 500,000 shares of no par common stock outstanding that were sold at an average price of $23 per share. The January 1 balance in Retained Earnings was $5,800,000.
July 30   Paid the cash dividends.
   22   Issued an additional 50,000 shares of common stock, using an underwriting company. The underwriter set the selling price at $30 per share and purchased all 50,000 shares from Akron, Inc. at this price, less a 7% underwriting fee.
   30   The underwriting company sold all 50,000 shares to investors.
August 8 Received a $39,000 bill for legal services from the law firm that had prepared the documents for the stock sale. Instead of cash, the firm agreed to accept 1,200 shares of common stock. As of this date the common stock is trading on stock exchanges at $34.50 per share.
Sept. 27 The company acquired land that was offered for sale at $400,000. Instead of cash, the seller agreed to accept 14,000 shares of common stock. The stock was trading at $29 per share.
Oct. 7   Because of increased profits, the board of directors increased the quarterly dividend to $350,000 to stockholders of record as of October 14.
Oct. 31   Paid the cash dividends.
Dec. 12   Issued 10,000 shares of a new Class B no par, $3 preferred stock. The new preferred stock was sold to an underwriter at a price of $52 per share less a 7% commission.
Dec. 31   Current year income was $40,000. (Omit journal entry.)

LG 29-6. **Prepare journal entries and stockholder's equity.** The December 31, 2007 balance sheet of Toledo, Incorporated shows the stockholders' equity accounts that you see below.

a. Journalize the transactions listed below. (For journal paper, you can make general journal copies from the general journal template in the appendix or print them out from the disk at the back of this book.)

b. Prepare the stockholders' equity section of the balance sheet as of March 31, 2008. The net income for January–March is $125,000. (*Suggestion:* After you prepare the journal entries, use T accounts to keep a record of the account balances that you will need for the stockholders' equity section.)

c. Prepare the stockholders' equity section of the balance sheet as of April 30, 2008. The net income for April is $70,000. Explain any differences between the March 31 and April 30 stockholders' equity sections.

d. Prepare tables for each type of stock to record the number of shares issued and to verify the number of common and preferred shares issued as of March 31 and April 30.

Account	Balance	Account	Balance
Common Stock, $1 par value, 100,000 shares issued	$100,000	Preferred Stock, $75 par value, 3%, convertible, 10,000 shares issued	$ 750,000
Paid-in Capital in Excess of Par, Common Stock	680,000	Paid-in Capital in Excess of Par, Preferred	$ 20,000
		Retained earnings	1,895,000

The preferred stock is convertible into 2.5 shares of common stock for each share of preferred stock.

2008

Jan. 12 The company sold 50,000 shares of common stock for $10 per share. The stock was sold by subscription, which required the buyers to immediately pay 25% of the total due and to pay the remaining 75% by April 10.

Feb. 11 The company purchased some production equipment usually sold for $24,000 by issuing 2,500 shares of common stock to the seller, who agreed to accept the stock instead of cash. At the time of the purchase, the stock was actively traded on stock exchanges at $11 per share.

24 Buyers of 20,000 shares of the stock sold on January 12 paid the remaining balance due on their stock subscriptions.

March 9 Owners of 2,000 shares of preferred stock converted their shares into common stock. Preferred dividends are not payable on preferred stock that is converted to common shares.

19 Buyers of 5,000 shares of the stock sold on January 12 paid the remaining balance due on their stock subscriptions.

April 3 The remaining buyers of the subscribed stock paid their balances in full.

7 The board of directors declared a $50,000 quarterly cash dividend.

LG 29-7. Prepare journal entries and stockholder's equity. The December 31, 2007 balance sheet of Hanover, Inc. shows the stockholders' equity accounts that you see below.

a. Journalize the transactions listed below. (For journal paper, you can make general journal copies from the disk at the back of this book.)

b. After you prepare the journal entries, use T accounts to keep a record of the account balances that you will need for the stockholders' equity section. Also prepare tables to record the number of shares of common stock and preferred stock.

c. Prepare the stockholders' equity section of the balance sheet as of June 30, 2008. The net income for March–June is $117,000.

d. Prepare tables for each type of stock to record the number of shares issued and to verify the number of common and preferred shares issued as of June 30, 2008.

Account	Balance	Account	Balance
Common Stock, $.10 par value, 200,000 shares issued	$20,000	Preferred Stock, $50 par value, 7%, convertible, 10,000 shares issued	$500,000
Paid-in Capital in Excess of Par, Common Stock	2,480,000	Paid-in Capital in Excess of Par, Preferred Stock.	10,000
		Retained earnings	410,000

The preferred stock is cumulative and 2 years in arrears. The preferred stock is convertible into 3 shares of common stock for each share of preferred stock.

2008

Mar. 12   The board of directors declared a $100,000 quarterly cash dividend to stockholders of record on March 17, payable on April 12.

25   Hanover, Inc. sold 25,000 shares of common stock at a price of $15.50 per share.

27   The company issued 2,000 common shares to the underwriter selling the stock. The underwriting company agreed to accept the shares instead of charging a cash commission.

April 12   Paid the dividends declared on March 12.

15   Owners of 3,000 shares of preferred stock converted their shares into common stock. Preferred dividends are not payable on preferred stock that is converted to common shares.

19   Issued 5,000 shares of a new Class B $100 par, 8%, non-convertible preferred stock. The new preferred stock was sold to an underwriter at a price of $105 per share less a 7% commission.

May 7   Received a $45,000 bill for legal services from the law firm that had prepared the documents for the preferred stock sale. Instead of cash, the firm agreed to accept 500 shares of Class B preferred stock. The preferred stock is trading on stock exchanges at $105 per share.

June 14   The board of directors declared a $100,000 quarterly cash dividend to stockholders of record on June 21, payable on July 12.

PRACTICE   Learning Goal 29, continued

Solutions are in the disk at the back of the book and at: www.worthyjames.com

LG 29-8. Prepare journal entries and stockholder's equity. June 30, 2008 is the year end for Middlebury Corporation. The table below shows the stockholders' equity accounts as of year end.

a. Journalize the transactions listed below. (For journal paper, you can make general journal copies from the disk at the back of this book.)

b. Prepare the stockholders' equity section of the balance sheet as of September 30, 2008. The net income for July–September is $136,000. (*Suggestion:* After you prepare the journal entries, use T accounts to keep a record of the account balances that you will need for the stockholders' equity section.)

c. Prepare the stockholders' equity section of the balance sheet as of October 31, 2008. The net income for October is $52,000. Explain any differences between the September 30 and October 31 stockholders' equity sections.

d. Prepare tables for each type of stock to record the number of shares issued and to verify the number of common and preferred shares issued as of September 30 and October 31.

Account	Balance	Account	Balance
Common Stock, no par, 125,000 shares issued	$1,225,000	Preferred Stock, $50 par value, $2, convertible, 15,000 shares issued	$750,000
Retained earnings	710,000	Paid-in Capital in Excess of Par, Preferred	60,000

The preferred stock is cumulative and 1 year in arrears. Each share of preferred stock is convertible into 4 shares of common stock.

2008

July 9   Middlebury Corporation sold 75,000 shares of no-par common stock for $12.00 per share. The stock was sold by subscription, which required the buyers to immediately pay 40% of the total cost and to pay the remaining 60% by October 9.

18   The company purchased land that was offered for sale at $140,000 by issuing 12,000 shares of common stock to the seller, who agreed to accept the stock for the land instead of cash. At the time the agreement was signed with the seller, the stock was actively traded on stock exchanges at $12 per share.

Aug. 24   Buyers of 30,000 shares of the stock sold on July 9 paid the remaining balance due on their stock subscriptions, and Middlebury Corporation issued the shares to the investors.

Sept. 5   Owners of 3,000 shares of preferred stock converted their shares into common stock. Preferred dividends are not payable on preferred stock that is converted to common shares.

14   Buyers of 15,000 shares of the stock sold on July 9 paid the remaining balance due on their stock subscriptions.

29   The board of directors declared a $40,000 quarterly cash dividend payable on October 17.

Oct. 3   The remaining buyers of the subscribed stock paid their balances in full.

17   The company paid the cash dividend.

23   The company sold 10,000 shares of its preferred stock by using an underwriting company that sold the stock for $55 per share and deducted a 7% underwriting commission from the sales proceeds.

PRACTICE

Learning Goal 29, continued

Solutions are in the disk at the back of the book and at: www.worthyjames.com

Instructor-Assigned Problems

If you are using this book in a class, these review problems may be assigned by your instructor for homework, group assignments, class work, or other activities. Only your instructor has the solutions.

IA-15. **Prepare journal entries and stockholder's equity.** The December 31, 2007 balance sheet of Sycamore Corporation shows the stockholders' equity accounts that you see below.

a. Journalize the transactions listed below. (For journal paper, you can make general journal copies from the template in the disk at the back of this book.)

b. Prepare the stockholders' equity section of the balance sheet as of September 30, 2008. The net loss for July–September is $52,300. (*Suggestion:* After you prepare the journal entries, use T accounts to keep a record of the account balances that you will need for the stockholders' equity section.)

c. Prepare the stockholders' equity section of the balance sheet as of October 31, 2008. The net income for October is $25,000. Explain any differences between the September 30 and October 31 stockholders' equity sections.

d. Prepare tables for each type of stock to record the number of shares issued and to verify the number of common and preferred shares issued as of September 30 and October 31.

Account	Balance	Account	Balance
Common Stock, $.50 par value, 250,000 shares issued	$125,000	Preferred Stock, $25 par value, 6%, convertible, 20,000 shares issued	$500,000
Paid-in Capital in Excess of Par, Common Stock	5,341,000	Paid-in Capital in Excess of Par, Preferred	$12,000
		Retained earnings	862,000

The preferred stock is convertible into 1.5 shares of common stock for each share of preferred stock.

2008

July 1 The company sold 80,000 shares of common stock for $24 per share. The stock was sold by subscription agreement that required the buyers to immediately pay 40% of the total due and to pay the remaining 60% by October 31.

July 10 The company purchased computer equipment by issuing shares of common stock. The retail price of the equipment was $280,000 and the company issued 11,200 shares of common stock to the seller, who had agreed to accept the stock instead of cash. At the time of the purchase, the stock was actively traded on stock exchanges at $26 per share.

Aug. 20 Owners of 15,000 shares of preferred stock converted their shares into common stock. Preferred dividends are not payable on preferred stock that is converted to common shares.

Sept. 9 Buyers of 50,000 shares of common stock paid the remaining balance due on their stock subscriptions.

Oct. 15 The board of directors declared a $50,000 quarterly cash dividend for stockholders of record as of October 20.

28 The remaining buyers of the subscribed stock paid their balances in full.

PRACTICE Learning Goal 29, continued

IA-16. **Prepare journal entries and stockholder's equity.** The June 30, 2008 balance sheet of Puuloa, Inc. shows the stockholders' equity accounts that you see below.

a. Journalize the transactions listed below. (For journal paper, you can make copies from the template in the disk at the back of this book.)
b. After you prepare the journal entries, use T accounts to keep a record of the account balances that you will need for the stockholders' equity section. Also prepare tables to record the number of shares of common stock and preferred stock.
c. Prepare the stockholders' equity section of the balance sheet as of September 30, 2008. The net income for July–September is $374,500.
d. Prepare tables for each type of stock to record the number of shares issued and to verify the number of common and preferred shares issued as of September 30, 2008.
e. What were the dividends per share for common shareholders on July 9? On October 18?

Account	Balance	Account	Balance
Common Stock, $.05 par value, 300,000 shares issued	$15,000	Preferred Stock, $100 par value, 6%, convertible, 7,500 shares issued	$750,000
Paid-in Capital in Excess of Par, Common Stock.	9,640,000	Retained earnings	2,800,000

The preferred stock is cumulative and one year in arrears. The preferred stock is convertible into 2 shares of common stock for each share of preferred stock.

2008

July 9   The board of directors declared a $120,000 quarterly cash dividend to stockholders of record on June 30, payable on August 15.

Aug. 5   Puuloa, Inc. sold 15,000 shares of common stock at a price of $48 per share.

12   The company issued 1,000 common shares to the underwriting company selling the stock.

15   Paid the dividends declared on July 9.

25   Owners of 6,000 shares of preferred stock converted their shares into common stock. Preferred dividends are not payable on preferred stock that is converted to common shares.

Sept. 10   Issued 10,000 shares of a new Class B $100 par, 9%, non-convertible preferred stock. The new preferred stock was sold to an underwriter at a price of $103 per share less a 7% commission.

28   Received a $50,000 bill for legal services from the law firm that had prepared the documents for the preferred stock sale. Instead of cash, the law firm agreed to accept 500 shares of preferred stock. The preferred stock is trading on stock exchanges at $104 per share.

Oct. 18   The board of directors declared a $150,000 quarterly cash dividend to stockholders of record on September 30, payable on November 5.

Your Questions?

It is *very* important to be aware of what you need to understand better. What do you need to understand better about this learning goal? On a separate piece of paper, write the questions that you want to discuss with your classmates, instructor, or supervisor. Try to be very specific about what is bothering you, such as explanations that you do not fully understand.

<table>
<tr><td>LEARNING GOAL 30</td><td># More Paid-in Capital and Retained Earnings Transactions</td></tr>
</table>

In Learning Goal 30, you will find:

Paid-in Capital Changes

Retained Earnings Changes

Treasury Stock

Definition

Treasury stock is stock that a company has issued and later purchased from investors, so that the stock is no longer outstanding. Treasury stock can be described as stock that is issued but not outstanding (no longer owned by investors).

Why It Happens

A company will purchase some of its own stock for several business reasons:

- The company hopes to purchase the stock at a low price and resell the shares at a higher price. In that way, the business can obtain more capital than it had at the time the shares were purchased without issuing any new shares.
- Reducing the outstanding shares also tends to reduce the amount by which the market price of the stock will decline, which makes investors happy.
- The company is trying to prevent another party from buying enough shares to control the company and change the management.
- The company may want additional shares of stock available for other purposes such as issuing stock to employees or using stock to purchase another company.

Treasury Stock, *continued*

Example of Purchase

The October 31 stockholders' equity of Greenville Corporation is shown below, before the purchase of treasury stock:

> **Greenville Corporation**
> **Balance Sheet (partial)**
> **October 31, 200X**
>
> Paid-in capital
>   Common stock $.10 par value, 20,000 shares issued   2,000
>   Paid-in capital in excess of par, common   438,000
>   Total paid-in capital   440,000
> Retained earnings   235,000
>   Total paid-in capital and retained earnings $675,000

On November 11, Greenville Company purchases 1,000 shares of its own common stock at the market price of $21 per share.

Treasury Stock	21,000	
Cash		21,000

The treasury stock is recorded by a debit to the Treasury Stock account at the actual purchase cost (the *cost method*). Treasury Stock is a ***contra equity account***, which means that it is a separate account that acts as an offset against the balances in stockholders' equity accounts.

Treasury stock has a debit balance because it is a reduction in stockholders' equity. In the example, the number of outstanding shares has decreased by 1,000 and the shares held in treasury have increased by 1,000. ***Outstanding shares*** means the shares of stock held by stockholders. The total authorized shares are unchanged.

continued ▶

Treasury Stock, *continued*

Example of Purchase,
continued

The stockholders' equity after the treasury stock purchase is:

Greenville Corporation
Balance Sheet (partial)
November 12, 200X

Paid-in capital
  Common stock $.10 par value, 20,000 shares issued,
    19,000 shares outstanding   2,000
  Paid-in capital in excess of par, common 438,000
    Total paid-in capital 440,000
Retained earnings 235,000
    Total paid-in capital and retained earnings 675,000
Less: treasury stock (1,000 shares at cost) . . . . **(21,000)**
    Total stockholders' equity $654,000

Notice the following:

- The number of outstanding shares is 1,000 less than the issued shares. Only outstanding shares can vote, receive dividends, and receive assets in liquidation.
- The total stockholders' equity is reduced by subtracting the cost of the treasury stock from the total paid-in capital and retained earnings.
- Legal capital is not affected.

TIP

Do not make the mistake of classifying treasury stock as an asset because it is recorded with a debit. Treasury stock is a temporary reduction in the amount of stockholders' equity.

Sale of Treasury
Stock: Overview

At some future time after the treasury stock is purchased, the corporation will usually sell the stock. Depending on the market price of the stock, the treasury stock will be sold above cost, below cost, or at cost. The three examples below show these situations. Be sure to note that no gain or loss is ever recorded.

Sale at Cost

Greenville Company sells 100 shares of treasury stock at $21 per share.

Cash	2,100	
Treasury Stock		2,100

Treasury Stock, *continued*

Sale Above Cost	Greenville Company sells 500 shares of treasury stock at $30 per share.

Cash	15,000	
Treasury Stock		10,500
Paid-in Capital from Treasury Stock		4,500

Sale Below Cost	Greenville Company sells the remaining 400 shares at $18 per share.

Cash	7,200	
Paid-in Capital from Treasury Stock	1,200	
Treasury Stock		8,400

Key Points

- Gain or loss is not recorded. Sales above and below cost are just expansions and contractions of paid-in capital from investors.

- When treasury stock is sold above cost, Paid-in Capital from Treasury Stock is credited for the difference above cost. Paid-in Capital from Treasury Stock is a source of capital that is shown as part of the paid-in capital section of stockholders' equity.

- When treasury stock is sold below cost, Paid-in Capital from Treasury Stock is debited for the difference below cost. If there is not a sufficient balance in this account Retained Earnings is debited.

- Each time that treasury stock is sold there is an increase in cash and an increase in total stockholders' equity. Total stockholders' equity increases by the amount of the cash received.

Other Methods

The method illustrated here is called the *cost method*, and it is the most popular technique for recording treasury stock transactions. However, other methods are also used, some of which are required by state laws.

Retirement of Stock

Overview

A corporation can also purchase shares of its stock for the purpose of permanently canceling the shares so they can never be reissued. This stock is called *retired stock*. When stock is retired, the related stock and paid-in capital accounts are reduced. For example, if one-third of the preferred stock is retired, the journal entry includes a debit to Preferred Stock and a debit to Paid-in Capital in Excess of Par, Preferred for one-third the amount in each account. Any difference between the cash paid and the reduction of the stock accounts is debited or credited to Retained Earnings.

Example

The stockholders' equity section of Trenton Enterprises balance sheet is shown below. Assume that the company pays stockholders $9 per share to retire 100,000 shares (one-half) of its common stock.

Stockholders' Equity		
Paid-in capital		
Preferred stock $100 par,		
7%, 10,000 shares issued	$1,000,000	
Paid-in capital in excess of par, preferred. . . .	95,000	$1,095,000
Common stock $.10 par value,		
200,000 shares issued	20,000	
Paid-in capital in excess of par, common. . . .	1,550,000	1,570,000
Total paid-in capital		2,665,000
Retained earnings		720,000
Total stockholders' equity.		$3,385,000

The general journal entry is:

Common Stock ($20,000 × 100,000/200,000)	10,000	
Paid-in Capital in Excess of Par, Common	775,000	
($1,550,000 × 100,000/200,000)		
Retained Earnings ($900,000 − $785,000)	115,000	
Cash (100,000 shares × $9)		900,000

Check Your Understanding

Write the completed sentences on a separate piece of paper.

Treasury Stock is a ⋯⋯⋯ ⋯⋯⋯ type of account. When treasury stock is purchased, total stockholders' equity ⋯⋯⋯ (increases/decreases). When treasury stock is sold, total stockholders' equity ⋯⋯⋯. Legal capital ⋯⋯⋯ (is/is not) affected. When treasury stock is sold, gain or loss ⋯⋯⋯ (is/is not) recorded. A purchase or sale of treasury stock changes the number of shares ⋯⋯⋯.

If 1,000 shares of treasury stock costing $12 per share were sold for $10 per share, the total increase in stockholders' equity would be $⋯⋯⋯. If 1,000 shares of treasury stock costing $12 per share were sold for $15 per share, the total increase in stockholders' equity would be $⋯⋯⋯. Prepare the correct journal entry for this transaction.

Answers

Treasury Stock is a contra equity type of account. When treasury stock is purchased, total stockholders' equity decreases (increases/decreases). When treasury stock is sold, total stockholders' equity increases. Legal capital is not (is/is not) affected. When treasury stock is sold, gain or loss is not (is/is not) recorded. A purchase or sale of treasury stock changes the number of shares outstanding.

If 1,000 shares of treasury stock costing $12 per share were sold for $10 per share, the total increase in stockholders' equity would be $10,000. If 1,000 shares of treasury stock costing $12 per share were sold for $15 per share, the total increase in stockholders' equity would be $15,000.

Cash	15,000	
Treasury Stock		12,000
Paid-in Capital from Treasury Stock Transactions		3,000

Stock Dividends

Definition

A *stock dividend* is a proportional distribution by a corporation of shares of its own stock to existing stockholders, with no change in par or stated value.

Example

Portland Corporation has 50,000 shares outstanding and declares a 5,000 share (10%) stock dividend. An investor who owns 500 shares will receive 50 (10%) more shares. Before the dividend the investor owned 1% of total shares (5,000/50,000 = 1%) and after the dividend the investor still owns 1% of total shares (5,500/55,000 = 1%). Each stockholder maintains the same percentage ownership as before the dividend.

continued ▶

Stock Dividends, *continued*

Effects of a Stock Dividend	A stock dividend has the following effects: ■ The number of outstanding shares increases, but authorized shares do not. ■ Some retained earnings are permanently transformed into paid-in capital. ■ There is no change in total stockholders' equity. ■ There is no change in par or stated value.
Why Stock Dividends Are Declared	A corporation may have several possible business reasons for stock dividends. ■ Stock dividends conserve cash, yet still offer something to stockholders. ■ Large stock dividends over the long term will reduce the market price of stock. This may be desirable if the stock is trading at a high price and the corporation wishes to make the stock more affordable to smaller investors. ■ The corporation may wish to increase the paid-in capital by reducing retained earnings, which makes less retained earnings available for cash dividends.

Rules for Recording Stock Dividends

If . . .	then . . .
the dividend is less than approximately 20 to 25% of the shares outstanding prior to the declaration (small dividend) . . .	use the *market value* per share of the stock, multiplied by the shares outstanding.
the dividend is 25% or more than the shares outstanding prior to the declaration (large dividend) . . .	use the *par or stated value* per share of the stock,* multiplied by the shares outstanding.

* Values for no-par stock vary, depending on state law.

Stock Dividends, *continued*

Examples:
Calculate Value

Assume that the board of directors of Arlington Corporation declares a stock dividend. Prior to the declaration 100,000 shares are outstanding with a par value of $.10 per share. The stock was originally issued at $5 per share. The current market value of the stock is $9 per share, and retained earnings is $200,000.

- **Example 1:** Assume that the stock dividend is 15,000 shares. The value to record is: 15,000 × $9 = $135,000 (small stock dividend).
- **Example 2:** Assume that the stock dividend is 30,000 shares. The value to record is: 30,000 × $.10 = $3,000 (large stock dividend).

Journal Entries

The journal entries for a stock dividend are recorded in two steps:

Step 1: Record the declaration.
Step 2: Record the distribution.

- **Example 1:**   Assume in the first example that Arlington Corporation declared the dividend on September 15, and the stock is distributed on October 1.

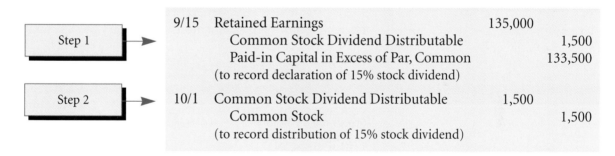

9/15	Retained Earnings	135,000	
	Common Stock Dividend Distributable		1,500
	Paid-in Capital in Excess of Par, Common		133,500
	(to record declaration of 15% stock dividend)		
10/1	Common Stock Dividend Distributable	1,500	
	Common Stock		1,500
	(to record distribution of 15% stock dividend)		

- **Example 2:**   Assume the same dates in the second example.

9/15	Retained Earnings	3,000	
	Common Stock Dividend Distributable		3,000
	(to record declaration of 30% stock dividend)		
10/1	Common Stock Dividend Distributable	3,000	
	Common Stock		3,000
	(to record distribution of 30% stock dividend)		

TIP

Large stock dividends are infrequent. Instead of large stock dividends, stock splits are declared by boards of directors.

continued ▶

Stock Dividends, *continued*

Analysis

The **Common Stock Distributable** account is a stockholders' equity account; it is not a liability. The purpose of the account is to show the legal capital created when the stock dividend was declared. When the stock is actually distributed, the amount is permanently reclassified into the Common Stock account.

Using Example 1 from the prior page, the paid-in capital section on the balance sheet before the distribution of shares is:

Stockholders' Equity		
Paid-in capital		
Common stock	$ 10,000	$(100,000 \times \$.10)$
Paid-in capital in excess of par	623,500	$(100,000 \times \$4.90 + \$133,500)$
Common Stock Distributable	1,500	$(15,000 \times \$.10)$
Total paid-in capital	635,000	

A stock dividend causes **no change in total stockholders' equity**. Notice that in both journal entry examples, an amount of retained earnings was simply moved into paid-in capital. This is because most state laws view additional shares issued as an increase in legal capital and paid-in capital. GAAP provides us with general rules for what values to use on financial statements, although exact amounts may vary by state law.

	Before Dividend	After Distribution	
From Example 1: Small Stock Dividend			
Stockholders' Equity			
Paid-in capital			
Common Stock, $.10 par	$ 10,000	$ 11,500	
Paid-in capital in excess of par	490,000	623,500	
Total paid-in capital	500,000	635,000	
Retained earnings	200,000	65,000	
Total stockholders' equity	$700,000	$700,000	NO CHANGE!
Total outstanding shares	100,000	115,000	

No Change in Business Value

Issuing a stock dividend has no effect on the value of the business that is issuing the stock. All that has happened is that some amount has been permanently transferred out of retained earnings into paid-in capital. Retained earnings is decreased and paid-in capital accounts are increased.

Stock Dividends, *continued*

Another Illustration (Small Dividend)

The illustration below shows this effect for a 10,000-share $1 par common stock dividend valued at $50,000. Retained Earnings is reduced by $50,000, and Common Stock and Paid-in Capital in Excess of Par are together increased by the same total. Notice that total stockholders' equity does not change.

Before Stock Dividend

Paid-in capital
Common stock $1 par value, 75,000 shares issued . . . . $ 75,000
Paid-in capital in excess of par, common 300,000
    Total paid-in capital 375,000
Retained earnings 500,000
    Total paid-in capital and retained earnings $875,000

After Stock Distribution

Paid-in capital
Common stock $1 par value, 85,000 shares issued $85,000
Paid-in capital in excess of par, common 340,000
    Total paid-in capital 425,000
Retained earnings 450,000
    Total paid-in capital and retained earnings $875,000

Effect on Stock Price

In principle, the market price of the stock should decrease by the reciprocal of the percentage increase in shares; more shares should decrease the price per share. For example, after a 10% stock dividend, stock that sells for $22 should sell at ($22 × 1/1.1) = $20. In practice, this does not always happen, especially for small stock dividends—when the price might actually increase!

Why? Investors often mistakenly believe that more shares will increase their future wealth or that the company has become more valuable. However, a stock dividend often occurs when a company simply wants to conserve cash. Also, a stock dividend ultimately reduces the size of future share price increases when compared to what would have happened if no stock dividend had been declared (because more shares are outstanding).

Check Your Understanding

1. Explain the effect that a stock dividend has on the following items:

   - the number of shares outstanding and the number of authorized shares
   - the amount of retained earnings and the amount of paid-in capital
   - the amount of total stockholders' equity
   - the par or stated value of the stock

2. Prepare general journal entries to record each of the following situations:

   Situation #1: Ash Grove Corporation has 100,000 shares of $1 par common stock outstanding. The market price of the stock is $28 per share.

   - The company declares a 10% stock dividend.
   - The company issues the stock.

   Situation #2: River Valley Corporation has 100,000 shares of $1 par common stock outstanding. The market price of the stock is $25 per share.

   - The company declares a 30% stock dividend.
   - The company issues the stock.

Answers

1. • The number of shares outstanding increases; the number of authorized shares is unchanged.
   • Retained earnings decreases and paid-in capital increases by the same amount.
   • Total stockholders' equity remains unchanged.
   • The par or stated value remains unchanged.

2. ***Situation #1*** (use market value):

Retained Earnings	280,000	
Common Stock Distributable		10,000
Paid-in Capital in Excess of Par		270,000

Common Stock Distributable	10,000	
Common Stock		10,000

Situation #2 (use par value):

Retained Earnings	30,000	
Common Stock Distributable		30,000

Common Stock Distributable	30,000	
Common Stock		30,000

QUICK REVIEW

- Treasury stock purchases can occur for several reasons, such as: Selling the treasury stock later at a higher price to obtain more capital; reducing outstanding shares so the market price of the stock will not decline; reducing shares available to unfriendly third parties; and using the stock for other purposes such as employee stock.

- Treasury stock is recorded at cost. Treasury stock is never an asset; it is shown in stockholders' equity as a contra-equity amount that reduces stockholders' equity. When treasury stock is sold, gains and losses are never recorded; only paid-in capital or retained earnings is affected.

- A stock dividend is a proportional distribution by a corporation of additional shares of stock to existing stockholders. A stock dividend has the following effects: Outstanding shares increase but authorized shares do not; some retained earnings is permanently reclassified into paid-in capital; there is no change in total stockholders' equity; there is no change in par or stated value.

- For a small stock dividend (less than approximately 20 to 25% of outstanding shares) market value is used. For a large stock dividend (25% or more of outstanding shares) the par or stated value is used.

- A stock split is a simultaneous decrease in par or stated value and a proportional increase in the number of shares. A stock split has the following effects: The per-share par or stated value is reduced; the number of issued and outstanding shares increases in the same proportion as the change in the par or stated value; stockholders receive new shares; the market price usually decreases because of the number of new shares outstanding.

- No journal entry is required to record a stock split because the balances in stockholders' equity do not change.

- Retained earnings is the part of the stockholders' equity that represents the cumulative amount of net income that is still retained in the business, less certain transactions or adjustments. Retained earnings has no relationship to the amount in the cash account and is not equivalent to cash. Also, retained earnings is not a claim on any specific asset.

- The amount of retained earnings available for dividends can be limited by a restriction on retained earnings as well as an appropriation of retained earnings.

- Items that affect retained earnings include net income, net loss, dividends, prior period adjustments, change in accounting principle, and some treasury stock sales below cost.

- The statement of retained earnings summarizes all the current period changes in retained earnings and shows exactly the same final balance of retained earnings as on the balance sheet.

VOCABULARY

Appropriation of retained earnings: a limitation on the use of retained earnings to pay dividends, recorded by a journal entry into a separate retained earnings account (page 599)

Change in accounting principle: a change from a currently used, generally accepted accounting principle to a different generally accepted accounting principle (page 601)

Common stock distributable: an account that shows the legal capital amount of stock that has been subscribed but not yet fully paid for (page 594)

Contra equity account: an account that has a debit balance and acts as an offset against the total of the balances in other stockholder equity accounts (page 587)

Deficit in retained earnings: a debit balance in retained earnings (page 599)

Outstanding shares: shares of stock held by stockholders (page 587)

Prior period adjustment: an entry to retained earnings to correct an accounting error of a prior period (page 600)

Restriction on retained earnings: a limitation on the use of retained earnings to pay dividends, usually reported in the footnotes to financial statements (page 599)

Retained earnings: the part of the stockholders' equity claim that comes from the cumulative amount of net income since the business was formed, *minus:* net losses, dividends, and some treasury stock transactions (page 599)

Retired stock: stock that has been repurchased by a corporation, cancelled, permanently removed from paid-in capital, and never reissued (page 590)

Statement of retained earnings: a financial statement that summarizes all the current period changes in retained earnings (page 602)

Stock dividend: a proportional distribution by a corporation of shares of its own stock to existing stockholders, with no change in par or stated value (page 591)

Stock split: a simultaneous decrease in the par value or stated value of stock and a proportional increase in the number of shares (page 597)

Treasury stock: stock that a company has issued and then repurchased, so the stock is no longer outstanding (page 586)

PRACTICE   Learning Goal 30

Solutions are in the disk at the back of the book and at: www.worthyjames.com

This learning goal is about paid-in capital and retained earnings transactions. Use these questions and problems to practice what you have just read.

Multiple Choice
Select the best answer.

1. Which of the following is *not* a reason for a corporation to purchase treasury stock?
   a. diminish or prevent decreases in the market price of the company's stock
   b. prevent another party from acquiring enough shares to get control of the business
   c. purchase shares at a higher price and reissue them at a lower price for paid-in capital
   d. use the shares for other purposes such as employee stock options

2. Which of the following best describes the treasury stock account?
   a. a contra equity account that reduces the amount of retained earnings shown in the stockholders' equity
   b. a contra equity account that is usually shown separately as a reduction in total stockholders' equity
   c. a type of retained earnings that increases total retained earnings when the treasury stock increases in value
   d. a paid-in capital account used when a stock dividend has been declared

3. Shares of treasury stock are
   a. increased when there is a stock split.
   b. increased when there is a stock dividend.
   c. entitled to receive all dividends.
   d. all of the above.

4. A treasury stock purchase
   a. reduces the number of outstanding shares but not the issued shares.
   b. has no effect on the legal capital.
   c. reduces the total stockholders' equity.
   d. all of the above.

5. When a company sells treasury stock, the journal entry can include a
   a. debit to Retained Earnings.
   b. a credit to Paid-in Capital in Excess of Par from Treasury Stock.
   c. credit to Treasury Stock.
   d. all of the above.

6. When stock is retired
   a. the amount retired is shown as a single reduction in total stockholders' equity.
   b. the paid-in capital accounts are permanently reduced.
   c. legal capital is permanently reduced.
   d. all of the above.

7. A stock dividend
   a. increases the number of issued and outstanding shares.
   b. increases the total stockholders' equity.
   c. reduces the par value per share of stock.
   d. all of the above.

8. A stock split
   a. increases the number of issued and outstanding shares.
   b. does not affect the total authorized shares.
   c. reduces the par value per share of stock.
   d. all of the above.

9. Komail Corporation had 1,000 shares of $1 par value common stock held as treasury stock and the stock had been purchased for $20 per share. The company then sold 500 of the shares for $24 per share. Because of the sale, the total stockholders' equity will
   a. increase by $500.
   b. increase by $2,000.
   c. increase by $10,000.
   d. increase by $12,000.

10. For a small stock dividend, the value to use for calculating the amount of the dividend is the
   a. par value per share.
   b. stated value per share.
   c. market value per share.
   d. book value per share.

11. How would a stock dividend and a stock split affect total stockholders' equity?

	Stock Dividend	*Stock Split*
a.	No effect	Decrease
b.	Decrease	No effect
c.	Increase	Decrease
d.	No effect	No effect

12. How would a 10% stock dividend affect retained earnings and paid-in capital?

	Retained Earnings	*Paid-in Capital*
a.	Decrease	Decrease
b.	Decrease	Increase
c.	Increase	Decrease
d.	No effect	No effect

13. How would issuing $1 par value treasury stock at a price $5 above cost affect Treasury Stock, Common Stock, and Paid-in Capital in Excess of Par From Treasury Stock?

	Treasury Stock	*Common Stock*	*Paid-in Capital in Excess of Par*
a.	Decrease	Increase	Increase
b.	Increase	Decrease	Decrease
c.	Decrease	Increase	No effect
d.	No effect	No effect	No effect

14. After a 3 for 1 stock split, the total par value amount in stockholders' equity is
   a. three times the pre-split amount.
   b. one-third the pre-split amount.
   c. twice the pre-split amount.
   d. unchanged.

15. Maxwell, Inc. declared a 3 for 2 stock split. Before the split, the company had 90,000 shares of $.15 par value common stock outstanding. After the split,
   a. the par value will be $.075 and the total shares will be 180,000.
   b. the par value will be $.10 and the total shares will be 135,000.
   c. the par value will be $.025 and the total shares will be 540,000.
   d. the par value will be $.05 and the total shares will be 450,000.

16. Which of the statements below is correct?
   a. A stock dividend increases total stockholders' equity, but a stock split does not.
   b. Neither a stock dividend nor a stock split affects the total par value in paid-in capital.
   c. Neither a stock dividend nor a stock split affects the total stockholders' equity.
   d. Both a stock dividend and a stock split require a reduction in retained earnings.

17. A proportional distribution of shares of its own stock to existing stockholders' with no change in par value and no change in total stockholders' equity is a

    a. stock split.

    b. cash dividend.

    c. stock dividend.

    d. liquidating dividend.

18. The board of directors of Munoz Corporation distributed a 10% stock dividend declared on 100,000 outstanding shares of $1 par value stock. The market value of the stock is $20 per share. Which of the following is correct?

    a. Retained Earnings decreases $10,000 and Paid-in Capital in Excess of Par increases $10,000.

    b. Retained Earnings increases $10,000 and Paid-in Capital in Excess of Par decreases $10,000.

    c. Retained Earnings decreases $200,000 and Paid-in Capital in Excess of Par increases $200,000.

    d. None of the above is correct.

19. After the board of directors declared a 15% stock dividend on $1 par value common stock, but before the stock is distributed, the following account(s) should be credited:

    a. Common Stock and Paid-in Capital in Excess of Par, Common

    b. Common Stock Distributable and Paid-in Capital in Excess of Par, Common

    c. Common Stock and Common Stock Distributable.

    d. Common Stock Distributable

20. The board of directors of Reese Corporation declared a 30% stock dividend on 250,000 shares of $1 par value common stock. The stock currently sells for $18 per share. The journal entry should include a

    a. debit to Retained Earnings and a credit to Common Stock.

    b. debit to Retained Earnings and a credit Paid-in Capital in Excess of Par.

    c. debit to Retained Earnings, credit to Common Stock, and a credit to Paid-in Capital in Excess of Par

    d. debit to Retained Earnings, credit to Common Stock, credit to Paid-in Capital in Excess of Par, and a credit to Treasury Stock, if there is a balance in the Treasury Stock account.

21. The difference between a restriction and an appropriation of retained earnings is that

    a. a restriction makes retained earnings unavailable for dividends, but an appropriation does not.

    b. an appropriation is legally binding, but a restriction is optional.

    c. a restriction is disclosed in footnotes, but an appropriation requires a journal entry.

    d. an appropriation is disclosed in footnotes, but a restriction requires a journal entry.

22. Which of the following would *not* appear on a statement of retained earnings?

    a. cash dividends

    b. stock dividends

    c. stock split

    d. prior period adjustment

23. Retained earnings is

    a. an asset.

    b. equivalent to the total cash available.

    c. equal to the cumulative amount of net income earned.

    d. equal to the cumulative amount of net income minus net losses, and dividends.

Discussion Questions and Brief Exercises

1. Why would a corporation purchase shares of its outstanding stock and hold the shares as treasury stock? Does a corporation record gain or loss when it resells the stock? Explain your answer.

2. What is the difference between stock that is authorized, stock that is issued, and stock that is outstanding?

3. When a corporation sells treasury stock, describe the effects on total assets, total stockholders' equity, net income, and paid-in capital. Is treasury stock an asset?

4. Describe the effect that a stock split has on each of the following: Par value per share, total par value, total shares outstanding, total shares issued, and total shares authorized.

5. Explain why a stock dividend has no effect on total stockholders' equity. Explain why a stock split has no effect on total stockholders' equity.

6. On March 1, Halim Corporation purchased 5,000 shares of its $1 par value common stock for $14 per share. On May 3, the company sold 3,000 of the shares for $18 per share. On June 28, the company sold the remaining shares for $13 per share. Prepare the journal entries for March 1, May 3, and June 29. For each date, describe the effects on total stockholders' equity.

7. Identify which items you have studied that increase retained earnings and decrease retained earnings. Briefly describe each item.

8. What is a prior period adjustment? Where does it appear in financial statements?

9. What is a change in accounting principle? Where does it appear in financial statements?

10. On January 2, the ledger accounts of Liu Corporation show the following balances: Common Stock $100,000; Paid-in Capital in Excess of Par, Common $1,220,000; and Treasury Stock $172,000. The common stock has a par value of $1 per share, 500,000 shares were authorized, and 105,000 shares were issued. The treasury stock consists of 10,000 shares purchased at $17.20 per share. On January 10, Liu Corporation completed a 2 for 1 stock split. What are the effects of the split on par value, the dollar amounts in each account, and the shares authorized, issued, and outstanding?

11. On July 1, 2007, the retained earnings balance for Baker Corporation was $720,000. The net loss for the fiscal year ended June 30, 2008 was $121,000. During the year the company paid cash dividends totaling $40,000 and also discovered an accounting error in which the prior year depreciation expense was overstated by $5,000. Prepare a statement of retained earnings for Baker Corporation for the year ended June 30, 2008.

12. What is the meaning of a restriction of retained earnings? Why are retained earnings restricted? How are retained earnings restrictions reported in financial statements?

13. Why would a board of directors declare a stock dividend instead of a cash dividend?

14. Explain the differences between a small stock dividend and a large stock dividend. What is the effect on stockholders' equity accounts?

15. Under what circumstances do you think a board of directors would decide to declare a stock split instead of a stock dividend?

16. What kind of account is "treasury stock"?

17. Miles Corporation currently has outstanding 120,000 shares of $1 par value common stock. Show the effect on par value per share, total par value, and total outstanding shares of each the following stock splits: 2 for 1, 3 for 1, 3 for 2, 4 for 3, and a reverse split of 1 for 2.

18. Travon Fuller owns 1,000 shares of Maples Corporation stock. There are 50,000 shares of stock outstanding, and the stock is currently selling for $27 per share. The company declared a 15% stock dividend. How many shares will Travon own after the dividend? What is his percentage ownership in the company before and after the dividend? Estimate the price of the stock after the dividend.

19. What factors determine the amount of cash dividends that a board of directors can declare?

20. What is a deficit in retained earnings? What causes it?

21. On a separate piece of paper (so that you can use this exercise again), complete the following table that compares the effects of stock dividends and stock splits. Enter "no change," "increase," or "decrease" as appropriate for each item.

Item	Stock Dividend	Stock Split
a. Total stockholders' equity	. . . .	. . . .
b. Total paid-in capital	. . . .	. . . .
c. Total retained earnings	. . . .	. . . .
d. Total par or stated value	. . . .	. . . .
e. Par or stated value per share	. . . .	. . . .
f. Total shares issued	. . . .	. . . .
g. Total shares authorized	. . . .	. . . .
h. Taxable income to stockholder	. . . .	. . . .

Solutions are in the disk at the back of the book and at: www.worthyjames.com

PRACTICE   Learning Goal 30, continued

Reinforcement Problems

LG 30-1. **Analyze stockholders' equity.** The stockholders' equity section of the Gilroy Corporation balance sheet is shown below.

Gilroy Corporation
Balance Sheet (partial)
March 31, 2008

Stockholders' Equity

Paid-in capital

Common stock, $.05 par, 100,000 shares issued, 90,000 shares outstanding	$ 5,000
Paid-in capital in excess of par, common	872,000
Total paid-in capital	877,000
Retained earnings	985,000
Total paid-in capital and retained earnings	1,862,000
Less: Treasury stock, common (10,000 shares at cost)	(70,000)
Total stockholders equity	$1,792,000

Answer the following questions:

a. What is the total stockholders' equity after declaration of a 10% stock dividend when the market price of the stock is $8 per share?

b. What are the account balances of the accounts affected by the declaration of the above dividend?

c. How many shares are issued and how many shares are outstanding after the stock dividend is distributed?

d. After the stock dividend, Gilroy Corporation declared and distributed a 2 for 1 stock split. How many shares are issued and outstanding after the stock split?

e. What is the total stockholders' equity after the stock split?

LG 30-2. **Journalize transactions.** Lexington Corporation completed the selected transactions that are shown below. Prepare the general journal entries to record the transactions. (For journal paper, you can make general journal copies from the disk at the back of this book.)

Transactions:

Oct. 5   Lexington Corporation declared a 10% stock dividend on 50,000 shares of $1 par value common stock that has a current market value of $30 per share.

30   Issued the shares from the dividend declared on October 5.

Nov. 11   Purchased 10,000 shares of treasury stock at a cost of $22 per share.

Jan. 17   The board of directors declared a $250,000 annual cash dividend. In addition to the common stock, there are also 18,000 shares of $100 par value, 5% preferred stock outstanding. (Use separate Dividends Payable accounts for preferred and common dividends.)

Feb. 14   Paid the cash dividend declared on January 17.

April 8   Sold 7,000 shares of the treasury stock at a price of $27 per share.

24   Sold the remaining shares of treasury stock at a price of $19 per share.

30   Declared a 5 for 4 stock split on the common stock. (Indicate the number of shares to be issued that will replace the old shares.)

PRACTICE   Learning Goal 30, continued

Solutions are in the disk at the back of the book and at: www.worthyjames.com

LG 30-3. **Journalize transactions.** In 2008, Nashville Corporation completed the selected transactions shown below. The December 31, 2007 stockholders' equity section of the balance sheet provides additional information.

Prepare the general journal entries to record the transactions. (For journal paper, you can make general journal copies from the disk at the back of this book.)

Nashville Corporation
Balance Sheet (partial)
December 31, 2007

Stockholders' Equity

Paid-in capital

Preferred stock, $75 dollar par, 8%, 25,000 shares issued and outstanding..		$ 1,875,000
Common stock, $1 par, 300,000 shares issued and outstanding.........	$ 300,000	
Paid-in capital in excess of par	5,450,000	5,750,000
Total paid-in capital..		7,625,000
Retained earnings..		4,290,000
Total stockholders equity.......................................		$11,915,000

Transactions:

April 4   Nashville Corporation purchased 10,000 common shares of treasury stock for $200,000.

May 27   Sold 7,000 shares of treasury stock at a price of $24 per share.

July 8   The board of directors declared a 25,000 share stock dividend on the common stock. At the time, the common stock was selling for $24.80 per share.

August 11   Issued 25,000 new common shares for the stock dividend.

Sept. 4   Sold 2,000 shares of treasury stock for $34,000.

20   Sold 50,000 new shares of common stock for $21.50 per share.

Oct. 1   The board of directors declared a 2 for 1 split of the common stock and issued the new shares to replace the old shares. (Indicate the number of new shares issued.)

Solutions are in the disk at the back of the book and at: www.worthyjames.com

PRACTICE   Learning Goal 30, continued

LG 30-4. **Journalize transactions and prepare a statement of retained earnings.** The year-end June 30, 2008 stockholders' equity section of the Bakersfield Corporation balance sheet is shown below. Also shown are the transactions for the first three months of the 2008–2009 fiscal year, beginning July 1.

a. Prepare the general journal entries to record the transactions. (For journal paper, you can make general journal copies from the disk at the back of this book.)
b. Prepare a statement of retained earnings for the three months ending September 30, 2008. During the period, the company incurred a net loss of $186,000.

Bakersfield Corporation
Balance Sheet (partial)
June 30, 2008

Stockholders' Equity

Paid-in capital

Preferred stock, $100 dollar par, 9%, 20,000 shares issued and outstanding..		$2,000,000
Common stock, $.10 par, 475,000 shares issued and outstanding	$ 47,500	
Paid-in capital in excess of par	4,840,000	4,887,500
Total Paid-in capital		6,887,500
Retained earnings		2,320,000
Total stockholders equity		$9,207,500

Transactions:

July 11   The accountants discovered an accounting error in the prior year that understated revenue and understated accounts receivable by $125,000.

23   Bakersfield corporation purchased 8,000 common shares of treasury stock for $11 per share.

Aug. 8   Sold 4,000 shares of treasury stock at a price of $14.50 per share.

24   The board of directors declared a 10% stock dividend on the common stock. At the time, the common stock was selling for $13 per share.

Sept. 5   Issued new common shares for the stock dividend.

Sept. 20   Sold 2,000 shares of treasury stock for $20,000.

22   The board of directors declared a quarterly $100,000 cash dividend payable on October 31 to stockholders of record as of Oct. 10, 2008. (Use separate Dividends Payable accounts for preferred and common dividends.)

LG 30-5. **Analyze effect of transactions.** During the current year, Palo Alto Properties, Inc. completed the transactions shown below.

Create a table in the format as illustrated. Enter the amounts of increases or decreases for each transaction into the appropriate categories in the table. Show decreases in ( ). If a transaction does not affect a category, enter "NE" for "No Effect."

Transactions:
1. Sold 50,000 shares of $1 par value common stock for $15 per share.
2. Declared a $25,000 cash dividend.
3. Declared a stock dividend for 12,000 new shares at a time when the stock was selling for $18 per share. Assume there are 200,000 shares outstanding before the dividend.
4. Purchased 5,000 shares of treasury stock when the stock was selling for $12 per share.
5. Distributed the common stock declared in transaction item #3.
6. Sold 2,000 shares of treasury stock for $16 per share that had a cost of $12 per share.
7. Recorded a prior period adjustment for an accounting error that overstated the prior three years' net income by a total of $238,000.
8. Paid the cash dividend declared in transaction #2.
9. Sold 1,000 shares of treasury stock for $10 per share that had a cost of $12 per share.
10. Assume a beginning balance of 40,000 shares of common stock issued and outstanding prior to the transactions above. The company declared a 2 for 1 stock split on 102,000 shares of $1 par value stock that sells for $15 per share.
11. Recorded current period net income of $77,000.

Format:

Item	Common Stock	Paid-in Capital in Excess of Par	Paid-in Capital: Treasury Stock	Common Stock Distributable	Retained Earnings	Treasury Stock

LG 30-6. **Prepare statement of retained earnings and a stockholders' equity section of the balance sheet.** In the previous problem (LG 30-5), assume that Palo Alto Properties, Inc. had the following beginning balances in the stockholders' equity accounts before recording the transactions: Common Stock, $1 par, $40,000; Paid-in Capital in Excess of Par, $450,000; Retained earnings, $840,000.

a. Prepare a statement of retained earnings for the year ended December 31, 2008.
b. Prepare the stockholders' equity section of the balance sheet as of December 31, 2008. Be sure to calculate and show the total shares as well as the dollar amounts. (*Hint:* Remember to adjust the par value for the split.)

LG 30-7. **Analyze changes and prepare stockholders' equity section of balance sheet.** The stockholders' equity section of the De Leon Corporation balance sheet as of December 31, 2007 is shown below. In the following year, the company earned net income of $109,000 for the year ended December 31, 2008. During 2008 the company declared and distributed a 10% common stock dividend at a time when the stock was selling for $25 per share, but it did not pay any cash dividends. The company later sold 1,000 shares of the treasury stock for $23 per share. There were no other stockholders' equity transactions during 2008.

Prepare the December 31, 2008 stockholders' equity section of the balance sheet. Be sure to calculate and show the number of shares as well as the dollar amounts.

De Leon Corporation
Balance Sheet (partial)
December 31, 2007

Stockholders' Equity

Paid-in capital

Preferred stock, $100 par, 7% 5,000 shares issued and outstanding		$ 500,000
Common stock, $1 par, 92,000 shares issued, 90,000 shares outstanding	92,000	
Paid-in capital in excess of par, common	815,000	
Paid-in capital from treasury stock transactions	20,000	927,000
Total paid-in capital		1,427,000
Retained earnings		1,210,000
Total paid-in capital and retained earnings		2,637,000
Less: Treasury stock, common (2,000 shares at cost)		(40,000)
Total stockholders equity		$2,597,000

LG 30-8. **Journalize transactions and prepare a statement of retained earnings.** During 2008, Muncie, Inc. completed the selected transactions shown below.

a. Prepare the general journal entries to record the transactions. (For journal paper, you can make general journal copies from the disk at the back of this book.)
b. Prepare a retained earnings statement for the year ended December 31, 2008.
c. After completing this problem, explain why prior period adjustments affecting revenues and expenses are recorded directly into retained earnings instead of being recorded as part of current year operations.

Transactions:

Jan. 5   The Muncie, Inc. board of directors declared a $250,000 semi-annual cash dividend. 100,000 shares of $50 par, $3 preferred stock are issued and outstanding. 500,000 shares of $.06 par common stock are issued and outstanding. (Use separate Dividends Payable accounts for preferred and common dividends.)

Feb. 15   Paid the cash dividends.

March 12   Purchased 8,000 common shares as treasury stock at a cost of $30 per share. No treasury shares were owned prior to the purchase.

PRACTICE Learning Goal 30, continued

LG 30-8, *continued*

April 20	The board of directors declared a 40,000 share common stock dividend. At the time of the dividend, the common stock was selling for $30 per share.
May 17	Distributed the shares for the common stock dividend.
July 8	The board of directors declared a $350,000 semi-annual cash dividend.
Aug. 17	Paid the cash dividends.
23	Sold 2,000 shares of the treasury stock at a price of $23 per share. (There is no balance in a Paid-in Capital from Treasury Stock Transactions account.)
Sept. 19	The board of directors declared and distributed a 3 for 2 split of the common stock.
Oct. 21	Sold 1,000 shares of treasury stock at a price of $22 per share.
Nov. 30	Recorded a prior period adjustment for inventory errors that had overstated expenses and understated the net income by $352,000 during the prior five years. (The error resulted in understated inventory, so the adjustment will also increase the Inventory account.)

Other information: The January 1 Retained Earnings balance was $2,740,000. Current year operations have resulted in a net loss for the year of $284,000.

LG 30-9. Journalize transactions, prepare a statement of retained earnings, prepare stockholders' equity section of balance sheet. During 2008, Evanston, Inc. completed the selected transactions shown below. The December 31, 2007 stockholders' equity section of the balance sheet provides additional information.

a. Prepare the general journal entries to record the transactions. (For journal paper, you can make general journal copies from the disk at the back of this book.)

b. Create T accounts for stockholders' equity accounts, enter the beginning balances, and post the journal entries that affect stockholders' equity into the T accounts. Also, prepare tables that record the number of shares of common stock, treasury stock, and preferred stock.

c. Using the balances from the T accounts, prepare the December 31, 2008 statement of retained earnings.

d. Using the balances from the T accounts, prepare the December 31, 2008 stockholders' equity section of the balance sheet.

e. Do you think that common stockholder dilution occurred during the year? Discuss.

Evanston, Inc.
Balance Sheet (partial)
December 31, 2007

Stockholders' Equity

Paid-in capital

Preferred stock, no par; $5; 130,000 shares issued and outstanding	$ 1,365,000
Common stock, no par, 200,000 shares issued and outstanding.	5,400,000
Total paid-in capital.	6,765,000
Retained earnings.	8,210,000
Total stockholders equity	$14,975,000

LG 30-9, *continued*

Transactions:

Jan. 4   The board of directors of Evanston, Inc. declared a semi-annual cash dividend of $500,000. (Use separate Dividends Payable accounts for preferred and common dividends.)

Feb. 18   Paid the cash dividend.

March 9   Sold 50,000 new common shares at $28 per share.

April 3   Purchased 15,000 shares of common stock as treasury stock for $22 per share.

June 8   The board of directors declared a 10% stock dividend on the common stock outstanding. The stock had a market price of $30 per share.

July 7   Distributed the shares from the June 8 stock dividend declaration.

11   The board of directors of Evanston, Inc. declared a semi-annual cash dividend of $375,000.

Aug. 20   Paid the cash dividend.

Sept. 9   Sold 5,000 treasury shares for $140,000.

Oct. 15   Accountants discovered errors that overstated revenue by $250,000 for the two prior years. (Reduce the asset Short-Term Investments).

Dec. 2   Sold 8,000 treasury shares for $17 per share.

Other information: Evanston, Inc. earned $414,000 net income for the year.

LG 30-10. Cumulative problem. This problem contains transactions discussed in Learning Goals 29 and 30. During 2008, Minneapolis Corporation completed the selected transactions shown below. The December 31, 2007 stockholders' equity provides additional information.

a. Prepare the general journal entries to record the transactions. (For journal paper, you can make general journal copies from the disk at the back of this book.)

b. Create T accounts for stockholders' equity accounts and enter the beginning balances. Post the journal entries that affect stockholders' equity into the T accounts. Also, prepare tables to record the balance of the common shares outstanding, treasury shares, and preferred shares outstanding.

c. Using the balances from the T accounts, prepare the December 31, 2008 statement of retained earnings.

d. Using the balances from the T accounts, prepare the December 31, 2008 stockholders' equity section of the balance sheet.

LG 30-10, *continued*

Minneapolis Corporation
Balance Sheet (partial)
December 31, 2007

Stockholders' Equity

Paid-in capital

Preferred stock, $50 par, 9%, 40,000 shares issued and outstanding	$2,000,000	
Paid-in capital in excess of par	100,000	$ 2,100,000
Common stock, $1 par, 250,000 shares issued, 240,000 outstanding.	250,000	
Paid-in capital in excess of par	8,750,000	9,000,000
Total paid-in capital		11,100,000
Retained earnings		15,980,000
Total paid-in capital and retained earnings		27,080,000
Less: treasury stock, common (10,000 shares, at cost)		(220,000)
Total stockholders' equity		$26,860,000

Transactions:

Jan. 4   The board of directors of Minneapolis Corporation declared a semi-annual cash dividend of $600,000. (Use separate Dividends Payable accounts for preferred and common dividends.)

Feb. 14   Paid the cash dividend.

March 7   Issued an additional 100,000 shares of common stock, using an underwriting company. The underwriter set the selling price at $40 per share and purchased all 100,000 shares from the company at this price, less a 7% underwriting fee.

18   The cost of legal services for the stock sale was $70,000. The law firm that prepared the documents agreed to accept 2,000 shares of common stock instead of cash. (The stock is not yet actively traded.)

May 11   Owners of 8,000 shares of preferred stock converted their shares into common shares. Preferred dividends are not payable on preferred stock that is converted to common shares. The stock is actively traded at $38 per share.

June 5   The company purchased some production equipment that had a dealer asking price of $500,000 by issuing 16,000 shares of common stock to the seller, who agreed to accept the stock instead of cash. At the time of the purchase, the stock was actively traded on stock exchanges at $34 per share.

July 8   The board of directors declared a semi-annual cash dividend of $600,000. (Use separate Dividends Payable accounts for preferred and common dividends.)

August 15   Paid the cash dividend.

21   The board of directors declared a 5 for 4 stock split of common stock. The stock was issued.

Nov. 20   Discovered a prior year accounting error that did not record $120,000 of commissions that are still owed to sales employees (Commissions Payable).

LG 30-10, *continued*

Dec. 12   The board of directors declared a 10% stock dividend on the common stock. At the time of the declaration, the stock was selling for $40 per share. Shares will be issued in January.

Dec. 29   Sold 10,000 shares of treasury stock for $38 per share.

Other information: The preferred stock is cumulative and two years in arrears. Each share of preferred stock is convertible into 4 shares of common. The net income earned for the current year was $2,970,000.

INTERNET EXERCISES

Use EDGAR and review the SEC website. Do an Internet search for EDGAR. (Use bookmark/favorites to save the location in an "Accounting References" folder.)

a. What is EDGAR? Click on the "About EDGAR" link.

b. Review the purpose of the SEC by clicking on the "What We Do" link. In your own words, describe the purpose of EDGAR. What part does EDGAR play in the function of the SEC?

c. Any interested party can find excellent information about large companies by examining forms 10-K, 10-Q, and 8-K. On the EDGAR home page, click the "Investor Information" link. Then, in the search box type in the form description "10-K." Using the information available, explain why these three forms are important.

d. Using the names of three large companies given by your instructor or selected by you, locate and view their most recent forms 10-K, 10-Q, and 8-K. (Use the option "exclude ownership forms" to save time.) Look at both financial statements and other information about the companies.

e. Compare the 10-K information you get in (d) above with the information available on the annual reports of the three companies you selected. Then compare the 10-Q information to the company quarterly reports and press releases. Do you see any advantage to using the EDGAR resource?

Your Questions?

It is *very* important to be aware of what you need to understand better. What do you need to understand better about this learning goal? On a separate piece of paper, write the questions that you want to discuss with your classmates, instructor, or supervisor. Try to be very specific about what is bothering you, such as explanations that you do not fully understand.

| LEARNING GOAL 31 | **Prepare Corporate Financial Statements** |

Overview of Statements

Same Basic Statements

Every type of business uses the same basic financial statements. These are the *balance sheet, statement of equity, income statement,* and *statement of cash flows*. Although a corporation has more complex transactions than a proprietorship, a corporation prepares the same type of statements. In this section we will review the corporate balance sheet, statement of stockholders' equity, and income statement.

In Learning Goal 31, you will find:

Balance Sheet, Statement of Stockholders' Equity, and Income Statement

Corporate Tax

Balance Sheet

Overview

The basic idea of a corporate balance sheet is the same as a proprietorship or partnership. A corporate balance sheet shows assets (wealth) and the creditors' and owners' claims on the assets. The essential difference in a corporate balance sheet is the owners' equity. As you have already seen, this part of the balance sheet is called *stockholders' equity* or *shareholders' equity* and is subdivided into various categories. Here we will focus on the stockholders' equity part of the balance sheet.

Basic Format

The basic format of stockholders' equity consists of two major sections: paid-in capital and retained earnings. Certain designated items are shown below retained earnings—for example, treasury stock.

Example

An example of the stockholders' equity section for Lahaina Corporation's balance sheet is shown on the following page. Notice the following elements:

- Name: The name of the company is followed by the word "Corporation." Instead of "Corporation," some companies use the word "Incorporated" or also "Inc."
- Sources of paid-in capital: The paid-in capital section shows the various sources of capital obtained by the company, except for net income or loss. Par value amounts (legal capital) are also disclosed as part of the paid-in capital. In the example, the total paid-in capital is $1,182,000.
- Retained earnings shows the capital that has been retained from all the net income less net losses and that was not paid out in dividends. In the example, the total of retained earnings is $998,000.
- The example shows a treasury stock amount. This indicates that the company has reduced its outstanding stock and its stockholders' equity by purchasing 3,000 shares of its own common stock at a cost of $45,000.
- The final item, "unrealized value gain in certain securities," is an accumulated other comprehensive income item. Accumulated other comprehensive income is a measure of cumulative value changes in certain asset and liability items, which are not reportable as part of net income but that affect stockholders' equity. Comprehensive income is discussed in detail later in this section.

Balance Sheet, *continued*

Example, continued

Lahaina Corporation
Balance Sheet (partial)
December 31, 2008

Stockholders' Equity

Paid-in capital

Preferred stock, $100 par, 4%, 4,000 shares issued and outstanding	$400,000	
Paid-in capital in excess of par, preferred.	2,000	$ 402,000
Common stock, $1 par, 66,000 shares issued, 63,000 shares outstanding	66,000	
Paid-in capital in excess of par, common.	704,000	
Paid-in capital from treasury stock transactions. . . .	10,000	780,000
Total paid-in capital		1,182,000
Retained earnings (see note 15)		998,000
Total paid in capital and retained earnings		2,180,000
Less: **Treasury stock**, common (3,000 shares at cost)	(45,000)	
Add: **Unrealized value gain in certain securities**. . .	18,000	(27,000)
Total stockholders' equity		$2,153,000

Note 15: $200,000 of retained earnings is restricted by the terms of the loan agreement with Forum Bank and Trust Company. Therefore, maximum retained earnings available for dividends is $798,000.

Condensed Presentation

So far, we have illustrated the stockholders' equity section of the balance sheet in a detailed format to clarify each item. However, in practice some parts of the stockholders' equity disclosure are more condensed than we have shown. This is illustrated below.

- The Paid-in capital name is omitted, because it is understood
- Preferred stock par and preferred paid-in excess of par amounts are combined.
- All common stock paid-in capital in excess of par is combined as one item called *additional paid-in capital*, sometimes called *capital surplus*.
- Subtotals are omitted.
- The name "Accumulated other comprehensive income" is used.

TIP

Sometimes the total par value of stock is referred to as ***capital stock***. For example, on the stockholders' equity section, the "capital stock" for preferred stock is $400,000 and for common is $66,000. The condensed version does not show these separately.

---

continued ▶

Balance Sheet, *continued*

Lahaina Corporation
Balance Sheet (partial)
December 31, 2008

Stockholders' Equity

Paid-in capital

Preferred stock, $100 par, 4%, 4,000 shares issued and outstanding	$400,000	
Paid-in capital in excess of par, preferred	2,000	$ 402,000
Common stock, $1 par, 66,000 shares issued, 63,000 shares outstanding	66,000	
Paid-in capital in excess of par, common	704,000	
Paid-in capital from treasury stock transactions	10,000	780,000
Total paid-in capital		1,182,000
Retained earnings (see note 15)		998,000
Total paid-in and retained earnings........................		2,180,000
Less: Treasury stock, common (3,000 shares at cost).....................	(45,000)	
Add: Unrealized value gain in certain securities	18,000	(27,000)
Total stockholders' equity..........................		$2,153,000

Lahaina Corporation
Balance Sheet (partial)
December 31, 2008

Stockholders' Equity

Preferred stock, $100 par, 4%, 4,000 shares issued and outstanding		$ 402,000
Common stock, $1 par, 66,000 shares issued, 63,000 shares outstanding	$ 66,000	
Additional paid-in capital	714,000	780,000
Retained earnings (see note 15)		998,000
Less: Treasury stock, common (3,000 shares at cost)		(45,000)
Add: Accumulated other comprehensive income...........................		18,000
Total stockholders equity		$2,153,000

Statement of Stockholders' Equity

Overview

Because of the numerous types of transactions that can affect stockholders' equity, many corporations present a detailed explanation of the current changes in stockholders' equity. This is called a ***statement of stockholders' equity***. This statement is similar in purpose to the statement of owner's equity that is prepared for a proprietorship but contains more complex elements. When a corporation prepares a statement of stockholders' equity, a statement of retained earnings is not prepared.

Statement of Stockholders' Equity, *continued*

Example

The statement of stockholders' equity that explains the changes in the Lahaina Corporation stockholders' equity is illustrated below. Notice that the final balances in each column correspond exactly to the amounts shown in the stockholders' equity section of the balance sheet.

Lahaina Corporation
Statement of Stockholders' Equity
For the Year Ended December 31, 2008

(Amounts in $000s)

	Preferred Stock $100 Par Value	Common Stock $1 Par Value	Additional Paid-in Capital	Retained Earnings	Treasury Stock	Accum. Other Compre- hensive Income	Total
January 1: 2,000 shares preferred, 40,000 common shares issued, and 34,000 shares outstanding	$200	$40	$400	$950	$(90)	$10	$1,510
Net income..................				154			154
Other comprehensive income: Unrealized value gain in certain securities						8	8
Comprehensive income							162
Issued 2,000 shares of preferred stock	202						202
Issued 20,000 shares of common stock		20	220				240
Sale of treasury stock (3,000 of 6,000 shares held)			10		45		55
Cash dividends on preferred stock				(16)			(16)
Stock dividend distributed on common stock		6	84	(90)			—
Balance, December 31	$402	$66	$714	$998	$(45)	$18	$2,153

Net Income

Income items are usually presented first. The first income item for the period, net income, is the $154,000 net income reported on the income statement for the current period.

continued ▶

Statement of Stockholders' Equity, *continued*

Comprehensive Income

The second income item is "other comprehensive income." The various terms that refer to comprehensive income can be confusing. To help sort this out, here are definitions of the elements of comprehensive income:

- *Comprehensive income* consists of net income (or loss) plus "other comprehensive income" (or loss). Together, these account for all the change in stockholder's equity except for investments and dividends. In the statement above, comprehensive income is $162,000, which consists of the net income of $154,000 combined with the $8,000 "other comprehensive income."
- *Other comprehensive income* generally refers to specific value changes in certain assets and liabilities *in the current accounting period*. The value changes in these items directly change the value of the stockholders' equity but are not considered to be part of net income. Instead, these items bypass the net income and can be reported either on the statement of stockholders equity or as a separate section on the income statement under the net income. Examples of designated comprehensive income items are **unrealized** (meaning not sold) **gains or losses** in certain investment securities and foreign currency translation adjustments for receivables, payables, and investments.
- *Accumulated other comprehensive income* is the cumulative amount of all the "other comprehensive income" for all accounting periods. This is a cumulative change to stockholders' equity. This cumulative amount is shown as a separate item in stockholders' equity on the balance sheet. Notice in the example that the net income of $154,000 flows into the retained earnings, whereas the other comprehensive income item of $8,000 flows into the accumulated other comprehensive income category.

The reason for this complexity is that the Financial Accounting Standards Board believed that it was important to present the net income as well as the value changes in certain key items. They called the combined amount "comprehensive income." At the same time, the value changes are not regarded as part of net income, so these items must be shown separately, both in the current period and in stockholders' equity.

Preferred Stock

This column shows that 2,000 shares of preferred stock were issued for $202,000 ($101 per share). Notice that par value of $200,000 is combined with the paid-in capital in excess of par of $2,000.

Common Stock

This column shows that 20,000 shares of $1 par value common stock were issued. Notice that par value of $20,000 is shown separately from the $220,000 paid-in excess, which is reported as part of "additional paid-in capital." The column also includes $6,000 from a small stock dividend.

Statement of Stockholders' Equity, *continued*

Additional Paid-in Capital	This column includes the following current period changes:

- $220,000 of paid-in capital in excess of par from the sale of stock
- $10,000 of additional paid-in capital from the sale of treasury stock at $10,000 in excess of its cost
- $84,000 of paid-in capital in excess of par from issuing a small stock dividend

Retained Earnings

This column includes the following current period changes:

- $154,000 increase for the net income
- $16,000 decrease for the cash dividends paid on the preferred stock
- $90,000 decrease for the market value for the stock dividends issued. Notice that the stock dividend did not cause any change in total stockholders' equity.

Treasury Stock

This column shows a $45,000 decrease in the cost of treasury stock held because some of the treasury stock was reissued. The total change in the stockholders' equity was $55,000 because the treasury stock was sold for $10,000 in excess of the acquisition cost.

Accumulated Other Comprehensive Income

This column shows a current "other comprehensive income" item (identified as an unrealized gain in certain securities) of $8,000. Therefore, the total accumulated amount of "other comprehensive income" items that have been reported so far is $18,000.

Instead of being presented on the statement of stockholders' equity, comprehensive income is sometimes shown as a separate amount on the income statement below net income. Example:

Net income	154,000
Other comprehensive income	8,000
Comprehensive income	$162,000

Check Your Understanding

A partial statement of stockholders' equity for Tech Corporation is presented below. The statement contains the January 1, 2008 account balances of stockholders' equity. The additional paid-in capital on January 1 consists entirely of paid-in capital in excess of par for the common stock. The following events occurred during the year:

- February: Sold an additional 100,000 shares of common stock for $18 per share.
- May: Sold an additional 10,000 shares of 6% preferred stock for $53 per share.
- June: Paid cash dividends of $80,000 to stockholders.
- September: Sold 5,000 shares of treasury stock for $22 per share that cost $17 per share. 6,000 shares of the common stock are held as treasury stock.
- The net income for the year was $248,000.
- There was a $30,000 unrealized gain on investments that is other comprehensive income.

a. Prepare a completed statement of stockholders' equity for 2008.
b. Prepare the stockholders' equity section of the balance sheet as of December 31, 2008. Use the detailed format.

Tech Corporation
Statement of Stockholders' Equity
For the Year Ended December 31, 2008

(Amounts in $000s)

	Preferred Stock $50 Par Value	Common Stock $1 Par Value	Additional Paid-in Capital	Retained Earnings	Treasury Stock	Accum. Other Compre-hensive Income	Total
January 1: 8,000 shares preferred, 92,000 common shares issued, and 86,000 shares outstanding	$400	$92	$1,500	$965	($102)	($20)	$2,835

Answers

a.

Tech Corporation
Statement of Stockholders' Equity
For the Year Ended December 31, 2008

(Amounts in $000s)

	Preferred Stock $50 Par Value	Common Stock $1 Par Value	Additional Paid-in Capital	Retained Earnings	Treasury Stock	Accum. Other Comprehensive Income	Total
January 1: 8,000 shares preferred, 92,000 common shares issued, and 86,000 shares outstanding	$400	$ 92	$1,500	$ 965	($102)	($20)	$2,835
Net income				248			248
Other comprehensive income: Unrealized value gain in certain securities						30	30
Comprehensive income							278
Issued 10,000 shares of preferred stock	530						530
Issued 10,000 shares of common stock		100	1,700				1,800
Sale of treasury stock (5,000 of 6,000 shares held)			25		85		110
Cash dividends				(80)			(80)
Balance, December 31	$930	$192	$3,225	$1,133	($17)	$10	$5,473

b.

Tech Corporation
Balance Sheet (partial)
December 31, 2008

Stockholders' Equity

Paid-in capital		
Preferred stock, $50 par, 6%, 18,000 shares issued and outstanding	$900,000	
Paid-in capital in excess of par, preferred	30,000	$ 930,000
Common stock, $1 par, 192,000 shares issued, 191,000 shares outstanding	192,000	
Paid-in capital in excess of par, common	3,200,000	
Paid-in capital from treasury stock transactions	25,000	3,417,000
Total paid-in capital		4,347,000
Retained earnings		1,133,000
Total paid-in and retained earnings		5,480,000
Less: Treasury stock, common (1,000 shares at cost)	(17,000)	
Add: Unrealized value gain in certain securities	10,000	(7,000)
Total stockholders equity		$5,473,000

Income Statement Overview

Introduction

The basic idea of a corporate income statement is the same as that of a proprietorship or partnership. A corporate income statement shows revenues, expenses, and net income. However, a corporate income statement can also have additional, more complex, elements.

Format

The illustration below shows the corporate income statement format.

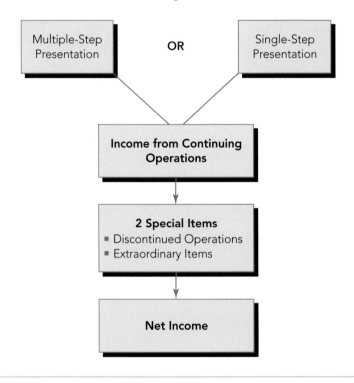

Income Statement Overview, *continued*

Multiple-step and Single-step

There are two equally acceptable income statement formats. The single-step presentation is the format that we used in the earlier Volume 1 learning goals. The advantage of single-step format is its simplicity because net income or ***income from continuing operations*** can be calculated in a single step by subtracting total expenses from total revenues. A multiple-step statement calculates the income in steps and shows subtotals. The advantage of the multiple-step statement is its greater disclosure of details. Both formats show exactly the same total dollar amounts.

Multiple-step Format

Net service *(or sales)* revenue
Less: Cost of goods sold *(for a merchandising or manufacturing company)*
Gross profit *(for a merchandising or manufacturing company)*
Less: Operating expenses *(detailed separately)*
Operating income
Add: Other revenues and gains *(not part of main operations)*
Less: Other expenses and losses *(not part of main operations)*
Income from continuing operations before tax
Less: Income tax expense
Income from continuing operations

Single-step Format

Revenues:
    Net service *(or sales)* revenue
    Other revenues and gains
Less: Expenses
    Cost of goods sold *(for a merchandising or manufacturing company)*
    Operating expenses *(detailed separately)*
    Other expenses and losses
    Income tax expense
Income from continuing operations

continued ▶

Income Statement Overview, *continued*

Examples:
Service Business

The Mega Corporation is a service company (no merchandise sold). In these examples, notice that the multiple-step statement breaks the income into subtotals of *operating income, income from continuing operations before tax*, and *income from continuing operations*.

Multiple-step

Mega Corporation
Income Statement (partial)
For the Year Ended December 31, 2008

Net service revenue		$ 870,000
Operating expenses		391,500
Operating income		478,500
Other revenue, gain, and expense:		
Rental revenue	$ 3,700	
Gain on sale of equipment	23,000	
Interest expense	(11,900)	14,800
Income from continuing operations before tax		493,300
Income tax expense		148,000
Income from continuing operations		$ 345,300

Single-step

Mega Corporation
Income Statement (partial)
For the Year Ended December 31, 2008

Revenues:	
Net service revenue	$870,000
Rental revenue	3,700
Gain on sale of equipment	23,000
Total revenues and gains.	896,700
Expenses:	
Operating expenses	391,500
Interest expense	11,900
Income tax expense	148,000
Total expenses	551,400
Income from continuing operations	$345,300

Income Statement Overview, *continued*

Key Points

The examples illustrate the following key points:

- A corporation is a separate legal entity, therefore the corporation pays income tax on the corporate income. Unlike a proprietorship or partnership, **income tax expense appears on the corporate income statement**.
- "Income from continuing operations" shows the income earned by the company from transactions that are typically part of, or related to, its normal activities. This number is very important to investors and lenders because it represents the results of a company's regular activities and has useful predictive value for what may happen next period. If a corporation does not have any other transactions that are considered to be *special items*, income from continuing operations is simply net income.

Example: Merchant or Manufacturing Business

Merchandising and manufacturing businesses have a large expense item called *cost of goods sold*, which is the cost of the merchandise sold to customers. Revenue is *sales* revenue. On a multiple-step statement, cost of goods sold is subtracted from net sales for a subtotal called *gross profit*.

We now return to the example of Lahaina Corporation, for which we have already seen the stockholders' equity section of the balance sheet and the statement of stockholders' equity. Lahaina Corporation is a merchandising company. Its multiple-step income statement to the level of income from continuing operations is illustrated below.

Lahaina Corporation Income Statement (partial) For the Year Ended December 31, 2008		
Net sales revenue..........................		$1,500,000
Cost of goods sold.........................		720,000
Gross profit		780,000
Operating expenses........................		603,000
Operating income.........................		177,000
Other revenue and loss		
Interest revenue	$ 4,100	
Loss on sale of equipment	(11,100)	(7,000)
Income from continuing operations before tax....		170,000
Income tax expense.......................		51,000
Income from continuing operations...........		119,000

Income Statement Special Items

Introduction

Special items are designated categories of events that must be reported separately from the income from continuing operations. Usually these special items appear on corporate income statements, although the items could appear on non-corporate income statements as well.

Special Item 1: Discontinued Operations

Most large businesses consist of a number of separate components, each having its own distinguishable operations and cash flows. These components are typically significant operating segments of a business, such as a division that provides a separate product or service or a subsidiary company. For example, if XYZ Electronics Company consists of a computer division and a printer division and if it also owns ABC real estate company, each one is a component of XYZ. The discontinued activity of any of the three components would be a *discontinued operation*.

Rules

Rule 1: If a component of an entity is either disposed of or offered for sale, then the component is defined as a ***discontinued operation***.

Rule 2: The following two items must be shown separately, under a separate heading (called discontinued operations).

- The operating income or loss of a discontinued operation must be shown separately, ***net of tax*** expense or tax savings (after subtracting the tax effect).
- Any gain or loss on the disposal of a discontinued operation must be shown separately net of tax expense or tax savings.

Income Statement Special Items, *continued*

Example

Lahaina Corporation sold its hotel reservation division in September of 2008. Up to the date of sale the division had operating income of $40,000. Also, the net assets of the division were sold at a gain of $90,000. Lahaina Corporation has a tax rate of 30%. These events are illustrated below.

Lahaina Corporation
Income Statement (partial)
For the Year Ended December 31, 2008

Income from continuing operations		119,000
Discontinued operations		
Income from hotel reservation division of		
$40,000 less income tax of $12,000	$28,000	
Gain on disposal of hotel reservation division of		
$90,000 less income tax of $27,000	63,000	91,000
Income before extraordinary item		210,000

Note: This example also illustrates the importance of showing discontinued operations as a completely separate category. Can you see how misleading it would be to include the $91,000 discontinued income as part of income from continuing operations?

Special Item 2:
Extraordinary
Gains and Losses

Extraordinary gains and losses, also called ***extraordinary items***, are gains and losses that result from events that are (a) unusual and (b) infrequent. The idea is that such an event is very abnormal and completely unrelated to business operations. This does require some judgment. For example, the occurrence of floods in some geographical areas may be quite unusual, but floods may occur frequently in other areas.

In general, extraordinary gains and losses result from events such as fires, floods, earthquakes, and foreign government expropriations. Items that would *not* be considered extraordinary include lawsuits, write-offs of asset values, strikes, and (based on past FASB responses) probably terrorist attacks.

Rule

Extraordinary items are shown net of tax in a separate section of the income statement, following discontinued operations.

continued

Income Statement Special Items, *continued*

Example

Lahaina Corporation had an uninsured fire loss during the year in the amount of $80,000. Lahaina Corporation has a tax rate of 30%. This event is illustrated below.

Lahaina Corporation		
Income Statement (partial)		
For the Year Ended December 31, 2008		
Income from continuing operations		119,000
Discontinued operations		
Income from hotel reservation division of		
$40,000 less income tax of $12,000	$28,000	
Gain on disposal of hotel reservation division of		
$90,000 less income tax of $27,000	63,000	91,000
Income before extraordinary item		210,000
Extraordinary fire loss of $80,000 less		
income tax savings of $24,000		(56,000)

Note: A loss creates a tax savings because it reduces taxable income. The amount of the reduction in the tax is the amount of the loss times the tax rate.

TIP

A significant change in how a company conducts its operations often results in major expenditures called restructuring charges. ***Restructuring charges*** are the expenses that result from events such as employee layoffs, major reductions in the level of operations, and closing plant facilities. All these events create additional expenditures. For example, employee layoffs often involve special termination pay and relocation costs, and terminating operations may require contract penalty payments and asset writeoffs.

Restructuring Charges Are Not Extraordinary

Many large corporations report restructuring charges. Restructuring charges that are part of a discontinued operation are included as part of the discontinued operations special item. If restructuring charges are not part of a discontinued operation, they are part of operating income. In this case, for a single-step format, the restructuring charges should be shown as a separate line item with operating expenses. In a multiple-step format, restructuring charges should be part of operating expenses.

In all cases, restructuring charges should be clearly explained in footnotes.

Income Statement Special Items, *continued*

**Completed
Illustration**

The completed multiple-step income statement for Lahaina Corporation that includes special items is illustrated below.

**Lahaina Corporation
Income Statement
For the Year Ended December 31, 2008**

Net sales revenue		$1,500,000
Cost of goods sold		720,000
Gross profit		780,000
Operating expenses		603,000
Operating income		177,000
Other revenue and loss:		
Interest revenue	$ 4,100	
Loss on sale of equipment	(11,100)	(7,000)
Income from continuing operations before tax		170,000
Income tax expense		51,000
Income from continuing operations		119,000
Discontinued operations		
Income from hotel reservation division of $40,000 less income tax of $12,000	28,000	
Gain on disposal of hotel reservation division of $90,000 less income tax of $27,000	63,000	91,000
Income before extraordinary item		210,000
Extraordinary fire loss of $80,000 net of tax savings of $24,000		(56,000)
Net income		$ 154,000

Note: This example includes all of the categories that are not part of continuing operations. However, a business may have none or only one of the special items. This would create *a change in the name* of "income from continuing operations." For example:

- If there were no special items, income from continuing operations would become "net income."
- If there were no discontinued operations, income from continuing operations would become "income before extraordinary item."

Check Your Understanding

Shown below is a multiple-step income statement to the level of income from continuing operations.

a. On a separate piece of paper (so you can do the problem again) enter the missing names and amounts.
b. Identify the two types of special items that would appear below income from continuing operations. Explain how these items are shown.

Wailuku Corporation
Income Statement
For the Year Ended December 31, 2008

_____		$2,850,000
Cost of goods sold		1,340,000
_____		
_____		
Restructuring charges	125,000	
Total _____		625,000
_____		885,000
Other revenues and loss:		
Interest revenue	$ 5,000	
Rental revenue		
Loss on sale of equipment	(15,900)	11,100
_____		
_____		270,000
Income from continuing operations		626,100

Answers

b. The two special items are discontinued operations and extraordinary gains/losses. Each item is shown "net of tax" with the tax effect identified. Discontinued operations is separated into two parts: income or loss from the discontinued operations and the gain or loss resulting from disposal. Each part is shown net of tax.

Wailuku Corporation
Income Statement
For the Year Ended December 31, 2008

Net sales revenue		$2,850,000
Cost of goods sold		1,340,000
Gross profit		1,510,000
Operating expenses	500,000	
Restructuring charges	125,000	
Total operating expenses		625,000
Operating income		885,000
Other revenues and loss:		
Interest revenue	$ 5,000	
Rental revenue	22,000	
Loss on sale of equipment	(15,900)	11,100
Income from continuing operations before tax		896,100
Income tax expense		270,000
Income from continuing operations		626,100

a.

Earnings Per Share

Overview

Earnings per share (EPS) is a calculation that shows the income per share of common stock. It is only used for common stock. Earnings per share is an extremely important number that is widely used by investors and analysts in a variety of ways. Here are two of the most important uses:

- Earnings per share is a technique that clarifies the comparison of income between companies of different sizes. For example, if Jones Company reports $1,000,000 of net income and has 100,000 common shares outstanding, its earnings per share is $10. If Smith Company reports $500,000 of net income and has 20,000 common shares outstanding, its earnings per share is $25. Even though Smith Company is smaller, the EPS calculation shows that each shareholder has a claim on more income.

- Earnings per share is part of a very widely used investment calculation called the ***price-earnings ratio (PE ratio)***. The price-earnings ratio is calculated by dividing the market price per share of a stock by the earnings per share. The price-earnings ratio is used to indicate if a company's stock is fairly priced, relative to the amount of income the company is earning (or expected to earn). Financial analysis books discuss this topic in greater detail.

Publicly traded companies are required to show earnings per share on an income statement. The disclosure is optional for other companies.

Basic Earnings Per Share

The calculation for basic earnings per share is:

$$\frac{\textbf{(net income} - \textbf{preferred dividends)}}{\textbf{weighted average of common shares outstanding}}$$

Analysis

- Preferred dividends declared in the period are subtracted from net income because preferred dividends reduce the amount of net income that is available to common stockholders.
- Weighted-average number of shares outstanding is calculated by using the period of time that shares are outstanding. The following examples demonstrate the calculation.

TIP

If preferred stock is cumulative, the preferred dividends for the period are subtracted from net income whether or not they were declared. Dividends in arrears are not used because these dividends were part of prior period EPS calculations. Most preferred stock is cumulative unless otherwise stated.

continued ▶

Earnings Per Share, *continued*

Example 1

Assume that Duluth Company has net income of $500,000 for the current year. Duluth company has outstanding 5,000 shares of $100 par value, $3 preferred stock. Also outstanding all year are 100,000 shares of common stock. Earnings per share is: ($500,000 – $15,000)/100,000 = $4.85 per share.

Example 2

Assume the same facts as Example 1, except that during the year, Duluth Company had transactions that caused the number of common shares to change. Specifically, on May 1 the company issued an additional 50,000 shares. On November 1, the company purchased 30,000 shares of treasury stock. To determine the denominator of the fraction, we calculate the weighted average number of shares by multiplying (weighting) the number of shares outstanding by the period of time (we will use months) they were outstanding.

Date	Shares	Months	Weighted Total
January 1	100,000	4	400,000
May 1	150,000	6	900,000
November 1	120,000	2	240,000
		12	1,540,000

Thus, the weighted average number of shares is: 1,540,000/12 = 128,333

Earnings per share is: ($500,000 – $15,000)/128,333 = $3.78 per share

Financial Statement Disclosure

Earnings per share information is disclosed on the income statement below net income. If there are special items, earnings per share must be disclosed at all the income levels for: (1) continuing operations, (2) discontinued operations, (3) income before extraordinary items (4) the extraordinary item, and (5) net income.

Earnings Per Share, *continued*

**Completed Income
Statement Example**

The example below shows the completed income statement for Lahaina Company with the earnings per share disclosure. The company had 4,000 shares of 4%, $100 par preferred stock outstanding, and 51,500 weighted average shares of common stock outstanding during 2008.

Lahaina Corporation
Income Statement (partial)
For the Year Ended December 31, 2008

Income from continuing operations		119,000
Discontinued operations		
Income from hotel reservation division of $40,000		
less income tax of $12,000	28,000	
Gain on disposal of hotel reservation division of		
$90,000 less income tax of $27,000	63,000	91,000
Income before extraordinary item		210,000
Extraordinary fire loss of $80,000 net of tax savings		
of $24,000		(56,000)
Net income.		$154,000
Earnings per share of common stock:		
Income from continuing operations		$2.00
Discontinued operations		1.77
Income before extraordinary item		3.77
Extraordinary loss		(1.09)
Net income.		$2.68

Computations for earnings per share:

- Income from continuing operations: ($119,000 – $16,000)/51,500 = $2.00
- Discontinued operations: $91,000/51,500 = $1.77
- Income before extraordinary item: ($210,000 – $16,000)/51,500 = $3.77
- Extraordinary loss: –$56,000/51,500 = ($1.09)
- Net income: ($154,000 – $16,000)/51,500 = $2.68

Most Useful

In practice, the earnings per share amount most useful to investors and analysts is *earnings per share from continuing operations*, although earnings per share for net income is probably the most widely quoted.

continued

Earnings Per Share, *continued*

Diluted Earnings Per Share	In a complex capital structure, a corporation may have various types of securities that potentially could become outstanding common shares. Examples are treasury stock, convertible preferred stock, convertible bonds, common stock subscribed, stock options, and a number of other items. When these items exist, a second earnings per share disclosure is required. It is based on a calculation that assumes the maximum number of shares that could potentially have been outstanding and is called *diluted earnings per share*. We will leave the details of this calculation to more advanced textbooks.
Not for . . .	Earnings per share are not calculated for comprehensive income.

Deceptive Statements

WARNING	Although the names, format, and amounts on a corporate income statement can seem complicated at first, it is really important to know them very well—especially if you are an investor, lender, or anyone else analyzing company operations. The format, the names used to describe income, and the calculations are all specifically prescribed by GAAP.
	You must be careful about this when using company information. Some companies use public relations and media documents or company websites to show income statement numbers with names for income that sound similar to GAAP required names, but which actually do not conform to GAAP. Names such as "Pro Forma Earnings," "Operating Earnings," and "Core Earnings" use calculations that have nothing to do with GAAP.
	For example, in recent years one well-known corporation announced that it had Pro Forma Earnings of $67.4 million. However, later it turned out that the company really had a net *loss* on a GAAP basis of $50.6 *billion!* How does this happen? A company uses its own computations with its own names and also omits unfavorable special items. Is this legal? Yes, provided that the company discloses that the statements are not based on GAAP. Unfortunately though, many people do not understand the difference.
	Know the difference—and ignore media releases and other information that does not conform to GAAP. Whenever non-GAAP data is presented by public companies, the Securities and Exchange Commission requires that GAAP calculations also be presented. The GAAP data are what you should look for and use.

Deceptive Statements, *continued*

"Reserve" Is Misleading	Be careful if you see the word "reserve" used on financial statements. This word is very misleading: *it does not mean a fund of cash.* The word usually means a reduction in an asset caused by an accrued expense or an estimated probable loss. Instead of reducing the asset account directly, the reduction is recorded in a separate offsetting account (credit balance) against the asset with the name reserve. A better word to use instead is "allowance." Actual cash reserves are always shown as part of the cash balance and use the word "cash."
Financial Statement Analysis	Financial statement analysis is an extensive topic. Learning Goal 30 in Volume 2 provides a detailed discussion of methods and examples of tools used in financial statements analysis.

Book Value

Definition	***Book value*** is another term for stockholders' equity. Most often book value refers to common stockholders' equity. *Note:* A second meaning for the term "book value" is completely different. Book value also means the undepreciated cost of a long-term asset. In other words, cost minus accumulated depreciation is the book value of a particular asset.
Example with Only Common Stock	Assume that the balance sheet of Sonora Corporation shows total assets of $2,000,000. Total liabilities are $800,000; therefore, the amount of stockholders' equity and book value is $1,200,000. ***Book value per share*** is the book value divided by common shares outstanding. Assume that the only stock is 100,000 common shares outstanding. The calculation of book value per share is: $1,200,000/100,000 = $12 per share.

continued

Book Value, *continued*

Example with Both Common and Preferred Stock

If stockholders' equity includes preferred stock, a value for the preferred stock must first be subtracted from the total equity because preferred stockholders have a priority claim on assets before common stockholders. Generally, the value to use for preferred stock is its call price (or par value if there is no call price) plus any cumulative dividends in arrears.

In the example above, assume that the stockholders' equity of Sonora Corporation includes 5,000 shares of 8%, $100 par value preferred stock with a call price of $103 per share. The preferred dividends are two years in arrears.

Stockholders' equity		$1,200,000
Preferred call price: (5,000 × $103)	$515,000	
Dividends in arrears: (5,000 × $100 × .08 × 2)	80,000	
		(595,000)
Book value		$ 605,000
Book value per share: $605,000/100,000 = $6.05 per share		

Why Book Value Is Useful

- Investors like to compare the book value per share to the market price per share. The idea is that book value represents an approximation of the amount that would be received in case of liquidation (although this is not certain), so a market price of the stock near book value is a very conservative value. "Value" investors look for stocks that are selling near or below book value. In fact, most stocks have a market price significantly above book value.
- Book value per share is used to evaluate the trend in stockholders' equity.
- Total book value may act as a reference point in negotiations and contracts.

Deferred Income Tax

Overview

As you know, corporations pay income tax. Unlike a proprietorship or partnership, income tax appears as an expense in the corporate income statement.

However, the amount of income before tax for accounting purposes and the amount of taxable income as determined by tax rules are calculated differently for certain types of revenue and expense items. When these items occur, the income tax expense shown on an income statement will be different from the amount of tax paid to taxing authorities based on the **income tax return** calculation. For example, two different methods of an expense calculation for a certain type of expenditure will eventually result in the same total expense after several periods. However, before that happens the amount of the expense each year on the income statement will be different than what is being paid to taxing authorities. These are called **temporary differences**. Eventually, an item that is greater in one period will *reverse*, and become less in a later period.

The difference between income tax expense on the income statement and the tax actually paid creates a balance sheet item called **deferred tax**. Deferred tax can be either a liability for future income tax or an asset that that will benefit the company by being an offset against future taxes.

Example 1 of
Temporary Difference

Because of a timing difference in how depreciation expense is calculated, the income before tax of San Benito Corporation is $100,000, but the depreciation allowed by taxing authorities results in a larger expense deduction. Thus, taxable income is only $80,000. The tax rate for the company is 30%. The journal entry to record the tax is:

> Higher future tax
> when timing
> difference reverses

Income tax expense ($100,000 × .3)	30,000	
Income Tax Payable ($80,000 × .3)		24,000
▶ Deferred Income Tax		6,000

Example 1, continued

Assume that in the next year all the other revenues and expenses are the same as the previous year except the depreciation item. Now the depreciation expense calculations reverse; the *timing* of the methods results in a greater depreciation expense on the income statement and a lower deduction allowed by taxing authorities. The result is that net income is $80,000 and taxable income is $100,000. The journal entry is:

Income tax expense ($80,000 × .3)	24,000	
Deferred Income Tax	6,000	
Income Tax Payable ($100,000 × .3)		30,000

The Deferred Income Tax liability becomes a current tax payable. After both periods, the total tax expense on the income statement is now the same as the tax actually paid, but the timing of the items was different.

continued ▶

Deferred Income Tax, *continued*

Example 2 of Temporary Difference

GAAP requires that a seller's product warranty expense and liability be recorded in the same year as the product is sold. Income tax rules allow a tax deduction only when the warranty liability is paid. The income statement of Humbolt Corporation shows income before tax of $50,000; however, the expenses include $10,000 of accrued warranty expense. The taxable income is $60,000 because the warranty expense is not deductible yet. The journal entry is:

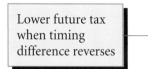

Lower future tax when timing difference reverses

Income tax expense ($50,000 × .3)	15,000	
Deferred Income Tax	3,000	
Income Tax Payable ($60,000 × .3)		18,000

A $3,000 deferred tax asset is recorded as a balance sheet item. The asset represents the benefit of a future lower tax liability. (Humbolt has paid more taxes than the income statement indicated it "should" have.)

Example 2, continued

Assume that total revenues and expenses are the same next year except that there is no longer a warranty expense because a different product is being sold. However, in this year the company pays for repairs on the items returned from last year, and the warranty liability is paid. The journal entry to record the tax is:

Income tax expense ($60,000 × .3)	18,000	
Deferred Income Tax		3,000
Income Tax Payable ($50,000 × .3)		15,000

The deferred tax asset is now realized in the form of a lower tax liability in the current period. After both periods, the tax expense on the income statement is the same as the tax actually paid, but the timing of the items was different.

Permanent Differences

Some items create differences between tax and accounting income that are not a matter of timing and do not reverse. These are called ***permanent differences***. For example, club dues paid for membership in social and athletic organizations are never deductible for income tax purposes but are an expense in determining accounting income.

Permanent differences do not create a deferred tax. The method for dealing with permanent differences is simply to apply the tax law rule for the item when calculating the tax expense on the income statement. Therefore, the tax calculation for the item will be the same for both accounting income and taxable income. In this example, club dues would be excluded as a deductible item when calculating tax expense for the income statement and tax payable for the balance sheet.

Other common permanent difference items are nontaxable municipal bond income, meals and entertainment expense limit, and penalties and fines.

QUICK REVIEW

- Every business prepares the same basic types of financial statements—the balance sheet, statement of owner's or stockholders' equity, income statement, and statement of cash flows. A corporation prepares all these statements, except that they may contain more accounts and complex transactions.

- The essential difference in a corporate balance sheet is in the owner's equity section, which is called stockholders' equity. The stockholders' equity section shows various types of paid-in capital and retained earnings, and it can also include treasury stock and accumulated other comprehensive income. Also, a "real-world" stockholders' equity section is frequently more condensed than the examples illustrated in textbooks.

- To clarify the changes in the various items of stockholders' equity, a statement of stockholders' equity is prepared. This statement provides a detailed breakdown of all changes in stockholders' equity account during the current accounting period.

- The idea of comprehensive income is to combine net income (or loss) plus value changes in certain specified items, which together account for all changes in stockholders' equity except for stockholder investments and distributions. The presentation of comprehensive income consists of three elements: comprehensive income, other comprehensive income, and accumulated other comprehensive income.

- A corporate income statement with no special items will present net income in either a multiple-step format or a single-step format. A corporate income statement with special items will show income from continuing operations presented in either a multiple-step format or a single-step format. The special items are then shown under the income from continuing operations.

- Two special items must be presented separately on the income statement, below income from continuing operations: discontinued operations and extraordinary items.

- Earnings per share (EPS) is an important calculation that is used by investors, analysts, and lenders. Earnings per share must be disclosed for various designated levels of income on the income statements of publicly traded companies.

- You must careful of deceptive non-GAAP financial statements. Be sure to base all analysis only on financial statements that conform to GAAP.

- Book value is a calculation that identifies the amount common stockholders' equity. Book value is often used as a conservative value to compare against stock price.

- Deferred income tax is caused by a timing difference in which a revenue or expense amount that is shown on the income statement is different from the amount calculated for the income tax return. An item that results in a lower tax liability than tax expense reported on the income statement creates a deferred tax liability that is realized as a higher tax payment at a future date. An item that results in a greater tax liability than the tax expense shown on the income statement creates a deferred tax asset that becomes a lower tax liability later. Permanent differences do not create a deferred tax item because the tax law rule is applied to both the income statement tax expense calculation and to the calculation of the tax liability to taxing authorities.

VOCABULARY

Accumulated other comprehensive income: the cumulative amount of other comprehensive income items (page 624)

Book value: another term for stockholders' equity, usually referring to common stockholders' equity (page 641)

Book value per share: common stockholders' equity per outstanding share (page 641)

Capital stock: another term for the total par value of stock (page 625)

Comprehensive income: net income (or loss) plus other comprehensive income, which together account for all current period changes in stockholders' equity except for investments and distributions (page 624)

Discontinued operations: the income or loss, net of tax, caused by discontinuing a significant component of a business (page 632)

Deferred tax: the difference between income tax expense on an income statement and actual income tax liability reported on the tax return for the same period, which is caused by timing differences in certain revenue and expense items (page 643)

Diluted earnings per share: an additional earnings per share calculation that is required for companies having complex capital structures that potentially could create additional outstanding shares of common stock (page 640)

Earnings per share (EPS): a calculation that shows the income per share of common stock (page 637)

Extraordinary gains and losses (extraordinary items): gains and losses resulting from events that are both unusual and infrequent (page 633)

Income from continuing operations: a subtotal of income that is calculated whenever discontinued operations items appear on an income statement (page 629)

Income tax return: the document that must be submitted to taxing authorities to show the amount of tax that is payable (page 643)

Net of tax: the amount remaining after subtracting the tax effect for a specified gain or loss (page 632)

Other comprehensive income: the current period value changes in certain specified items that affect stockholders' equity but are not considered to be part of net income (page 624)

Permanent difference: a difference between accounting income and taxable income as the result of a revenue or expense item being allowed for one income calculation but not the other (page 644)

Price-earnings ratio (PE ratio): a ratio that is used by investors and analysts to help determine if a stock is fairly priced, under priced, or over priced (page 637)

Restructuring charges: expenses that result from a major change in business operations (page 634)

Statement of stockholders' equity: a detailed explanation of the current changes in stockholders' equity (page 622)

Temporary difference: timing differences when a revenue or expense item is recognized as an item on the income statement and when the item is recognized for the purpose of calculating income tax liability (page 643)

Unrealized (gain or loss): the potential gain or loss that would occur, based on current market value, of an investment that has not yet been sold (page 624)

PRACTICE   **Learning Goal 31**

Solutions are in the disk at the back of the book and at: www.worthyjames.com

This learning goal is about corporate financial statements. Use these questions and problems to practice what you have just read.

Multiple Choice
Select the best answer.

1. An income statement of a proprietorship or partnership can report all the same items as an income statement of a corporation except
   a. extraordinary gains and losses.
   b. discontinued operations.
   c. income tax expense.
   d. income from continuing operations.

2. A detailed explanation in table format of all current period changes in stockholders' equity is called a(n)
   a. statement of stockholders' equity.
   b. statement of retained earnings.
   c. stockholders' equity section of the balance sheet.
   d. income statement.

3. Which of the following is *not* an example of a special item that could appear on a corporate income statement?
   a. extraordinary gain or loss
   b. comprehensive income
   c. discontinued operations
   d. gain on sale of discontinued operations

4. Restructuring charges should be reported on financial statements as
   a. an adjustment to the beginning balance of retained earnings.
   b. part of operating income on the income statement.
   c. part of discontinued operations on the income statement.
   d. either (b) or (c), depending on circumstances.

5. Hartford Corporation incurred an extraordinary flood loss of $100,000. Hartford Corporation pays tax at rate of 30%. How should the company report the flood loss?
   a. $100,000 loss as part of income from continuing operations
   b. $100,000 loss as a special item
   c. $100,000 loss less a $30,000 tax savings as a special item
   d. $100,000 loss less a $30,000 tax savings as part of income from continuing operations

6. New Haven, Inc. sold a division of its company during the year for a $400,000 gain. Prior to the date of sale, the year-to-date net loss for the division was $1,000,000. The company's tax rate is 30%. What will be reported on the income statement as a special item?
   a. $420,000 loss
   b. $1,000,000 discontinued operations loss less a $300,000 tax savings
   c. $400,000 gain less $120,000 income tax
   d. both (b) and (c)

7. On an income statement, "Income from continuing operations"
   a. would have a different name if there were no discontinued operations.
   b. must be presented by using the multiple-step format.
   c. must be presented by using the single-step format.
   d. none of the above.

8. Comprehensive income
   a. does not include net income.
   b. includes net income plus "other comprehensive income."
   c. is reported on the balance sheet as part of stockholders' equity.
   d. none of the above.

Solutions are in the disk at the back of the book and at: www.worthyjames.com

PRACTICE   Learning Goal 31, continued

9. "Accumulated other comprehensive income"
   a. is reported on the balance sheet as part of stockholders' equity.
   b. is reported on the income statement.
   c. includes current period net income.
   d. none of the above.

10. An extremely important number that is widely used by investors and analysts and is part of the price-earnings ratio is
    a. net income.
    b. comprehensive income.
    c. earnings per share.
    d. total stockholders' equity.

11. Jamestown, Inc. reported $850,000 of net income for the year. During the year, the company had 50,000 shares of $100 par, 8%, preferred stock outstanding and 400,000 shares of common stock outstanding. What is the basic EPS for the year?
    a. $2.13
    b. $17
    c. $1.89
    d. $1.13

12. The Cedron Corporation balance sheet shows $3,250,000 of stockholders' equity. 175,000 shares of no par common stock are outstanding, and 25,000 of common shares are held as treasury stock. The balance of retained earnings is $2,000,000. What is the book value per share of the stock?
    a. $20.00
    b. $32.50
    c. $11.43
    d. $18.57

13. The Roxbury, Inc. balance sheet shows a stockholders' equity that consists of the following items: 200,000 shares of $.05 par value common stock outstanding that has a paid-in capital in excess of par balance of $3,590,000. The retained earnings balance is $800,000. Treasury Stock shows a balance of $50,000, which is the cost of 2,500 shares. What is the book value per share of the stock?
    a. $21.75
    b. $17.95
    c. $22.00
    d. some other amount

14. The stockholders' equity of Zhao corporation consists of the following: 3,000 shares of $100, 6%, preferred stock outstanding that has a call price of $105 per share and was sold at $101 per share. The stockholders' equity also shows 50,000 shares totaling $775,000 of no par common stock and $500,000 of retained earnings. The preferred stock is one year in arrears. What is the book value per share of the common stock?
    a. $24.90
    b. $25.26
    c. $31.56
    d. some other amount

15. A stock dividend is reported as a(n)
    a. adjustment to the beginning balance of retained earnings.
    b. current period reduction in retained earnings.
    c. deduction from operating income on the income statement.
    d. special item on the income statement.

16. What items create the difference between income from continuing operations and net income?
    a. discontinued operations, extraordinary gains/losses, and change in accounting principle
    b. extraordinary gains/losses and change in accounting principle
    c. discontinued operations and change in accounting principle
    d. discontinued operations and extraordinary gains/losses

17. A statement of stockholders' equity
    a. shows the beginning and ending balance of stockholders' equity.
    b. shows the beginning and ending balance of retained earnings.
    c. is often prepared instead of a statement of retained earnings.
    d. all of the above.

18. Elmira, Inc. had 250,000 shares of common stock issued and 200,000 shares outstanding during the year. Operating income before tax for the year was $890,000 and net income was $630,000. What was the earnings per share (EPS) for the year?
    a. $3.56
    b. $4.45
    c. $3.15
    d. some other amount

19. On January 1, Flatbush Corporation had 500,000 shares of common stock issued and outstanding. On April 2, the company sold 300,000 additional shares. On October 31, the company purchased 150,000 shares of treasury stock. Also outstanding all year were 100,000 shares of $100, 8%, preferred stock. The company reported net income of $2,750,000 for the year. What is the earnings per share for the net income?
    a. $2.79
    b. $3.68
    c. $3.94
    d. some other amount

20. Which of the following items would be reported as part of net income?
    a. comprehensive income
    b. discontinued operations
    c. prior period adjustment
    d. accumulated prior effect of change in accounting principle

21. Which of the following items is reported as part of stockholders' equity on the balance sheet?
    a. comprehensive income
    b. other comprehensive income
    c. accumulated other comprehensive income
    d. deferred income

Discussion Questions and Brief Exercises

1. Compare and contrast the statement of retained earnings and the statement of stockholders' equity.

2. Your friend Daleesha Ames is studying for an accounting exam. She is not clear about the meaning of the following four terms: operating income, income from continuing operations, income before extraordinary item, and net income. Can you explain to her what these terms mean and how they are calculated?

PRACTICE   Learning Goal 31, continued

Solutions are in the disk at the back of the book and at: www.worthyjames.com

3. What two special items appear on an income statement? What do they mean and how are they shown?

4. Where does income tax expense appear on a corporate income statement?

5. On January 1, Shenandoah Corporation had 450,000 shares of $1 par common stock outstanding. On May 1, the company purchased 10,000 shares of treasury stock for $30 per share. On June 1, the company declared a 2 for 1 stock split. On June 2, how many shares of stock are outstanding? How many are in treasury? How many shares are issued? What is the total cost and cost per share of the treasury stock?

6. In (5) above, Shenandoah Corporation also had 150,000 shares of $100, 9%, preferred stock outstanding during the year. The net income for the year ended December 31 was $3,850,000. What are the earnings per share?

7. As an investor, does it matter to you if earnings per share are increasing or decreasing? Do you think that some earnings per share amounts on the income statement might be more important to you than others? Why?

8. Why are preferred dividends subtracted from income when calculating earnings per share?

9. Explain the concept of book value. Why is the preferred stockholders' equity claim subtracted from total stockholders' equity when calculating book value?

10. Professor Rodriguez explained the income statement presentation of earnings per share in class today with the following information, but class was over before she could complete the example. Can you complete the example by showing the proper earnings per share presentation on the income statement? Information (special items are net of tax): Income from continuing operations, $2,475,000; gain from discontinued operations, $600,000; extraordinary earthquake loss, $385,000; weighted average shares outstanding during year: 800,000; annual preferred stock dividends: $680,000.

11. Fallon Corporation has short-term investments in stocks and other financial securities. The value of these investments frequently changes, and at the end of the year the company had a $120,000 unrealized loss on the investments. Fallon Corporation reported $340,000 of net income. What is the amount of other comprehensive income? What is the amount of comprehensive income? Where are these items usually shown on financial statements?

12. On January 1, Zephyr Cove, Inc. had 400,000 common shares outstanding. On May 1, it issued 275,000 more shares. On August 31, 100,000 shares of treasury stock were purchased. On December 1, 75,000 of the treasury shares were sold. To calculate EPS, what is the weighted average number of shares for the year?

13. During the current year, Sparks, Inc. discontinued and sold its mining operations, which were a major segment of its business. The loss on the mining operations during the current year was $1,250,000. The recorded gain on the sale was $200,000. Income from continuing operations for the year was $11,300,000. The current tax rate for Sparks, Inc. is 40%. On which financial statement would these events be shown? Show the correct presentation and discuss the reason for this method of presentation.

14. Which of the following items probably qualify as "extraordinary"? Explain your reasons.
   a. loss resulting from a lawsuit
   b. loss from repairs made to a defective product
   c. loss caused by a tsunami (tidal wave)
   d. loss from sale of long-term investments
   e. flood loss (business located next to a river)
   f. loss from a labor strike
   g. expropriation (takeover) of a business by a foreign government
   h. business property condemned for public use a federal, state, or local agency

15. What is the difference between "net income" and "comprehensive income"?

16. Give examples of two items that would be "other comprehensive income."

17. Give examples of how a company can present misleading income statement information in its public relations and media documents.

18. What is the cause of deferred income tax?

19. The Deferred Income Tax account can be either an asset or a liability. How does this happen?

20. MacTavish Corporation reported $200,000 warranty expense on its 2008 income statement. However, income tax rules do not permit this item to be a tax-deductible expense on the income tax return until the expense is actually paid, which occurred in 2009. The company's tax rate is 40%. MacTavish Corporation had pre-tax accounting income of $2,000,000 in 2008 and $3,000,000 in 2009. Prepare the 2008 and 2009 journal entries to record the income tax expense, deferred tax, and income tax payable.

21. On a separate piece of paper (so that you can use this exercise again without seeing answers), complete the following table by checking the appropriate spaces to indicate on which financial statement an item is presented.

Item	Income Statement	Statement of Stockholders' Equity	Balance Sheet
a. Net income	_____	_____	_____
b. Sale of treasury stock	_____	_____	_____
c. Balance of treasury stock	_____	_____	_____
d. Comprehensive income	_____	_____	_____
e. Accum. other comprehensive income	_____	_____	_____
f. Prior period adjustment	_____	_____	_____
g. Cash and stock dividends	_____	_____	_____
h. Total stockholders' equity	_____	_____	_____
i. New shares of stock issued	_____	_____	_____

Reinforcement Problems

LG 31-1. **Prepare stockholders' equity section of a balance sheet.** Shown below are selected account balances of Cumberland Enterprises, Inc. as of December 31, 2008.

Prepare the stockholders' equity section of the company's balance sheet using a detailed format.

- Retained earnings: $2,820,000
- Common stock, $1 par: $450,000
- Accumulated other comprehensive income: ($410,000)
- Paid-in capital in excess of par, preferred: $220,000

- Treasury stock: $550,000
- Preferred stock, 7%, $50 par: $3,750,000
- Paid-in capital from treasury stock transactions: $180,000
- Paid-in capital in excess of par, common: $4,100,000

Other information: 500,000 shares of common stock were issued and 450,000 shares are outstanding. 75,000 shares of preferred stock are outstanding. The terms of a bank loan restricts $1,000,000 of retained earnings as unavailable for dividends.

LG 31-2. **Prepare a multiple-step income statement.** Shown below are selected account balances of Alexandria Corporation as of the fiscal year ended June 30, 2009. The income tax rate is 40%.

Prepare the company's multiple-step income statement for the fiscal year. (Disregard earnings per share for this problem.)

- Interest expense: $42,000
- Operating expenses: (*detailed separately*) $1,150,000
- Gain on sale of equipment: $84,000
- Net sales revenue: $3,520,000
- Interest revenue: $23,000

- Loss from discontinued operations: $125,000
- Loss on sale of discontinued operations: $450,000
- Gain on land condemnation by state: $270,000
- Cost of goods sold: $1,600,000

LG 31-3. **Prepare multiple-step and single-step income statements.** Shown below are selected account balances of Pasadena Corporation as of the fiscal year ended December 31, 2008. The income tax rate is 40%.

a. Prepare a multiple-step income statement for the fiscal year. (Disregard earnings per share for this problem.)
b. Prepare a single-step income statement for the fiscal year. (Disregard earnings per share for this problem.)

- Interest expense: $75,000
- Sales and marketing expenses: $310,000
- Administrative expenses: $520,000
- Other operating expenses: $540,000
- Gain on sale of equipment: $125,000
- Net sales revenue: $5,800,000
- Extraordinary loss from earthquake: $150,000

- Loss from discontinued operations: $210,000
- Gain on sale of discontinued operations: $130,000
- Restructuring charges (not part of discontinued operations): $1,120,000
- Interest revenue: $10,000
- Cost of goods sold: $2,700,000

PRACTICE   Learning Goal 31, continued

LG 31-4. Prepare a statement of stockholders' equity. The selected events and account balances shown below involve the activities of Irvine Valley Corporation during the company's 2008 fiscal year.

Prepare the company's statement of stockholders' equity for the year ended December 31, 2008.

Account balances on January 1, 2008:
- Common Stock, $.10 par value, 490,000 shares outstanding $49,000
- Retained Earnings: $5,380,000
- Paid-in Capital in Excess of Par: $7,056,000
- Treasury Stock: 20,000 shares at cost, $220,000
- Accumulated Other Comprehensive Income: $150,000

Events:
- Net income for the year was $850,000.
- Irvine Valley Corporation has an operating division in Mexico. When converting the value of the assets and liabilities of this division from pesos to dollars to report on the financial statements, a decrease in the value of the peso caused a decrease in the division's dollar value that is a foreign currency translation loss of $120,000.
- During 2008 the company issued 100,000 new shares of common stock a price of $15.30 per share.
- During 2008 the company sold 10,000 shares of treasury stock at $18 per share.
- During 2008 the company paid $1,000,000 of cash dividends.
- During 2008 the company declared and issued a 5% stock dividend at a time when the stock was selling for $17 per share.

LG 31-5. Analyze a statement of stockholders' equity. A statement of stockholders' equity is shown below for Fullerton, Inc. As of January 1, the preferred stock had been sold at par value and additional paid-in capital consisted only of paid-in capital in excess of par for the common stock.

LG 31-5, *continued*

Use the statement to answer the questions about the company.

Fullerton, Inc.
Statement of Stockholders' Equity
For the Year Ended December 31, 2008

(Amounts in $000's)	Preferred Stock $75 Par Value	Common Stock $1 Par Value	Additional Paid-in Capital	Retained Earnings	Treasury Stock	Accum. Other Comprehensive Income	Total
Balance, January 1..........	$3,750	$550	$13,200	$8,700	$(425)	$154	$25,929
Net income				891			891
Other comprehensive income: Unrealized value loss in certain securities						(40)	(40)
Comprehensive income							851
Issued *xxx* shares of common stock		50	1,325				1,375
Sale of treasury stock (5,000 shares of 25,000 shares)			70		85		155
Cash dividends on preferred stock				(225)			(225)
xxx % stock dividend on common stock		72	2,088	(2,160)			—
Balance, December 31	$3,750	$672	$16,683	$7,206	($340)	$114	$28,085

Questions:
a. What is the par value of the company's common stock?
b. As of January 1, what was the average price per share for common stock sold?
c. What was the amount of comprehensive income in the current period? What does it consist of?
d. What was the cost of the treasury stock sold? What was the cost and the selling price per share?
e. What was the increase in stockholders' equity from the sale of the treasury stock?
f. How many new shares of common stock were issued?
g. What percentage was the stock dividend (large or small dividend)? How many shares were issued? (The stock dividend was declared after all sales of stock.)
h. What was the market price of the stock at the time of the stock dividend?
i. What was the effect of the stock dividend on total stockholders' equity?
j. What total amount of stockholders' equity should appear on the balance sheet?

PRACTICE   Learning Goal 31, continued   *Solutions are in the disk at the back of the book and at: www.worthyjames.com*

LG 31-6. Prepare a statement of stockholders' equity and the stockholders' equity section of a balance sheet. The account balances and selected transactions of Great Falls Corporation during the company's 2008 fiscal year are shown below.

a. Prepare the company's statement of stockholders' equity for the year ended December 31, 2008. (Use a single column for all preferred stock paid-in capital. Use one column for common stock and a separate "additional paid-in capital" column for all other common stock capital in excess of legal capital.)

b. Prepare the stockholders' equity section of the balance sheet as of December 31, 2008.

Selected account balances on January 1, 2008:
- Preferred Stock: $100 par, 8%; 11,000 shares outstanding; $1,100,000
- Common Stock: $.10 par value, 770,000 shares issued; $77,000
- Paid-in Capital in Excess of Par, Common: $6,250,000
- Paid-in Capital from Treasury Stock Transactions: $50,000
- Retained Earnings: $150,000
- Treasury Stock: 15,000 shares; $120,000

Events:
- Net income for the year was $240,000.
- In January, Great Falls Corporation sold 5,000 new shares of the preferred stock at a price of $103 per share.
- In April, the company issued 40,000 new shares of common stock at a price of $9 per share.
- In August, the company sold 10,000 shares of treasury stock at a price of $7.40 per share.
- During the year, the company experienced cash flow problems and had not paid any preferred dividends. In November, the company paid only a quarterly cash dividend on the preferred stock.
- In December, Great Falls Corporation declared a 40,000-share common stock dividend, with the stock to be distributed on January 3. The market price of the common stock at the time was $8.50 per share.
- Also during December, accountants discovered a prior year accounting error that understated 2007 net income by $120,000.

LG 31-7. Prepare a single-step income statement with earnings per share. Missoula Corporation has the selected account balances and information shown below for the fiscal year ending October 31, 2008.

a. Prepare a single-step income statement, including full earnings per share disclosure, for the 2008 fiscal year.

b. Calculate the price-earnings ratio for net income at October 31, 2007 and October 1, 2008. Interpret the results of your calculations.

Selected account balances on October 31, 2008:
- Net Sales: $3,440,000
- Cost of Goods Sold: 1,510,000
- Operating Expenses: 748,000
- Interest Revenue: 7,000
- Interest Expense: 69,000
- Extraordinary flood loss: 130,000
- Tax savings from flood loss: 52,000
- Rental Revenue: $36,000
- Loss on Sale of Equipment: 35,000
- Income Tax Expense: 484,000
- Discontinued Operations Loss: 97,000
- Tax savings from discontinued operations loss: 39,000
- Gain on sale from discontinued operations: 185,000
- Tax on gain on sale from discontinued operations: 74,000

LG 31-7, *continued*

Common shares outstanding during the year: 300,000 shares
The market price of the stock:
- October 31, 2007: $36.75 (earnings per share for net income was $1.40)
- October 31, 2008: $45.50
No preferred stock has been issued.

LG 31-8.   Record deferred tax transactions. In each of the independent situations below, on a separate piece of paper (so you can use this problem again), complete the table and record the correct journal entry for each year.

a.   Amity Corporation made a $100,000 charitable contribution in 2008. This contribution is fully deductible for accounting purposes, but tax rules limit the deduction to $80,000 for calculation of the taxable income, while permitting the balance of the contribution to be used as a deduction next year.

	2008	2009
Pre-tax accounting income	$700,000	$900,000
Charitable contribution	_____	_____
Taxable income	========	========
Income tax payable @ 40%		

b.   Bagwell Sales Company, Inc. uses a depreciation method for calculating income tax liability that permitted $300,000 of deductible expense more than the depreciation expense used for accounting purposes. In 2009 this difference reversed, and tax rules permitted $300,000 less than used for accounting purposes.

	2008	2009
Pre-tax accounting income	$5,000,000	$4,700,000
Depreciation difference	_____	_____
Taxable income	========	========
Income tax payable @ 40%		

c.   Accelerated Corporation uses a different method for recording depreciation expense on a plant and equipment asset for accounting purposes than for tax purposes. The asset cost $100,000, and one-fourth of that amount is recorded each year as depreciation expense on the income statement. For tax purposes, the company uses a method that allows a $50,000 deduction in the first year, $25,000 in the second year, and $12,500 in each of the last two years.

	2006	2007	2008	2009
Pre-tax accounting income	$1,000,000	$1,500,000	$2,000,000	$3,000,00
Depreciation difference	_____	_____	_____	_____
Taxable income	========	========	========	========
Income tax payable @ 40%				

LG 31-8, *continued*

d. In 2008, the income statement of Goodtime Corporation reported $500,000 income from continuing operations before tax. As an expense item on the income statement, the company reported $30,000 of meals and entertainment expense. This expenditure is never deductible for the calculation of taxable income. The company's tax rate is 40%. Prepare the general journal entry to record the tax expense and tax liability.

LG 31-9. **Cumulative problem—journal entries, income statement, statement of stockholders' equity, and stockholders' equity on a balance sheet.** Coeur d' Alene Enterprises, Inc. completed the selected 2008 transactions that are shown below.

a. Prepare the general journal entries to record the transactions. (For journal paper, you can make general journal copies from the disk at the back of this book.)
b. Enter the January 1 balances shown below as beginning balances in T accounts. Then post the transactions into the T accounts. Open new T accounts as necessary.
c. Prepare tables to record the shares of preferred and common stock outstanding and shares of treasury stock.
d. Prepare a 2008 multiple-step income statement, including earnings per share.
e. Prepare a statement of stockholders' equity for 2008.
f. Prepare the stockholders' equity section of the balance sheet as of December 31, 2008.
g. Calculate the book value per share as of December 31, 2008.

Selected January 1 account balances:
- Preferred Stock, convertible into 4 shares of common for each share of preferred; $80 par, 8%, callable at $85, 16,000 shares issued and outstanding: the preferred was sold at par.
- Common Stock, $1 par value, 450,000 shares issued and outstanding: $450,000
- Paid-in Capital in Excess of Par, Common: $7,100,000
- Paid-in Capital from Treasury Stock Transactions: $188,000
- Retained Earnings: $8,290,000
- Accumulated Other Comprehensive Income $115,000

Year-end December 31 income statement information:
- Net sales revenue: $7,450,000
- Cost of goods sold: 4,110,000
- General and administrative expense: 1,167,000
- Sales and marketing expense: 488,000
- Extraordinary loss, earthquake damage: 450,000
- Restructuring charges: $250,000
- Rental revenue (miscellaneous income): 70,000
- Interest expense: 134,000
- Loss on sale of land: 86,000
- Loss from discontinued operations: 80,000
- Loss on sale of discontinued division: 270,000

Other information:
- The tax rate for Coeur d' Alene Enterprises is 40%.
- Coeur d' Alene Enterprises changed its method of valuing inventory in 2008. This qualifies as a change in accounting principle. The accumulated prior effect of the change would have decreased prior years' net income by the $150,000.
- For the year, the company had $65,000 of unrealized losses on certain short-term investment securities.

LG 31-9, *continued*

Selected transactions:

Jan. 3   The board of directors issued new common shares for a 4 for 3 stock split declared in December of the prior year.

Mar. 8   Declared a semi-annual cash dividend of $200,000.

April 12   Paid the dividend.

May 2   Issued 4,000 shares of preferred stock for land to be used for future development. The asking price for the land was $345,000. The preferred stock is regularly traded, and at the time of the agreement, the stock had a market price of $85 per share.

June 1   Owners of 5,000 shares of preferred stock exercised the right to convert to common shares.

Aug. 30   The company purchased 30,000 shares of treasury common stock at $23 per share.

Sept. 7   Declared a semi-annual dividend of $250,000.

Oct. 12   Paid the dividend.

Dec. 1   Sold 25,000 shares of treasury stock for $19.40 per share.

1   Sold 40,000 new common shares at a price of $19.20 per share.

LG 31-10. **Cumulative problem—journal entries, income statement, statement of retained earnings, and stockholders' equity on balance sheet.** Twin Falls Corporation completed the selected 2008 transactions that are shown below.

a. Prepare the general journal entries to record the transactions. (For journal paper, you can make general journal copies from the disk at the back of this book.)

b. Enter the January 1 balances shown below as beginning balances in T accounts. Then post the transactions into the T accounts. Open new T accounts as necessary.

c. Prepare tables to record the shares of preferred and common stock outstanding and shares of treasury stock.

d. Prepare a 2008 single-step income statement. (Disregard earnings per share for this problem.) Twin Falls Corporation uses the income statement to show comprehensive income or loss. Be sure to record the net income amount in the Retained Earnings T account.

e. Prepare a statement of retained earnings for 2008.

f. Prepare the stockholders' equity section of the balance sheet as of December 31, 2008.

g. Calculate the book value per share as of December 31, 2008.

Selected January 1 account balances:

■ Preferred Stock, $100 par, 6%, cumulative, 25,000 shares issued and outstanding: $2,500,000

■ Common Stock, $1 par value, 200,000 shares issued and outstanding: $200,000

■ Paid-in Capital in Excess of Par, Common: $3,900,000

■ Retained Earnings: $5,200,000

Year-end December 31 income statement information:

■ Sales revenue: $4,850,000

■ Cost of goods sold: 1,720,000

■ General and administrative expense: 545,000

■ Sales and marketing expense: 773,000

■ Extraordinary gain, land condemnation: 315,000

■ Organization expense: 133,000

■ Restructuring charges: $524,000

■ Interest revenue: 40,000

■ Interest expense: 55,000

■ Loss on sale of land: 90,000

■ Loss from discontinued operations: 150,000

LG 31-10, *continued*

Other information:
- The tax rate for Twin Falls Corporation is 40%.
- The interest revenue is municipal bond interest revenue, which is not taxable.
- For the year, the company had $75,000 of unrealized gains on certain short-term securities.

Selected transactions:

Jan. 3   The board of directors declared a semi-annual cash dividend in the amount of $400,000. The preferred dividends are one year in arrears.

Jan. 30   Paid the dividend.

Feb. 1   Sold 100,000 shares of common stock by using an underwriting company that sold the stock for $19 per share and deducted a 7% commission from the sales proceeds.

April 12   The board of directors declared a 10% common stock dividend when the stock was selling for $18 per share.

May 1   Issued the shares for the stock dividend.

July 3   The board of directors declared a semi-annual cash dividend in the amount of $400,000.

Aug. 1   Purchased 30,000 shares of treasury stock for $12 per share.

Aug. 5   Paid the dividend.

Sept. 23   Issued 2,000 shares of preferred stock in exchange for equipment that usually sells for approximately $210,000. The preferred stock trades regularly on an exchange and had a value of $102 per share at the time it was issued for the equipment.

Oct. 19   Discovered an accounting error that overstated the prior year's income by $90,000. Service revenue was overstated and accounts receivable were overstated.

Nov. 1   Sold 10,000 shares of treasury stock for $17.50 per share.

Dec. 1   Split the common stock 5 for 4.

Your Questions?

It is *very* important to be aware of what you need to understand better. What do you need to understand better about this learning goal? On a separate piece of paper, write the questions that you want to discuss with your classmates, instructor, or supervisor. Try to be very specific about what is bothering you, such as explanations that you do not fully understand.

Glossary

Account: a detailed, historical record of all the increases and decreases of a specific item in the accounting equation (page 395)

Account form: a balance sheet format in which assets are placed on the left side of a page, and liabilities and owner's equity are placed on the right side (page 300)

Account numbers: unique identification numbers assigned to accounts (page 445)

Account payable: a legal obligation to pay money, usually as the result of a purchase and usually requiring payment in less than 90 days (page 154)

Account receivable: the legal right to collect an amount owed by a customer (page 7)

Accounting: a system of activities that has the objective of providing financial information that is useful for decision making (page 218)

Accounting cycle: a recurring, sequential pattern of accounting activities (page 521)

Accumulated other comprehensive income: the cumulative amount of other comprehensive income (page 624)

Added value: the value created when a new resource is created (page 11)

Annual report: a document, usually prepared by a large corporation, that contains audited financial statements, footnotes, and management discussion and analysis (page 280)

Appropriation of retained earnings: a limitation on the use of retained earnings to pay dividends, recorded by a journal entry into a separate retained earnings account (page 599)

Articles of incorporation: a formal application to a state authority for the purpose of creating a corporation (page 541)

Asking price: the price that is asked by a willing seller (page 546)

Asset: business property (page 37)

Authorized shares: the number of shares a corporation is authorized to sell, as permitted by the state that grants the charter (page 546)

Balance sheet: a report that shows the assets and claims on assets as of a specific date (page 300)

Bid price: the price that is offered by a willing buyer (page 546)

Board of directors: a group of responsible individuals who are elected by shareholders and who act on behalf of shareholders to safeguard their interests and supervise management (page 538)

Book of original entry: a journal (page 449)

Book value: another term for stockholders' equity, usually referring to common stockholders' equity; also, the undepreciated cost of a long-term asset (page 641)

Bookkeeping: another name for the processing functions in the accounting process (page 221)

Bylaws: a corporate constitution that establishes authority, rules, and procedures for conducting the affairs of a corporation (page 541)

Callable preferred stock: preferred stock that can be purchased from stockholders by the issuing corporation at a fixed price (page 570)

Capital statement: another name for the statement of owner's equity (page 294)

Capital stock: another term for the total par or stated value of issued stock (page 567)

CEO (chief executive officer): usually, the president of a corporation (page 539)

CFO (chief financial officer): usually, the vice president of finance (page 539)

Change in accounting principle: a change from a currently used, generally accepted accounting principle to a different generally accepted accounting principle (page 601)

Charge: to debit an account (page 428)

Chart of accounts: a listing of account names and identification numbers (page 445)

Charter: the legal document that creates a corporation (pages 70, 541)

Closely held corporation: a corporation with no publicly traded stock (page 542)

Common stock: ownership shares issued by all for-profit corporations (page 70)

Common stock distributable: an account that shows the legal capital amount of stock that has been subscribed but not yet fully paid for (page 594)

Comparability: the quality of information that makes it comparable between companies and over time (page 282)

Compound entry: an entry containing three or more accounts (page 460)

Comprehensive income: net income (or loss) plus "other comprehensive income" that together account for all current period changes in stockholders' equity except for investments and distributions (page 624)

Conceptual framework: the organized reasoning that explains the basic nature of accounting (page 356)

Consistency: the quality of information that is prepared using the same methods and procedures (page 282)

Contra equity account: an account that has a debit balance and acts as an offset against the total of the balances in other stockholder equity accounts (page 587)

Controller: the chief accounting manager of a corporation; usually is responsible for all accounting functions and reports to the vice president of finance (page 540)

Convertible preferred stock: preferred stock that is convertible into common stock (page 569)

Corporation: a business created by law that is a combined legal and economic entity and is owned by one or more individuals as stockholders (pages 70, 536)

Cr.: the abbreviation for "credit" (page 427)

Credit: a right-side entry or the right side of an account (page 427)

Cumulative dividend: a feature of preferred stock requiring that all dividends declared must be first applied to preferred dividends in arrears plus current preferred dividend before common stockholders can receive a dividend (page 568)

Date of record: the date by which stock ownership must be officially recorded for the owner to receive a dividend (page 565)

Debit: a left-side entry or the left side of an account (page 427)

Declaration date: the date that a board of directors approves a dividend (page 565)

Deferred revenue: another name for unearned revenue (page 127)

Deferred tax: the difference between income tax expense on an income statement and actual income tax liability reported on the return for the same period (page 643)

Deficit in retained earnings: a debit balance in retained earnings (page 599)

Dilution: a reduction in the percentage ownership of existing stockholders in a class of stock; also a reduction in earnings per share due to issuance of new shares (page 560)

Discontinued operations: the income or loss, net of tax, caused by discontinuing a significant component of a business (page 632)

Dividends: non-liquidating distributions of assets from a corporation to its stockholders (page 558)

Dividends in arrears: dividends not declared on cumulative preferred stock (page 568)

Double-entry: a system of recording financial changes that requires at least two changes in the accounting equation so that it will stay in balance (page 94)

Dr.: the abbreviation for "debit" (page 427)

Earnings per share (EPS): a calculation that shows the income per share of common stock (page 637)

Economic entity: any activity or operation for which the financial condition or financial information is to be reported (page 63)

Economic entity assumption: assumption that it is possible to identify an individual economic entity for which financial reporting is to be done (page 64)

Economic resource: a resource that can be valued or measured in dollars (page 4)

Elements of financial statements: the basic components of financial statements (page 358)

Entity: another term for economic entity (page 63)

Entry: the recording of a change in an account; usually refers to recording in ledgers or journals (page 396)

Equity: a claim on asset value (page 47)

Ex-dividend date: the date before which a stock must be purchased to allow enough time for the buyer's name to be officially recorded to receive a dividend—usually two business days before the date of record (page 565)

Expense: a decrease in owner's equity caused by using up resources in operations (page 112)

Extraordinary gains and losses: gains and losses resulting from events that are both unusual and infrequent (page 633)

Fiduciary duty: a special responsibility of trust that requires honest behavior and decision making that is in the best interests of others who rely on this duty (page 539)

Financial Accounting Standards Board (FASB): the highest standard-setting authority in accounting (page 360)

Financing activities: inflows and outflows of cash that are caused by borrowing and by owner's investments and withdrawals (page 308)

Footing: the balance of an account; the total of a column of numbers (page 396)

For-profit corporation: a corporation that raises capital and operates to earn profits (page 542)

Furniture, fixtures, and equipment: long-lived (more than a year) non-real estate assets used in operations (page 153)

General journal: an all-purpose journal that can record all types of transactions (page 450)

General ledger: a book or computer file that contains all of the ledger accounts (page 443)

General partnership: a partnership in which all partners have personal liability and full management authority (page 70)

Generally Accepted Accounting Principles (GAAP): the rules and methods that accountants must follow (page 358)

Historical cost principle: the requirement that transactions be recorded at the original transaction value (page 40)

Income from continuing operations: a subtotal of income that is calculated whenever discontinued operations appear on an income statement (page 629)

Income statement: a report that explains the operational changes in owner's equity for a specific period of time (page 286)

Income tax return: the document that must be submitted to taxing authorities to show the amount of tax that is payable (page 643)

Incorporator: the person who completes the application process to create a corporation (page 539)

Intangible assets: assets that have no physical substance, usually legal rights (page 154)

Inventory: the goods that a merchant has in stock for the purpose of selling to customers (page 153)

Investing activities: inflows and outflows of cash that are caused by acquiring and disposing of primarily long-term assets and making and collecting loans (page 308)

Investment bank: a company that advises and assists corporations in selling stock to the public (page 545)

IPO (initial public offering): the first time that stock is offered for sale to the public (page 545)

Issued shares: the number of shares sold or issued for other reasons (page 546)

Journal: a chronological record of transactions (page 443)

Journalizing: recording information into a journal (page 450)

Leasing: renting property (page 40)

Ledger: a book or computer file that contains accounts (page 443)

Ledger accounts: accounts that are found in a ledger (page 443)

Legal capital: a minimum amount of paid-in capital that must be maintained for the protection of creditors and that can never be paid to stockholders until the corporation is liquidated and creditors are paid in full (page 554)

Legal entity: the entity that has legal ownership of assets and legal responsibility for debits (page 68)

Liability: a debt; a creditor's claim on assets (page 48)

Limited liability: owner or investor personal liability that is limited to a fixed amount; for stockholders, usually the amount of legal capital (page 555)

Limited partnership: a partnership in which certain partners do not have personal liability (page 70)

Liquidating dividend: a dividend that exceeds the balance in retained earnings (page 564)

Liquidity: how quickly an asset can be turned into cash (page 303)

LLC (limited liability company): a business entity that has both corporate limited liability and partnership profit/loss allocation features (page 543)

Managerial accounting: a kind of accounting that focuses on the detailed information needs of a specific company, rather than on the general public (page 280)

MD&A: "management discussion and analysis"; found in annual reports (page 281)

Measurement: another name for the valuation analysis part of transaction analysis; sometimes used to describe all elements of transaction analysis (page 220)

Negotiable stock: stock that can be freely transferred to a new owner (page 537)

Net assets: a synonym for owner's equity (page 48)

Net cash flow: the net change in cash during any specific time period (page 309)

Net income: when revenues are greater than expenses (pages 16, 290)

Net loss: when expenses are greater than revenues (pages 17, 290)

Net of tax: the amount remaining after subtracting the tax effect for a specified gain or loss (page 632)

Net worth: a synonym for owner's equity (page 48)

Nonprofit corporation: a corporation that is organized for the purpose of facilitating charitable or educational goals (page 542)

No-par stock: stock without a par value (page 555)

Normal or natural side: the side of an account that records increases; the positive side (page 397)

Note payable: a legal obligation to pay money as the result of a borrower signing a written promise to pay, called a "promissory note" (page 155)

Note receivable: a legal right to collect money as the result of a borrower signing a written promise to pay, called a "promissory note" (page 153)

Objective evidence: proof or documentation provided for a transaction (page 40)

Operating guidelines: the principles, constraints, and assumptions part of the conceptual framework that gives guidance to accountants (page 358)

Operating statement: another name for the income statement (page 287)

Organization chart: a chart that shows functional title and levels of authority in an organization (page 539)

Organization expense (organization cost): alternative account names used to record the costs of organizing and forming a corporation (page 562)

Other comprehensive income: the current period value changes in certain specified items that affect stockholders' equity but are not considered to be part of net income (page 624)

Outstanding shares: shares of issued stock that are held by stockholders (page 587)

Owner's equity: an owner's claim on assets (page 48)

P & L statement: another name for the income statement (page 287)

Paid-in capital: the part of stockholders' equity that comes from investments in the corporation, primarily by stockholders (page 553)

Paid-in capital in excess of par (or in excess of stated value): paid-in capital that exceeds the legal capital as it is presented in stockholders' equity (page 556)

Par value: a minimal amount per share that is paid in and establishes a stockholder's limit of liability (page 555)

Participating preferred stock: a preferred stock that receives additional dividends, based on a formula, after the common stockholders are paid (page 570)

Partnership: a business with two or more owners acting as partners (page 69)

Payment date: the date a dividend is paid (page 565)

PE (price-earnings) ratio: a ratio that is used by investors and analysts to help determine if a stock is fairly priced, underpriced, or overpriced (page 637)

Personal liability: being personally responsible to make good (to ensure payment of) all business debts (page 68)

Preemptive right: the right of existing stockholders to maintain the same percentage ownership in the same class of stock (page 560)

Preferred stock: a type of stock that gives its owners dividend and liquidation preference over common stockholders (page 556)

Prepaid expense: an advance payment made to a provider of

services before the services are received (page 153)

Prior period adjustment: an entry to retained earnings to correct an accounting error of a prior period (page 600)

Profit and loss statement: another name for the income statement (page 287)

Property: any resource that can be owned (page 5)

Proprietorship: a noncorporate business that is owned by one person (page 67)

Public Company Accounting Oversight Board (PCAOB): a federal government organization that supervises and enforces the disclosure and auditing standards that accountants must apply to corporations whose stock is publicly traded (page 280)

Publicly held (publicly traded) corporation: a corporation having stock that is traded on public stock exchanges (page 542)

Recognition: recording a transaction (page 221)

Relevance: the quality of information that makes it significant or important (page 282)

Reliability: the quality of information that makes it free from material error or bias (page 282)

Report form: a balance sheet format in which assets are placed at the top of a page and liabilities and owner's equity are placed below the assets (page 300)

Residual claim: the owner's right to share in assets only after the creditors are paid (page 560)

Restriction on retained earnings: a limitation on the use of retained earnings to pay dividends, usually reported in the footnotes to financial statements (page 599)

Restructuring charges: expenses that result from a major change in business operations (page 634)

Retained earnings: the part of stockholders' equity claim that comes from the cumulative amount of net income since the business was formed, less net losses, dividends, and certain stockholders' equity transactions (page 557)

Retired stock: stock that has been repurchased by a corporation, canceled, permanently removed from paid-in capital, and never reissued (page 590)

Revenue: an increase in owner's equity caused by making sales to customers (page 116)

Secondary offering: a sale of stock to the public at some time after the initial public offering (page 545)

Secret reserves: undervalued assets received for stock; also, undervalued assets in general (page 562)

Security: the particular asset or assets a creditor can claim for nonpayment of a debt (page 50)

Service potential: the future benefits that an asset provides (page 38)

Services: the use of labor or the use of someone's property (page 5)

Shareholder: another word for stockholder (page 70)

Single-entry: an accounting system that does not record all parts of transactions and does not use the concept of the accounting equation (page 94)

Stakeholders: people and organizations that use accounting information (pages, 221, 280)

Start-up costs: a name that refers to the costs related to organizing and forming a corporation or any other business (page 562)

Statement of cash flows: a report that explains the change in the cash balance during a specific period of time (page 307)

Statement of condition: another name for the balance sheet (page 301)

Statement of earnings: another name for the income statement (page 287)

Statement of owner's equity: the financial statement that explains all the changes in owner's equity (page 293)

Statement of position: another name for the balance sheet (page 301)

Statement of retained earnings: a financial statement that summarizes all the current period changes in retained earnings (page 602)

Statement of stockholders' equity: a detailed explanation of the current changes in stockholders' equity (page 622)

Statements of financial accounting standards (SFAS): the official pronouncements of the Financial Accounting Standards Board (page 360)

Stock dividend: a proportional distribution by a corporation of shares of its own stock to existing stockholders, with no change in par or stated value (page 591)

Stock premium: another term for paid-in capital in excess of par (page 556)

Stock split: a simultaneous decrease in the par value or stated value of stock and a proportional increase in the number of shares (page 597)

Stockholders (shareholders): owners of a corporation; owners of shares of stock (page 539)

Stockholders' equity: the owner's equity of a corporation (page 552)

T account: the simplest form of an account, in the form of a T, showing name above the T and increases on one side and decreases on the opposite side (page 396)

Transaction: any event that causes a change in the accounting equation (page 96)

Transfer agents: companies that specialize in keeping records of stock ownership (page 546)

Treasury stock: stock that a company has issued and then repurchased, so the stock is no longer outstanding (page 586)

Trial balance: a sequential listing of all the non-zero accounts with their debit or credit balances shown in separate columns (page 503)

Unearned revenue: a liability created by receiving a payment from a customer before services are performed or goods are provided (page 127)

Underwriter: an investment bank that manages the issuance of a new stock, usually by agreeing to buy the stock from the issuing corporation, minus a commission charge, and then selling the stock to the public; also, any entity willing to assume risk

Unrealized gain or loss: the potential gain or loss that would occur if an investment that has not yet been sold were to be sold (page 624)

Value chain: the sequence of activities that consumes resources for the purpose of adding value (page 14)

Vendor: any seller of goods or services (page 50)

Watered stock: stock that is issued for overvalued assets (page 562)

Withdrawals: a decrease in the owner's capital caused by the owner's withdrawal of cash or other assets out of a business for personal use (page 190)

Subject Index

Essential Math Index

A comprehensive basic math review with explanations, problems, and solutions is included on the disk in the back of this book. The index for this math review is included here for easy reference to the topics covered. The Table of Contents for the Volume 1 math review is also on the disk. The math review continues on the disk with Volume 2.

READ CAREFULLY: YOU ARE AGREEING TO THE TERMS AND CONDITIONS OF THIS LICENSE

GRANT OF LICENSE and OWNERSHIP

The enclosed computer programs and data ("Software") are licensed, not sold, to you by Worthy & James Publishing and in your purchase or adoption of the accompanying textbooks you agree to these terms. Worthy & James Publishing reserves all rights not granted to you. You own only the disk(s) but Worthy & James owns the Software itself. This license allows you to use and display your copy of the Software on a single computer (that is, with a single CPU) at a single location for academic or non-commercial use only, provided that you comply with the terms of this Agreement. You may make one copy for backup, or transfer your copy to another CPU, provided that the Software is usable on only one computer.

RESTRICTIONS

You may not transfer or distribute the Software or documentation to any other person or entity, including the use of networks for simultaneous use on more than one computer. You may not deconstruct, reverse engineer, disassemble, decompile, modify, or adapt the Software, or create derivative works directly or indirectly from the software. This Software is copyrighted.

TERMINATION

This license is effective until terminated. This license agreement terminates automatically if you fail to comply with the terms of this license agreement. Upon termination, you shall destroy the software. All provisions of this agreement in respect to limitation and disclaimer of warranties, limitation of liability, remedies and damages, and ownership rights shall survive termination.

COMPLETE AGREEMENT and GOVERNING LAW

This agreement is the complete agreement between you and Worthy & James Publishing and supersedes any and all other agreements or communications or proposals, written or oral between you and Worthy & James Publishing. This agreement shall be construed in accordance with the laws of the United States of America and the state of California. **IF YOU DO NOT AGREE TO THE TERMS OF THIS AGREEMENT DO NOT OPEN THE DISK PACKAGE.**

WARRANTY LIMITATION FOR SOFTWARE MEDIA

BY OPENING THE SEALED SOFTWARE MEDIA PACKAGE, YOU ACCEPT AND AGREE TO THE TERMS AND CONDITIONS BELOW. IF YOU DO NOT AGREE TO THESE TERMS AND CONDITIONS, **DO NOT OPEN THE PACKAGE**.

THIS SOFTWARE MEDIA IS PROVIDED TO YOU ON AN "AS IS" BASIS, WITHOUT WARRANTY. IF THE SOFTWARE MEDIA IS DEFECTIVE, YOU MAY RETURN IT FOR A REPLACEMENT WITHIN 60 DAYS FROM DATE OF PURCHASE WITH PROOF OF PURCHASE. THIS IS YOUR ONLY REMEDY AND OUR ONLY OBLIGATION. WE DO NOT WARRANT THE MEDIA FOR FITNESS FOR ANY PARTICULAR USE, THAT ITS USE WILL BE UNINTERRUPTED OR ERROR-FREE, OR AGAINST THE LOSS OF DATA. WORTHY & JAMES PUBLISHING, ITS OWNERS, EMPLOYEES, AGENTS, AUTHORS, AFFILIATES, AND PARTNERS, TO THE FULLEST EXTENT PERMITTED BY APPLICABLE LAW HEREBY DISCLAIM TO YOU AND ANY THIRD PARTY, WITH RESPECT TO THIS MEDIA AND CONTENTS HEREIN, ALL EXPRESS, IMPLIED, AND STATUTORY WARRANTIES OF ANY KIND, AND ANY REPRESENTATIONS OR WARRANTIES ARISING FROM USAGE, CUSTOM, OR TRADE PRACTICES. IN NO EVENT SHALL WORTHY & JAMES PUBLISHING, ITS OWNERS, EMPLOYEES, AGENTS, AUTHORS, AFFILIATES, AND PARTNERS BE LIABLE TO YOU OR ANYONE ELSE FOR ANY CLAIM ARISING OUT OF OR RELATING TO THIS MEDIA FOR ANY TYPE OF DAMAGES, INCLUDING BUT NOT LIMITED TO DIRECT, CONSEQUENTIAL, SPECIAL, INCIDENTAL, PUNITIVE, INDIRECT, OR ANY OTHER, EVEN IF ADVISED OF THE POSSIBILITY OF SUCH DAMAGES. ANY LIABILITY FOR US, WHETHER OR NOT IN TORT, NEGLIGENCE, OR OTHERWISE, ALSO SHALL BE LIMITED IN THE AGGREGATE TO DIRECT AND ACTUAL DAMAGES.

DISCLAIMER

The content of the disk software media that accompanies this book is designed to provide only general educational support and is sold with the understanding that the publisher and author are not engaged in providing accounting, financial, tax, legal, or any other kind of professional services. If professional services are needed, competent professional help should be sought. Although every effort has been made to ensure that the Software media contents are as accurate and useful as possible, the Software may contain errors and omissions, and the publisher and author make no warranties, express or implied, for fitness of use of this Software.